Anne Frank and Etty Hillesum

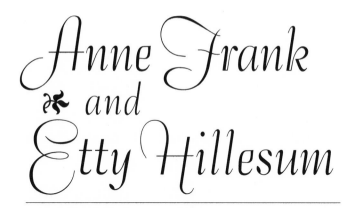

Anne Frank and Etty Hillesum

INSCRIBING SPIRITUALITY AND SEXUALITY

DENISE DE COSTA

Translated by
Mischa F. C. Hoyinck and Robert E. Chesal

RUTGERS UNIVERSITY PRESS
New Brunswick, New Jersey, and London

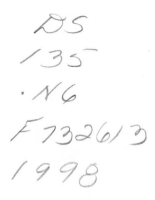

First published in the original Dutch as *Anne Frank & Etty Hillesum: Spiritualiteit schrijverschap seksualiteit,* in 1996 by Uitgeverij Balans, Amsterdam, the Netherlands

First published in English in 1998 by Rutgers University Press, New Brunswick, New Jersey

This study and its translation into English were sponsored by Nederlands Wetenschappelijk Onderzoek (NWO), the Dutch Organization for Scientific Research.

Library of Congress Cataloging-in-Publication Data

Costa, Denise de, 1958–
    [Anne Frank & Etty Hillesum. English.]
    Anne Frank and Etty Hillesum : inscribing spirituality and sexuality / Denise de Costa ; translated by Mischa F. C. Hoynick and Robert E. Chesal.
    p.   cm.
    ISBN 0-8135-2549-7 (alk. paper). —ISBN 0-8135-2550-0 (alk. paper)
    1. Frank, Anne, 1929–1945. 2. Hillesum, Etty, 1914–1943.
3. Jews—Netherlands—Biography. 4. Holocaust, Jewish (1939–1945)—Netherlands.
5. Psychoanalysis and feminism. 6. Feminist criticism.   I. Title.
DS135.N6F732613   1998
940.53'18'092—dc21   97-49649
                                                       CIP

British Cataloging-in-Publication data available.

Manufactured in the United States of America

❧ CONTENTS

✺ IN LOVING MEMORY

What connection is there between writing and death?
Writing can console.
Otherwise, this book would not have been written.

My father, David de Costa, loved to write letters to his two daughters: reflective, encouraging letters full of good advice. A few of them were devoted to the history of his ancestors. Several versions of his lineage exist. One of these stories begins in Portugal, in the late seventeenth century, when a certain Da Costa, a Jew, fled the Inquisition in his native country and boarded a vessel bound for the East Indies. On the island of Ambon in the Moluccas (today part of Indonesia), he started trading in pepper and cloves. During the Dutch rule over the colony, between 1650 and 1660, he was given the choice of becoming a Dutch citizen or leaving the island. He opted for the former, probably partly because the Netherlands was known for its tolerance toward Jews.

The Da Costas acquired a certain status. In the nineteenth century one of them, whose name had meanwhile been changed into the more Dutch-sounding De Costa, was appointed regent of Ambon. This was my father's grandfather.

My father was born in the Dutch East Indies, in the city of Batavia, now Djakarta. There, he grew up and lived through World War II. Later, he witnessed the horrors of the Bersiap period—when the Indonesians fought to gain independence from Dutch colonial rule—and, like his Portuguese ancestor, he wanted to leave the country. He wanted to go to sea, but his father had different ideas and sent him to the Netherlands to complete his education.

He moved to Amsterdam, where he studied electrotechnical engineering and met his future wife, Wijntje Heineke. She was a nurse, originally from a small Dutch village called Loosdrecht, near Amsterdam. They married and had two daughters, whom he taught to be "East Indian." His use of the term exemplified himself: He had class and showed a quiet respect for the things and the people around him. It also meant that he encouraged his daughters from a young age to explore and develop their talents. He was deeply committed to their studies and work, and every milestone filled him with pride and joy. He was looking forward to seeing me, his older daughter, defend my doctoral thesis. A man who loved the rituals that mark the special occasions in life, he would have enjoyed the defense ceremony more than anyone.

While I was putting the finishing touches on my manuscript, in the beautiful autumn of 1995, my father had a stroke and died.

> Yesterday. Sunday. Night.
> At my parents' home
> I stood at the open window.
> A fall sky and a full moon.
> All I could think was:
> Father and Mother
>
> Today. Monday. Morning.
> In my parents' village
> I stood looking at the old church.
> Here, long ago, they said
> "I do" and pledged love and loyalty.
> All I could think was:
> Father and Mother
>
> Today. Monday. Around noon.
> It won't be long and then we'll carry my father,
> Borne by love,
> Outside, into the light.
> The leaves are falling.
> The sun breaks through the clouds.
> Fall is falling in our hearts.
>
> Monday. The evening falls.
> The moon lights up my father's grave,
> May he rest in peace.
> It is fall. And evening.
> And all I can think is:
> Father and Mother.

On the day I defended my doctoral thesis, I put flowers on his grave.

I dedicate this book to my father. And to my mother. I finished this book at her kitchen table, while she was tearing old papers belonging to my father into a thousand tiny pieces: the silent sound of grief and unfathomable sadness.

⚡ ACKNOWLEDGMENTS

My work on this dissertation has been exhausting, pleasurable at times, but also burdensome.

I would like to thank my co-supervisors, Rosi Braidotti and Maaike Meijer, for their guidance. Rosi kept a bird's-eye view on my work in two ways: Often she wrote her comments on an airplane; also, she looked mainly at the big picture, keeping an eye out for connections to other ways of thinking. Maaike stayed closer to the ground, as it were; with painstaking attention to detail, she pointed out every word or sentence that needed work. Although they were both extremely busy and always pressed for time, they received each new version of my chapters with enthusiasm, and inspired me to persevere when things became difficult.

In the late 1980s, Rosi Braidotti was scouting for talent, and I was looking for a supervisor. I was not the only one. Rosi had a million-dollar idea: She initiated the Ph.D. seminar, so that all her Ph.D. candidates could supervise and help one another. And so I, a proverbial loner, became part of a group that truly practiced the interdisciplinarity professed by women's studies. I learned to be critical of other people's work and to have my own work critiqued. I realized how cooperation and comparing notes with colleagues can broaden and add depth to scholarly work. Berteke Waaldijk, Baukje Prins, Annemie Halsema, Anne-Claire Mulder, and Christa Stevens, who were working on their own dissertations, took the time to enrich my book with their insights.

For a while, I shared an office in the attic of a university building with Jann Ruyters, Geertje Mak, Inez van der Spek, and Christien Franken. This was hardly the ideal place for working in silence, but it provided fertile ground for friendships.

Three people whom I could always rely on for support are Anneke van de Meulen, "the boss" of the Utrecht University Women's Studies Department, and Sylvia Koene and Louise van Tetterode, who were the department's foundation. Their interest and their helpfulness are unsurpassed and proved indispensable.

From very early on, Dineke Stam and Yt Stoker of the Anne Frank House helped me find relevant information. I appreciate their enthusiastic contributions and the openness with which they approached my work. I am also most grateful to David Barnouw of the Rijks Instituut voor Oorlogs-Documentatie (RIOD), the Netherlands State Institute for War Documentation, for supplying me with additional information on Anne Frank.

I would like to express my deepest thanks to Hanneke Starreveld, a friend of Etty Hillesum, for her friendship, intelligence, and wisdom, which she so generously shared with me after we first met at a conference about Etty Hillesum at the International School for Philosophy in Leusden on December 21, 1991. I am also thankful for her confidence in me and for granting permission to publish a previously unknown letter of Etty Hillesum's in this book.

I am indebted to Agnès Vincenot and Frits Smeets for their help with translations. Agnès made a great many last-minute corrections to my translations from French, and Frits translated the English. Agnès's patient and thoughtful way of living and working is like a breath of fresh air, and I respect her deeply for it. And I would like to thank Frits and Jola for the friendship that developed during a time when, as everyone knows, friendships tend to be neglected.

I thank Marijke too, for never being insulted by my urge to read and write and for being ever willing to take a jog together out in the polder.

My thanks to Carlos for his detective work, which helped trace the diaspora of the Sephardic Da Costa family.

My gratitude goes to Thera, who has been my best friend since kindergarten, and to Marjon, my best friend from college. They were my guardian angels in troubled times and accompanied me during the defense of my thesis.

"Are you going to thank me in your book too?" asked Luc.

"Yes."

"Because I would always sit quietly and read or play with my Lego blocks while you worked on the computer?"

"Exactly!"

But not just for that. Luc and Wouter were the ones who brought me back, day after day, from a history of war to a present full of love and living beings.

Anne Frank and Etty Hillesum

❧ *Introduction*

Anne Frank was a girl, Etty Hillesum a young woman. Both came from well-to-do Jewish families. Both lived in Amsterdam during the German occupation of the Netherlands, and both died in concentration camps—Anne Frank in Bergen-Belsen and Etty Hillesum in Auschwitz-Birkenau.[1]

Both left behind diaries, letters, and short stories, which have drawn responses in the form of reviews, articles, novels, documentaries, music, plays, and visual art. By adding this book to the body of literature on their writing, I hope to change the process of canonization so that, from now on, their texts will be read differently. What I hope to contribute is a women's-studies perspective. "Women's studies"—an umbrella term for feminist research into the differences between women and men, or the feminine and the masculine—has as its ultimate goal "put[ting] an end to the absence and/or subordination of women and the feminine in Western culture" (Buikema and A. Smelik, 1995, 11). This research can take many forms. The term is plural because it refers to many different schools of thought and scientific approaches. Although the theoretical and methodological underpinnings of women's studies are now generally accepted and respected, there has been little research into sex and gender differences at the time of the Holocaust. After all, the Nazis' aim was to destroy all Jews, regardless of sex, age, social class, or any other factor which divided Jews themselves. Anne Frank saw her fellow Jews being deported from Amsterdam to the transit camp Westerbork:

> In the evenings, when it's dark, I often see rows of good, innocent people, accompanied by crying children, walking on and on, in the charge of a couple of these men, bullied and beaten until they almost

1

drop. Nobody is spared—old people, children, babies, expectant mothers, the sick—they all join in the death march. . . .

I get frightened when I think of close friends who have been delivered into the hands of the cruelest brutes the world has ever seen. And
all because they are Jews.   (AF*b*, 316; adapt. MH/SL)

To explore the differences of how women and men experienced and perceived the Holocaust would cloud the issue, because life and death did not
depend on gender difference but on the difference between Jew and Gentile.
It could also be argued, however, that by emphasizing differences, women's
studies counteracts the rigidity of the Nazi conceptualization, which ultimately lumped all Jews together. Without losing sight of this context, women's-
studies research into the Holocaust[2] aims to let women's voices speak.

Such an endeavor is needed because, until recently, studies of the Nazi
persecution and destruction of the Jews have largely been based on the
accounts of men, on the assumption that the male perspective is universal
and objective. This approach ignores the significance of sex and gender differences in the construction of history and society. Western culture is based on
a far-reaching dichotomy between the sexes to the extent that women and men
have divergent experiences, speak different languages, and are seen and
heard in dissimilar ways. This dichotomy was also present in the Third Reich.
Sexism was an integral element of racist thinking.[3] Nazi anti-Semitism propagated stereotypical images of Jewish men as both wealthy capitalists and
communist revolutionaries. Jewish women were absent from this propaganda.
They were murdered simply for their ability to give birth to the next generation of Jews.[4]

My analysis of Anne Frank's and Etty Hillesum's texts takes a dual approach:
I focus both on the context of the Holocaust and on the writers as female
subjects. My research focuses on differences rather than equality. The philosophy of difference to which I adhere is diametrically opposed to that of the
Nazis. I view difference as positive. The Nazis separated people into categories
and hierarchies, and thereby stigmatized them. At the top was the "racially
pure German" man. Right below him was his "racially pure" German wife,
who, as a woman, was subordinate to him, but could play an important role
in bringing Nazi ideals to fruition.[5] At the bottom of the hierarchy were "the
others": Jews, Gypsies, homosexuals, the mentally and physically weak or
handicapped, communists, and dissidents. The Nazis believed that all these
"others" were inferior and needed to be eliminated, so that all differences

would eventually disappear. In this way, only one race would survive, the Germans. This concept of difference is rooted firmly within European culture:

> In the European history of philosophy, "difference" is a central concept insofar as Western thought has *always* functioned by dualistic oppositions, which create subcategories of otherness, or "difference-from." Because in this history "difference" has been predicated on relations of domination and exclusion, to be "different-from" came to mean to be "less than," to be *worth* less than.   (Braidotti 1994a, 147)

If there is a lesson to be learned from the Holocaust, it is that the risks inherent in superannuated European thinking are enormous. Etty Hillesum reached this conclusion even before she knew about Auschwitz. While still living in relative freedom in Amsterdam, she tried to come to grips with the "hopelessly unnatural theories of race, nation, and so on" (EH, 20, H'83, 9; adapt. MH/SL),[6] which cast one group as good and the other as evil. In exploring the hatred the Dutch felt for the Germans, Hillesum had the courage to search her own soul as well. She dared to acknowledge that "Nazi barbarism awakens the very same barbarism in us" (EH, 22; trans. MH). However understandable it might have been for her to hate the Germans, she did all she could to resist this emotion. She was determined to express not hatred, but unconditional love. At Westerbork she wrote: "It is the only way one can live life these days, out of blind love for one's tormented fellow creatures—regardless of their nationality, race or religion" (EH, 671; trans. MH).

She would not allow herself to be swept up by the pervasive mechanism of hatred. Whereas Nazi ideology predicted a better future once "the other" had been removed, Hillesum's ideal society was one in which hatred had been eradicated. To her mind, hatred—which she believed came from the idea that all evil resides in others and that same and self are purely good—was destroying the world. Etty Hillesum was extremely suspicious of this dualism, as she kept repeating: "I see no alternative [but that] each of us must turn inward and root out and destroy everything that motivates us to destroy others. And let us be well aware that every atom of hatred we add to this world makes it even more desolate" (EH, 560; H'83, 180; adapt. MH/SL).

Here, she linked evil in the outside world with imperfections in the self. One finds a similar train of thought in Julia Kristeva's* essay about the stranger

---

*Julia Kristeva, born in Bulgaria in 1941, is a professor of language and literature at the University of Paris, a permanent visiting professor at Columbia University in New York, and a psychoanalyst. She has published widely in the interdisciplinary field of language, literature, philosophy, and psychoanalysis.

in Western civilization. Treading in the footsteps of Freud, Kristeva described the outsider as the hidden side of our identity; in this view, the alien is part of ourselves and no longer only associated with another race or nation.

> Freud's personal life, [as] a Jew wandering from Galicia to Vienna and London, with stopovers in Paris, Rome, and New York (to mention only a few of the key stages of his encounters with political and cultural foreignness), condition[ed] his concern with confronting the other's discomfort as ill-ease in the continuous presence of the "other scene" [the unconscious] within us.   (Kristeva 1991, 181 [1988])[7]

This psychoanalytical ethos is cosmopolitan in nature. It suggests that human solidarity is based on recognition of "the other" in oneself, so that everyone embodies "the other" and there are no outsiders.

The Nazis wanted no part of such ideas. Freud himself suspected that there was some connection between anti-Semitism and criticism of psychoanalysis. When Hitler became chancellor of Germany, in 1933, Freud's books were burned. After the Anschluss, Freud left Austria very reluctantly, only after much persuasion. In 1938 he fled to London, where he died one year later. His four elderly sisters (another sister, Anna Freud Bernays, had emigrated to the United States years before) stayed behind in Vienna. They were eventually arrested and murdered in concentration camps (Wantoch, 1989).

The writings of Anne Frank and Etty Hillesum have only been partly recovered. While the Nazis were doing their best to destroy the Jews, Frank and Hillesum were working on their personal development. Though their freedom to do so grew more restricted, language was a channel of expression no one could take away from them. Both devoted themselves to writing; in language they found a new home, a safe haven to which they could retreat.

While in hiding, Anne Frank began to seek an explanation for the war. At times she would draw the conclusion that God had foisted this hardship on the Jews. On those occasions, however, she also expressed faith that he would lift the suffering again (AF*a*, 600). At other times, she placed the blame on people: "People simply have an urge to destroy, an urge to kill, to murder and rage, and until all mankind without exception, undergoes a great change, wars will be waged; everything that has been built up, cultivated, and grown will be cut down and disfigured, to begin all over again after that!" (AF*a*, 628; adapt. MH/SL).

Anne Frank was having bouts of depression, resulting from nearly two years of life indoors and various traumatic experiences. But she fought her despondent moods with a large dose of optimism. She clung to her dreams of the extraordinary future that awaited her: "I have made up my mind now to lead a different life from other girls and, later on, different from ordinary housewives" (AF*a*, 629; adapt. MH/SL).

In the Dutch, Anne actually wrote *lijden* (to suffer, to endure) rather than its homonym *leiden* (to lead), tinging this hopeful passage with bitterness. This excerpt dates from May 1944, just a few months before her arrest, which marked the beginning of her suffering in Westerbork, Auschwitz-Birkenau, and finally Bergen-Belsen.

Anne Frank was confronted with the consequences of being "the other" in at least two ways. From a very young age, she had felt the effects of anti-Semitism. She was only a preschooler when her family decided to flee the Nazis. They left their hometown of Frankfurt am Main for Amsterdam. Seven years later, the Nazis occupied the Netherlands, and two years after that, the Franks went into hiding. Hence Anne knew very well what it meant to be Jewish, and in that sense to be "the other." She pondered this and discussed it with her boyfriend in the Secret Annex, Peter van Pels. Anne was dismayed when Peter turned away from religion: "Though I am not Orthodox either, it still hurts every time I realize how alone, scornful, and how wretched he really is" (AF*a*, 684; adapt. MH/SL).

She needed God in order to develop into a good person, while "upholding [her] own sense of honor and obeying her own conscience" (AF*a*, 605). Even though life was being made difficult for her because she was a Jew, she kept her faith.

Anne Frank was "the other" not only as a Jew, but also as a woman. In the Secret Annex she became more aware of her sexually subject status and its inherent exclusions. In her diary she distanced herself from the traditional roles of housewife and mother, but did so without denying her womanhood:

> I know that I'm a woman, a woman with inner strength and plenty of courage!
> If God lets me live, I shall achieve more than Mother ever has, I shall not remain insignificant, I shall work in the world for mankind!
>
> (AF*a*, 601; adapt. MH/SL)

She was not writing about the difference between men and women, but about differences between women: between girl and woman, mother and daughter. She did not want to be like her mother. She wanted, after the war, to see the world and to be financially independent.

If Anne had survived the war, she would have been twenty in 1949, the year in which Simone de Beauvoir's magnum opus, *The Second Sex,* was published. Anne might have discovered the book and been inspired by it. Beauvoir criticized the thinking that categorized "women," "Jews" and "blacks" as essentially different from, and inferior to, "white, Christian men."[8] *The Second Sex* explores the position of women and describes them as men's vassals. Beauvoir saw man as the subject, woman as the object. Man is one, woman the other. Beauvoir was deeply convinced that this way of thinking oppressed women. She made an explicit appeal for equality of the sexes, arguing that women were not inferior to men. Because men and women occupied different positions, which offered them unequal opportunities, Beauvoir called on women to live as men did: to forget about having children and to find employment outside the home, which she saw as the shortest road to equality.

Anne had not yet begun to think about motherhood. She dreamed of a career as a journalist or writer. In the Secret Annex, she discovered a passion, linked to her Jewishness and her adolescence, for writing, from which she drew strength and comfort. One of the most important developments in feminism and women's studies in the 1980s is the recognition of how sexual difference is intertwined with other differences, such as ethnicity, class, and age. Whereas Beauvoir began by analyzing the position of "white, middle-class" women, women's studies is now attempting to outgrow this preoccupation by also examining differences among women and within groups of women.[9] This book was born out of the same impulse.

In France, Hélène Cixous was one of the first to claim that her drive to write was fueled by a combination of her Jewish background and her womanhood. In *Coming to Writing* (1991a [1976]), she linked the desire to write with being in the position of "the other." She asserted that writing could be a reaction to discrimination or exile. Cixous herself had come from a society in which it was difficult for a Jewish woman to live in freedom, and there she discovered that writing could be an avenue for personal development:

> Writing, dreaming, delivering; being my own daughter of each day. The affirmation of an internal force that is capable of looking at life without dying of fear, and above all of looking at itself, as if you were simultaneously the other—indispensable to love—and nothing more nor less than me.   (Cixous 1991a, 6 [1976])[10]

Anne Frank most certainly took the same route. Her diaries display a critical yet loving exploration of the self, in which she often saw herself as someone else in need of advice. But this someone else is the other in herself, which is not the same as "the other" in the discriminative, monolithic sense disputed by Beauvoir. In her final diary entry, she described two sides of herself. One Anne showed herself to the outside world as a cheerful, bubbly, lighthearted girl, "nothing but a frolicsome little goat who's trying to break loose" (AF*a*, 698; adapt. MH/SL). The other Anne was more withdrawn and did not express herself in public but was much sweeter, purer, and wiser. This Anne did come out in the diary. For a long time she had hardly known this hidden side of herself. Before going into hiding, she had lived "a heavenly life" (AF*a*, 515), her days filled with admirers and girlfriends, with school adventures in the Amsterdam quarter known as the Rivierenbuurt. Then she was rudely cast out of this Eden. In response she closed the gap between past and future by writing, which became a vehicle in her quest to regain paradise (Cornell 1988, 130). She found it again both on earth (in her dream of becoming a writer) and in heaven (in her faith in God and her guardian angel). Writing in her diary was Anne's way of going into hiding internally, in order to remain or become whole.

On first reading the writings of Etty Hillesum, a self-taught but born philosopher, I was immediately tempted to link them with the work of several twentieth-century women philosophers who had influenced my own intellectual development.

When Hillesum's development is seen in the context of twentieth-century thought on women and the feminine, it becomes apparent that her views on sexual difference changed over time. Although they were rooted in stereotypes about women—the very inequalities Beauvoir sought to eliminate in both her private life and intellectual work—they developed into an outspoken view on the feminine that brings to mind Luce Irigaray's philosophy of sexual difference. Although Irigaray has taken a direction very different from Beauvoir's, she still shows great respect for her: "To respect Simone de Beauvoir is to follow the theoretical and practical work for social justice that she carried out in her own way; it is to maintain the liberating horizons which she opened up for many women, and men" (Irigaray 1993c, 13–14 [1990]).[11]

In the 1970s, Beauvoir's life and philosophy were a great inspiration to many second-wave feminists. Simultaneously, some women philosophers—particularly in Paris—began challenging her concept of equality because it still implied that man and the masculine were the norm. So, while some were seeking the "masculinization of woman" which Beauvoir in fact propounded, others were exploring the implications of a "feminization of woman." Whereas Beauvoir opted for equality, Luce Irigaray worked on a philosophy of difference. One of the best-known philosophers whose theories center on sexual difference, Irigaray developed a partly pragmatic, partly utopian strategy to support the process of woman becoming woman. She believes that women should not live by masculine norms and values, but should turn inward to find out which the characteristics traditionally attributed to women truly fit them, and which do not. In this way, women can change themselves from objects into subjects without denying their sexual identity. As a result, their femininity will no longer be defined by men; Women will decide for themselves what femininity means. This vision amounts to a reversal of values. While the masculine is traditionally the norm and, by corollary, the norm takes on a masculine connotation, Irigaray was the first to use the feminine as a strength and as an alternative to Beauvoir's brand of feminism.

Reading Etty Hillesum's oeuvre in the context of Beauvoir's and Irigaray's philosophies makes clear that she faced the same problem as they did: How to define woman in Western culture (De Costa 1993b). However, one major difference between Hillesum and Beauvoir is that in her earlier writings the former still clung to the traditional stereotype of women. In her first diaries, she wondered whether she was a real woman because she led such a cerebral life: "I am not really a 'natural woman,' at least not sexually. I am no tigress, and sometimes that makes me feel inferior. My instinctive physical urges are diverted and weakened in many ways by all sorts of intellectualizations, which I am sometimes ashamed of" (EH, 130; H'83, 43–44; adapt. MH).

She associated the feminine so closely with the physical that she regarded this spiritualization process—which is how she described her development—as a process of becoming human: "Perhaps the true, inner emancipation of women has yet to begin. We are not yet full human beings; we are still bitches. We are still bound and tied by centuries-old traditions. We are still waiting to be born as people, that is the great task that lies before us women" (EH, 73; H'83, 27–28; adapt. MH).

From this, it is clear that Hillesum wavered between the concepts of Beauvoir and Irigaray, briefly summed up by the quotations: "One is not born, but rather becomes, a woman" (De Beauvoir 1988, 295 [1949])[12] and "I am born a woman, but I must still become this woman that I am by nature" (Irigaray 1996, 107 [1992]).[13] Beauvoir saw the feminine identity primarily as a cultural construct that was an obstacle to the self-actualization of women. She rejected any notion of feminine specificity. Irigaray, on the other hand,

advocates searching for a feminine potential. In the struggle for emancipation, unity, and equality, Beauvoir called on women to become "humans."
Irigaray's goal is for women to become women. In the latter's view, a recognition of women's difference will earn women respect as different but equal,
without forcing them to compromise. It is in the specificity of women's lives
that Irigaray finds her leads for a radical critique and transformation of the
phallocentric, male-defined Western culture.

When she first started thinking about her identity, Etty Hillesum assumed
that she had to rid herself of feminine characteristics in order to become a
whole person. Later, she came to realize that femininity was not exclusively
bound to the body. She could also draw on an ancient bond between the
feminine and the soul. Woman's task, which she had taken on, lost its negative connotation (to renounce one's body) and was transformed into a
positive act (to use one's spiritual strength). She discussed this with her friend
Julius Spier:

> And I explained to him once again that I believed that this would
> be woman's historical task for the years to come: to guide man to his
> soul, by way of hers. And none of the eroticism need be lost. But one
> must put everything in its rightful place, einordnen. And I also believe
> that the most important and pioneering men of the future will be those
> who have such a strong feminine side—and at the same time are still
> real men, like him [Spier] and like Rilke for instance—that they act as
> the, how shall I say it, signposts to the regions of the soul. And not
> those "he-men," those Führers and heroes in uniform, not the ones they
> call "real men." But then, maybe real men only exist in the minds of
> women anyway.   (EH, 301; trans. MH)[14]

At this point, she no longer associated the feminine only with the body;
she also saw a connection with the soul and with emotions. She recognized
that women felt more whole as human beings than men did: "It really is true,
I think: Men can only reach their own feelings through ours, women's feelings" (EH, 312, trans. MH).

As she sorted out what it meant to be a woman, she began to see herself
as part of a larger whole that was both of this world and beyond. She was
gathering inner strength which she intended to use in order to ease humanity's suffering. This strength she believed to have a divine source. During her
self-discovery, she also developed a very personal spirituality. Although the
Jewishness of this faith is debatable, her writings indicate that she ultimately
decided not to run from the fate of the Jews. She reached this decision
through self-knowledge and the discovery of a deep, inner spirituality. She

was convinced that suffering was part of life and did not want to evade it: "Ultimately what matters most is to bear the pain, to cope with it, and to keep a corner of one's soul unsullied, come what may" (EH, 150; H'83, 146).

She recognized that the Nazis were not after individuals, but numbers. More than once, Hillesum was offered a chance to go into hiding, but she knew that if she accepted, someone else would be deported in her place. Still, she continued to emphasize that this was her own choice, and in so doing relativized the Nazis' power. She did not feel trapped within their jaws, but rather held in God's embrace. Her acceptance of the *"Massenschicksal"* (mass or common fate; EH, 511) was no passive deed:

> And I shall wield this slender fountain pen as if it were a hammer, and my words will have to be so many hammer strokes with which to beat out the story of our fate and of a piece of history as it is and never was before. Not in this totalitarian, massively organized form, spanning the whole of Europe. Still, a few people must survive if only to be the chroniclers of this era. I would very much like to become one of their number.   (EH, 511; H'83, 146–147; adapt. MH)

Anne Frank and Etty Hillesum represented "the other" in more ways than one: as women and as Jews. Anne Frank's and Etty Hillesum's place in the symbolic order was not self-evident. Therefore, they each needed a strong will and a great desire to enter, insofar as possible, the realms of language and culture. Both Anne Frank and Etty Hillesum defied women's accepted, pre-ordained roles: to be shackled to the body and a housewife's chores. They refused to accept the limitations and duties women were subjected to. They searched for other ways to live and found new possibilities in language.

Because they were Jews, their freedom of movement grew increasingly restricted as the war continued, until the only path that remained open was the one that led to their death. Anne Frank and Etty Hillesum were caught between fear and hope, rebellion and resignation, the will to live and acceptance of death. In that no-man's-land, they found a reality that is everywhere: God. So it was not only in language, but also in the divine, that they found a home. There, they found comfort and support, but, most importantly, a chance to be themselves. In their discourse on spirituality they created an opportunity for self-actualization. They wrote and kept faith while staring death in the face. Writing and faith allowed them to make sense of life, however little of it was left to them.

Anne Frank wrote more than just diaries. She left behind short stories that are virtually unknown and, unlike the diaries, have only been translated into a few languages. What is more, the only versions of the diary that most people know of is the one published by her father, Otto Frank, in 1947, and—even worse—the stage plays and films based on it. A particularly distorted version of her life and work was the stage play written by the American writers Frances Goodrich and Albert Hackett.[15] This play was extremely popular both in the United States and abroad, and the film based on it was generally well received. The "stage or celluloid Anne" is, however, quite different from the Anne who emerges in the diary.

The "diary Anne" has many faces. Sometimes she is sweet and kind; at other times inconsiderate and indifferent. She has strong feelings of love and hate. Every day, she struggles with fears of arrest and deportation. She knows there is a Jewish ghetto not far from the Secret Annex. She is an eyewitness to the deportation of Jews from Amsterdam to the Westerbork transit camp. Along with the others in the hiding place, she listens to Radio Oranje (the voice of the Dutch government-in-exile in London), and so she is aware of the mass killings in Poland.

She fights fear and depression brought on by the Nazi terror, and tries to stay cheerful and optimistic in spite of it all. She knows that her chances of surviving the war are very slim, but she keeps herself afloat with dreams and fantasies of life "after the war." She hopes to become a journalist, or better yet, a novelist. In short, the "Anne of the diary" is a rich, complex personality.

The "stage Anne" is but a watered-down version of this. The play de-emphasizes the context—the persecution and destruction of the Jews—as well as the less favorable sides of Anne's character. She is portrayed as a cheerful and optimistic girl. The distortion of the diary is obvious at the end of the play, when the writers have her say: "In spite of everything I still believe that people are really good at heart." This sentence has become one of the most quoted and famous in the entire diary, and yet it was taken completely out of context. When Anne wrote these words, she was in a serious mood; she realized how hard it is for young people to grow up in wartime:

> "For in its innermost depths, childhood is lonelier than old age." I read this saying in some book, and I've always remembered it, and found it to be true. Is it true then that grown-ups have a more difficult time here than we do? No. I know it isn't. Older people have formed their opinions about everything and don't waver before they act. It's twice as hard for us young ones to hold our ground, and maintain our opinions, in a time when all ideals are being shattered and destroyed, when people are showing their worst side, and do not know whether to believe in truth and right and in God.

Anyone who claims that the older ones have a more difficult time here certainly doesn't realize to what extent our problems weigh down on us, problems for which we are probably much too young, but which thrust themselves upon us continually, until, after a long time, when we think we've found a solution, but the solution doesn't seem able to resist the weapons which reduce it to nothing again. That's the difficulty in these times: ideals, dreams and cherished hopes rise within us, only to meet the horrible truth and be shattered. It's really a wonder that I haven't dropped all my ideals, because they seem so absurd and impossible to carry out. Yet I keep them, because in spite of everything I still believe that people are really good at heart.

I simply can't build up my hopes on a foundation consisting of confusion, misery, and death, I see the world gradually being turned into a wilderness, I hear the ever-approaching thunder, which will destroy us too, I can feel the sufferings of millions and yet, if I look up into the heavens, I think that everything will turn out all right, that this cruelty too will end, and that peace and tranquillity will return again. In the meantime, I must uphold my ideals, for perhaps the time will come when I shall be able to carry them out! (AF*a*, 693–694; adapt. MH/SL)[16]

Thus the phrase "in spite of everything I still believe that people are really good at heart" can be explained as a survival mechanism. This contrasts starkly with the playwrights' interpretation. They turned this sentence into the concluding statement of the play, suggesting that it was Anne's final statement, her conclusion. That was not the case, however. Anne wrote for another two weeks, and ended with a description of the two sides of her character. Three days later, she was torn away from her writerly existence, leaving her no time to think of a fitting conclusion.

Anne Frank's diaries are a description of her thoughts, feelings, and actions during the time in hiding. Anne found out while writing that she was a "little bundle of contradictions" (AF*a*, 697). Both the secretive, serious Anne and the "frolicsome little goat who's breaking loose" (AF*a*, 698) are committed to paper. In choosing to portray only her cheerful and optimistic side, the playwrights created a very flat and one-sided character. Moreover, they ignored something which Anne Frank must have heard about: the terrors of the camps. She wrote the sentence in question in mid-July 1944, before she was sent to Auschwitz. What went on in her mind when she arrived in the camps? Six weeks later, on the night of September 5, 1944, she set foot in Auschwitz-Birkenau. Within two months, she was deported to another camp: Bergen-Belsen.

"Now Anne, who had written that she still believed that people were good at heart, sees it all, all there is to see, this young girl so eager for experience.

If she could have kept her diary there in hell, what belief would she have recorded? Can we project Anne into the future?" (Rosen 1992,85).

This rhetorical question is worth raising, and contains an implicit criticism of the playwrights Goodrich and Hackett. Until the last moment, Anne stayed by her sister Margot's side. Margot died, weak and exhausted, at the end of winter, in February or March 1945. Anne died soon thereafter. Contrary to what the play suggests, her story has no happy ending.

The play and its success can be interpreted as a desperate attempt to cling to a simplified Enlightenment ideal, based on an optimistic view of the future and a great faith in humanity. This ideal holds that humans have the capacity to gain more and more knowledge and insight, and thus to become ever more capable of influencing the course of history. Furthermore, because people are good and reasonable by nature, Western civilization will be marked by ever greater rationality, liberty, and emancipation. This widely accepted concept of humanity has been disrupted by modern European history. The mass murder of all those who did not fit the norm occurred at the heart of so-called civilized Western culture. The Shoah is impossible to understand by reasoning from a one-dimensional Enlightenment concept. The irreconcilability of the Enlightenment and the Holocaust became apparent in the immediate postwar period. Many people—not only Nazis but many camp survivors as well—tried to forget the war. They attempted to go on living as if nothing had happened. They suppressed the traumatic events. This reaction was encouraged at the personal level, but also in a much wider sense. The 1950s was a period of reconstruction in Western Europe. People had to work hard, and there was little time for mourning and dealing with trauma. Despite everything, people held on to the Enlightenment ideal: that people are essentially good, and that an increase in rationality would lead to more happiness on earth.

In the long run, however, it proved impossible to suppress the memory of Europe's greatest genocide. The past few decades have seen the publication of growing numbers of books by people who experienced the Holocaust, people who want to bear witness to the events in writing: "It has been suggested that testimony is the literary—or discursive—mode par excellence of our times, and that our era can precisely be defined as the age of testimony" (Felman and Laub 1992, 5).

The history of the Anne Frank play shows a parallel shift. The original version placed minimal emphasis on the persecution of the Jews and on the ultimate murder of the people in hiding. The stress was on faith in humanity and the future. Anne's optimistic phrases were quoted out of context and given undue weight.

In 1956, the play was performed in the Netherlands in Dutch translation for the first time. In 1984, it was adapted by Mies Bouhuys, and in 1995 it was staged again to mark the fiftieth anniversary of the war's end. This time, however, the final scene was drastically different from the original version by Goodrich and Hackett. The upbeat note had been removed from the play's end. The light from the outside world, which pierces the darkness of the hiding place, brings not enlightenment but Nazis, who are making their way up the stairs. The actors stand with their backs to the audience, facing the staircase. They stretch their arms upward. Then they turn around and stand side by side. Each in turn utters the name of the person he or she played and his or her (estimated) date and place of death. This ending casts a hush over the audience—as in a commemoration of the dead—before they begin to applaud. Apparently it took half a century for the theatergoing public to be able to look back and face the painful realities of the past.[17]

This book does not aim to provide an in-depth analysis of the varying degrees of distortions of Anne Frank's character and background in the years since the war. I focus primarily on the notebooks and loose sheets that Anne Frank herself filled with writings. She did not hide from the paradoxes of youth and adulthood, nor those of life and death; she tried to face them and name them. If Anne is ambiguous, her oeuvre most certainly is too. There are three versions of the diaries, two of which were published only a decade ago. I will go into this more deeply in the first chapter on Anne Frank, but I would like to briefly comment on it here.

Anne Frank kept a diary for the entire period she was in hiding. In the spring of 1944, she began rewriting this diary after hearing a speech by Gerrit Bolkestein, minister of education, art, and science of the Dutch government-in-exile, broadcast by Radio Oranje. Bolkestein urged the people living under Nazi occupation in Holland to save their letters and diaries so they could be collected and kept for posterity. A few weeks later she decided to prepare her original diary for publication. She rewrote the entries on loose sheets in very neat and flowing handwriting. She made changes in style as well as content. Because she hoped that publication would earn her respect as a human being, but above all recognition as a writer, she tried to improve her writing style. For the same reason, she omitted certain passages that she considered unsuitable for publication, probably out of embarrassment. She left out nasty remarks about her mother and overt references to her own sexual awakening. In this way, she constructed herself as someone who conformed more closely to the dominant norms and values of the day. And thus, two Annes were born: the Anne of the original diary, who wrote only for herself, and the Anne of the second version, who was concerned with the preconceived notions of the outside world.

Of the eight people who hid in the Secret Annex, Anne's father, Otto Frank, was the only one to survive the camps. After the war, he decided to publish his daughter's diary, posthumously fulfilling her wish to become a writer. The manuscript which he offered to publishers was based largely, but not fully, on the rewritten version of the diary. Otto Frank also made some changes of his own. *Het Achterhuis,* the version that was published in the Netherlands in June 1947 and has been translated into dozens of languages, differs considerably from the original version.

Otto Frank died in 1980. In his last will, he left the diaries to RIOD. In 1986, the RIOD published a scholarly, unexpurgated edition of the diaries. The wonderful layout of this critical edition presents all existing versions of each diary entry on the same page, making it possible to identify and interpret the differences between the various versions.[18]

It is especially interesting to see how Anne Frank censored her own diary (De Costa 1994). She left out the passages referring to her female identity, or more precisely, the process of becoming a woman: the conflicts with her mother, her increased awareness of her body and sexual feelings, and her first menstrual periods. Her father censored the diary along the same lines, sometimes at the explicit request of prudish publishers (Frank 1986a, 69).

These facts are particularly interesting in light of the following paradox: Despite the fact that Holocaust-related literature centers more often on men's than women's experiences, the most widely read book about the persecution of the Jews is the diary of Anne Frank. However, this apparent contradiction is dissolved when one asks the question, "Which Anne Frank do we actually think we know?" The image propagated by the media has, to a great extent, been shaped to conform to conservative social values. This is why I prefaced the section on Anne Frank with a chapter describing the texts she herself wrote—the two versions of her diaries, the stories, and the Secret Annex descriptions.

The second chapter on Anne Frank examines the origin of her passion to write. Diary writing—an activity girls in particular are drawn to—appears to fill a void that is created by adolescence and, in Anne Frank's case, by forced isolation as well. Writing can serve to block out feelings of desperation and depression. This healing effect is explained by Julia Kristeva in an essay on adolescent writing (Kristeva 1990). Nonetheless, certain thoughts and feelings described in Anne Frank's diary call into question Kristeva's view that writing is a very masculine, even phallic, exercise, "if not the phallus par excellence" (Kristeva 1990, 11).

When Luce Irigaray published her dissertation (Irigaray 1974), she was fired by her mentor, Jacques Lacan, because of their sharply differing views on the phallocentric character of psychoanalytic theory. Julia Kristeva, however, has proven to be a much more loyal, obedient daughter. She does not question "the Law of Father Lacan," but continues to defend phallocentrism. For many researchers trained in feminist theory, this in itself is sufficient reason to disregard her work. However, I believe there is no need to throw out the baby with the bathwater, as it were. Inspired by Irigaray's productive method of transformation from within, I have tried to rewrite Kristeva's discourse—which appears to relegate women and the feminine to the background—in order to reveal the importance of the mother-daughter relationship to the writing process. In discussions of how Anne Frank's parents influenced her development, Edith Frank-Holländer has always received less attention than Otto Frank. However, a psychoanalytic reading of Anne Frank's texts points toward a very different balance. In short, the realm of the feminine and the maternal is not abandoned upon entry into the symbolic order of language and culture; it continues to have an impact on Anne's development from girl into woman. Though this reading is a departure from the traditional reading reception-history of Anne Frank's diaries and her other writings, I demonstrate that her urge to write is best explained by the mother-daughter relationship, rather than the father-daughter relationship.

Although Anne Frank was persecuted for being a Jew, it is sometimes claimed that her Jewish background is a controversial issue because her family was not Orthodox and her writings display few Jewish elements. For example, Anne Frank and Primo Levi have been referred to as authors who owe their worldwide acclaim partly to "erasing Jews and Judaism in favor of humanity as a whole" (Dresden 1991, 238; trans. MH). In Anne Frank's case at least, I think the perceived lack of Jewishness has more to do with the reception of the diaries than with their actual content (De Costa 1994).

Chapter 3 focuses on her religious development, which left a clear mark on her diaries and stories. Anne Frank thought about believing or not believing in God, and about the relationship between Jews and Christians and between

Orthodox and Reformed Jews, and she incorporated her ideas in her diaries and fiction. She also staked out a very specific position on the place of women in Jewish tradition. A psychoanalytical approach to her writings—with extra attention to apparently marginal, implicit textual characteristics—reveals a link between her spirituality and her adolescence. While in Jewish tradition, menstruation is surrounded by taboos, Anne Frank's first menses made her realize that she possessed divine powers. Although the Jewish religion is deeply patriarchal, she found ways of continuing to believe in God without being untrue to herself. Using dreams and fantasies, she created a God who met her needs. She sought a God who could guide her through adolescence and provide comfort in the hard times in which she lived. She eased the burden of living by summoning up a guardian angel in the shape of her beloved late maternal grandmother.

Seen from an Irigarayan perspective, this process of "becoming divine" can be clearly traced and analyzed. I apply Irigaray's views on the need, sense, and meaning of religion to discover the spiritual dimension of Anne Frank's oeuvre. A typical feature of Irigaray's theories is a critical stance toward existing discourses, particularly toward "in-difference"—the implicit disregard of women and the feminine that pervades virtually all of Western thought. So, while Irigaray's work helps to reveal Anne's "double otherness," it also presents a dilemma: her double outsider position calls into question Irigaray's presence in this book. In the intermezzo this problem is examined in detail. To recognize the "multiple other" in Anne Frank—a stubborn, curious, intelligent girl who loved life, the youngest inhabitant of the Secret Annex, a Jew during the occupation—is to challenge Irigaray's rock-solid certainty that "sexual difference is one of the major philosophical issues, if not the issue, of our age" (Irigaray 1993a, 5 [1984]).[19]

How can this view be reconciled with the image of Anne Frank that emerges from her writings, let alone with the central trauma of the twentieth century: the murder of six million Jews? According to Irigaray, all evil in Western culture is fundamentally due to the lack of sexual difference in that culture. Working toward a culture of sexual difference, one of true respect between man and woman, and respect for both the masculine and the feminine, would constitute a first step toward acceptance of, and respect for, all other differences—of class, ethnicity, age, and religion (Irigaray 1996 [1992]). But how can this point of view, which puts the male-female difference before all other differences, be brought into line with the peril to which Anne Frank was constantly exposed because of her Jewish background? My answer to this question can be found in the Intermezzo, where I will also return to Julia Kristeva's theories. I analyze how Kristeva's and Irigaray's theories facilitate, or limit, my attempt to explore the relationship between Jewishness and femininity.

Etty Hillesum is far less well known than Anne Frank, even though two long letters of hers had been illegally published already during the war.[20] It was not until 1981 that excerpts of her diaries were published in Dutch (Hillesum 1981), followed six months later by a selection of her letters (Hillesum 1982). Finally, in October 1986, a complete edition of all remaining diaries and letters to and from Etty Hillesum was published (Hillesum 1986).

Just like Anne Frank, Etty Hillesum wanted to become a writer. When she left for Westerbork in 1942, she gave her diaries to a friend for safekeeping and asked her to pass them on to Klaas Smelik, who was a writer himself, in case she should not survive her captivity. In September 1943 she was deported from Westerbork to Auschwitz, where, according to Red Cross records, she was murdered on November 30 of the same year.

After the war, Hillesum's friend tried to honor her wishes, but no one wanted to publish the writings. Publishers probably suspected that readers would not be receptive to "war books." There was a tendency to look forward rather than back; people wanted neither to remember nor to mourn (however, see also note 1, on p. 254).

This attitude appears to have changed in the 1980s, the heyday of postmodernism. According to Jean-François Lyotard, the postmodern is part of the modern, because it represents everything in modernity that is hidden, obscure, and impenetrable. The postmodern is not the end of the modern, but signifies a different relationship to the modern. In a postmodern outlook on life, one must experience the "unbearable darkness of being" rather than close one's eyes to the unfathomable and complex elements that life largely consists of.

Forty years after they were written, Etty Hillesum's diaries and letters were published and reached a large audience. Although they met with some criticism, her writings were mostly praised for their philosophical depth and mystical sensibility. At the same time, there also was a tendency to ignore the ambiguities in her work. Just as in the initial reception of Anne Frank's diary, complexities and paradoxes were avoided. A striking example of this desire was the photograph on the cover of a collection of critiques on Hillesum's writings (Gaarlandt 1989). This cover shows Hillesum staring pensively into the camera. Her chin rests on her left hand. The cigarette she held in the original photograph has been retouched out of the picture. Over time, Etty Hillesum may have developed into a "demi-saint" (De Costa 1991, 142), but she also had worldly, "unsaintly" traits. It was especially difficult for her to deal with this incongruity, this inner contradiction: "You are actually better off being either a complete whore or a true saint. At least then you have peace of mind and you know what you are. In my case, the ambivalence is really quite extreme" (EH, 51; trans. MH).

As her diaries and letters demonstrate, Hillesum's strength lay in her very capacity to accept the paradoxes and complexities of life and in herself. She continually strove to incorporate these contradictions into a larger whole, without eliminating the ambiguities. She applied this not only to her inner life, but also to the outside world. Amid the misery of the war, she remained sensitive to the beauty of being alive. She often wrote about how intensely she enjoyed the good side of life. At the same time she was painfully aware of the discrepancy between text and context. During the mass deportations of Jews she wrote:

> 3 JULY 1942, FRIDAY EVENING, 8:30. Yes, I am still at the same desk, but it seems to me that I am going to have to turn a new leaf and find a different tone. I must admit a new insight into my life and find a place for it: What is at stake is our impending destruction and annihilation, we can have no more illusions about that. They are out to destroy us completely, we must accept that and go on from there. [. . .] At least, now I know and I shall not burden others with my fears. I shall not be bitter if others fail to grasp what is happening to us Jews. I work and continue to live with the same conviction, and I find life meaningful— yes, meaningful—although I hardly dare say so in company these days.
>
> Living and dying, sorrow and joy, the blisters on my feet and the jasmine behind the house, the persecution, the unspeakable horrors— it is all as one in me and I accept it all as one mighty whole and begin to grasp it better if only for myself, without being able to explain to anyone else how it all fits together. I wish I could live for a long time so that one day I would find a way to explain it, and if I am not granted that wish, well, then somebody else will perhaps do it, carry on from where my life has been cut short. And that is why I must try to live a good and faithful life to my last breath: so that those who come after me do not have to start all over again, need not face the same difficulties. Isn't that doing something for future generations?
>
> (EH, 486–487; H'83, 130–131; adapt. MH)

Etty Hillesum invited her future readers to follow her line of reasoning. The act of wiping out her cigarette, however, suggests the opposite: It is symbolic of a much wider censorship. The removal of the cigarette can be considered to be more than a metaphor for the omission of Etty Hillesum's worldly traits; it is also symptomatic of the avoidance of the contradictions in her texts. The reception of Hillesum's works shows a tendency toward a non-ambiguous interpretation of author and texts. Ambiguities are "retouched" in one way or another, changing the overall image significantly. Another example of this can be found in the English translation (Hillesum 1983) of the Dutch-language selection from the diaries. Not only is it regrettable that the English-speaking world is unable to read all of Hillesum's works, but, what is worse, the existing English edition leaves much to be desired in some places. To illustrate this point, here is a new translation of an excerpt from Hillesum's diaries:

> A poem by Rilke is as real and as important as a young man falling out of an airplane, that is something you must not forget. [Both are] part of this world and you cannot obliterate one with the other. Go to sleep.
>
> You must accept every paradox; of course, you'd like to fuse everything into a unity and to somehow simplify everything in your mind, to make life easier for yourself. But life isn't like that. It consists of contradictions that all have to be accepted as part of life, and we should not accentuate one at the cost of the other. Just let it all spin around, and maybe it'll somehow fall into place.   (EH, 92; trans. MH)

In the English edition of her diaries, entitled *Etty: A Diary 1941–43* (1983), this passage reads as follows:

> A poem by Rilke is as real and as important as a young man falling out of an aeroplane. That's something I must engrave on my heart. All that happens in this world of ours and you must not leave one thing out for the sake of another. Now go to sleep. Accept your inner conflicts, try to bridge them, *to simplify them, for then your life will become simpler as well.* Mull them all over and perhaps they'll fall into place.
>
> (H'83, 34; italics added)

In the original Dutch, Hillesum describes her understanding of the tendency to simplify, but she herself advocates acceptance of life's paradoxes. In Arnold J. Pomerans's translation, Hillesum's plea appears inverted: she is in favor of simplifying conflicts so that life will also become simpler and more bearable. Hillesum's acceptance of life's complexities is therefore rewritten into an appeal for simplification! How can this major disparity between the original and the English translation be accounted for? Is it simply a matter of careless translating or bad editing? Or is something else going on? I suspect that both the "retouched" cigarette and the erroneous translation are part of the same (conscious or unconscious) attempt to make Hillesum's works more accessible and comprehensible, by portraying certain aspects as simpler and less ambiguous than they really are.

Chapter 4, the first chapter on Etty Hillesum, gives an overview of her work with all its contradictions and inherent complexities.

While the Anne Frank part of this book draws on the insights of Julia Kristeva and Luce Irigaray, the Etty Hillesum part deals primarily with another theorist: Hélène Cixous. In her semimonthly seminars between 1985 and 1988, Cixous regularly discussed Hillesum's diaries and letters, a selection of which was published in French during that period (Hillesum 1985 and 1988). However, only a tiny fraction of Cixous's thought on Etty Hillesum has been published.[21] By analyzing Cixous's responses to the diaries and letters—and by using Cixous's knowledge and methods—I want to reassess the literary, philosophical, and spiritual value of Etty Hillesum's works. In the process, I will describe and comment on the scope and limitations of Cixous's theoretical concepts.

Of the three French theorists—Kristeva, Irigaray, and Cixous—the latter relates most explicitly to the position of "the other," and not only in terms of sexual difference. As a Jew and an Algerian she grew up amidst differences: "I had the 'luck' to take my first steps in the blazing hotbed between two holocausts, in the midst, in the very bosom of racism, to be three years old in 1940, to be Jewish, one part of me in the concentration camps, one part of me in the 'colonies'" (Cixous 1991a, 17 [1976]).[22]

Cixous's mother, a midwife, was an Ashkenazic Jew of Austro-Hungarian descent who had fled to Algeria from Germany. Her father was a Sephardic Jew from Spain, who had moved to Algeria after living in Morocco. As a child, Cixous was exposed to several languages: Yiddish, German, French, and Arabic.[23] Outside the home, life was full of danger: imperialism, colonialism, anti-Semitism, racism, and sexism were all rampant. Having grown up in a phallocentric and anti-Semitic world, Cixous described herself as a *juifemme*, a "Jewoman":

> You are, you too, a Jewoman, trifling, diminutive, mouse among the mouse people, assigned to the fear of the big bad cat. To the diaspora of your desires; to the intimate deserts. And if you grow, your desert likewise grows. If you come out of the hole, the world lets you know that there is no place for your kind in its nations.
>
> (Cixous 1991a, 7 [1976])[24]

Against this backdrop, Cixous has called for the practice of difference. Although she refuses to order differences of any kind (cultural, class, sexual, or ethnic) into a hierarchy that favors the heterosexual white male, she does acknowledge their existence. In her literary theories, she explores the influence of differences on texts.

Chapter 5 examines Cixous's thoughts on culture, language, and writing in general, as well as her analysis of Etty Hillesum's diaries and letters. To Cixous, Hillesum belongs to a category of authors who come to writing through adversity and who end up proclaiming the richness of life in their work. Cixous suspects that there is a (tragic) link between periods of violence in history and the gift of writing and thinking (Cixous 1992, 113). For those who have no place in the world, language can be a sanctuary. This relationship to language is not unfamiliar to Jews. There have been times when language was the only thing they had left. Cixous has a special place in her heart for authors *sans abri*—homeless writers. But this does not mean that she uncritically accepts life's misery because she is only interested in its literary and poetic expression. She is political in a poetic way; poetry and politics are closely related. Cixous believes that a text should establish both an aesthetic and an ethical relationship to reality. The literature she values most is produced by sources that, in times of violence and terror, are often silenced. Often those who suffer most from the violence and terror are the ones able to heal, to open their hearts and minds to a way of living that transcends power and war. This ability engenders a style of writing Cixous calls *écriture féminine*. Such writing cannot take place in a vacuum, separate from life; it is nourished by life and continuously interacts with it.

In chapter 5, I will apply Cixous's explorations of what constitutes *écriture féminine* to Etty Hillesum's relationship to writing. Rejecting the commonly held opinion that Etty Hillesum is otherworldly, I will focus mainly on the passages that discuss the extreme times in which she lived, and based on these, I will analyze her motives for writing. She wanted to be a chronicler, not to report on all the anti-Jewish legislation and atrocities, but to write about the things that are easily overlooked under such circumstances:

> Years from now, schoolchildren will be taught about yellow stars and ghettos and Nazi terror and it will make their hair stand on end. But parallel to that textbook history, there is another one. [. . .] Perhaps it is worth being part of history. One can at least see for oneself what else there is, besides that which ends up in the history books.
>
> (EH, 375; H'83, 109; adapt. MH)

At odds with the spirit of the times, Etty Hillesum remained open to love and the beauty around her. That was her way of putting up a fight. She had a gift for staying attuned to the things that brightened the dark period in which she lived.

There is another way in which Hillesum fought the totalitarian regime that held so many in an iron grip. She liberated herself from it by focusing on another reality. Through meditation, or "listening within," as she called it, she was trying to establish an ethical base. She attempted to bring out the good in herself and others and to rid the world of evil. Inspired by Rilke's *Weltinnenraum* [inner universe],[25] she tried to describe her inner reality. The diary genre proved to be eminently suitable for this. In a year and a half, she filled eleven notebooks. Though her focus was inward, diary writing was not a way of burying her head in the sand. It was her way of actively contributing to the improvement of society:

> And I see no other solution, I really see no other solution but to turn inward, to your own core, to extinguish all the rottenness there. I no longer believe that we can improve anything in the outside world that we have not first improved in ourselves. And that to me seems to be the only lesson to be learned from this war, that we must *only* look inside ourselves and nowhere else.
>
> (EH, 254; H'83, 71; adapt. MH)

In writing, Etty Hillesum sought ways to counter Nazi power structures. In terms of content, her writings come close to Cixous's norms for *écriture féminine*. However, writing must also display a change in style to be considered *écriture féminine*, and it is debatable whether Etty Hillesum's texts fit the bill in this respect. In chapter 5, I will argue that Hillesum's writing changed along with her thinking. In her diaries, she developed a way of thinking and living that differed radically from the mainstream; in the end, she also mentioned an alternative way of writing that would fit in with this. Time ran out before she could develop these ideas, although first attempts can be found in her last diaries and letters.

The spiritual development in Etty Hillesum's texts is the theme of the sixth and final chapter. Reviews that pursue this subject tend to emphasize the spiritual inspiration she received from her friend and mentor Julius Spier. In Western, patriarchal culture, the desire to locate "the "man behind the woman" is not uncommon. The influence of women is apparently being considered much less interesting. I counter this phenomenon by turning my attention to Hillesum's friend Henny Tideman, whose influence on Hillesum's spiritual growth was substantial, and cannot be ignored in the search for Hillesum's sources of inspiration.

I also defy the patriarchal man-behind-the-woman syndrome by emphasizing the authenticity of Hillesum's spirituality. Nourished by the people and
books around her, she eventually arrived at a unique concept of religion and
the divine. While many other people were rejecting religion because it could
not be reconciled with the horrors of war, Etty Hillesum saw no reason to
renounce God. On the contrary, she grew even closer to her private deity.

Although Hillesum wrote profoundly and impressively about her spiritual development, I distrust the existing tendency to declare her a saint. As
soon as a woman finds a place in the symbolic order—in this case, in the
spiritual discourse—she is written out of it again. She is declared holy and
thereby placed beyond reality. Cixous, too, interprets Hillesum's diaries in this
way: "There is a name for her particular make-up, her nature, that which forms
her destination, and I will go so far as to call it that: saintliness" (Cixous, seminar 03/22/1986; trans. MH)[26]

Cixous expresses surprise that this should be so, because the mystical
tradition into which Hillesum seems to fit presumably does not exist in Judaism.
Her diaries show a changing relationship to God; limited at first, it eventually
developed into an all-encompassing, exclusive, and absolute love. In her first
diaries, she was not yet saintly; she was still "a little woman," as she often put
it. But before long, according to Cixous, she entered the realm of holiness:
"But very soon she starts becoming a non-woman and a saint" (Cixous, seminar 03/22/1986; trans. MH).[27] I disagree with Cixous. To challenge her point
of view, I draw on Irigaray's theories about the relationship between the divine
and the feminine. In the process of "becoming divine," Etty Hillesum did not
leave behind her femininity; in fact, her spiritual awakening coincided with
her exploration of what it means to be a woman. She did not disavow her
femininity. On the contrary, her spirituality and particularly the mystical
inspiration that emanates from her later diaries and letters are steeped in feminine specificity. In chapter 6 I show that her mystical encounter with God
can, in the end, no longer be interpreted as a sublimation of her love for Spier,
but must be seen as a love affair resulting in a powerful instance of symbolic
motherhood: Etty Hillesum carries God within her and, like a midwife, assists
in the birth of God in herself and others.

In the epilogue, I will draw a parallel between writing then and reading now.

Anne Frank

Chapter 1 ❧ Ode to My Fountain Pen

The first and second chapters of this book focus on Anne Frank the writer. In chapter 2 I investigate her motives for writing, drawing mainly on the psychoanalytic and literary theories of Julia Kristeva. This chapter, however, is devoted to the material to be analyzed: Anne Frank's texts.*

Anne Frank became posthumously famous with *Het Achterhuis*—published in the United States under the title *Anne Frank: The Diary of a Young Girl* (New York: Doubleday, 1952), a selection of her writings compiled by her father, Otto Frank. That text, while it certainly provides a good impression of Anne Frank's talent for writing, is unsuitable for scholarly research. Not until 1986 did RIOD publish a complete and comparative edition of Anne Frank's diaries. The English translation, *The Critical Edition,* appeared in 1989. However, it, too, is incomplete; it contains neither the "book of beautiful quotations" nor the tales Anne set down in an account book. Some of the latter were published in Dutch in 1949, followed by a wider selection in 1960. Eventually, in 1982, the whole account book was published in Dutch. In English a selection of Anne Frank's tales was first published in *The Works of Anne Frank* (New York: Doubleday, 1959) and later in *Tales from the House Behind* (New York: Bantam, 1966). Finally a wider selection, called *Anne Frank's Tales from the Secret Annex,* was published (New York: Doubleday, 1983).

I have decided to follow *The Critical Edition* in calling the original diaries the *a* version. The rewritten version is called the *b* version (see "The Loose

---

*I have deliberately chosen to use the word "texts" rather than "diaries"; until recently relatively few people knew that Anne Frank not only kept a diary but also wrote in other genres. She wrote short stories, worked on a novel, and kept a "book of beautiful quotations." Moreover, many of her diary entries were written in the form of letters.

Sheets"). The *c* version—the text published in *Anne Frank: The Diary of a Young Girl*—receives hardly any attention in this book, because I am interested in Anne Frank's own writing, rewriting, and editing. These days, there is even a *d* version, which refers to a revised and expanded edition of the diary edited by Otto Frank and Mirjam Pressler. They based it on the text from *The Diary,* but expanded it with passages from the *a* and *b* versions. The "Pressler" edition, as the *d* version is also referred to, was first published in Germany and then in the Netherlands (both in 1991). In 1995 the book was published by Doubleday in New York. Doubleday, which in 1989 had published *The Diary of Anne Frank: The Critical Edition,* confused matters by calling its 1995 publication *The Definitive Edition.* In my view there can never be a definitive edition of Anne Frank's diaries because not all of the original diaries were recovered and Anne Frank did not live long enough to edit them fully herself.

Anne Frank's texts consist of three notebooks that were saved, a rewritten version on loose sheets, an account book full of tales and descriptions of the Secret Annex, and finally, the "book of beautiful quotations." I will describe the texts in the same order.

⎡*The Diaries of Anne Frank* (A Version)
THE FIRST DIARY

Friday, June 12, 1942, was Anne Frank's thirteenth birthday. One of the presents she received was an album, the kind meant for collecting little poems from family and friends. It was almost square in shape, with a red-and-white-checked cover. She decided to use it as a diary. That same day she wrote on the front page: "I hope I shall be able to confide in you completely, as I have never been able to do in anyone before, and I hope that you will be a great support and comfort to me" (AF*a*, 177).

Right from the start she treated the diary as a living person with whom she corresponded. She wrote, for instance:

> I'll start with the moment I got you, or rather saw you lying on my birthday table, . . .
> Soon after seven I went to Daddy and Mommy and then to the living room to open my presents, the first to greet me was *you,* possibly the nicest of all.   (AF*a*, 177–178; adapt. MH/SL)[1]

Apparently she knew how to keep a diary. She consistently started her notes by recording the day of the week and date and then putting down her thoughts in the first person, after which she signed the entry "Anne Frank" or "Anne," often underlining them. On her birthday she wrote only the first dedication. On Sunday she continued by reporting on her birthday, introducing her friends in passing. She immediately took to diary writing: "Now I must stop next time I'll have so much to write in you again, that is to tell you, bye-bye, we're going to be great pals" (AF*a*, 186).

On Monday, June 15, 1942, she introduced her classmates. After each of their names, she concisely characterized them and their relationship to herself. Although her comments suggest that she was part of a wide social circle, she remarked that she had never had a best friend. Apparently she missed an intimate friendship.

On Tuesday, June 16, 1942, she continued her list, also including the boys in her class. Her next entry is dated a week after her birthday, Friday, June 19, and is only a few lines long. After this she did not write for ten days. On Tuesday, June 30, she returned to her diary and realized: "I still have to give an account of the whole week" (AF*a*, 192).

She summed up the most important events of the preceding days and devoted a little more space to her encounters with Hello, her boyfriend.

In those earliest diary entries she wrote of the things important to her: most of all, the pleasures surrounding her birthday. She enumerated every last present she received. She also wrote down the names of many people she knew: her friends, both boys and girls, and classmates. She appears to have had an active social life. Her school activities, her friendships with girls and her boyfriend are what occupied her mind, what she wrote about. Apparently, and remarkably, the war was not an issue at all. When she introduced herself in her diary, she wrote that her family had come from Germany, but she never mentioned the reasons why they emigrated to the Netherlands:

> I was born on 12 June 1929 in Frankfurt a/M. I lived in Frankfurt until I was 4, then my father Otto Heinrich Frank went to Holland to look for a post; that was in June. He found something, and his wife Edith Frank-Holländer moved to Holland in September. Margot and I went to Aachen, to our grandmother Rosa Holländer-Stern, Margot went on to Holland in December, and I followed in February, and was put on Margot's table as a birthday present.   (AF*a*, 189)

Frank continued by describing her days at school in Amsterdam. But even when she reported being transferred from a Montessori to a Jewish secondary school, she made no mention of the fact that this move was not voluntary but on German orders. It was one of the Nazi measures meant to isolate the Jews from the rest of the population. Otto and Edith Frank probably tried to spare their children from talk of the war; perhaps they managed to do this until the threat became too ominous to remain hidden. Besides, Anne herself would most likely have tried to ignore the German occupation as best she could.

Her carefree life ended abruptly on Sunday, July 5, 1942. The next Wednesday, in hiding, she wrote:

> I still have a whole lot to write in my diary, on Sunday Hello came over to our place, on Saturday we went out with Fredie Weiss, and over to oasis of course. On Sunday morning Hello and I lay on our balcony in the sun, on Sunday afternoon he was going to come back, but at about 3 o'clock a policeman arrived and called from the door downstairs, Miss Margot Frank, Mother went down and the policeman gave her a card which said that Margot Frank has to report to the S.S.
>
> (AF*a*, 206; adapt. MH/SL)

On that day one thousand people, mostly German Jews, received orders to report for labor in Germany. It was the beginning of the deportation of the Jews. Like Margot, many of those called up were teenagers who had to leave without their parents.[2] Margot's order to report prompted Otto and Edith Frank to go into hiding with their two daughters, a move they had long since prepared for. Very early on Monday morning, the Franks left for the "secret annex" to Otto Frank's office building. His daughter reported succinctly on this dramatic turn of events in her life. Once over the initial shock, she displayed an optimistic attitude:

> It's not really all that bad here, for we can cook for ourselves, and downstairs in Daddy's office we can listen to the radio. I can write all the names and everything openly in my diary now. [. . .] and I don't think we'll be bored here just yet. [. . .]
>
> We have things to read as well and we are going to buy all sorts of games.
>
> Of course, we are not allowed to look out of the window at all or to go outside. Also we have to do everything softly in case they hear us below.
>
> Now I shall stop because I still have a lot to do.　　(AF*a*, 222)

A few days later, on Sunday July 12, 1942, her mood had changed. She felt lonely and isolated. She felt alienated, especially from her mother. She missed Moortje, her cat, which she had to leave behind. In her next diary entries she wrote of the war for the first time. She listed the facts: the German attack and occupation in May 1940, the anti-Semitic laws that increasingly restricted the Jews' freedom of movement, and finally the decision to go into hiding. At first she had emphasized all the possibilities that remained; now she realized the limitations of being in hiding. When she wrote: "I *can't* write down everything that goes on inside me and that I'm accused of, because it's *so* bad" (AF*a*, 226), she was referring to her distress at being in hiding and to her alienation from her family.

On August 1 she wrote: "So far I have put almost nothing in my diary other than thoughts and have never got around to nice stories I might read out aloud one day. But from now on I won't be so sentimental or a bit less and keep closer to reality" (AF*a*, 227).

She stuck to her resolve for no more than a few sentences. Then her feelings got in the way again:

> Here we are then, it all starts early in the morning, we get up at 7 and line up for the bathroom, then we go upstairs to have breakfast, then it's time to do the dishes and some sort of household chore or other. And so it goes until evening in the evening we usually do an hour of exercises, and I practice hard at my dance steps. It's very cozy here in our small room, but I feel anything but at home. The fact that we can *never* go outside bothers me more than I can say, and then I'm really afraid that we'll be discovered and shot, not a very nice prospect, needless to say. (AF*a*, 227)

She went on to describe a number of incidents that were bothering her. Depressed, she ended her entry with: "So something happens every day, but I am too lazy and too tired to write everything down" (AF*a*, 228).

For two weeks she wrote nothing. "There is little change in our life here" (AF*a*, 229) was how she resumed. She did mention the bookcase that was installed in front of the door to the Secret Annex, to camouflage it. The next entry is dated August 22, and the following one is from September 21, 1942: "I haven't written anything for ages, but no doubt I'll make up for it" (AF*a*, 233).

She wrote extensively and humorously about an event in the Secret Annex. Peter van Pels, one of her housemates, read a certain book against his parents' explicit wishes, and this caused a scene. That day she ended as follows:

> I would just love to correspond with somebody, so that is what I intend to do in future with my diary. I shall write from now on in letter form, which actually comes to the same thing.
>
> Dear Jettje, (I shall simply say,)
>   My dear friend, both in the future as well as now I shall have a lot to tell you. [. . .] Regards to everyone and kisses from
>
> *Anne Frank*
> (AF*a*, 237)

Anne lived up to her promise. The diary continues in the form of letters to a certain Jettje, a character whom she immediately provided with a context:

Jettje was surrounded by people to whom Anne sent her regards. She liked the letter form, because that same day she wrote another letter, this one addressed to a certain Emmy:

> I have some time left tonight dearest Emmy, and so I shall drop you a few lines, this afternoon I wrote a fairly sheepish letter to Jettje, [. . .]. [So, *tabeb,*] just as in "Joop ter Heul." Incidentally, have you read "Joop ter Heul"? How are things with Janeau? Are you all right, you two, or do you still squabble every day and make up in the evenings, that is the best bit of all for sure. [. . .]
>
> [N]ow I must stop,
>
> dearest Emmy regards to Georgette from
>
>

Anne Frank.
> (AF*a*, 238–239; adapt. MH)[3]

From September 21, 1942, Anne wrote letters in her diary nearly every day. On September 28, 1942, she added the following entry to the dedication on the front page: "I have had a lot of support from you so far, and also from our beloved club to whom I now write regularly, I think this way of keeping my diary is much nicer and now I can hardly wait for when I have time to write in you" (AF*a*, 177).

"You" refers to the diary, but who are "our beloved club"? Does this refer to the club mentioned on the first pages of the diary, when Anne Frank introduced her friends and also mentioned a club ("the little Bear, minus 2," AF*a*, 185)? This club consisted of Sanne, Jacque, Ilse, Hanneli, and Anne herself. Anne Frank did indeed write two letters to Jacque (Jacqueline), her classmate and friend. They are both farewell letters. Although both are dated September 25, the first appears to have been written either immediately before or after the Franks went into hiding:

> Dear Jacqueline,
>
> I am writing this letter in order to bid you good-bye, that will probably surprise you, but fate has decreed that I must leave (as you will of course have heard a long time ago) with my family, for reasons you will know.   (AF*a*, 243)

Anne probably copied this letter into her diary on September 25 and added the second one in the same sitting. A few days before, on September 22, she had written: "Tomorrow I think I'll write my farewell letter to Jacqueline, it should have been done 2 months ago" (AF*a*, 241). In this letter she thanked Jacqueline for her letter (which, in reality, was never written; see Van Maarsen 1996, 56 [1990]), inquired about other girlfriends (Ilse and Lies[4]), and urged Jacqueline not to keep her letters.

A few years ago Jacqueline van Maarsen wrote a book about the war and her relationship with Anne Frank. She says she looked for a farewell letter at the Frank house after they had gone into hiding, but was unable to find it (Van Maarsen 1996, 56). Anne probably was not allowed to send the letter because that would have been too risky. The same goes for the second letter. It is striking how in her first farewell letter Anne called Jacqueline her best friend, while her description of her classmates suggests that she was disappointed in Jacqueline (see AF*a*, 187 and 243).

Jacqueline was the only one from the "little Bear club" to whom Anne wrote letters, making it quite unlikely that "our beloved club" referred to "the little Bear club." The girls she wrote to had different names: Emmy, Jetje, Kitty, Pop, Marianne, Conny, Pien, and Lou. Who are they? If we compare these names to the ones she listed at the beginning of the diary—the names of her friends and classmates—we find that only Jacqueline appears in both sets.

The solution to the riddle lies in the letters themselves. In the fall of 1942, Anne wrote to her pen pals that she was reading Cissy van Marxveldt's novels: *De Kingford School, De Stormers,* and particularly the *Joop ter Heul* series, which she liked very much. Cissy van Marxveldt was the pen name of Sietske Beek-De Haan (1889–1948), the author of girls' books that were very popular in the Netherlands in the 1930s and 1940s.[5] Between 1919 and 1925 she wrote four novels about the life of Joop ter Heul: *De H.B.S.-tijd van Joop ter Heul* [Joop ter Heul's high school years], *Joop ter Heuls problemen* [Joop ter Heul's problems], *Joop van Dil-ter Heul* [Joop ter Heul gets married] and *Joop en haar jongen* [Joop and her son]. It is clear from Anne's letters that she devoured these books. During the same month in which she wrote the letters to her friends, she read the entire four-book series, more than seven hundred pages in all. She was obviously inspired by the *Joop ter Heul* series. This intertextual relationship became apparent in her second letter, addressed to Emmy (see AF*a*, 238), in which the word *tabeh* [so long] alludes to other literature. Anne used *tabeh* to say good-bye and mentioned that she had adopted this farewell from the Joop ter Heul novels.[6] The books had a profound influence: she did not merely adopt a few expressions but also modeled her diaries after *Joop ter Heul,* for *De H.B.S.-tijd van Joop ter Heul* is an epistolary novel. The main character, Joop, writes letters to her friend Net. At some point her father demands that she cut down on her letter writing so that she can devote more time to her homework. To compensate Joop starts writing in some old notebooks of her sister's, "because once in a while I have to vent my bottled up feelings" (Van Marxveldt 1985, 16 [1919]; trans. MH).

Joop wrote to Net once a month, and the rest of the time she kept a diary. Incidentally, the other three *Joop ter Heul* novels are first-person narratives.[7] So it was the first book in the series that gave Anne Frank the idea of writing diary letters. While Joop wrote to Net, Anne wrote her first letter to Jetje and parenthetically added: "I shall simply say" (AF*a*, 237). As for her new pen pal's name, she might have chosen Jet because it rhymed with Joop ter Heul's Net. In any case, the name Jetje does not appear in the *Joop ter Heul* novels. Mirjam Pressler, who translated the Critical Edition of Anne Frank's diaries into German, mentions in her translation that the names Anne Frank used were derived from the *Joop ter Heul* series. Pressler wrote more extensively about this in another book about Anne Frank, in which she mistakenly referred to Jetje as a character from *Joop ter Heul* (Pressler 1993, 34 [1992]).

Waaldijk (1993, 332) and Nussbaum (1994a, 529) were both equally misled by a note in the English Critical Edition (1989, 223), and so mistakenly credited Pressler with being the first to discover the origin of the names. On June 12, 1986 (Anne Frank's birthday), literary critic Sietse van der Hoek wrote in the Dutch daily *De Volkskrant* that Anne Frank's Kitty referred to Kitty Egyedi, a prewar friend. The next day a response from his colleague Theodor Holman was printed in the evening newspaper *Het Parool*. Holman had been convinced by editor Nienke van der Meulen of Bert Bakker publishers that there could be no mistake; from the complete version of the diaries, which appeared in the Dutch Critical Edition, it was clear that "Kitty" was derived from the *Joop ter Heul* series (see also Heebing 1994, 238). Jacqueline van Maarsen, too, realized that "Kitty" was "Joop ter Heul's" friend only after reading the Critical Edition (Van Maarsen 1996, 54–56). She also points out that intertextuality is effective only if there is a common frame of reference: The influence of the *Joop ter Heul* series had never before been detected because the only people to read the original diary had been men, or women who had grown up outside the Netherlands. These readers were therefore unfamiliar with Cissy van Marxveldt's girls' books. This can be linked to Maaike Meijer's theory of heterogeneity (1988): She juxtaposes the myth of monolithic literature and a monolithic history of literature with a literary polysystem, consisting of various reading and writing circuits, including women's and children's literature. Because children's literature is often subdivided into girls' and boys' books, her system could be extended to include girls' literature, to which Cissy van Marxveldt's oeuvre belongs (Meijer 1988, 338). The importance and scope of girls' literature should not be underestimated: One of the most famous diaries in the world, to which countless politicians, opinion makers, and artists have referred, turns out to have been inspired by girls' literature and could itself be included in that genre.[8]

In the *Joop ter Heul* series, the main character has other friends apart from Net, who together form the "Jopopinoloukicoclub," a name inspired by the first letters of their first names: Joop (Josephine), Pop (who is actually called Emilie), Pien (Philipine), Noortje, Loukie (or Loutje), Kitty, and Conny. Most of these names can be found in Anne Frank's diary letters: Dearest Kitty, Dear Pop, Dear Conny, Dear Pien, Dear Lou. Their last names, which Anne sometimes added, correspond to those in the *Joop ter Heul* novels.[9]

Moreover, Anne sometimes sent her regards, which once again points to the fact that she was writing to characters in the *Joop ter Heul* books: she asked Pop to give her regards to Betty, Pop's sister in the novels. Pien is asked to give her regards to Kaki, and Kitty to give them to François: These are their respective boyfriends. To Conny, Anne wrote:

> Dearest Conny,
>
> How are you and Nanny, poor soul you are so lonely, yes but here's a fine prospect, you can stay with me, I was with your mother the whole morning, and she agrees, I hope that this diversion is to your liking, so come as quickly as possible.   (AF*a*, 249)

This passage obviously does not refer to the actual situation in the Secret Annex, where no friends could just be invited to sleep over. The fourth *Joop ter Heul* novel, *Joop en haar jongen,* offers an explanation. One day Joop receives a letter from Conny, who for health reasons is staying in the province of Limburg in the south of the Netherlands with "Nanny," probably a companion her mother selected for her. Conny complains to Joop: "And now I am like a bird, flapping its wings against the bars of it cage and breaking them in his stubborn attempts to escape from its prison" (Van Marxveldt 1985, 465 [1925]; trans. MH).

Feeling sorry for Conny, Joop asks her mother if Conny can come and stay with her. In effect Anne Frank imitated Joop and repeated what had happened to Joop and her friend. It is not hard to imagine that the above quotation must have moved her deeply, since she often must have felt like a caged bird herself in that hiding place (see also note 31).

As the previous example shows, Anne sometimes inscribed the *Joop ter Heul* history into her life. At other times, however, she made up her own stories. For example, she wrote Kitty a letter to comfort her (AF*a*, 248–249). We can gather from her consoling words that Kitty had been dumped by her darling Henk. This scene cannot be traced to any of Van Marxveldt's novels.

Kitty is the character who for a long time is not concerned with love at all. After school she goes into stock brokerage and is the only member of the club with a job. It is not until the very end that she becomes engaged to François. There is a character named Henk in *Joop ter Heul*, but he has nothing to do with Kitty. Henk is the man who is engaged to be married to Lotte Boom, causing Lotte to turn down a proposal from Joop's brother Kees.[10]

A few of the names in the diary are new. Emmy and Jet are not found on the list of classmates and friends from before the Franks went into hiding, nor do they appear in the *Joop ter Heul* novels. These are the girls to whom Anne wrote her first two letters. A week later she wrote to "the whole club in general" and then to Jetje and Emmy, whom she told: "I only write to you once a month and Jacqueline isn't included [either]" (AF*a*, 223).[11] From this it can be deduced that Emmy and Jet had nothing to do with the Joop series. Who they were and where they came from remain a mystery.[12] It is possible that Anne first made up her own names (choosing Jet because it sounded like Joop's Net) and only later hit upon the idea of writing to the Joop ter Heul girls.

The diary mentions a third name, Marian(ne),[13] which does not appear in the Joop books. Through her Anne gave her regards to Jaap and made all kinds of inquiries: "How are you two getting on and how is Gabi's singing. When is the little one due, it can't be long now. Is your mother all right, and how is your bank-papa?" (AF*a*, 248).

Some confusion arises when this passage is compared to the Joop novels. There Jaap is the first boyfriend of Joop's pen pal Net. I was unable to find any Gabi.[14] However, Kitty's sister Georgien does take singing lessons. "The little one" refers to Joop's sister's baby, and "bank-papa" is Joop's father-in-law, who works at a bank.

Anne wrote to Marianne a few more times and twice asked her to give regards to Jaap. Possibly Marianne had the same function for Anne Frank as Net had for Joop. What they have in common is that they are pen pals of Anne Frank and Joop ter Heul, and that their boyfriends bear the same name.

Still, Anne preferred writing to Kitty, one of Joop's friends:

Dear Kitty,
    Yesterday I wrote to Emmy and Jettje but I prefer writing to you, you know that don't you and I hope the feeling is mutual.   (AF*a*, 240)

Perhaps their almost identical surnames (Kitty's is Franken) explains why Anne preferred Kitty. Also Kitty was one of the most cheerful and enterprising girls in the Jopopinoloukicoclub. According to Van Maarsen, Anne Frank identified most with Kitty Franken (Van Maarsen 1996, 55). However true this may be, it did not mean that she wrote to Kitty Franken more often. She wrote to everyone in turn.

The writing of letters lasted from September 21 to November 13, 1942. Anne often asked her friends to say hello to their boyfriends and other loved ones for her and sometimes inquired briefly about their lives. And she told them a great deal about her own life in hiding, so that the letters kept their diary function (of describing and processing one's own life). She wrote about everything that occupied her time: the household chores and the novels and textbooks she read. She wrote to her pen pals about the persecution of the Jews in Amsterdam; the news of this reached her through the people who helped the inhabitants of the Secret Annex. She also wrote of her relationship to the others in the hiding place. She mentioned that they intended to allow yet another person to join them. She also described her fears, for example when strange people entered the office building downstairs. And she kept her friends abreast of the progress of the war, in particular the Allied landings in North Africa. After November 13, one final letter of this volume appears. It is addressed to Kitty and dated December 5.

Finally, this first diary contains an entry dated May 2, 1943, six months after the final letter. This entry is not in the form of a letter, but it is a description of the moods of the people in hiding and a comparison with life before the war. It is likely that Anne started a new diary at the end of 1942, because the first one was practically full. As early as October 26 she wrote: "Dearest Phienny, Daddy has asked Mr. Kleiman for a diary" (AF*a*, 288), and a few days later: "I simply can't wait to ask Mr. Kleiman for the new diary" (AF*a*, 291).

However, this second diary has not survived. It is highly likely that more than one diary has been lost, because the missing entries cover a period of more than a year. The next original diary entries by Anne Frank do not appear until December 21, 1943.

THE SECOND (RECOVERED) DIARY

Anne Frank's next diary, a notebook with a hard black cover, immediately makes a totally different impression. In her first diary she regularly pasted in loose sheets, pictures, and a letter from her father. She also alternated her handwriting, switching from cursive writing to printing and back. Her second diary was a lined notebook, resulting in a more even and regular impression. The regularity is further enhanced by Anne's almost continuous cursive writing, with few lapses into printing. Moreover, she no longer pasted in as many things as she had in the first diary.

Her second diary starts with the inscription:

> Diary of
> Anne Frank
> from 22 December 1943 to 17 April 1944.
> "Secret Annex"
> A'dam C.
> In part letters to "Kitty."   (AF*a*, 427)

In her first letter to Kitty, Anne Frank wrote:

> Dear Kitty,
> Father has tracked down another new diary for me and this one is
> of a respectable thickness, as you will see for yourself in good time.
>   (AF*a*, 427; adapt. MH)

She wrote almost daily in this diary, on average three to three and a half pages per sitting, mostly in the form of letters to Kitty. She signed off alternately as Anne, Anne Frank, Anne Mary Frank (her first and middle names were actually Anneliese Marie), sometimes underlining her name and sometimes using the possessive: "Yours, Anne M. Frank," for example.

Because all the entries from December 1942 to December 1943 are missing, the entry dated March 7, 1944, in which she surveyed her life, is important. First she described her carefree but lighthearted school days, then the sudden transition to life in hiding, full of fears and tension: "Then the first half of '43. My inexpressible sadness, my fits of crying and my loneliness, how I began to see all my faults and shortcomings which were much greater than I ever thought" (AF*a*, 517–518).

She described how she tried in vain to develop a closer relationship with her father and how lonely she felt in that period. In the second half of 1943, she felt less sad. She accepted her distance from her parents, God came into her life, and she fell in love with Peter, the boy who—with his parents—was a fellow resident of the hiding place.

In this, the second of the recovered diaries, she wrote about her inner emotions rather than the events in the Secret Annex: "Lately, I haven't felt at all like writing about what's been going on here. I've been much more concerned with personal matters" (AF*a*, 523).

She often wrote of her longing for friendship and love, and of her feelings of loneliness. She benefited from writing letters to her so-called pen pal, Kitty: "But, still, the brightest spot of all is that at least I can write down my thoughts and feelings, otherwise I would be absolutely stifled" (AF*a*, 534).

She wrote to Kitty that she was thinking about her deceased grandmother. As Anne herself had to deal with feelings of abandonment, even while in the midst of her family and the others hiding in the Secret Annex, she realized how lonely the old woman must have been. She also recalled her grandmother's loyalty and goodness. These memories contrast sharply with her feelings toward her mother. The emptiness that resulted from a lack of motherly love, at least in Anne's mind, gave rise to a strong craving for friendship. She discovered Peter and Margot as like-minded people. She identified with the other teenagers in her surroundings and believed that they too felt this lack of motherly love.

> Aren't the grown-ups idiotic and stupid? Just as if Peter, Margot, Bep and I don't all feel the same about things, and only a mother's love, or that of a very, very good friend, can help us.
> The two mothers here just don't understand us at all! (AF*a*, 505)[15]

Her attitude toward Margot shows a particularly noticeable change from the first diary, where Anne saw Margot and her mother as "hand in glove" and felt excluded. Anne was keenly aware of this change: "How Margot and I really only know each other well for a little while, but that, even so, we don't tell each other all that much, because we are always together" (AF*a*, 547).

Sometimes she discussed her problems with her sister. Once in a while they wrote each other notes, which Anne Frank copied into her diary. She also tried to combat her loneliness by approaching Peter: "My longing to talk to someone became so intense that somehow or other I decided to speak to Peter" (AF*a*, 444).

She visited him in his attic and was touched by the look in his eyes and his insecurity, combined with masculinity. She emphasized to Kitty that she was not in love. She simply felt a need for friendship, and if Peter had been a girl, she wrote, she would have felt equally good (AF*a*, 446). By day she denied any feelings of love, but at night she dreamed of Peter Schiff (whom she called Petel), a boy she had fallen in love with at primary school. The dream upset her for weeks on end. More than a month later, she wrote:

> I have to keep myself under control—time and again, I long for my Petel, I long for every boy, even for Peter—here. I want to shout at him: "Oh say something to me, don't just smile all the time, touch me, so that I can again get that delicious feeling inside me that I first had in my dream of Petel's cheek.
> I feel completely confused, I don't know what to read, what to write, what to do, I only know that I am longing.   (AF*a*, 483)

She became more and more focused on Peter and could hardly concentrate on anything else. To Kitty she confessed: "Peter Schiff and Peter van Pels have grown into one Peter, who is beloved and good, and for whom I long desperately" (AF*a*, 501).

She admitted she was in love and suffered because this love at first remained unrequited. Weeks later deliverance finally seems near. On March 19, 1944, Anne wrote to Kitty that she had had the most wonderful evening ever in the Secret Annex. The previous evening Peter and she had stood at the open attic window. Because it was already quite dark, they dared broach some intimate subjects:

> We told each other so much, so very very much, that I can't repeat it all, but it was lovely, the most wonderful evening I have ever had in the "Secret Annex." [. . .]
>
> It was wonderful, he must have grown to love me as a friend and that is enough for the time being. I am so grateful and happy, I just can't find the words. I must apologize Kitty, that my style is not up to standard today. I have just written down what came into my head!
>
> (AF*a*, 547–548)

In the days that followed, she and Peter talked a great deal. She steered the conversation in the direction of sexuality and asked Peter, who had had a better sex education, about the facts of life. In return she intended to tell him "what a girl really looks like there" (AF*a*, 566). She thought it would be quite complicated to explain this well and practiced her explanation in a letter to Kitty (AF*a*, 567).

Although she was excited about her bond with Peter, she did not forget her other fantasies. She told Peter of her passion for writing, then and in the future:

> Oh yes, I don't want to have lived for nothing like most people. I want to be useful or give pleasure to the people around me yet who don't really know me, I want to go on living even after my death! And therefore I am grateful to God for giving me this gift, this possibility of developing myself and of writing, of expressing all that is in me!
>
> (AF*a*, 569)

A few days later, on March 28, 1944, Gerrit Bolkestein addressed the nation on Radio Oranje:

> History cannot be written on the basis of official decisions and documents alone. If our descendants are to understand fully what we as a nation have had to endure and overcome during these years, then what we really need are ordinary documents—a diary, letters from a worker

in Germany, a collection of sermons given by a parson or a priest. Not until we succeed in bringing together vast quantities of this simple, everyday material will the picture of our struggle for freedom be painted in its full depth and glory.   (Frank 1989, 59)

The historical material would be collected in a special center set up for this purpose—later named RIOD. The people in the Secret Annex, who gathered around the illegal radio every evening to catch the latest news from London, also heard Bolkestein's address. The next day she wrote:

Dear Kitty,
    Bolkesteyn [*sic*], an M.P., was speaking in the Dutch News from London, and he said that they ought to make a collection of diaries and letters after the war. Of course, they all made a rush at my diary immediately.
    Just imagine how interesting it would be if I were to publish a [novel] of the "Secret Annex," the title alone would be enough to make people think it was a detective story.   (AF*a*, 578; adapt. MH)[16]

The idea of writing a novel about her experiences in hiding was slowly forming in her mind. Bolkestein's call for documents greatly intensified her drive to write. She was aware that her ability to cope with her problems—her partly unrequited love, her mood swings, and her despair over the endless war—was due to her writing: "I can shake off everything if I write; my sorrows disappear, my courage is reborn!" (AF*a*, 588).

She scrutinized her talents critically: "I know that I *can* write, a couple of my stories are good, my descriptions of the 'Secret Annex' are humorous, there's a lot in my diary that speaks, but—whether I have real talent remains to be seen" (AF*a*, 586).

We see from this passage that Anne Frank wrote not only a diary but also fiction. Her unfinished novel *Cady's Life* is contained in this second notebook (Frank 1989, 144).

Ten days later, on the last pages of her diary, she wrote of finally getting Peter to kiss her. She reported it in minute detail to Kitty and shared her worries about whether she should tell her parents and what they would think of her if they knew. She did not know what to make of it herself. On the one hand she found herself too young to be making love. But on the other she knew she lived in extraordinary circumstances and was developing at a faster rate than other girls her age. It was not only love but also fear that drove her into Peter's arms. "Oh Anne, how shameful! But honestly, I don't think it is; we are shut up here, shut away from the world, in fear and anxiety, especially just lately. Why, then, should we who love each other remain apart? Why should we not kiss each other in these times?" (AF*a*, 609–610).

On Sunday, April 9, the warehouse of 163 Prinsengracht was burglarized. Anne described the incident in detail in her diary. In the general panic that swept through the hiding place, it was suggested that her diary be burned in case they were discovered. To Anne this was the worst fate imaginable: "This, and when the police rattled the cupboard door, were my worst moments; not my diary, if my diary goes I go with it!" (AF*a*, 595).

THE LAST DIARY

Anne Frank's last diary is again a ruled notebook. It has a green-and-gold-marbled cover and black binding. On the first page of her new diary Anne wrote: "Someone's been a real darling again and has torn up a chemistry notebook for me to make a new diary, this time the someone was Margot" (AF*a*, 613).

In layout and handwriting this diary closely resembles the previous one. Anne pasted in even fewer loose sheets and pictures, and her writing is mainly cursive. The entries average three to three and a half pages each (Frank 1989, 158). In the beginning she wrote virtually every day; later this frequency decreased considerably. All entries are in the form of letters to Kitty.

The front page bears the following inscription:

> Diary of Anne Frank
> from 17 April 1944 to
> "Secret Annex"
> A'dam C.
> Partly letters to "Kitty."
> The owner's maxim:
> *Schwung muss der Mensch haben!* [Zest is what man needs!]
>
> (AF*a*, 612)

The inside of the back cover reads: *"Soit gentil et tiens courage!* [Be nice and have courage!]" (AF*a*, 699). In her first entry she wrote that a carpenter was screwing iron plates to the front door panels and that everyone in the hideout was taking extra precautions in order to minimize the risk of discovery. She also wrote that her father expected "large-scale operations" from the Allied forces, but that she could hardly imagine being liberated anymore (AF*a*, 613). Despite this the hope of liberation is a recurring theme in the diary. The long-expected invasion is the talk of the day. At long last, on Tuesday, June 6, 1944, the big moment arrived. Anne Frank underlined the date in her diary and wrote:

Dearest Kitty,

"This is *the* day," came the announcement over the English news at 12 o'clock and quite rightly "this is *the* day," the invasion has begun!

(AF*a*, 666)[17]

She reported on the radio broadcasts in great detail. The rest of this diary also deals much more with the war than its predecessors.[18] Like the others in the Annex, Anne was optimistic and hoped the war would be over by the end of 1944. One of her last letters to Kitty, dated July 21, 1944, ends:

Do you gather a bit what I mean, or have I been skipping too much from one subject to another? I can't help it; in anticipation of sitting on school benches next October I feel far too cheerful to be logical! Oh, boy oh boy, hadn't I just told you that I didn't want to be too hopeful? Forgive me, I haven't got the reputation of being a "little bundle of contradictions" for nothing! (AF*a*, 696)

Another recurring theme in the last diary is Anne's relationship with Peter. On the first few pages of the notebook, she told Kitty that she had explained everything about girls' bodies to Peter:

The evening ended by each giving the other a kiss, just next the mouth, it's really a lovely feeling!

Perhaps I'll take my book of beautiful quotations up there sometime, to go more deeply into things for once, I don't get any satisfaction out of lying in each other's arms day in, day out, and would so like to feel that he's the same. (AF*a*, 613; adapt. MH/SL)[19]

These remarks signal the beginning of a certain ambivalence toward Peter. The second diary testifies to a growing closeness between the two young lovers, but this one shows a diminishing intimacy between them, at least on Anne's part. She was no longer obsessed with him in her diary; when she did mention him, it was often in negative terms. She doubted whether it was right to give herself so completely to him. She realized she would not want to marry him, because she felt he lacked character, willpower, and courage. Uncertain what she should do, she informed her father "that when we are together, Peter and I don't sit miles apart" (AF*a*, 624). Initially Otto Frank reacted calmly. He told his daughter to be careful, and that seemed to settle the matter. But later on he appeared less than pleased with this "necking" (AF*a*, 629) and forbade her to go up to Peter's attic every evening. Anne's reaction was to write letters, first to Kitty and then to her father. In harsh tones she told him that she had learned to care for herself because her parents had deserted her. She wrote that this loneliness was precisely what had driven her into Peter's arms. She asked, or rather demanded, that her father treat her as an adult and trust her.

Her father would have to understand that she was her own person and perfectly capable of making her own decisions (AF*a*, 629–631). Otto Frank was visibly upset by this letter full of accusations. This in turn upset Anne, and she confessed to Kitty her regrets over having written it: "As far as Mommy is concerned all of it is true, but to accuse the good Pim, who has done and still does do everything for me—no, that was too low for words" (AF*a*, 634; Anne often called her father Pim).

She was ashamed of the letter and vowed to be forgiving, as her father had been. She wanted to make a fresh start, but without denying her feelings for Peter, however ambivalent they may have been:

> I want to start from the beginning again and it can't be difficult, now that I have Peter. With him to support me I *can* and will! I'm not alone any more; he loves me. I love him, I have my books, my storybook and my diary, I'm not so frightfully ugly, not utterly stupid, have a cheerful temperament and want to have a good character!   (AF*a*, 635)

In the following weeks she was silent about Peter. She explained herself to Kitty: "After my laborious conquest I've got the situation a bit more in hand now, but I don't think my love [for Peter] has cooled off, he's a darling, but I soon closed up my inner self from him, if he wants to force the lock again he'll have to work a good deal harder than before!" (AF*a*, 652).

A week later Anne wrote that she felt worse than she had for months. Although there were some enjoyable moments in the Secret Annex, she was also very worried. One of the people who had helped to smuggle food into the hideout had been arrested; their supplies were dwindling. They had heard that the Netherlands was in the grip of a wave of anti-Semitism and that German refugees would be expelled from the country after the war.[20] For obvious reasons this weighed heavily on those in the Secret Annex.

Among the reasons Anne gave for her depressive mood was her disappointment in Peter. A few weeks later she analyzed the finer points of her disenchantment. Apart from his "dislike of religion and all his talk about food and various other things" (AF*a*, 675), she also complained about his reserved nature, which prevented them from getting through to each other. She accused him of weakness of character and was irritated by his mocking of religion and his tendency to take the path of least resistance. "Laziness may *appear* attractive, but work *gives* satisfaction" (AF*a*, 684).

She also noticed that Peter had started to lean on her, a development she disliked. She began wondering how to boost his self-respect, how to show him the importance of improving himself and standing on his own two feet.

I know very well that I conquered him instead of him conquering me. I created an image of him in my mind, pictured him as the quiet, sensitive, lovable boy, who needed affection and friendship! I needed a living person to whom I could pour out my heart; I wanted a friend who'd help to put me on the right road. I achieved what I wanted, and, slowly but surely, I drew him toward me.   (AF*a*, 692)

Anne wrote to her fictitious pen pal Kitty of her disappointment in both her father and in Peter. She longed for intimacy but was unable to find this with either one of them. She did not know whether Peter was superficial or shy, but either way, her great expectations had not been fulfilled. It felt as if Pim, too, had shut her out. He had continued playing the role of the father who treated her as "a girl-like-all-others" (AF*a*, 691), and, moreover, he had shown too little of himself. Frank was unable to open up to anyone who refused to do the same, which explains why her relationships with her father and Peter failed to develop as she would have liked.

In her last diary entry, dated Tuesday, August 1, 1944, she also blamed herself in the intimacy issue. Anne confessed to Kitty that she found it hard to get close to someone. She saw herself as a dual personality; on the one hand she had a cheerful, superficial side, full of optimism and zest for life, and on the other she had a side "that is much better, deeper and purer" (AF*a*, 697). This was her vulnerable side, which needed protection from the outside world, so that no one could even guess at its existence.

I'm afraid they'll laugh at me, think I'm ridiculous, sentimental, not take me in earnest. [. . .]

Therefore the nice Anne is never present in company, has not appeared one single time so far, but almost always predominates when we're alone. I know exactly how I'd like to be, how I am too . . . inside. But alas I'm only like that for myself. And perhaps that's why, no I'm sure it's the reason why I say I've got a happy nature within and why other people think I've got a happy nature without. I am guided by the pure Anne within, but outside I'm nothing but a frolicsome little goat who's breaking loose.   (AF*a*, 698)

These reflections on herself are the last words in Anne Frank's diary. Three days later the Secret Annex was discovered and its inhabitants were deported.

The last diary heralds Anne Frank's other texts. Her writing ambitions were not limited to the diary genre. In the spring of 1944 she wrote: "I want to send in to 'the Prince' to see if they will take one of my fairy tales, under a pseudonym, of course, but because all my tales so far have been too long, I don't think I have much of a chance" (AF*a*, 616; adapt. MH).[21]

A few days later she mentioned having written a good short story, "Blurry, the Explorer." Reading it out loud had been a success (AF*a*, 618). She wrote that she was working on a story about a fairy named Ellen, which she wanted to present to her father on his birthday (AF*a*, 633). This was not the only connection Anne drew between her father and her writing; her unfinished novel *Cady's Life* is an adaptation of her father's life story (AF*a*, 647).[22]

On Thursday, May 11, 1944, Anne told Kitty how much reading and studying she had done and then went on:

> You've known for a long time that my greatest wish is to become a journalist someday and later on a famous writer. Whether these leanings towards greatness (insanity!) will ever materialize remains to be seen, but I certainly have the subjects in my mind. In any case, I want to publish a book entitled *het Achterhuis* after the war; whether I shall succeed or not, I cannot say, but my diary will be a great help.
>
> (AF*a*, 647)

Nine days later, on Saturday, May 20, 1944, she came out with the truth:

> Dear Kitty,
> At long last after a great deal of reflection I have started my "Achterhuis," in my head it is as good as finished, although it won't go as quickly as that really, if I ever get to finish it.[23]   (AF*a*, 653; adapt. MH)

The Loose Sheets (B Version)

Anne Frank usually wrote in her diary every day, or at least once every few days. This pattern was broken, however, in the summer of 1944. In July she made only four entries: on the sixth, eighth, fifteenth, and twenty-first of the month. This hiatus can probably be explained by the fact that she had started editing her diaries to prepare them for publication, in compliance with Minister Bolkestein's request on Radio Oranje. Most likely the editing and rewriting took up so much time that she could hardly keep her current diary up to date.

She rewrote her original diary entries on separate, unlined sheets of copying paper. These sheets, which were colored salmon-pink, rose-pink, ivory, and blue, were all recovered after the war. Anne folded the sheets double, so that each sheet yielded four pages. She wrote 324 pages and rewrote all the entries up to the one dated March 29, 1944.

From her diary we can see that she began the rewriting process on May 20, 1944 (see the previous section). She was able to work on it until August 4. This means that she must have written an average of four to five pages per day. At the same time, she was also writing her current diary.

Anne Frank's editing work can be more precisely dated by studying the comparative handwriting analysis done by the Dutch State Forensic Science Laboratory. This institute analyzed the Frank diaries on behalf of RIOD (Frank 1989, 102–165), which commissioned the analysis to provide a scientific response to the various attacks on the authenticity of these writings. A team of experts headed conducted a two-part analysis, consisting of document examination and handwriting identification. Their findings convincingly established—with a probability bordering on certainty—that the text known as the diary of Anne Frank had indeed been written by Anne Frank.

In one part of the analysis, the writing in different texts in Anne Frank's hand was compared. From various handwriting characteristics it can be deduced that she must have worked particularly hard on the loose sheets between July 15 and August 1. In that period she completed 162 pages, averaging about 11 a day (Frank 1989, 159). These findings lend credence to the assumption that Anne Frank had no time to write in her current diary in July 1944 because she was too busy rewriting.

The loose sheets can be divided into three periods. The first period begins when Anne started keeping a diary and extends through 1942. For this period a comparison can be made between the original version (*a*) and the rewritten version (*b*); the original diary can be seen as a prototext for the rewriting. For the next period, from December 1942 to December 1943, there is no prototext; the original diary was never recovered so we have access to the rewritten version only. The third period begins on December 22, 1943, and ends on March 29, 1944, the date of the last entry that Anne Frank rewrote. For the third period we have both versions, so the original can be compared with the edited diary.

JUNE 1942–NOVEMBER/DECEMBER 1942

The first part of the rewritten version is characterized by a great number of corrections in the text, which suggests that Anne wanted to create nicely flowing prose. She made an effort to rewrite her diary into a text which could captivate the reader. This is also apparent from the content. Although she stayed largely true to the original contents of the diary, she omitted some parts and expanded others. She added information for clarity; for example, she wrote: "Pim (that's Daddy's nickname)" (AF*b*, 246).

Anne Frank opted not to have her rewritten diary start on her birthday, as the original diary had, but a week later: on June 20, 1942. She expounded on her reasons for keeping a diary. It was meant neither for others to read nor for posterity, she stated, for it seemed unlikely that either she or anyone else would be interested in the diary later on. She kept a diary so she could get things off her chest.[24] Despite her wide circle of family and acquaintances, she sorely missed a true friend, someone with whom she could be honest and open. The diary was meant to fulfill this longing for intimacy and was therefore given a name: Kitty. This suggests that the diary itself was her friend (AF*b*, 180–181).[25] But her role as a diarist writing for herself did not last long. In the next passage, she wrote: "No one will grasp what I'm talking about if I begin my letters to Kitty just out of the blue, so I'll start with a brief sketch of the story of my life, much as I don't like to" (AF*b*, 182; adapt. MH/SL).[26]

She then continued with a description of her life, and this time—in contrast to the original diary—she also included her Jewish background and the German occupation:

> And, as we are Jewish we emigrated to Holland in 1933. . . . After May 1940 good times rapidly fled, first the war, then the capitulation, followed by the German invasion, which is when the sufferings of us Jews really began. Anti-Jewish decrees followed each other in quick succession and our freedom was strictly limited. Yet things were still bearable, despite the star, separate schools, curfew, etc. etc.
>
> (AF*b*, 182–183)

She continued by describing her daily activities: the Ping-Pong club, eating ice cream at Oasis, her admirers, her school escapades. She wrote humorously about getting into trouble for talking in class and having to write essays as punishment for her misconduct. Her essays were quite creative, and she got compliments from the teacher.

In the next passages, Anne again described in detail what anti-Jewish measures were taken. This had not been mentioned in the prototext-text, the original diary. She complained about not being allowed to take the tram. She recalled how, on a walk, her father tried to prepare her for the possibility of going into hiding. She wrote down the dialogue of that moment for the benefit of future readers; she wanted to explain what going into hiding meant and why it was necessary.

> "But Father, when would it be?"
> He spoke so seriously that I grew very anxious.
> "Don't you worry about it, we'll arrange everything. Make the most of your carefree young life while you can."
> That was all. Oh, may the fulfillment of these somber words remain far distant yet.
>
> (AF*b*, 204–205)

This excerpt shows that Anne Frank had a talent for building tension in the text.

Anne located the next entry in the Secret Annex. She expansively informed her future audience—whom she addressed as Kitty in all her diary entries—about the hasty move from her home on the Merwedeplein to the house on the Prinsengracht. She carefully described her new abode, as well as the people she now had to deal with: her fellows in hiding and their helpers. After this, there are no entries for an entire month: "Dearest Kitty, I have deserted you for a whole month, but honestly, there is so little news here that I can't find amusing things to tell you every day" (AF*b*, 219).

She documented life in the Secret Annex: its events, incidents, and arguments. Disagreements were hardly mentioned in the original diary, but in the rewritten version they receive far more attention. Mr. and Mrs. Van Pels quarreled regularly, which was completely alien to Anne because her parents did not. Unaware that grown-ups could bicker like that, she was all the more upset by it because she often became the subject of their squabbles:

> Nothing I repeat nothing about me is right; my general appearance, my character, my manners are discussed from A to Z. I'm expected (by order) to simply swallow all the harsh words and shouts in silence and I am not used to this. In fact I can't! I'm not going to take all these insults lying down, I'll show them that Anne Frank wasn't born yesterday.[27] Then they'll be surprised and perhaps they'll keep their mouths shut when I let them see that I am going to start educating them. That's no way to behave! Plain barbarism!   (AF*b*, 253; adapt. MH)[28]

Anne's tirades were not limited to the pages of her diary. In the Secret Annex as well she was more than just the target of arguments; she was often an active participant. She clashed frequently with her mother and Margot, whom she felt to be strangers (AF*b*, 249).

She also wrote of parties (birthdays, Sinterklaas,[29] and Hanukkah), of day-to-day worries (for instance about food), and of war reports: the British landing in North Africa and the terrible news of the persecution of Jews in Amsterdam. She also wrote down what she did during the day. At first she did not get around to studying, but at the end of September she mentioned that she had started schoolwork. She wrote that she did not want to be behind in school after the war.

One of the main differences between the *b* version and the original diary is that in the rewritten version Anne wrote exclusively to Kitty, as she had originally intended to do. The other girls' names were edited out of the *b* version. She did write, however: "Mr. Kleiman brings a few special books for me every other week I'm thrilled with the Joop ter Heul series. I've enjoyed the whole of Cissy van Marxveldt very much, and I've read 'een Zomerzotheid' 4 times and I still laugh about some of the ludicrous situations that arise" (AF*b*, 240).

I was hoping that this clue would lead me to the origin of the names Jetje, Emmy, and Marianne. Unfortunately no such characters are to be found in *Een Zomerzotheid.*

In the original version one of the last entries in the first diary concerns the arrival of the eighth dweller in the Secret Annex: the dentist Pfeffer.[30] This was an important event, because Anne was to share her room with him from then on. Her last entry in this diary was devoted to the Sinterklaas party. The next original diary was never found, but the rewritten version on loose sheets was recovered. By reading the loose sheets, we can trace Anne Frank's footsteps. However, this must be qualified. We have seen that the *b* version is sometimes identical to the *a* version, but that there are substantial differences as well. Anne Frank often shifted emphasis, leaving certain things out and adding information in other places. Therefore the rewritten version of the diary from November 1942 to December 1942 cannot be accepted indiscriminately as a representation of Anne Frank in that period. The *b* version is an interpretation, an adaptation of the original texts, written in the spring and summer of 1944.

NOVEMBER 1942–DECEMBER 1943

According to my division, the second part of the loose sheets ranges from November 19, 1942, to December 6, 1943. Anne reordered this rewritten version so that there are on average only three or four entries per month. In some months there are even fewer entries: in January, February, May, June, and October, she had the Anne Frank character write to Kitty only twice a month. In other months there are many more entries. In March she wrote seven letters, in July and August six.

Her report on Mr. Pfeffer's arrival is much more detailed than in the original version. His stories of the outside world were of especially great interest to Anne Frank and her coinhabitants. The first *b* entries that have no counterpart in the *a* version, dated Thursday and Friday, November 19 and 20, 1942, show that the Frank and Van Pels families were scared by Pfeffer's accounts of the difficult situation of the Jews in Amsterdam. To avoid causing unnecessary worries or emotional upsets, the helpers had not said too much about the anti-Semitic terror, but with Pfeffer, the bad news of raids and deportations reached the Secret Annex anyway. Anne wrote to Kitty that she herself saw rows of people being marched off by the Germans at night (AF*b*, 316). The news severely darkened the mood in the house. Everyone in the hiding place realized that, compared to other Jews, they were well off—a thought that did not cheer them up, however. They were afraid of being discovered and also worried about the fate of friends and acquaintances: "I get frightened when I think of close friends who have now been delivered into the hands of the cruelest brutes the world has ever seen. And all because they are Jews" (AF*b*, 316).

The rumors of the horrors faced by the Jews, the shootings and the bombardments of Amsterdam that scared her to death, all these made her yearning for peace ever stronger. She closely followed the news on the radio and reported on these developments in her diary letters. The events in Italy gave her hope: Mussolini's retreat in late July 1943 and Italy's surrender on September 8, 1943. But her fears and worries remained. Anne Frank regularly reported on the helpers they depended on for supplies. They often fell ill and had trouble providing the hiding place with food. The people in the hiding place also worried about the warehouseman, because it was uncertain whether he could be trusted. Burglaries gave more reason to fear detection. The tension and the confinement led to many arguments. "Relations between us are getting worse all the time" (AF*b*, 405), she wrote in mid-September 1943. There were quarrels with Mr. Pfeffer, who turned out to be difficult to live with; Mr. and Mrs. Van Pels argued frequently, which upset her. She did not get along with her mother, and moreover she was a prime focus in the many quarrels about the upbringing of teenagers. She took valerian pills against anxiety and depression. Like the others she suffered from mood swings and gloominess. On Sundays in particular she felt bad: "I wander from one room to another, downstairs and up again, feeling like a songbird who has had his wings clipped and who is hurling itself in utter darkness against the bars of his cage" (AF*b*, 411; adapt. MH).[31]

Anne confessed to Kitty that her bleakness not only had to do with the deportations and her fear of detection, but also with her feelings of abandonment. She felt guilty about this and blamed herself for being ungrateful.

Aside from the moods and arguments that determined the atmosphere, Ann wrote of the activities and events in the Secret Annex. She described the household chores, often with a good dose of humor, such as the day when they had to make sausages, or when they had to fill packets of gravy. She also wrote of "day-killing subjects," school subjects she and Margot studied to kill time. For example, they taught themselves shorthand. Frank also mentioned that she loved mythology, especially the Greek and Roman gods. Everyone also eagerly awaited Saturdays, when Miep Gies or another one of their helpers would bring a fresh load of five library books. "Reading, learning and the radio are our only amusements" (AF*b*, 366), she wrote. At one point Otto Frank applied for a prospectus from the Leidse Onderwijs Instellingen (LOI, the Leiden Teachers Institutes) to give them something useful to do. Margot opted for Latin, but this was considered too difficult for Anne.

> To give me something new to begin as well, Father asked Kleiman for a children's Bible so that I could find out something about the New Testament at last. "Do you want to give Anne a Bible for Hanukkah?" asked Margot, somewhat perturbed. "Yes—er, I think St. Nicholas Day is a better occasion," answered Father.
> Jesus just doesn't go with Hanukkah.   (AF*b*, 412; adapt. MH)

Anne Frank did not just spend time reading and learning. She also devoted many hours to writing. "Dear Kitty," she wrote on Wednesday, August 4, 1943:

> Now that we have been in the "Secret Annex" for over a year you know something of our lives, but some of it is quite indescribable; there is so much to tell, everything is so different from ordinary times and from ordinary people's lives. But still, to give you a slightly closer look into our lives, now and again I intend to give you a description of an ordinary day.   (AF*b*, 381)

That day, she described an evening and night in the Secret Annex; for the next few days, she described their lunch hour. Then she wrote:

> An interruption in my sketches of life in the "Secret Annex." A few weeks ago I started to write a story, something that was completely made up and that gave me such pleasure that my pen-children are now piling up.
> Because I promised to give you a faithful and unadorned account of all my experiences, I'll let you judge whether small children may perhaps take pleasure in my tales.   (AF*b*, 387)

What follows is a story entitled "Kaatje,"[32] inspired by the neighbors' daughter, whom Anne sometimes watches from the window.[33]

Another one of her stories, "Ode to My Fountain Pen," is about the fountain pen her grandmother gave her for her ninth birthday: "At thirteen the fountain pen came with us to the 'Secret Annex,' where it has raced through countless diaries and compositions for me" (AF*b*, 414).

The fountain pen accidentally ends up in a newspaper with dirt and is shoved into the stove, where it burns brightly. Anne ends the story as follows:

"I have one consolation, although a slender one, my fountain pen has been cremated, just what I want later!" (AF*b*, 414).

DECEMBER 1943–MARCH 1944

The third part of the loose sheets starts on Wednesday, December 22, 1943, the date from which there are original entries again, allowing a comparison with the previous version.

Anne Frank's first entry was a humorous account of the illness she had just suffered. In the original version she merely mentioned this in passing, but in the rewritten version she reported in detail on her bout of flu, ending with: "I'm fit as a fiddle again, 1 centimeter taller, 2 lbs. heavier, pale, and with a real appetite for learning" (AF*b*, 428).

She also wrote that there was little else to tell: "It is drizzly weather, the stove smells, the food lies heavily on everybody's tummy, causing thunderous noises on all sides, the war at a standstill, morale rotten" (AF*b*, 429).

Two days later she wrote again of the atmosphere in the Secret Annex; everyone was still prey to mood swings and she also characterized herself as "himmelhoch jauchzend, zu Tode betrübt [*sic*]" (AF*b*, 430, a famous line from Goethe: "On top of the world, in the depths of despair."). She was aware how much luckier she was than many other Jewish children, but the mere thought of a normal, peacetime school life made her long intensely for freedom, pleasure, and fresh air. She was ashamed of these feelings, which she felt made her look ungrateful. So she shared them only with Kitty:

> Especially at this time of the year, with all the holidays for Christmas and the New Year, and we are stuck here as if we're outcasts. Still I really ought not to write this because it seems ungrateful but, no matter what they think of me, I can't keep everything to myself, so I'll remind you of my opening words "Paper is patient."* (AF*b*, 430–431)

The next entry is dated January 2, 1944. She had been browsing through her old diaries and was unpleasantly surprised by her vehement criticisms of her mother. She distanced herself from the earlier Anne Frank in this respect. The original version shows no such mercy. To the contrary, on January 6, 1944, the *a* version describes all the disappointment and resentment Anne felt toward her mother. She was probably not ready to modify her image of her mother as early as January 1944. She most likely changed her mind in the late spring or the summer of that year (in any case, after May 20), when she was

---

*This well-known German aphorism fit Anne Frank's life perfectly.

rereading her diaries in order to rewrite them. So in terms of content, this passage should actually be dated months later.

The next passage, dated Wednesday, January 12, 1944, also gives a skewed impression of reality. In the original version Anne wrote that Margot and her mother got along very well together, but that she felt very distant from both of them. These feelings have been edited out of the rewritten version completely. Instead she inserted a remark about how much better she and Margot had learned to get along lately and how the two sisters agreed that their relationship with their parents was not nearly as good as the latter seemed to think.

In the original diary Anne Frank made three confessions on January 6, 1944. The first one pertains to her negative image of her mother; the second one concerns physical intimacies. Anne omitted both of these from the rewritten version. She included nothing about her disappointment in her mother and nothing about the physical changes she had gone through and what she felt about them. Only the third confession, about Peter, is included in the loose sheets, albeit in a modified form. In the original version she wrote: "My longing to talk to someone became so intense that somehow or other I decided to speak to Peter" (AF*a*, 444).

In the *b* version she changed this to: "My longing to talk to someone became so intense that somehow or other I took it into my head to choose Peter" (AF*b*, 444).

This difference tells us that Anne Frank later looked back critically on her falling in love with Peter. This becomes even more apparent in the following comparison. In the original diary she wrote: "When I lay in bed that night all I could do was cry, cry terribly, but having to make sure no one could hear me. In bed I thought over all the things I would say to Peter today and I couldn't stop sobbing. I fell asleep very late" (AF*a*, 445).

Months later she rewrote this passage to read:

> When I lay in bed and thought over the whole situation, I found it far from encouraging and the idea that I should beg for Peter's patronage was simply repellent. One can do a lot to satisfy one's longings, which certainly sticks out in my case, for I have made up my mind to go and sit with Peter more often and to get him talking somehow or other.   (AF*b*, 445)

With hindsight Anne distanced herself from her lovesick behavior toward Peter van Pels. But her feelings for Peter Schiff, her old love, remained unchanged. She copied the description of the dream, and its attending emotions, almost verbatim into the edited version of her diaries.

In the case of Peter van Pels it is particularly clear how she rewrote her own writings, because her feelings for him changed so profoundly in the time that elapsed between the *a* and *b* versions. At the beginning of 1944 she fell in love with Peter, but six months later she had already fallen out of love again. For this reason she omitted considerable parts from the original in the edited version of her diary. Anne's exclamation "Oh, sweetheart!" (AF*a*, 514) did not survive the editing process. In early March 1944 she looked back at her life and wrote about the past few months: "At the beginning of the New Year the second great change, my dream . . . and with it I discovered Peter, discovered a second and equally hard conflict, discovered my longing for a boy; not for a girlfriend but for a boyfriend" (AF*a*, 518; adapt. MH/SL).

In the loose sheets she wrote more succinctly and less explicitly: "At the beginning of the New Year the second great change, my dream, . . . and with it I discovered my boundless desire for all that is beautiful and good" (AF*b*, 518).

On March 19, 1944, Anne informed Kitty that she had experienced the best and the most beautiful evening in hiding. Less than five months later, she omitted this entire passage. In retrospect the event no longer seemed important enough to be published.

In addition to the changes relating to her mother and Peter, Anne made other striking alterations in tone or tenor. She did not copy her revealing notes on sexuality and corporeality into the *b* version.

These discrepancies between the original diary and the rewritten version prove once more that the *a* and *b* versions are not identical and that the *b* version cannot entirely replace the original—an awareness that will help to avoid inaccurate interpretations. There is a period of more than a year (December 1942 to December 1943) from which the original diaries were lost. The image of Anne Frank that emerges from the rewritten version is of course partly based on the original diaries. But it is also partly the result of the psychological changes she had undergone. At the age of fifteen, she was not merely copying her diaries, but adding and omitting, and thus creating an image to her liking. Obviously, this led to shifts, changes, and discolorations.

The last entry on the loose sheets dates from Wednesday, March 29, 1944. In this case Anne copied the original almost verbatim. The entry concerns Minister Bolkestein's call for personal accounts of life in occupied Holland, followed by a description of the wartime situation outside the hideout: hunger, the black market, illnesses and bombings: "You don't know anything about all these things, and I would need to keep on writing the whole day if I were to tell you everything in detail" (AF*b*, 578–579).

The Account Book

Not only three original diaries and a sheaf of loose sheets survived the war. So did an account book in which she wrote short stories. Some of the texts are excerpts from her diary, others are fairy tales, other fictional writings, or memories of her schooldays. The account book makes a truly booklike impression. The texts are done in very neat handwriting, probably copied from draft versions. On the title page she wrote: "Tales and events from the Secret Annex."

The account book starts with a table of contents in four columns. The first column lists the page numbers. The second column, labeled "heading," lists the titles of the stories. The third column, called "what type," gives a genre classification, for instance "Secret Annex"—the most frequently used category—or "Jewish Secondary School," or "Fiction." The fourth column lists the dates, most likely those on which Anne either conceived of or recorded the stories.

By closely studying the diaries, I have tried to pinpoint when she started the account book. I found the first clue in a diary entry on the loose sheets, dated Saturday, August 7, 1943, when Anne told Kitty that she had started writing stories a few weeks earlier.

The second clue came in an entry approximately six months later, on Tuesday, March 7, 1944, in which she reflected on the previous period: "Then the second half of 1943 . . . I started to think, to write, and I discovered myself" (AFa, 518).

As she had been keeping a diary since June 1942, "writing" did not refer to the diary. She did not start rewriting her diaries until May 1944. Therefore it is likely that "writing" refers to her stories in the account book.

On May 7, 1944, she wrote: "I have my books, my storybook, and my diary" (AFa, 635), "storybook" most likely referring to her account book.

The first stories in the account book have all been classified as "Secret Annex"–type stories. The stories are adaptations of diary entries. The dates in the fourth column roughly correspond to the dates of the various diary entries, namely March 24, 1943, and December 8 and 10, 1942. Since the original diary covering these dates is missing, the only comparison possible is between the loose sheets and the account book. The stories entitled "Sausage Day" and "The Dentist" can both be found in the entry dated Thursday, December 10, 1942, in the *b* version of the diary. The burglary, described in "Were We Burgled?" is described in the diary on Thursday, March 25, 1943. There are few differences, except that she used people's real names on the loose sheets, while substituting their pseudonyms in the account book: Pfeffer, the dentist, became Dussel, and the Van Pels family became the Van Daans.

Several stories in the account book are dated in the first week of August 1943. These are descriptions of daily life in the Secret Annex, which can also be found on the loose sheets of the same dates. On August 4, 1943, Anne promised to describe to Kitty what their daily rituals were like. These descriptions are then also included in the account book.

Some other stories are dated February 1944. These are not just "tales from the Secret Annex"; Anne labels two of them "Fiction" and another one "Response to Criticism." One of the fictional stories concerns a flower girl who finds comfort in God and nature. The other "made-up" story is about an old woman and her granddaughter. (I return to this short story in chapter 3.) Anne's "Response to Criticism" is a critical analysis of the prudishness in the Netherlands and a plea for a more relaxed attitude toward nudity. These texts show that she was able to express herself well in various genres. Descriptions, fantasies, and reflections were written with apparent ease. Childish stories alternate with adult, journalistic texts.

In her original diaries and in the loose sheets, Anne referred to her stories a few times. She mentioned "Eve's Dream," "Blurry, the Explorer," "The Fairy Ellen," and the unfinished novel *Cady's Life.* From her diaries it is clear that some of the stories were meant for children. She asked her pen pal Kitty to judge whether the story entitled "Kaatje" was fit for children.

Sometimes she read her tales and descriptions to others and noted the audience's reactions. She copied the story about Ellen, the fairy, onto special stationery and presented it to her father as a gift.

The "Book of Beautiful Quotations"

On Tuesday, April 18, 1944, Anne referred to her "book of beautiful quotations." Kissing Peter was all right but ultimately unsatisfactory. She resolved one day to bring her "book of beautiful quotations" upstairs with her. This book, too, survived. It is a long, narrow account book in which she took down quotations in neat handwriting, with very few corrections. The book is not full; she used only forty-three pages. The front page reads: "Secret Annex 14 August 1943/an invention of Pim's."

Anne mentions the source of each quotation and included a date that probably refers to the day on which the quotation was copied. Judging by the dates, she started the book in June 1943 and added to it until July 1944. The first quotation, dated June 1943, is taken from Alice Bretz's *Het Lied der Duisternis* [Song of darkness]. Under the quotation she notes that the book was written after the author had gone blind. About friendship with God and gratitude, it is actually quite a moralistic quotation that says that God is not to blame for the misery of the world: "Thanking the Lord is something too many of us forget all too easily. We do remember to ask God for something, but seldom remember to thank him for everything he has already done for us" (trans. MH).

The book contains several quotations of a religious nature, for example, a conversation between Galileo and a cardinal about science and religion.

A number of quotations concern daughters. The second, for instance, is dated August 1943—the same date mentioned on the front page—and was taken from Multatuli's *Vorstenschool* [Royal college]. The quotation is about giving and taking, in the context of a conversation between mother and daughter. The queen mother expresses an interest in the activities of her daughter, Louise, who responds by launching into a detailed account of her exploits. But then Louise suddenly exclaims: "But mother . . . what a rude daughter I have been . . . I neglected to inquire as to your well-being!" (trans. MH).

There is also a quotation from F. de Clercq Zubli's *Het eeuwig lied* [The eternal song], in which a young woman named Joep discusses her writing ambitions with her mother. Joep wants to write fairy tales, and her mother encourages her. Joep had started to write when she went deaf. Her mother reminds her: "You had to express yourself, even if only to become clearly aware of what had gone on inside you. Every truthful book is someone's attempt to understand his own thoughts" (trans. MH).

After her son is born, Joep asks her mother whether she had found it difficult to raise a son. The mother answers: "I don't believe our upbringing should be aimed at creating men or women but people. I believe that all problems can be solved from a purely human point of view, not a female point of view, or a male" (trans. MH).

In this book the mother-daughter dynamics are ideal. A third quotation concerns trust. According to the mother, mothers do not have a right to their children's trust; this would be an abuse of motherhood. Anne, herself struggling with her relationship with her mother, quoted pages and pages from this idyllic book.

She also quoted Zoltan J. J. Harsangi's *Een Hemelbestormer* [A revolution in heaven], in which Galileo has a discussion with his daughter, Celeste. From Sigrid Undset's *Kristin Lavransdatter,* she cites the dramatic passage in which Lavran, on his deathbed, tells his daughter about his childhood—something she wished her father would do—and finally orders her not to mourn his death, because he sees death as God's grace.

Religion is a recurring theme, as are mother-daughter and mother-father relationships. In addition there are quite a few quotations pertaining to social injustice, for example by Multatuli, Thomas Moore, and Jacob van Maerlandt.

Furthermore, she quotes "Verschillende versjes van allerlei" [Various and sundry rhymes], some of which are in German and exhort the reader to behave well: Be generous, be just, share your joy—but not your pain—with others, and so on. She also quotes Goethe a few times.

A number of short quotations were signed "Rea," for example: "If I look myself in the eye, I will always recover the truth!" Her reflections on love, a quotation from her own diary (AF*a*, 506), are also signed "Rea." Was this perhaps an alias? "Rea" appears in the diaries twice. It ends the following rhyme: "Here I sit and learn all day/For Him; that is the only way!" (AF*a*, 501).

The second time it appears is at the end of the following entry:

> The following was written a few weeks ago, it doesn't count any longer, but because my verses are so few and far between I'll write it down all the same:
>
> > Once more the day has been a blight
> > For me just like the darkest night!
>
> > *Anne. (Rea.)*
> > (AF*a*, 567)

This last signature does indeed suggest that Rea is an alias, perhaps derived from Rhea in Greek mythology, one of Anne's favorite school subjects.[34]

On the last page she quotes her mother's "birthday poem from mama," dated May 12, 1944, her father's birthday (born 1889) and also her parents' wedding anniversary (1925):

> Nineteen hundred forty four
> His fifty-fifth year
> No end to war
> Baldness near
> Little money
> No food on the table
> Gifts a long forgotten fable
> A can of syrup
> no more could we get
> These are modest times indeed, and yet
> Pim has the spirit to say,
> "The war is going our way!"
>
> > (trans. MH)

The book contains two more mottoes, one of which also appears in the diary (AF*a*, 693): "For in its innermost depth, childhood is lonelier than old age." The book of beautiful quotations ends with: "Those who cannot listen cannot tell stories" (trans. MH).

The Writing Conditions

Anne Frank must have spent a great deal of time writing. One of the tales in the account book gives an impression of where and when she wrote. This story may actually be one taken from the original diary, although it is of a date for which the original did not survive (July 13, 1943). The story, entitled "The Best Table," deals with her request to her roommate for more use of the table.

> From two thirty to four o'clock I sit there every day, while Dussel is sleeping. The rest of the time, the room, plus the table, are off limits. Inside, in our common room, it is far too busy in the afternoon. One can't work there and besides, father sometimes likes to work at the writing table in the afternoon. (Frank 1982, 20; trans. MH)

She asks permission to use the table twice a week between four and five-thirty. After some sulking and grumbling she is granted permission. If this is a true story, Anne Frank was able to write for an hour and a half every day in relative isolation. From mid-July 1943, she was granted an extra three hours a week. But even then she was not really alone; the story shows that, between two-thirty and four, Pfeffer/Dussel was asleep in the same room. It was a narrow room, and the two did not get along very well, so Anne's writing conditions were far from ideal. It appears from the story that reading and studying could also be done in the living room, but that she could not get enough peace and quiet there to write. Miep Gies, one of the people who helped the Franks and their fellows in hiding, committed her memories to paper in the late 1980s. About Anne Frank: "She wrote in her diary in two places, her own room or her parents' room. Although everyone knew that she was writing, she never wrote when other people were present. Obviously Mr. Frank had spoken about this matter and given instructions for no one to disturb her" (Gies 1987, 95).

Elsewhere in the book, Miep Gies also recalls Anne Frank writing in her parents' room (Gies 1987:146). This memory is practically identical with her 1959 testimony in a libel suit:

> At the time when she lived in Prinsengracht, Anne Frank did a lot of writing. . . . Once . . . when I went up into the Annex and opened Anne's door, I saw her sitting at a table and writing in an account book. She was obviously startled, got up and quickly shut the book.

My immediate impression was that she was embarrassed at being caught at her writing. Just then Mrs. Frank came into the room. She took the situation in straight away and said to me: "Yes, we have a writer for a daughter." (Frank 1989, 25)[35]

Dearest Kitty,
    At last, at last I can sit quietly at my table in front of a crack of window and write you everything. (AFa, 660)

There were precious few places in the Secret Annex where Anne could be alone. Whenever circumstances allowed she withdrew into her parents' room or into the room she shared with Pfeffer. Bent over notebooks, loose sheets, or account books, with her back to the door, she devoted herself to her greatest passion: writing. In this chapter I describe her surviving texts. These texts can be classified into various genres and themselves refer to other literature, ranging from Cissy van Marxveldt to Greek myths and from women's magazines to the Bible. For Anne reading and writing were inextricably intertwined.

Chapter 2 ❧ *In White Ink*

What prompted Anne Frank to start writing? How, and why, did this writing develop into a passion? These are the questions I deal with in this chapter, using psychoanalytical perspectives that can help to unearth her unconscious motives. In 1907 Sigmund Freud gave a lecture on the creative writer and fantasy, in which he traced the origin of writing to childhood. Toward the end of his lecture, Freud admitted that he had dealt more with fantasy than with the writer, leaving a number of questions unanswered, for instance: What moves one to write down inner fantasies? Another subject Freud did not deal with was the connection between adolescence and writing. Freud associated childhood with play, adolescence with fantasy, and writing with adult daydreaming. The writing adolescent was left out of the picture.

This omission was remedied by Julia Kristeva in her lecture "The Adolescent Novel" (Kristeva 1990), which may be regarded as a supplement to Freud's lecture. Kristeva described adolescence as a period of transition and a discourse of love. It is a time when familial (parental) love is no longer sufficient, giving rise to feelings of emptiness and loneliness. The gap can be filled by language; in this respect writing adolescents repeat their first childhood years. Kristeva explained this in detail in *Black Sun: Depression and Melancholia* (1989 [1987a]), in which she described the human condition as a fundamental state of depression. Psychoanalysis presupposes the existence of an original unity (a symbiosis between mother and child), which is broken as the child grows up. This breach causes chronic depression. The remedy is language; linguistic signs serve to replace the original wholeness. Language is supported by the desire to coincide with it, to recognize oneself in words.

The transition from the semiotic, presymbolic phase[1] to the symbolic order is reactivated, so to speak, during adolescence. In this transition from childhood to adulthood, the old, familiar structures are left behind before any new structures can replace them. The depressive position can be painfully clear and thus fuel the drive to write: Again linguistic signs are used to fill a void.

Anne Frank started her diary on her thirteenth birthday (June 12, 1942) and kept writing it until August 1, 1944, when she was fifteen. As noted in the previous chapter, most entries date from around the time of her fifteenth birthday. This is because all the original entries from December 1942 to December 1943 (the *a* version) were lost, and because she did not start editing and rewriting the diary (the *b* version) until May 1944. Overcome by loneliness, she often pondered her relationship with her parents. Her sense of abandonment was not only due to her age. When she went into hiding in July 1942, she had to leave behind many people, pets, and possessions she loved. This gave the depressive position an added weight. Incidentally, Kristeva defines adolescence not as an age but as a certain mental structure that often occurs in people passing from childhood into adulthood. The conditions of war brought on an early adolescence in Anne Frank. In this chapter I analyze her motives to write, working from within the context of Kristeva's notions of adolescence, concepts she expressed primarily in *The Adolescent Novel*. However, it should be noted that Kristeva mainly analyzed texts about adolescence written by adults and, what is more, that she focused on male adolescence only. For these reasons her concepts can have only limited relevance to an analysis of Anne Frank's work.[2]

While it is true that her discoveries in psychoanalysis and linguistics, and in particular her insights into the workings and importance of semiotics, have a tremendous potential for bringing about change in a feminist direction, she is a controversial theoretician because she hardly develops the implications of her own theories; she even seems to obstruct them at times, for instance in her analysis of creative writing. She argues that writing as an artistic expression is rooted in the semiotic phase, in which the sound, rhythm, and intonation of language are more important than grammatical structures. In this pre-oedipal period, which precedes entry into the symbolic order, "the law of the father" is overshadowed by the mother-child dyad. The semiotic does not disappear once the child grows older and enters the symbolic order, the realm of language and culture; it keeps playing a role, albeit unconsciously or in the background. With regard to language, Kristeva—paraphrasing Mallarmé—calls the semiotic "the music in the letters." The semiotic can be heard in the sound, rhythm, and musical aspects of language. In Anne Frank's diary there is one incomprehensible sentence that is semiotically highly charged: "Bokkie Pepertje Sokkie Tokkie Pepertje—Pokkie Pepertje Pokkie" (AF*a*, 264).

Kristeva places the issue of writing within the scope of sexual difference, positing that women who write are in greater danger of developing insanity than are their male colleagues because the symbolic order is based on a male model. Therefore it is an order in which women find it difficult to gain a foothold. Women who devote themselves to creative writing are more likely to regress than men, because for women the pull of the semiotic is harder to resist.

In women's studies this theory has been criticized for its exclusion mechanism, in that Kristeva locks the mother up in the semiotic. Although the mother's function is initially positive (bonding and identification), it ends up negative; because of the incest taboo, both boys and girls must leave the realm of the mother. In heterosexual mores only boys are allowed to substitute for the mother by seeking a woman in the symbolic order. Girls are offered no substitute; what is more, based on their gender they must identify with the devalued position of the mother (Hoogland 1992, 47).

Critics of Kristeva's theory have sought to determine whether it is possible to rewrite her insights, particularly her emphasis on the semiotic, into a theory in which the mother remains an active presence in the symbolic order rather than being written out of language and culture. One of the first to do this has been Kaja Silverman (1988), who reassesses the nearly forgotten negative Oedipus complex, an old idea of Freud's that had never been developed. Silverman compares the complex to Kristeva's view on mothers in Western culture. She accuses Kristeva of wasting a good opportunity, for although Kristeva emphasizes the mother's role in facilitating the child's entry into the symbolic order, she makes no attempt to locate the mother herself in the symbolic order except as an (unconscious, sublimated) object of desire and as such, the artist's and writer's muse.

Kelly Oliver (1993a) gives Kristeva more credit, interpreting her theoretical concepts in such a way that there is room for the mother in the symbolic order. However, I suspect that all her interventions in Kristeva's text lead to a theory that is ultimately "beyond Kristeva." I return to Oliver's theory later in this chapter.

This digression into Kristeva's theories may seem to have no bearing on Anne Frank's texts. However, this chapter has two aims. One is to provide a psychoanalytical explanation for her passion for writing. The other is to ana-lyze the relationship between the semiotic and the symbolic order, paying par-ticular attention to the presence or absence of the mother in the text. This is meant to reveal the significance writing had for Anne, and to clarify whether the role of the mother can be extended into the symbolic order. By critically comparing her diaries with Julia Kristeva's theories, I will attempt both to unveil Anne's motives for writing and to propose a fundamental rereading of Kristeva's theories.[3]

The Diary as a Transitional Object

Adolescence is a no-man's-land between childhood and adulthood. Because of physical and psychic changes, the child's old, familiar way of life no longer fits, while a new one has yet to be found. Freud's psychoanalysis is based on two periods and the relationship between them: childhood and puberty, or adolescence.

A baby's drives are directed at fulfilling primary needs, especially through breast-feeding (or its equivalent, bottle-feeding). The first sexual object is the mother's breast. In *Transformation of Puberty,* Freud wrote: "There are thus good reasons why a child sucking at his mother's breast has become the proto-type of every relation of love. The finding of an object is in fact a refinding of it" (Freud 1953, 7, 222 [1905]).[4]

This relationship (which is primarily sexual, since it is guided by the libido and concerns only the satisfaction of needs) slowly evolves into a love rela-tionship between mother and child. Later the child learns to love others as well, becoming attached to its caretakers, those who provide love and affection.[5] During latency, the limbo between early childhood and puberty, the libido is tempered. Puberty brings on renewed sexual energy, caused by numerous physical changes; for girls this includes breast development and the first men-strual period. It would seem most logical at this point for the child to fall for (or rather, fall back on) the same sexual objects as before, especially the par-ents whom he or she has loved all along. Freud deduced from the fantasies of adolescents that their object choices indeed referred to early childhood. But a long time passes between infancy and the renewal of sexual feelings in puberty; the incest taboo takes root, so that adolescents know they are not allowed to focus their sexual desires on the parents.

The adolescent must start looking for new objects on whom (sexual) love may be focused. This struggle between conscious and unconscious wishes and desires, between reality and fantasy, is difficult but necessary:

> At the same time as these plainly incestuous fantasies are overcome and repudiated, one of the most significant, but also one of the most painful, psychical achievements of the pubertal period is completed: detachment from parental authority, a process that alone makes possible the opposition, which is so important for the progress of civilization, between the new generation and the old.
>
> (Freud 1953, 7, 227 [1905])[6]

So puberty can be characterized as a process of separation, one to which Anne also testifies in her diaries:

> I don't fit in with them and that's something I've been feeling very much, especially lately. They get so soppy with each other that I would rather be on my own. And then they say how nice it is for the four of us to be together, and that we get on so well, but it never occurs to them for one moment that I might not feel like that at all.   (AFa, 223)[7]

Adolescence is a period of transition from primary to secondary love objects. A similar transition takes place in childhood. In Freud's model there are three phases in child development. First there is the autoerotic phase, in which the child's libido is directed at parts of its own body. Because the child is unable to distinguish between its own body and that of the mother, the child's libido includes the pleasures of breast-feeding. In the second phase the libido is turned toward the self. This is the narcissist phase; the child perceives itself as an individual and focuses all its energy on this self-image. It is not until the third, or "object-oriented," phase that the child can see the other as separate from itself. Finally the libido is directed at the other.

In the third phase the child's awareness of being detached can lead to separation anxiety. Many children find something to comfort themselves with: an object that reminds them of their mother, such as a teddy bear or a small blanket to suck on or cling to. Their own thumbs may also function as transitional objects. Most children need these objects to make the separation process easier. At a very early age, a transitional object usually replaces the absent mother's breast, the object of the child's primary relationship. Unlike Freud, D. W. Winnicott, who first described the transitional-object phenomenon, does not interpret the mother's breast in a literal sense: "I include the whole technique of mothering. When it is said that the first object is the breast, the word 'breast' is used, I believe, to stand for the technique of mothering as well as the actual flesh" (Winnicott 1953, 95).

Winnicott believes that it is the mother's task to teach the child the primary experience of "disenchantment." In the beginning the baby's needs are satisfied instantly. This gives the child the illusion of a reality outside itself that it has created. The child experiences the breast as an extension of itself, as a consequence of its needs. It has the illusion that "the breast" is part of itself and therefore under its control. This phase does not last very long, since the mother's ultimate task is to guide the child toward independence. To achieve this the mother builds in little frustrations and disappointments from very early on. These are metaphorically described as "weaning." The child must learn that its needs cannot always be met immediately. It must come to understand that the mother is not just there for it, sharing the mother's love and care with others, and learn that the mother also needs time to herself. According to Winnicott a good mother is a "good-enough mother": She starts out by completely adapting to the child's needs but gradually stops doing so based on the child's growing ability to deal with the mother's limitations. Kristeva calls this the "mother function": Both identification and negation are introduced long before the child enters the symbolic order. Both Freud and Lacan believe that these processes only start once the child enters the symbolic order—the domain of the father—but Kristeva emphasizes the child's earlier development and the role of the mother. The transitional object's importance is closely linked to this: It helps the child to accept more easily its increasing independence from its mother.

Adolescence is a second period of separation and detachment, during which the child may again feel a need for a transitional object. Adolescents can no longer fall back on their familiar and safe childhood existence, but they have few intimate relationships in the adult world that can compensate for this loss. The primary love objects are released before secondary objects can replace them, leaving an emotional vacuum that may be filled by transitional objects. One excellent example is a diary. "The teenage diary becomes a safe, private, all-accepting partner—a transitional object—which facilitates the passage into adulthood" (Sosin 1983, 93).

The diary supplants intimacy with the parents and is a precursor to intimacy with others. In the famous passage with which Anne Frank started her diary, she wrote: "I hope I shall be able to confide in you completely, as I have never been able to do in anyone before, and I hope that you will be a great support and comfort to me" (AF*a*, 177).

Even before she actually started writing the diary (two days later), she had a very clear view of its function: The diary would be "someone" she could rely on and trust. In short, her diary would assume the role parents fulfill in childhood. A few pages later she also confessed to lacking an intimate friend:

"But I've never had a real friend, I thought at first that Jacque would be one, but it turned out badly. She's always having little secrets and going off with other girls such as J. R." (AF*a*, 187).[8]

A diary often functions as a transitional object in the period when adolescents are at an awkward in-between stage, when they are "neither fish nor fowl nor good red herring." They seem not to belong to any group; they are too grown up to rely on their parents, but too inexperienced to forge an intimate relationship with peers. The resulting feelings of loneliness and abandonment may be cushioned by keeping a diary. When Anne Frank started editing her diaries, from May 20, 1944, on, she wrote on the first pages:

> And now I touch the root of the matter the reason why I started a diary; it is that I have no such real friend.
>
> Let me put it more clearly, since no one will believe that a girl of 13 feels herself quite alone in the world, nor is it so. I have darling parents and a sister of sixteen. I know about thirty people whom one might call friends, I have strings of boyfriends, anxious to catch a glimpse of me and who, failing that, peep at me through mirrors in class. I have relations, darling aunts and a good home, no I don't seem to lack anything, save "the" friend. But it's the same with all my friends, just fun and joking, nothing more. I can never bring myself to talk of anything outside the common round or we don't seem to be able to get any closer, that is the root of the trouble. Perhaps I lack confidence, but anyway, there it is, a stubborn fact and I don't seem to be able to do anything about it. Hence, this diary. In order to enhance in my mind's eye the picture of the friend for whom I have waited so long I don't want to set down a series of bald facts in a diary like most people do, but I want this diary, itself to be my friend, and I shall call my friend Kitty. (AF*b*, 180–181)

Here we are dealing with two time frames. Anne dated this entry June 20, 1942, pretending that it had been written when she still lived on the Merwedeplein amid neighbors, classmates, and boyfriends. Despite all these relationships, she was unable to find real intimacy, and so she felt the need for a diary. She was well aware that this might be her own doing, but she did not know how to change it. In this respect Kitty is obviously a transitional object: Since she had no one to confide in, a diary seemed a suitable replacement.

However, when Anne wrote this passage, she had already been in hiding for almost two years. All contact with old acquaintances was strictly forbidden, since it could jeopardize the safety of everyone in the hiding place. For nearly two years, Frank had kept a diary, mostly written in the form of letters to Kitty. Kitty symbolized the friends she missed in real life. When even the most superficial contact with her peers had been cut off, Kitty became more than a transitional object; she became a symbolic replacement for friendship in general. Friendship had become impossible, due not only to the inner troubles Anne was experiencing as an adolescent, but also to external circumstances—the persecution of the Jews.

Increasing Narcissism

Aside from its function as a transitional object, a diary can also reflect an increase in narcissism (Deutsch 1951, 83 [1944]). As the distance between child and parents grows, the object libido is withdrawn. Since there is no replacement for the parents yet, the libido is temporarily directed at the self, bringing on a period of intensified narcissism (Baruch 1968, 430; Van Dam a, 138). The emotions that the child felt for the parents are now transferred to itself (Dalsimer 1986, 73). The adolescent turns inward. Fantasies and imagination become temporary replacements for broken ties with the past. As Anne put it: "Lately I haven't felt at all like writing about what's been going on here. I've been much more concerned with personal matters" (AFa, 523).

Her strong inward focus leads her to the discovery that she is actually "a little bundle of contradictions" (AFa, 697). She feels that she has a split personality: an outer and an inner self. The outer self is extroverted, cheerful, spontaneous, and superficial and always comes out in the company of others. But Anne loves her inner self more. This self is purer, sweeter, and deeper, though also very shy (see quotations on pp. 45; AFa, 697–698).

This introspection is caused not only by the withdrawal of the libido but also by the drastic physical changes of puberty. "In the three months I have been here I have gained 17 pounds, an enormous amount isn't it!" (AFa, 284).

Undoubtedly this weight gain was partly attributable to lack of exercise. But Anne was not only getting heavier, she was also growing taller. On her fourteenth birthday, her father wrote a poem for her which mentions that she had grown ten centimeters (AFb, 428).[9]

Like *Alice in Wonderland,* an adolescent girl might follow her own growth with mixed feelings of uncertainty, fear, curiosity, and awe and show a heightened interest in the physical and psychological processes involved (Dalsimer 1986, 8).

Keeping a diary can be an attempt to get a grip on these changes. Anne, too, was fascinated by the upheaval in her body. In the early part of her diary she showed great curiosity and excitement about her impending menstrual period. Her letter to Kitty dated October 20, 1942, ends with the postscript:

> I forgot to tell you the important news that I shall probably be hav-
> ing my period soon. I noticed that because I keep having a kind of
> sticky discharge in my panties and Mother has told me about it. I can
> hardly wait it seems so important to me, it's only a pity that I shan't be
> able to wear sanitary napkins because you can't get them any more,
> and the little tampons Mother wears can only be worn by women who
> have had a baby. Well farewell my child.　　　　　　　　(AF*a*, 287)

This last phrase can be interpreted in two ways. At the surface, it appears
that Anne simply closed her letter to Kitty in an unusual way, referring to her
pen pal as "my child." But implicitly this closing statement is also a reaction to
what she had just written. In this sense it signals Anne's farewell to childhood
(Van Dam a, 135).

A year later Anne reread her first diary and scribbled under this entry: "I
shall never be able to write such things again!" (AF*a*, 287). Subjects she had
first dealt with without hesitation later embarrassed her deeply: "I really blush
with shame when I read the pages dealing with subjects that I'd much better
have left to the imagination. I put it all down so bluntly!" (AF*a*, 304).

She recognized herself in an article by journalist Sis Heyster, published in
the women's magazine *Libelle*:

> She writes roughly something like this—that a girl in the years (time)
> of puberty becomes quiet within and begins to think about the won-
> ders that are happening to her body. I experience that too and that is
> why I get the feeling lately of being embarrassed in front of Margot,
> Mother, and Father. Funnily enough, Margot, who is much shier than I
> am, isn't at all embarrassed.　　　　　　(AF*a*, 442; adapt. MH/SL)

In chapter 3 I discuss the significance of menstrual periods to Anne Frank
and show that her physical development into womanhood coincided with
her spiritual development. While experiencing her first menstrual periods,
she created a guardian angel and, with it, a divine discourse suited to both
her age and the difficult conditions in which she lived.

But first I continue my discussion of the adolescent psyche in order to
make a connection with writing in general.

A Discourse of Love

Adolescence is a turbulent time without much support or stability. In the
Secret Annex, Anne Frank experienced her first menstrual period; her girl's
body transformed into that of a woman. Her thoughts and feelings changed
as well, and ranged from curiosity to embarrassment, excitement to depression, hope to despair:

Dear Kitty,

If you could read my pile of letters one after another, you would certainly be struck by the many different moods in which they are written.   (AF*b*, 415)

As mentioned before, Julia Kristeva's description of adolescence emphasizes psychical structures rather than age (Kristeva 1990). An adolescent is a subject in progress. As the parents' influence weakens, so does the superego, the conscience they have instilled in the child. The adolescent's psychic structure therefore becomes much less restrained and more open. But this liberation does not automatically lead to relief; it can give rise to depression. In Anne this depressive position was worsened by the fact that she had to do more than detach herself from her primary love objects. The Nazi regime forced her to pack up and go, changing her life practically overnight. The early diary entries, written at home on the Merwedeplein, testify to a life full of contact with her peers. Suddenly that all disappeared. From then on she lived hidden away from the world; all contact with the outside was out of the question. She was filled with nostalgia for everything she had to leave behind. A week after she moved into the Secret Annex she wrote about her cat:

I miss Moortje every moment of the day and no one knows how often I think of her; whenever I think of her I get tears in my eyes. Moortje is such a darling and I love her so much, I dream up all sorts of plans in which she comes back again because she's such a darling and I can trust her with everything.   (AF*a*, 226)

It seems that Moortje had been a transitional object for her. In that sense Kitty, or the diary, can be seen as a replacement for the cat. After a year and a half Anne's feelings about Moortje remained unchanged:

What I also understand so well is my longing for Moortje. I have been longing, often consciously but much more often unconsciously, for trust, love and caresses all the time I've been here. This longing is sometimes stronger and sometimes weaker, but it's always there.

(AF*a*, 305)

It is no wonder that Anne Frank was struggling with depression. In the middle of "normal" adolescent development, her farewell to parental love and care, she had also had to part with everything familiar. Moortje, her transitional object at home, could not go into hiding with her, and the transition from primary to secondary love objects was slowed down by the fact that she had no contact with peers, except for Peter and Bep and her older sister, Margot. She was all alone:

Still, I can't refrain from telling you that lately I have begun to feel deserted, I am surrounded by too great a void. I never used to feel like this, my fun and amusements, my girlfriends, completely filled my thoughts. Now I either think about unhappy things, or about myself. And at long last I have made the discovery that Father, although he's such a darling, still cannot take the place of my entire little world of bygone days. Mother and Margot have long since ceased to count in my feelings.

(AF*a*, 318; adapt. MH)

Kristeva interprets such feelings of depression as a lack of love. With their interplay of physical and psychological powers, the adolescent's thoughts and emotions form a discourse of love, or rather a discourse of heartbreak. The adolescent pines for love, but love does not come easily. Her parents are not the same people they used to be, and the love that she once gave them is withdrawn. In this period the adolescent is alone and narcissist. She keeps her love to herself because no new love objects have crossed her path. This situation reactivates the depressive position. Kristeva agrees with the idea widely accepted by psychoanalysts that adolescence is in fact the Oedipus complex revisited (Blos 1962, 100; Dalsimer 1986, 52; Deutsch 1951, 102 [1944]; A. Freud 1986, 139 [1936]). Nevertheless she gives it a specific twist, inspired by the Kleinian analyst Hanna Segal, in particular by her "Notes on Symbol Formation" (Segal 1988, 49–65).

Segal explains the child's entry into language by emphasizing the depressive position. In the first phase of development, the child does not feel the need for language. The child and the mother are one; to the child the rhythms, sounds, and notes of the semiotic are sufficient. But the child's eventual realization that it is separate from the mother triggers the depressive position. To live with this realization the child must accept language as a substitute for the mother. The child's need to learn language, to enter the symbolic order, is born once the mother/child symbiosis is broken and the child starts seeking a replacement for the loss of oneness. The child's awareness of disconnectedness, separation anxiety, which is in fact *la condition humaine,* opens the its mind to the symbolic reality of language. The child leaves the semiotic to enter the symbolic order by way of the depressive position:

> The symbol is felt to represent the object. The symbol is used not to deny but to overcome loss. . . . The word "symbol" comes from the Greek term for throwing together, bringing together, integrating. The process of symbol formation is, I think, a continuous process of bringing together and integrating the internal with the external, the subject with the object, and the earlier experiences with the later ones.

(Segal 1988, 57, 60)

The speaking subject is actually denying the loss of the mother, since what she is saying is: "I have not lost her, because I can retrieve her in language." Language is in fact a translation of the mother: "It will be recalled that separation from the object starts the so-called depressive phase. Upon losing mother and relying on negation, I retrieve her as sign, image, word" (Kristeva 1989, 74 [1987a]).[10]

By departing from oneness while denying the fundamental loss of symbiosis with the mother, the child gains access to the land of signs. But this does not relieve the pain. The human raison d'être is rooted in the depressive position; mourning the loss is often a lifelong process.

The depressive position is experienced in varying degrees. According to Kristeva adolescence is a resurgence of the depressive condition, resulting from the realization—just as in early infancy—of detachment from the parents. The love between parents and child can no longer be freely exchanged. The adolescent feels abandoned and, in a sense, relives the first separation from the mother, experiencing emptiness and lovelessness. Anne Frank was aware of this process, as we see from the following entry, which was written at a time when she had already tried to become closer to her peers. In other words the transition from primary to secondary objects of love was well under way. For the first time in her life, Anne felt close to Margot, Peter, and Bep, people of her own generation. She wrote down what this bond consisted of:

> Aren't the grownups idiotic and stupid? Just as if Peter, Margot, Bep and I don't all feel the same about things, and only a mother's love, or that of a very, very good friend, can help us.
> The two mothers here just don't understand us at all! . . .
> Only great love and devotion can help Bep, Margot, Peter, and me, and none of us here gets it. And no one, especially the stupid "know-alls" here, can understand us, because we are much more sensitive and much more advanced in our thoughts than anyone here would ever imagine in their wildest dreams!
> *Love, what is love? I believe love is something that can't really be put into words. Love is understanding someone, caring for someone, sharing their ups and downs. And in the long run that also means physical love, you have shared something, given something away and received something, no matter whether you are married or unmarried, or whether you are pregnant or not. It doesn't matter in the least if you've lost your honor, as long as you know that someone will stand by you, will understand you for the rest of your life, someone you won't have to share with anyone else!*
>
> (AF*a*, 505–506; adapt. MH/SL)

A few weeks later Anne Frank copied these sentences, which she herself had underlined, into her "book of beautiful quotations." Apparently she was pleased with her philosophical reflections on adult, heterosexual love. At the same time she recognized how people her age craved mother love. Her passage from childhood into adulthood is very apparent; she blamed adults for not providing love and understanding and had begun looking for solidarity among her peers, all the while thinking about the nature of love between men and women. These thoughts about love echo the call of the semiotic: The loved one will always be there for you, and only you.

In this phase of her life, Anne was too old for the one type of love but too young for the other. This lack of love, the depressive position, left her torn between the semiotic and the symbolic order, the order of language, signs, translations, and replacements.

This phase mirrors early childhood, the initial passage from the semiotic into the symbolic. After all, the speaking subject can in psychoanalytic terms be construed as the subject denying the loss of the mother by trying to recover her in language. An adolescent may temporarily regard language as an unacceptable translation of the original unity or wholeness. This constitutes a recurrence of the depressive position. While the speaking subject denies the loss of the mother by accepting her substitute (language), the depressive subject denies the possibility of recovering the mother in language. She denies the denial. She refuses to accept language as a substitute for the mother (see also De Martelaere 1993, 75).

This raises two important questions. What position did Anne Frank occupy in this phase? And how, in her case, did the transition from the speaking to the writing subject unfold?

Adolescent Writing

Anne Frank often felt empty and lonely; she seemed unable to find a substitute in the symbolic order for the original wholeness. In daily life she had trouble expressing herself in speech; she found the spoken word insufficient to represent her thoughts and feelings. Once, pondering her relationship to Peter, she wrote in her diary:

> I really don't honestly know how to begin, and however would he be able to, when he finds talking so much more difficult than I do? If only I could write to him, then at least I would know that he would grasp what I want to say, because it is so terribly difficult to put it into words!   (AFa, 534)

And to Margot she once wrote (on the subject of her closeness to Peter and how this would affect Margot): "Let's not talk about it anymore, but if you still want anything please write to me about it, because I can say what I mean much better on paper" (AF*a*, 552).

To Anne the difference between speaking and writing was considerable. Both are expressions of language, but writing is more solid, less volatile than speaking. Writing gives shape to words and anchors them down, and that is exactly what Anne needed. Writing, even letter writing, allows one to stay turned inward. In conversation the speaker is easily distracted due to the other's remarks or facial expressions. For adolescents there is even more at stake in writing: In depression, the subject runs the risk of regressing to the semiotic phase if she denies the symbolic order as a substitute of the original symbiosis. Anne Frank's defense was writing. This strengthened her bond with the symbolic order, with language and culture, while enabling her to open herself to semiotic influences.

Kristeva draws a distinction between three registers within writing; seen as a whole, these registers reveal the potential value of writing to the adolescent. Kristeva's first register is the semiotically productive activity of written signs; the second is the production of a novelistic fiction; and the third is hiding the writing from the judgment of others (Kristeva 1990, 9–10). The first register emphasizes writing as an activity, a physical, muscular movement requiring motor skills. By comparing this dimension of writing to mastery of anal control, Kristeva puts writing into a Freudian context. Freud stressed the erogenous significance of the infant's anal zone; a bowel movement could be a pleasurable or erotic experience. In his view the child experiences feces as a part of its own body that can be released or held on to at will. This creates an opportunity for power. In his analysis of anal eroticism, Freud endorsed and incorporated the ideas of Lou Andreas-Salomé.[11] According to Salomé the first taboo children are taught is the prohibition of deriving pleasure from anal activity, and as a result, children begin to suspect that they are not allowed to enjoy any of their urges. As soon as children are toilet trained, the anal "remains the symbol of everything that is to be repudiated and excluded from life" (Freud 1953, 7, 187 [1905]).[12]

When Kristeva postulates that writing gives narcissist satisfaction and can therefore be called a form of masturbation, she means writing in terms of the first register: as a muscular movement that the writer applies to her- or himself alone. The fact that adolescents tend to like writing has some bearing on the resurfacing of the repressed: It refers to the semiotic phase. After all, this is the phase in which the child experiences itself as all-encompassing. The child and the mother are one, and everything centers on the pleasurable release of urges.

These aspects of writing can clearly be traced in the process of diary writing. It is a solitary, muscular activity. It provides pleasure, through the activity itself—the motion of pen-on-paper—and through the product which flows from the pen. In addition, the link between diary writing and the anal phase can be seen from the context where this activity takes place. Diary writing is usually a reclusive act, performed in solitude. The diary is often shrouded in secrecy. This is symbolized further by its outward appearance; a real diary has a lock, after all. Anne's first diary had a lock, but her later notebooks did not. She kept her notes in an old briefcase of her father's and retreated whenever she wanted to write in her diary.

A diary writer is not only physically self-involved, but psychologically too. Diary writing is narcissist because the writer temporarily withdraws her outward libidinal drive, directing it inward onto herself. As an object the diary is—like the contents of one's bowels—an expression of oneself.

According to Helene Deutsch (1951, 12 [1944]), the first phase of puberty is analogous to the phallic phase of childhood; in both phases the child is interested in anatomical differences and physiological processes. This would also explain the secrecy surrounding the diary: Everything is sexually charged. However, I recognize only part of this in Anne Frank. Though she expressed great curiosity about physical processes, she was not consumed by it. Deutsch also theorized that the secrecy of diary writing could be a kind of revenge on the mother. Because the mother has kept secrets from her daughter, the daughter takes revenge by keeping her intimate secrets to herself (Deutsch 1951, 10 [1944]). Indeed, Anne did not always receive straight answers to her questions about her body:

> With us it's all pretty neatly arranged, before I was 11 or 12 I didn't realize that there were two inner lips as well, you couldn't see them at all. And the funniest thing of all was that I thought that the urine came out of the clitoris.
> When I asked Mother once what that stub of a thing was for, she said that she didn't know, she still pretends to be ignorant even now!
> (AFa, 566; adapt. MH)[13]

It seems to me that the aura of secrecy and retreat surrounding diary writing reflects the semiotic, physical act of writing as well as its content. The prevailing theories about adolescent diary writing only consider content. Kristeva has added the interesting idea that writing as an activity (regardless of content) can also be a reason to retreat. She arrived at this view through the basic principle underlying her scholarly project: an ongoing effort to draw more attention to the semiotic processes in our symbolic-oriented culture. In Kristeva's theory the semiotic is not a passing phase but a level that coexists with the symbolic.

Kristeva's second register of writing, the production of a novelistic fiction, is in keeping with Freud's concept of creative writing as a product of fantasy. He elaborated on this theme in his lecture *The Writer and Fantasy,* which I mentioned earlier. He opened his argument like this: "We laymen have always been intensely curious to know . . . from what sources that strange being, the creative writer, draws his material" (Freud 1959a, 9, 143, [1907]).[14]

Of course Freud tried—and managed—to locate the origin of writing in childhood. Most of all, he said, children love to play. When playing, the child creates its own world with the help of the objects at its disposal. The game is motivated by one deep wish: to be grown up. Children act out adult life.

In time, play develops into fantasy. While play is the distinguishing characteristic of early childhood, fantasy is the trademark of adolescence. In adolescent fantasy the tangible and visible objects of play have disappeared; in fantasy, the imagination is less visible than it was in actual play. Just like play, fantasies are guided by drives. According to Freud unfulfilled desires are the driving force behind fantasies.

This process can be seen in Anne's writings too, particularly in her account book. The fantasies, which she committed to paper in the shape of fairy tales or children's stories, often revolve around a barely disguised wish for freedom. In "Fear" (Frank 1994, 37–39), a wartime story, the first-person narrator is scared out of her wits by the bombings (just as the writer was) and at one point runs out the door, out of town, and into the woods. There her fear disappears.

Another of Anne's stories, "Blurry, the Explorer," begins like this: "Once, when he was still very small, Blurry felt a great desire to escape from the fussing care of his mother bear and see something of the wide, wide world for himself" (Frank 1994, 47).

Freud believed that desires are triggered by a circumstance in the present. A desire evokes memories from childhood, when a similar desire was fulfilled, thereby creating a daydream or fantasy oriented at future wish fulfillment. In other words, a fantasy wavers between three time levels: present, past, and future. A creative writer, therefore, is actually a "dreamer in broad daylight" (Freud 1959a, 9, 149 [1907]),[15] because:

A strong experience in the present awakens in the creative writer a memory of an earlier experience (usually belonging to his childhood) from which there now proceeds a wish which finds its fulfillment in the creative work. The work itself exhibits elements of the recent provoking occasion as well as of the old memory. (Freud 1959a, 9, 151 [1907])[16]

A similar process must have taken place when Anne Frank wrote her short story "Kaatje."[17] Most likely the "Kaatje" character was based on the girl Anne Frank had secretly watched from the window of the Secret Annex. "[Kaatje] is the girl next door. In fair weather I can watch her playing in the yard through our window. . . . [Kaatje] has a small cat that is so black that it looks like a Moor" (Frank 1994, 3).

She lost herself in the fantasy that she was Kaatje, that she could go outside and had a cat to take care of. The story describes the everyday routines that govern Kaatje's life: church, school, daydreams. The story ends like this: "[Kaatje] sighs. To be interrupted just as you are thinking of a glorious future" (Frank 1994, 5).

In writing this story Anne identified with the girl "out there" who led a normal life like the one she once had, a life she missed terribly.

Because Kristeva was schooled in the Lacanian tradition, she regards writing as an imaginary activity, that is to say one that refers to actions that are initially presymbolic but later become part of the symbolic in a specific way. Writing is nourished by fantasies. However, these fantasies cannot present themselves to our mind's eye in their purest form; they are filtered by culture's prohibitions, codes, and taboos. Hence Kristeva's register of producing a novelistic fiction is characterized by an interaction between the symbolic and the semiotic, between the conscious and the unconscious, between the law of culture and unbridled fantasy. The writing process is therefore a combination of fantasy and filter. In this theory "filter" can be replaced by "superego." After all, the filter contains all present ideologies and codes of representation—in other words, all the values, norms, and taboos that determine the symbolic order in form and content. In an entry in Anne's diary, her superego can be seen looking over her shoulder. She wrote that she had been crying one night:

> One large sob brought me back to earth again, and I quelled my tears because I didn't want them to hear anything in the next room.
> Then I began trying to talk some courage into myself. I could only say: "I must, I must, I must. . . ." Completely stiff from the unnatural position, I fell against the side of the bed and fought on, until I climbed into bed again just before half past 10. It was over!

And now it's all over, I must work, so as not to be a fool, to get on to become a journalist, because that's what I want! I know that I *can* write, a couple of my stories are good, my descriptions of the "Secret Annex" are humorous, there's a lot in my diary that speaks, but—whether I have real talent remains to be seen. . . .

I am the best and sharpest critic of my own work, I know myself what is and what is not well written. Anyone who doesn't write doesn't know how wonderful it is; I used to bemoan the fact that I couldn't draw at all, but now I am more than happy that I can at least write.

(AFa, 586–587)

Anne was very serious about working hard, being critical of her own work, and keeping her ultimate goal, to become a writer, foremost in her mind. A number of her short stories, for example "Eve's Dream," show how the conscience became a personal theme. In her dream, Eve meets an elf who counsels her about the right way to live. This allows Eve to become a better person and when she grows up, she suddenly understands the true nature of the elf: "She knew, as if in a flash, that it had been her own conscience which, in her dream, had shown her what was right. She was deeply thankful that, in her childhood, she had had the little elf as a guide and example" (Frank 1994, 15).

Anne's short stories "Give," "The Wise Old Dwarf," and "The Fairy" are also quite moralistic. These tales from the account book clearly show the interaction between filter and fantasy. When the filter is very fine-meshed, the written text is full of clichés and stereotypes. But because the adolescent's psychical structure is characterized by a weakening superego, the filter becomes coarser and leaves numerous openings for the repressed material.

I believe that in Anne Frank's case the filter is sometimes quite finely meshed, which accounts for her rather stereotypical fairy tales. It is striking, however, that the filter or superego we observe is not just the parents' voice, but to a far greater extent her own set of norms and values. She was contemplating the nature of conscience and developing a superego that felt like her own, even though she had inherited it from her parents. Actually her superego—which had lost some of its power due to the revival of libidinal drives and the separation process from her parents—is reinforced rather than renewed. Adolescents may feel the need for a reinforced superego, especially as a mechanism with which to resist their physical drives, or the id (A. Freud 1986, 109–142 [1936]). This might explain the highly moralistic tone of some of her tales, which are about how one should live and how to distinguish right from wrong. It seems that writing stories functioned as a way to reinforce her superego, which was weakened by the increased distance between herself and her parents. In other words, it is as if she herself refined the filter, as if she rewrote it in her own words.

The mechanisms governing Kristeva's second register of producing a novelistic fiction were enhanced by the conditions of war. In terms of literary genre, Anne Frank's oeuvre can be considered utopian: "She used her diary to both depict an imaginary better place and to prove the possibility of positive changes in the present" (Chiarello 1994, 128).

Referring to the second register of writing, Kristeva points out that adolescents can derive pleasure from writing because they experience for the first time how close their self-expressions in language are to themselves. Writing is a living discourse, not an empty one. Because language enables adolescents to express unconscious contents, they feel that language allows them to express their true selves. Anne experienced this mainly while writing her diary. The filter was coarse then, because she was writing for herself and not for others. The opposite is true of the stories in the account book, which she would sometimes read aloud to others. Kristeva's filtering theory greatly clarifies the difference between the diaries and the account book. The account book was written with an audience in mind and is highly moral in tone. The writing is stereotypical, having passed through a fine-meshed filter. Because Anne's original diary was written for herself only, it passed through a much coarser filter. To Margot she once wrote:

> I'll be happy to let you read what I've written in my diary today sometime, but I'm not ready yet. Later on, say in a month's time, if I've got any further with it, I might show it to you. Just let Mommy say I don't know anything about life then!
>
> You know why I think you'd be interested? Because although I can't express myself properly anywhere else, even in my tales, in my diary I can completely.
>
> It cries with pain or joy just as I sometimes do myself!   (AF*a*, 521)

Kristeva calls this second register "the production of a novelistic fiction." This raises the question of whether Anne Frank's diaries should be considered fiction. I believe they are, because diaries are about the construction of an identity. The diaries are, among other things, her story about herself: She constructs herself fictionally (Heebing 1991, 196). It is precisely through writing that she can shape herself, develop her superego and gain self-knowledge. The edited diaries, the *b* version, have even stronger fictional features. They were edited with a view to publication, so they were more finely filtered than the original. This version, more than the a version, is a construction; it is partly based on her self-image and partly motivated by her desire to paint an attractive picture for her future audience.[18]

The second register of adolescent writing is in line with one of the main characteristics Kristeva attributes to the adolescent psyche: openness. This is particularly true in the sense that the adolescent's psychical structure creates openings to the repressed, sparking off her psychical reorganization. The underlying cause of this process is the increasing detachment of the superego.

Kristeva defined the third register of writing as protection from appraisal by another. In this register she emphasizes writing's function as a refuge. Because writing is a solitary activity (writing testifies to a "solitary economy"), the writer can live out her wildest fantasies without risk. An adolescent's psychical structure is fluid, not fixed. Writing offers an opportunity to experiment with this psychic freedom without much danger. In this register too, writing can be regarded as a semiotic practice: "I will see writing as a semiotic practice that facilitates the ultimate reorganization of psychic space, in the time before an ideally postulated maturity" (Kristeva 1990, 10).

As is evident in Anne Frank's case, writing can serve to maintain order, to keep the peace. For example, she can express the anger and frustration she feels toward her mother without her mother noticing. Sometime before her fifteenth birthday, she became aware that her diary fulfilled this purpose:

> Dear Kitty,
>
> This morning when I had nothing to do, I turned over some of the pages of my diary and several times I came across letters dealing with the subject "Mother" in such a vehement way that it quite shocked me and I asked myself: "Anne, is it really you who mentioned hate, oh, Anne, how could you?" I remained sitting with the open page in my hand, and thought about it and how it came about that I should have been so brimful of rage and seemed so full of hate that I had to confide it all in you. [. . .]
>
> I hid myself within myself, I only considered myself and quietly wrote down all my joys, sorrows and contempt in my diary. . . .
>
> Those violent outbursts on paper were only giving vent to anger which in a normal life could have been worked off by stamping my feet a couple of times in a locked room or calling Mummy names behind her back. [. . .]
>
> I soothe my conscience now, with the thought that hard words are better on paper than that Mother should carry them in her heart.
>
> yours, *Anne*
>
> (AF*b*, 438–439; adapt. MH)

This passage is from the *b* version, dated January 2, 1944. In the original diary there is no such entry, suggesting that while Anne was editing her diaries (from May 1944 onward), she was struck by the harshness of her criticisms of her mother and wished to justify herself to a future audience rather than to the fictitious Kitty.[19]

Sonja Heebing, who surveyed teenagers about diary writing, mentions its therapeutic effect (Heebing 1991, 197). Many adolescents feel that writing is a good way to get things off your chest, to write difficult matters out of your system. In other words a diary functions as an emotional safety valve. Anne Frank was well aware that this "acting out" function was very important, not only because of her adolescence but also because she was in hiding:

> Yes, Kitty, Anne is a crazy child, but I do live in crazy times and under still crazier circumstances.
> But, still, the brightest spot of all is that at least I can write down my thoughts and feelings, otherwise I would be absolutely stifled.
> <div align="right">(AF<i>a</i>, 534)[20]</div>

The conditions in the hiding place made it very hard for her to keep any distance from the others. She did not have a room of her own, and as the youngest child in the Secret Annex she was raised, lectured, and advised from all sides. Her diary writing was one of the few opportunities she had to get away from all the well-meant advice. She felt that her diary was the only thing she had to herself (AF*a*, 533, 548). To her, writing was also one of the few ways to go through adolescent processes (Van Dam a, 150) and to work on forming her identity (Dalsimer 1986, 45).

The Phallus par Excellence

Adolescent writing reactivates the process of symbol appearance, motivated by feelings of loneliness and abandonment. Libidinal drives that were first directed at the parents are now directed inward, toward the self, making such a narcissistic activity as writing possible. Moreover, writing makes the depressive position bearable. The very act of writing is in itself pleasurable in the first register, where writing is a motor skill and a narcissistic activity. Another compensation is provided by the second register, where fiction is produced; the adolescent recognizes the text as authentic, partly because she or he appropriates the filter and partly because she or he is open to repressed fantasies and can determine the relationship between fantasy and filter her- or himself. In the third register, writing gives access to a world in which fantasies can safely be acted out. All three registers can be identified in Anne Frank's diaries and short stories.

The drive to write is fueled by a lack of love. The process of developing from a child into an adult is accompanied by heartache, which activates the depressive position. This depression is staved off by writing.

Hanna Segal sees a close link between the symbolic order, symbol formation, and depression. Kristeva, however, rejects this relationship where writing is concerned. Adolescent writing may be a reactivation of the depressive position, but it sustains itself from a manic position. Like any depressive, the writing adolescent cannot recover the lost object—the all-encompassing love of the mother—in normal, everyday language. However, the young writer does not accept this depressive void; he or she endures the depression by looking for something, a fetish, to fill the void and as such, to replace the original symbiosis.[21] She or he, the writer, does not assume a depressive position so much as a perverted one, putting the depression in parentheses and filling the chasm with a literary creation, a literary product. Writing transforms the fundamental feelings of depression, gloominess, and dejection into rhythm, signs, and forms:

> Literary creation is that adventure of the body and signs that bears witness to the affect—to sadness as imprint of separation and beginning of the symbol's sway; to joy as imprint of the triumph that settles me in the universe of artifice and symbol, which I try to harmonize in the best possible way with my experience of reality. But that testimony is produced by literary creation in a material that is totally different from what constitutes mood. It transposes affect into rhythms, signs, forms. The "semiotic" and the "symbolic" become the communicable imprints of an affective reality, perceptible to the reader (I like this book because it conveys sadness, anguish, or joy) and yet dominated, set aside, vanquished.   (Kristeva 1989, 22 [1987a])[22]

The ego, the sense of self, triumphs through the fetish of the text. When Anne had been deeply shaken by a burglary that aroused the fear of discovery, she wrote: "I trust to luck, but should I be saved and spared from destruction, then it would be terrible if my diaries and my tales were lost" (AF*a*, 481).

She cannot imagine a life without her diaries and her tales: her "oeuvre" is her crutch. According to Kristeva writing is actually quite a phallic phenomenon, "if not the phallus par excellence" (Kristeva 1990, 11). This, again, points to Kristeva's Lacanian education. To Jacques Lacan the phallus is the ultimate symbol for the object of desire. The phallus signifies that which the subject has lacked since she left the original wholeness. Defining writing as the phallus par excellence implies that writing creates the illusion of approaching the original wholeness. I can follow Kristeva's argument in the sense that writing acts as a fetish and creates a feeling of wholeness and fullness. However, I object to the male connotations of the phallus as the symbol for the ultimate object of desire. Even though we are dealing with the phallus, not the penis—with a symbol, not with reality—the link between penis and phallus is undeniable. Thus writing is drawn into male discourse, and this is where my doubts lie. Kristeva takes this reasoning very far: "Refusal of loss, triumph of the ego through the fetish of the text, writing becomes an essential phallic compliment, if not the phallus par excellence. It depends, for this very reason, on an ideal paternity" (Kristeva 1990, 11).

We hear nothing more of the mother and her influence on writing. "Ideal paternity" refers to Freud, who in the origin of the "ego-ideal" (an example or model for the child) presumes that the child identifies with the "father in his own personal prehistory" (Freud 1961, 19, 31 [1923]).[23] Freud's scant notes on this concept have been developed by Kristeva (Kristeva 1987c, 19–56 [1983b]).

In the first phase of life, the child finds itself in the chaotic fullness of the mother-child dyad. There are no object or subject positions since the child cannot take any distance; there is nothing but symbiosis. The child wants to be everything to the mother, wanting to satisfy all her needs. This archaic situation changes as soon as the child notices that the mother also desires another, "a third term . . . the phallus desired by the mother" (Kristeva 1987c, 41 [1983b]).[24] Apparently the child is unable to satisfy all the mother's needs, because the mother also desires something or someone who is in any case "not I." This awareness punctures the original fullness and results in a void. Therefore the child revises its desire: "I also want to be that other, so I can be everything to my mother." Hence the birth of the child's own desire, namely to be the third term, or in Lacanian terms: to be the phallus, the object of desire. This third term is like an ideal, a model. By striving "to be the other," the child places itself outside the earlier semiotic body. This primary identification takes place through language: "In being able to receive the other's words, to assimilate, repeat, and reproduce them, I become like him: One. A subject of enunciation. Through psychic osmosis/identification. Through love" (Kristeva 1987c, 26 [1983b]).[25]

The subject originates through identification with the speaking other, idealized by the child. Like Freud, who called this figure the "father in individual prehistory," Kristeva also calls it a father, the "imaginary father," to be precise. Kristeva apparently believes that in the child's perception it is the father rather than the mother who facilitates the transition from the semiotic to the symbolic order: It is he who meets the child halfway. The mother must stay where she is, static and unchangeable; only the dynamic father can cross boundaries. Although Kristeva, like Freud, indicates that this "father" is actually a condensation of the two parents, she prefers to call this conglomerate "father" because the identification takes places along the lines of language, and hence in the symbolic order:

> The child will not start speaking or learning. In order to do this, there must be what I in accordance with Freud call a "father in individual prehistory": a sort of conglomerate of both parents, of both sexes, which should however be considered a father, albeit not the strict, Oedipal father, but a living and loving father. Why a father and not a mother, if we know it is the mother who first cares for, hugs and nurtures us? Because this will allow for an intrapsychic and social institution which does not coincide with the physical entity of the mother, who is too close to the child and may cause short circuits leading to inhibition and psychosis. This "imaginary father"—the prime meridian of our archaic loves—takes on the role of the loving third term with which the ego identifies in its infancy. He makes it possible for our libidinal drives to be directed at the symbolic order, for the physical and the psychic to be separated—making space for play, for giving, for exchange, a space beyond separation and absence. In and through this transference onto a loving other, the sign and meaning are developed.
>
> (Kristeva 1986, 174–175 [1983a]; trans. MH)·

In this way Kristeva implies that the mother has no place in the symbolic order. This opinion is further underlined by her statements that the primary identification process coincides with the onset of the rejection of the pre-oedipal mother. The mother is perceived as an "abject": as something despicable that deserves repudiation:

> In short, primary identification appears to be a transference to (from) the imaginary father, correlative to the establishment of the mother as the "ab-jected." Narcissism would be that correlation (with the imaginary father and the "ab-jected" mother) enacted around the central emptiness of that transference.
>
> (Kristeva 1987c, 41–42 [1983b])[26]

Earlier in this chapter, when I described the same process in reference to adolescence, I was reasoning from the psychoanalytic premise that adolescence is a repetition of childhood. In adolescence, as in childhood, the primary objects of love are rejected and the libido is transferred to the self. At the same time feelings of depression arise. Using theories on the father in individual prehistory, we can refine our understanding of these processes of adolescence. Following Kristeva's argument, we can hypothesize that adolescence is not a process of rejecting both parents, but one of rejecting the mother and simultaneously idealizing the father. By extension we could postulate the following scenario: Physical and psychological forces make the female adolescent withdraw her libido from the primary love objects, in particular the mother—toward whom she even feels defensive—while at the same time she is seeking a chance to identify with others. The father is the first available candidate. This transition creates a void, which in turn presents an opportunity to take up the symbolic to fill the void. One expression of this is writing, so Kristeva can characterize writing as the phallus and make the whole process appear to depend on an ideal father.

"Mans" Instead of "Mams"

To respond adequately to Julia Kristeva, it is necessary to analyze Anne Frank's diaries with regard to these issues. Kristeva's theory leads me to hypothesize that, in adolescence, Anne Frank rejected her mother and began to idealize her father. As I will show in this section, such a structure can indeed be found here and there in the diaries. However, this is only one side of the story. In the next section we will see that Anne Frank's relationship with her mother was much more complicated—and less unambiguously negative—than it initially appears.

Especially in the first diary (written in the summer and autumn of 1942), Anne Frank juxtaposed her father and mother, writing lovingly and respectfully of Pim but negatively about her mother. Anne could not stand her mother and felt better understood by her father (AF*a*, 233, 249, 260). The entry quoted below is reproduced in its entirety because of its telling associations:

> This morning Miep told us that last night they were dragging Jews from house after house again in South Amsterdam. Horrible. God knows which of our acquaintances are left. A crippled old woman was sitting on Miep's doorstep because she couldn't walk, and so the bastards went to get a car, meanwhile the poor person had to wait out in the cold (she wasn't allowed to go indoors) and there was terrible shooting. You just can't imagine how awful it all is; I am only so glad that we are here. There was another argument yesterday, and Mother made the most awful fuss, she told Father just what she thought of me and had a horrible crying fit, so, of course, off I went too, and I'd got such a frightful headache already. Finally I told Daddy that I'm much more fond of

"him" than Mother, to which he replied that I'd get over that. But I don't believe it. I simply can't stand Mother, and I have to force myself not to snap at her all the time and to stay calm with her, I could easily slap her face, I don't know how it is that I have taken such a terrible dislike to her. Daddy said that I should sometimes offer to help her, when she doesn't feel well or has a headache; but I won't since I don't love her and I don't feel like it. I would certainly feel it for Father, I noticed that when he was ill. Also it's easy for me to picture Mother dying one day, but Father dying one day seems inconceivable to me. It may be very mean of me, but that's how I feel. I hope that Mother won't *ever* read "this" or any of the other things. (AF*a*, 266–267; adapt. MH/SL)

Anne Frank began this entry with an account of the Nazis' degrading treatment of an old woman. This fragment blends seamlessly into a description of one of her fights with her mother. Apparently she associated the old woman with her mother and herself with the snarling, hateful enemy. The passage also points to her death fantasies. In effect she wrote: "I hate my mother, I wish she weren't there" (Van Dam a, 142–143).

Because the original diaries written between late 1942 and December 1943 are missing, we have only the edited version for this period at our disposal. In this document Anne's mother plays a much less prominent role, which means one of two things: she either stopped writing about her mother in the original diary, or she considered the negative passages about her mother in the original diary unfit for publication. The latter is more likely; from later diary entries it is clear that she was ashamed of her nastiness.

Anne Frank seems to fit into Kristeva's analysis, which links the father to the symbolic order, to language, and negates the mother's influence. Together with her father, Anne studied and read English and German; they taught and tested each other (Dalsimer 1986, 53; Waaldijk 1993, 334). Together they composed poems for Saint Nicholas Day (AF*b*, 424–426).[27]

Anne's passion for writing and her excellent command of the Dutch language can be interpreted partly as a reaction against her mother, as the following quotations illustrate:

I know that I can discuss things and argue better than Mother, . . . and because of this (you may laugh) I feel superior to her in a great many things. If I love anyone, above all I must have admiration for them, admiration and respect, and Mother fails completely in these two requirements!   (AF*a*, 544)

Please bear in mind, dear Kitty, that the two ladies here speak terrible Dutch, . . . if you could hear their [gibberish] you would burst out

laughing: we don't pay attention to it any more, it's no good correct-
ing them either. When I write about Mother or Mrs. v. P. I won't repeat
their actual words but put them in proper Dutch.

(AF*b*, 233; adapt. MH)[28]

Anne tried to rid herself of her mother in many ways. In one diary entry
she fended her off very creatively by using a pun. Having been in hiding for
a year and a half at that point, Anne felt awful; she longed for more freedom
of movement, fresh air, and a supportive mother:

> Crying can bring such relief, but only if you can cry on someone's
> shoulder and despite everything, in spite of all my theories, and how-
> ever much trouble I take, each day I miss having a real mother who
> understands me. And that is why, with everything I do and write, I
> think of the Momsie that I want to be for my children later on. The
> Momsie who doesn't take everything that is said in general conversa-
> tion so seriously, but who does take what I say seriously. I have noticed,
> though I can't explain how, that the word Momsie tells you everything.
> Do you know what I've found to give me the feeling of calling my
> Mother something that sounds like Momsie? I often call her Mom;
> then from that comes Moms: the incomplete "Momsie," as it were,
> whom I would so love to honor with the extra "ie" and yet who does
> not realize it. It's a good thing that Moms doesn't realize it, because it
> would only make her unhappy.
>
> That's enough of that, writing has made my zu tode bedrübt ease
> a little!*   (AF*a*, 432; adapt. MH/SL)

Unfortunately in this quotation the English translation does not do justice to the original Dutch. In Dutch, Anne replaced the normal "mams" (mommy)
by the near homophone "mans" (manly). This allowed her to act out her
negative feelings toward her mother without her noticing it and to perform
a linguistic castration on her mother. She disabled her by cutting a leg off the
letter "m." Gone is the primordial mother she once fused with; the phallic,
pre-oedipal mother no longer exists. Immediately following this entry, Frank
wrote that she hoped she to become like her father (AF*a*, 433). After having
mutilated her mother in language, which amounted to rejecting the illusion
of maternal omnipotence, she turned toward the father, who—as a father in
individual prehistory—was her ideal and paragon.

If we link Anne Frank's diary entries to Kristeva's psychoanalytical notions,
we can postulate that while the mother is masculinized (in the process of

---

*Anne misspelled—and somewhat misused—Goethe's *zu Tode betrübt* (in the depths of
despair) as if it were a noun meaning "sadness" or "depression."

phallic omnipotence and castration) and thus deprived of her motherhood, the father is made "feminine" and his sphere of influence expanded.

The Multiple Mother

At first reading, the content of Anne Frank's diaries seems to support the idea that she was resisting her mother and identifying with her father. In this light it seems plausible to read her diaries as an illustration of Kristeva's emphatic statement: "Matricide is our vital necessity, the sine-qua-non condition of our individuation. . ." (Kristeva 1989, 27–28 [1987a]).[29]

The Oedipus complex was reawakened in the adolescent Anne. In itself this is a fairly common phenomenon in puberty, and in her case, it provided an impulse to write. After all, Frank did not want her parents to discover the negative feelings she had toward her mother. In her letters to Kitty, however, she could give free rein to her emotions. Writing was a way of "acting out" feelings, especially those concerning her mother.

And yet Anne's diaries can be read in another way. While on the surface the diaries testify to her alienation from her mother, a different current of emotions runs underneath. Not only did she somehow long for a bond with her mother, she also identified with women (instead of with a man, such as the father in individual prehistory):

> After I came here, when I was scarcely 13, I began to think about myself rather early on and to know that I am a person. Sometimes when I lie in bed at night I have a terrible desire to feel my breasts and to listen to the quiet rhythmic beat of my heart.
>
> I already had these kinds of feelings subconsciously before I came here, because I remember one night when I slept with Jacque I could not contain myself, I was so curious to see her body, which she always kept hidden from me and which I had never seen. I asked Jacque whether as a proof of our friendship we might feel each other's breasts. Jacque refused. I also had a terrible desire to kiss Jacque, and that I did. I go into ecstasies every time I see the naked figure of a woman, such as Venus in the Springer History of Art, for example. Sometimes it strikes me as so wonderful and exquisite that I have difficulty not letting the tears roll down my cheeks.
>
> If only I had a girlfriend!
>
> (AFa, 443; see also Van Maarsen 1996, 24)

It is striking that the sexual feelings Anne confessed to were focused on the symbol of the mother: the breasts. Breasts are the object of both masturbation and homosexual impulses (Dalsimer 1986, 56). The question Anne asked Jacque can be interpreted as an archaic longing to merge with the mother (Van Dam a, 140).

The emotions Anne experienced on seeing a Venus point to her receptiveness to images of women, or female ideals. It seems she was looking for adult role models. She found one in the Venus in her art history book and another in Miep Gies; to Anne, Miep was a paragon of womanhood: "Miep and Jan have just come back from their vacation, and now I can see a lot of Miep again" (AF*a*, 237). "I can still sit for hours just looking at Miep" (AF*a*, 244).

Miep Gies wrote a book about her memories of the war, in which she recalled Anne observing her: "As for me, Anne often seemed to be studying me. I could see her admiration for my independence and confidence in the face of everything. She seemed to admire my femininity too" (Gies 1987, 124–125).

Anne also tried to find ideals in her mother, but was disappointed:

> I don't pass judgment on Mother's character, for that is something I can't judge. I only look at her as a mother, and she just doesn't succeed in being that to me; I have to be my own mother. I've distanced myself from them all, I am my own skipper and later on I shall see where I come to land. All this comes about particularly because I have in my mind's eye an image of what a perfect mother and wife should be; and in her whom I must call Mother I find no trace of that image.
> (AF*b*, 296; adapt. MH/SL)

She accused her mother of regarding her daughters more as friends:

> Now that is all very fine, of course, but still a friend can't take a mother's place. I need my mother as an example that I can follow, I want to be able to respect her, and though my mother is an example to me in most things she is precisely the kind of example that I do not want to follow.   (AF*a*, 440)

Kitty can be interpreted partly as a substitute for a friend and partly as a substitute for an ideal mother. Since Anne could not keep in touch with friends she had had before going into hiding, she created Kitty to compensate for these lost friendships. But Kitty also has motherly characteristics: she never laughs at Anne, she is dependable and Anne can confide in her completely (Van Dam a, 127). In that sense, Kitty replaces the mother. She is imagined to be another person, but is in fact, just like the pre-oedipal mother, part of Anne: Kitty is a product of Anne's fantasies of perfect harmony. The connection between Kitty and the mother is made even more evident in one of Anne's first letters to Kitty: "[B]ut you have a great advantage Kitty, that is that you can discuss everything with your mom, I can't, and though I am very close to Pim, still a woman is different" (AF*a*, 248).

According to Heiman van Dam, it is at this point that the return of the repressed begins. In Van Dam's view, this quotation signals a secret wish to communicate with the mother, and keeping a diary is Anne's way of verbally communicating with her mother, whom she resists out of fear of her own homoerotic impulses. In other words, Van Dam explains Anne's conflict with her mother as resistance to a repressed libidinal desire for her mother. Writing to the empathic Kitty replaces, or allows Anne to sublimate, this desire. In this interpretation the mother emerges as someone with whom she would like to identify but does not, to avoid her homosexual feelings. Kitty, or writing, is a substitute for culturally taboo feelings (Van Dam a, 130–131).

Although Kristeva would formulate this differently (the mother-daughter relationship is characterized by fear of, and resistance to, regression to the pre-oedipal stage), both interpretations relegate the mother-daughter relationship to the realm of repudiation. "Resistance" and "fear": negative words for feelings that might just as well be regarded more positively. After all, Van Dam's theory offers no explanation for Anne's positive homosexual feelings as evidenced in the quotation about Jacque.

I believe that Anne did not resist all aspects of the mother, but only a particular image: the pre-oedipal, all-encompassing mother, the one with whom the child is fused in early infancy. This image threatens to become reality again in the hiding place, where any distance between mother and daughter is nearly impossible.

In order to form her own identity, the child must separate herself from this archaic mother. This process may be relived in adolescence, because the relationship to primary love objects is no longer self-evident but under reevaluation. The transition from primary to secondary objects of love may create a void, a feeling of "not belonging anywhere," which causes a yearning for the original wholeness, symbolized in a desire for the mother's breast. The fact that Anne Frank had these feelings is, I believe, the main reason why she wrote negatively about her mother. Although she sometimes wanted to curl up in her mother's embrace, she also wanted to grow and progress; that is why she did not give in to her archaic fantasies. At times these fantasies must have been quite overpowering: Their strength explains the often vehement language that Anne needed to keep her mother at a distance. Mother was allowed neither to be a friend nor to smother her: "Mother always treats me just like a baby, which I can't bear" (AF*a*, 229; adapt. MH). So, not matricide but love for the mother is vital. This love does not, as Kristeva supposes, disappear on entering the symbolic order. It is a recurring desire. In her fundamental critique of Kristeva, Silverman (1988, 120–126) developed Freud's notion of the negative Oedipus complex, in the sense of a daughter's feelings of love and desire for the mother. Her theory is in line with a passage in which Freud toyed with the idea that his concept of the Oedipus complex (love for the opposite-sex parent and distance from the same-sex parent) might be too simplistic and schematic (Freud 1961, 19, 33 [1923]). In effect, Freud believed that the Oedipus complex contained both the well-known, "normal," positive component and a negative variety: identification with the same sex parent. Freud never developed the concept of this negative variety; he quickly replaced it with the notion of the pre-oedipal stage. Silverman prefers to call it the "negative Oedipus complex." After all, seeing the mother-daughter relationship in the light of the Oedipus complex implies that the mother-daughter relationship is not limited to the presymbolic stage but is also viable in the symbolic order. The negative Oedipus complex acknowledges the impact of language, of the symbolic order, on the love between mother and daughter. Entry into the symbolic order marks a farewell to the mother and the beginning of a longing for her. This longing is not pre-oedipal, but oedipal (the negative variety) and, as such, part of the symbolic order. Silverman removes the barriers; whereas Kristeva places the father (of individual prehistory) in limbo between the semiotic and the symbolic, Silverman opens the symbolic order to the mother.

A longing for the mother is unmistakably present in the writings of Anne Frank. This longing may have been intensified by the life-threatening, terrifying persecution of the Jews. The German occupiers established a reign of terror in Holland, aimed at the destruction of all Jews. It was impossible for Jews to lead a normal life, and in this context one can easily understand the emergence of fantasies of returning to the safety of mother's embrace. It is from this same point of view that Kristeva analyzes the work of Marguerite Duras; Kristeva comments that the twentieth century is marked by Hiroshima and Auschwitz, and that Duras's women are aware of this (Kristeva 1989, 219–259 [1987a]; Doane and Hodges 1992, 73–78). Duras's female characters suffer from chronic melancholy due to a futile longing for the pre-oedipal mother. They cannot commit the necessary "matricide," because there is nothing in the symbolic order that motivates them to do so. They do not want to live in the world of Hiroshima and Auschwitz; they wish to return to their origins.

Interpreted in this way, Duras's books seem to confirm Kristeva's theory, particularly the notion that matricide is essential to make life in the symbolic order possible. But Anne Frank's diaries cannot be construed in this manner. She was not a Durasian character suffering from "the malady of death" (Kristeva 1989, 221 [1987a]). She compensated for regression fantasies with negative remarks about her mother. This was a healthy attempt to distance herself from the omnipotent mother of yore. The physical proximity with her mother, due to the confined conditions of the Secret Annex, compelled Anne to express herself more vehemently in writing than she might otherwise have done (AF*b*, 438–439). Because they lived in such close quarters, her desire for the mother converged with her fear of the ever-present mother. She was put under even greater pressure by the other adults in the Secret Annex, who interfered in her upbringing. In a sense her diary saved her; it offered some privacy and the possibility of a somewhat normal adolescence, at least on paper.[30]

Again Anne Frank cannot be read as a Durasian character; she longed not only for warmth and safety but also for independence and a useful role in society. Whereas Duras's women focus their drives only on the semiotic, Anne Frank channeled them into the symbolic too. Her diaries show a desire not only for the maternal but for independence as well. Rather than sacrifice one for the other, she wanted them to coexist.

This oscillation might explain her love for the father. She created an image of her father as a "motherly" figure. She did not doubt his love for her. He let her go her own way as much as possible but sometimes guided her gently in the desired direction. Otto Frank bears a close resemblance to Kristeva's description of the father in individual prehistory: "A sort of conglomerate of both parents, of both sexes, which should however be considered a father, albeit not the strict, Oedipal father, but a living and loving father" (Kristeva 1986, 174 [1983a]; trans. MH).

The relationship between father Pim and daughter Anne also suggests a reliving of childhood, the time when the child distances itself from the mother and enters the symbolic via identification with the father in individual pre-history. Kristeva herself indicated that this father was actually an amalgam of both parents; Anne's father, "a father who loves like a mother" (Oliver 1993a, 82), appears to be a prototype. He does not represent the strict, punitive father figure who lays down the law, but the loving father who listens to his child and offers her guidance.

Kelly Oliver (1993a) sees in this motherly father an opportunity to bend Kristeva's ideas toward Silverman's negative Oedipus complex. Oliver's interpretation method is not unknown in women's studies. It is used to reformulate phallocentric theories to make room for women or the "feminine." Since Kristeva's theories also tend toward phallocentrism, a resistant reading is particularly effective. Oliver puts it this way: "Reading against the grain of her writing, Kristeva's texts take us deeper into the maternal body" (Oliver 1993a, 70).

Although Kristeva persists in speaking of a father, she attributes so many traditionally maternal characteristics to him that the father in individual prehistory can almost be regarded as a mother. In fact the father is "not-him," but part "of her." In this view the male characteristics of the ideal father are relegated even further to the background.

The father in individual prehistory is the third term that can dissolve the mother-child symbiosis, enabling mother and child to break out of the dyad. Rather than being something or someone outside the mother, this third term is part of the mother, an aspect of her. It is, namely, her desire for something other than the child. The mother wants to be more than an extension of the child. She wants to play a role in other arenas of life as well. This is the mother the child must learn to accept.[31] Daughters in particular must cut loose from the archaic mother while also identifying with the woman in her. This woman is not just their mother, but someone who has a position in society. Such a mother is an ideal mother, according to Kristeva. In response to Winnicott's ideas, she has said:

> Nobody knows what the good-enough mother is. I wouldn't try to explain what that is, but I would try to suggest that maybe the good enough mother is the mother who has something else to love besides her child, it could be her work, her husband, her lovers, etc. If for a mother the child is the meaning of her life, it's too heavy. She has to have another meaning in her life. And this other meaning in her life is the father of prehistory.   (Kristeva, quoted in Weir 1993, 88–89)

This describes exactly the sort of mother Anne Frank held to be ideal, the mother she wanted as a model. She wanted to identify with women who fulfilled a useful role in society. She did not reject motherhood but felt that motherhood should be appreciated more explicitly by society:

> In no way do I mean by this that women should turn against childbearing, on the contrary, nature has made them like that and that is all to the good. I merely condemn all the men, and the whole system, that refuse ever to acknowledge what an important, arduous, and in the long run beautiful part, women play in society.   (AF*a*, 678)

At the same time, however, she did not look upon motherhood as a life's fulfillment:

> And if I haven't any talent for writing books or newspaper articles, well, then I can always write for myself. But I want to succeed; I can't imagine that I would have to lead the same sort of life as Mother and Mrs. v. P. and all the women who do their work and are then forgotten, I must have something besides a husband and children, something that I can devote myself to! (AF*a*, 587; adapt. MH)

This conviction is exactly what made it so difficult for her to identify with her mother. She was reacting against a mother who had lost herself in her family: She wanted to become a woman/mother who also desired something else. In Kristeva's words, this "something else" is the father in individual prehistory. This notion can be applied to a wide range of "other things," but to many women in the first half of the twentieth century only a husband qualified as a possible third term. A role in society, especially a paid job outside the home, was usually beyond their reach. This was probably true for Edith Frank-Holländer too: she had to confine her loves and passions to her family. Her status as a refugee was yet another obstacle to finding a position outside the home. Before she went into hiding, she had been active in the Reform Jewish community, but in the Secret Annex she could do little more than devote herself to the tasks of a housewife, mother, and spouse.

Through her mother's desire for the third term, the father in individual prehistory, Anne Frank took her first steps in the symbolic order. Like her mother she focused on Otto Frank at first. But she was not the kind of girl to leave it at that. She loved her father dearly, but her love for him was not only directed toward him as a person. In her identification with him, she also desired to have what he had: another fulfillment in life besides a family. To her, writing was both an opportunity to be someone in the wider world and an activity in which she, as part of the symbolic order, kept the bond with the semiotic intact. Her father in individual prehistory is indeed an amalgam of both parents and should therefore be called *parent* of individual prehistory. Mother and father move in opposite directions, but both move: The mother guides the child in her transition from the semiotic to the symbolic, while the father leaves the symbolic order to become part of the semiotic.

Written in White Ink

Kristeva continues to stress the importance of the phallus and the father, which makes it difficult to regard her as a theoretician who does not sacrifice the mother to the father. Nevertheless, I believe it is possible to read Kristeva in this way, as do other critics of Kristeva, such as Weir (1993) and Oliver (1993). To conclude this chapter I return to Kristeva's description of adolescent writing, because I want to emphasize that I reject her qualification of "the phallus par excellence." To me this term suggests that phallocentric culture is immutable and that there is no room for the influence of the feminine or the maternal on adolescent writing. In my search for an alternative description, I came across Kristeva's introduction to the issue of "primary identification with the father in individual prehistory." There she discusses the primary, archaic identification that is part of the oral phase (Kristeva 1987c, 24–26 [1983b]). It is a pseudo-identification, because there is no subject or object yet. The child becomes that which she ingests. Obviously this archaic or zero identification can be linked to the primary stage of symbiosis, to the mother's breast or the mother's milk as the ultimate signifier:

> The infant *becomes* the breast through its incorporation. . . . [T]his archaic semiotic identification with the mother's breast, which is merely a reduplication, becomes the first in a series of reduplications. It prefigures and sets in motion the logic of object identifications in all object relations, including both discourse and love. (Oliver 1993a, 72)

The primary identification with the mother's breast and the mother's milk becomes the model for all subsequent identifications. In later development this material turns into language: The child ingests words and identifies with them.

This interpretation makes it possible to associate adolescent writing with the mother's breast. I propose this association as a counterbalance to the description of adolescent writing as "the phallus par excellence." Kristeva characterizes writing, or its product, the oeuvre, as a fetish. A fetish serves to fill the void that is created when the mother falls from her pedestal and spoken language is not accepted as a substitute. Since the mother's breast acts as the signifier of the original wholeness, the specific linguistic act of writing can be understood as its replacement. Writing, like the mother's breast to the infant, can be experienced as part of oneself. The liquids involved, mother's milk and ink, serve the same purpose; both nourish the child's growing independence and help it to break away from the archaic mother.

From Anne Frank's diaries it is clear that the fantasy about the archaic mother never disappears completely. It resurfaces time and again, in veiled wishes and desires. Ultimately this fantasy was the source that inspired her to write; writing filled the void that resulted not from the castration complex but from the "weaning complex."

We may wonder, with many feminists, why a phallic economy? Why not, for example, an economy of the breast? Why not a weaning complex instead of a castration complex? (Oliver 1993a, 29).

I believe it is no longer tenable to define writing as "the phallus par excellence" and to mention only the ideal father's influence on this activity. The male connotations create a smoke screen that clouds our vision of the complicated relationship between writing and the feminine/maternal. Clearly this relationship is not only positive. But it can unleash tremendous energy and an urge to create. Undeniably Kristeva is right to argue that both the semiotic and the symbolic contribute to this. However, I disagree with Kristeva's definition of the mother image (which she seems to believe is the only possible mother image) and, above all, with her exclusion of the mother from the symbolic order. "The" mother does not exist; there are many mother images (just as there are many father images). If we are to believe Kristeva, women must sever themselves from the pre-oedipal mother without compensation or substitution in the future symbolic order. In light of Anne Frank's diaries, however, this thesis is no longer defensible. In writing, she oscillated, relating to various mother images.

Hélène Cixous worded this relationship between the maternal and the writing woman very beautifully and aptly in "The Laugh of the Medusa," her polemic call on women to write:

> Even if phallic mystification has generally contaminated good relationships, a woman is never far from "mother" (I mean outside her role functions: the "mother" as "nonname" and as source of goods). There is always within her at least a little of that good mother's milk. She writes in white ink. (Cixous 1981a, 251 [1975b])[32]

In the second part of this book, on Etty Hillesum, I discuss in more detail Cixous's thought on the possibilities for an *écriture féminine*. Chapter 5 in particular focuses on the relationship between writing and a female, libidinal economy in the context of Hillesum's texts.

The next chapter, which concludes the first part of the book, returns to Anne Frank's need for female role models in her adolescence. This time, however, I explore a different angle, namely her relation to the divine, using Luce Irigaray's insights as a guide.

Chapter 3 ❧ *Guardian Angel*

> Then Granny appeared, so that I consider her my guardian angel to
> whom I pray every night and send my kisses. Then came Hanneli, so
> clearly that I pray for her every night and she seems to be a symbol of
> the sufferings of all my friends and all Jews, thus when I pray for her
> I pray for all Jews and all those in need.   (AF*a*, 447)

In the idealization and identification processes Anne Frank went through,
two figures played an especially important role: Oma [Granny]—Rosa Holländer-
Stern, her mother's mother—and Hanneli (also known as Hannah or Lies)
Goslar, one of Anne's best friends.

In this chapter I explore in detail these relationships of love and
friendship in search of further support for my argument that Anne Frank
experienced both a positive and a negative Oedipus complex. Both relationships, her love for her grandmother and her friendship with Hanneli, bear
witness to a continuing bond with the semiotic and the maternal, unbroken
by entry into the symbolic order. I believe that when the negative Oedipus
complex occurs in girls, it constitutes a mother-daughter dynamic that shifts
and develops in pace with the process of becoming a woman. Breaking
the symbiosis between mother and daughter is a precondition not only of
subjectivity and language but also of the desire for the mother (Silverman
1988, 160). The mother-daughter relationship in the symbolic order is not
one of unambiguous repudiation, as many a classical psychoanalyst would
have us believe; it is, at the very least, ambivalent. This idea was at the
core of the previous chapter, in which I discussed Anne's relationship to
her mother, Edith Frank-Holländer, in the context of Julia Kristeva's psychoanalytical reflections.

This chapter is based on Luce Irigaray's theories, and in particular one of her main premises: the "sexual in-difference" of Western culture. Despite the fact that this culture is fundamentally based on a differentiation between the sexes, the differences are not equally respected. Much of what is attributed to men is also seen as the norm; much of what is considered feminine is also regarded as inferior. Irigaray applied this template not only to philosophy, "the discourse on discourse" (Irigaray 1985b, 74 [1977]), but also to psychoanalysis and religion. In this chapter I focus mainly on Irigaray's vision of divine discourse, because these insights allow me to investigate an important theme in Anne Frank's writings: her religious development and the role she attributed to her grandmother. According to Irigaray people need ideals in order to develop; "to believe in God" is, in a sense, to strive for an ideal existence. But while the worldly reality to which this "existence" refers is assumed to be universal, it is in fact male-defined. And it is precisely this bias that Irigaray criticizes: Western discourse on God is phallocentric and patriarchal. Women lack a God of their own who can function as an ideal and a role model. By applying Irigaray's cultural and religious critiques, or to put it another way, by exploring what constitutes her vision (Brügmann 1986), I can interpret her religious development as a creative process in which she sought and found ideals in the feminine. The first half of this chapter is devoted to this investigation. The second half deals with Anne's relationship with Hanneli Goslar. Irigaray believes that friendship or love between women is only possible if there is a third term, an ideal, which allows for distance and, hence, respect for each other's differences. By applying this view to Anne Frank, we will be able to continue along the path taken in the previous chapter: to describe and analyze the transition from primary to secondary love objects. Anne could only stop repressing her feelings for Hanneli after she had inscribed herself in the divine discourse in which her grandmother (the guardian angel) and God together form a third term. The quotation that begins this chapter shows that Hanneli Goslar was more than just a friend to Anne; she was a symbol for the suffering of her friends, all Jews and others in need. The fact that she no longer suppressed her thoughts about Hanneli also means that she was sometimes able to face up to the suffering outside her safe hideout. Hanneli Goslar functioned as a movie screen onto which Anne projected her fears of discovery and deportation. In order to cope with these fearful premonitions, she turned her beloved late grandmother into a guardian angel.

In the next three sections of this chapter, I analyze the relationship between grandmother and grandchild. The first section describes Anne's diary entries about her grandmother; the second and third deal with the idealization process that occurred when Anne accorded her grandmother a place in her spiritual growth. The fourth through seventh sections discuss the relationship between corporeality and spirituality. These are linked to the eighth section, which is about Hanneli Goslar. Rather than conclude this chapter with the final entry in the diary, the ninth section describes the last months of Anne's life, based on the accounts of Goslar and other women who were in the camps with her.

Rosa Holländer-Stern

Anne Frank was very close to her mother's mother. Rosa Holländer-Stern was a widow when she fled Nazi Germany in March 1939, spending the last years of her life with her daughter's family in Amsterdam. It is apparent from the very first entries in the diary, in which Anne Frank introduced herself, how important her grandmother was to her:

> In the summer of 1941 Granny Holländer fell very ill (she was staying with us by then), she had to have an operation and my birthday didn't mean much. It didn't in the summer of 1940 either, for the fighting in the Netherlands was just over then.
> Granny died this winter 1941–1942. And no one will ever know how much she is in *my* thoughts and how much I love her still.
> The celebration of this 1942 birthday was to make up for everything then, and Granny's little light shone over it.   (AF*a*, 189)

In September 1942 she glued a picture of her grandmother into her diary; in the caption she wrote that she often thought of her and of the love and peace Granny had brought into the home (AF*a*, 190). Granny is not mentioned again until December 29, 1943.[1]

> I was very unhappy again last evening. Granny and Hanneli came into my mind. Granny—oh, darling Granny, how little we understood of what she suffered, or how sweet she always was to us, how interested she was in everything that concerned us, and besides all this, she knew a terrible secret which she carefully kept to herself the whole time. How faithful and good Granny always was; she would never have let one of us down, whatever it was, however naughty I had been, Granny always stuck up for me. Granny—did you love me, or didn't you understand me either? I don't know. No one ever talked about themselves to Granny. How lonely Granny must have been, how lonely in spite of us! A person can be lonely, even if he is loved by many people, because he is still not the "One and Only" to anyone.
>   (AF*a*, 435)[2]

Thoughts of her grandmother resurfaced a week later in a dream: "Then Granny appeared, so that I consider her my guardian angel to whom I pray every night and send my kisses" (AF*a*, 447).

The late grandmother had undergone a metamorphosis and had been turned into a guardian angel, a substitute for God; Anne prayed "to" the guardian angel. The apparitions were not limited to dreams. On Friday nights, at sundown, Sabbath candles were lit in the Secret Annex. On March 3, 1944, Anne wrote: "When I looked into the candle this evening (Friday night at 5 to 8) I felt calm and happy. Oma seems to be in the candle, and it is Oma too who shelters and protects me and who always makes me feel happy again" (AF*a*, 508).

These extracts show that Anne idealized her grandmother; she was sweet, peaceful, and loved Anne unconditionally. Anne elevated her to the status of guardian angel but at the same time identified with her; both were lonely, despite the family members around them. Anne placed both herself and her grandmother in an outsider position. In the following sections I provide a psychoanalytic explanation for this complex relationship between grandmother and granddaughter.

A Family Romance

In the fall of 1943, Anne Frank was more frightened than ever. It was precisely during this period of fear and depression that images of her grandmother started to surface. Why did she start remembering her beloved grandmother just then? In the previous chapter I discussed the psychoanalytic idea that adolescence can trigger a regression to childhood. The same idea can explain why Granny appeared as a guardian angel.

It is reasonable to assume that in the fall of 1943 Anne regressed to her state of mind at the age of four. The fears she experienced in the Secret Annex in 1943 might unconsciously have triggered fears she had as a little girl.

When the Nazis came to power in 1933, the Franks' plans to leave Frankfurt and emigrate crystallized. Edith took her two daughters to her mother in Aachen, and Otto left for Amsterdam, where he managed to find a home for his family in the fall of 1933. Although there is some confusion about the exact dates of the move (see Frank 1989, 7, and AF*a*, 189), it is clear that Edith and Margot left for Amsterdam before Anne did. The profound effect this period had on Anne is plain to see in the diary entry in which she sums up the most important events in her life; the months she spent alone with Granny are mentioned explicitly. She was three and a half years old at the time. For a child that young, a few months of separation from her primary love objects can seem an eternity. This possibly traumatic event may have lain at the root of her feeling that she did not belong to the others. This feeling is voiced so frequently that, taken as a whole, Anne Frank's diaries could be interpreted as a "family romance." Coined by Freud (1959b, 9, 235–241 [1908]), the term denotes a fantasy about family relationships that may occur in puberty. It is a fantasy in which the child is not her parents' offspring but an adoptee.

From the very first entry right up to the last, the theme of the family romance plays an important role in Anne Frank's diary. For example, on July 12, 1942—soon after the Franks had moved into the Secret Annex—Anne wrote that she felt estranged from her family (AF*a*, 223.) Two years later, on July 15, 1944, she mentioned:

> Now I want to come to the chapter of: Father and Mother don't understand me. My father and mother have always thoroughly spoiled me, been sweet to me, defended me against upstairs, and have done all that parents could do. And yet I've felt so terribly lonely for a long time, so left out, neglected and misunderstood.   (AF*a*, 690; adapt. MH)

The "family romance fantasy" is part of the process in which the adolescent separates from her parents. In Freud's words:

> The liberation of an individual, as he grows up, from the authority of his parents is one of the most necessary though one of the most painful results brought about by the course of his development. [. . .] For a small child his parents are at first the only authority and the source of all belief. [. . .] Small events in the child's life which make him feel dissatisfied afford him provocation for beginning to criticize his parents. [. . .] There are only too many occasions on which a child is slighted, or at least *feels* slighted, on which he feels he is not receiving the whole of his parents' love, and, most of all, on which he feels regrets at having to share it with brothers and sisters.
> (Freud 1959b, 9, 237–238 [1908])[3]

Freud's theory applies well to Anne Frank's fantasies. She once asked herself the following question: "Is it just chance that Daddy and Mummy never rebuke Margot and that they always drop on me for everything?" (AF*a*, 294).

Anne sometimes imagined herself as an adopted child. She remembered once having pretended to be an orphan for a full six months:

> I have an odd way of sometimes, as it were, being able to see myself through someone else's eyes. Then I view the affairs of a certain Anne

Robin at my ease, and browse through the pages of her life as if she were a stranger.

Before we came here (when I didn't think about things as much as I do now) I used at times to have the feeling that I didn't belong to Mansa, Pim, and Margot, and that I would always be a bit of an outsider, sometimes I used to pretend for a good six months that I was an orphan, until I reproached and punished myself, telling myself it was all my own fault that I played this self-pitying role, while I was really so fortunate.   (AF*b*, 455; adapt. MH)

The explanation for this outsider feeling may lie in the possibly traumatic event Anne experienced as a little girl. In the fall of 1943, the separation anxiety she had felt as a child returned. Again it involved a process of separation from the parents, only this time of a different nature. In 1933 their parting had been a temporary one. In 1943 the separation was an essential part of the growth process.

As time passed, Anne "liberated" herself from her parents. This was often hard on her. Time and again she succumbed to depression, which was worsened by her frightful existence in the hideout and worries about the future. As a little girl, she had clung to her grandmother and had grown to love the old woman deeply; faced with the same emotions in 1943, she created an angel in her grandmother's image to protect her from fears and loneliness.

She incorporated this theme in a tale dated February 22, 1944. "The Guardian Angel" is about an old woman and her fourteen-year-old granddaughter: "The girl's parents had died when she was quite small, and the grandmother had always taken good care of her" (Frank 1994, 35).

When the grandmother dies, the girl becomes inconsolable and terribly lonely. She is overwhelmed by feelings of loss until one day her grandmother appears in a dream: "You mustn't think, now that I am dead, I no longer look after you; I am in heaven and always watch you from above. I have become your guardian angel, and I am always with you, just as before" (Frank 1994, 36).

In this short story the guardian angel mediates between heaven and earth, between life and death. She has the divine power to offer love, consolation, and protection. She is almost physically present, the grandmother transformed. In the dream she appears in the shape of the old woman.[4]

Her Mother's Mother

While Anne allowed her grandmother to play an important spiritual role, it seems she deliberately excluded her mother from her religious life. On a few occasions Anne mentioned that she was irritated that her mother had admonished her to read her prayer book (AF*a*, 267; AF*b*, 290). Later she reported an incident in which she kept her mother out of her own religious life. Anne refused to share the intimacy of prayer with her mother:

> Dear Kitty,
> Oh dear, I've got another terrible black mark against my name. I was lying in bed yesterday evening waiting for Father to come and say my prayers with me, and wish me good night, when Mother came into my room, sat on my bed, and asked very nicely, "Anne, Father can't come yet. Shall I say your prayers with you tonight." "No, Mansa," I answered. Mother got up, paused by my bed for a moment, and walked slowly toward the door. Suddenly she turned around, and with a distorted look on her face said, "I don't want to be cross with you; love cannot be forced!" There were tears in her eyes as she left the room. I lay still in bed, feeling immediately that I had been horrible to push her away so rudely. But I knew too that I couldn't have answered differently. (I couldn't pretend and pray with her against my will.)
> (AF*b*, 353; adapt. MH)

It seems that Anne's religious upbringing was the subject of a silent struggle in the house. Apparently she and Pim had once prayed together every evening, a ritual her mother was not part of. By occasionally foisting a prayer book on her daughter by day, Edith tried—in vain, as it turned out—to influence this aspect of her upbringing.

A year later Anne started developing a more personal relationship to God. Neither father nor mother played a part in this new religious awareness. Only her mother's mother, Rosa Holländer-Stern, was given a special and important role: the guardian angel.

In the previous chapter I discussed Anne's image of the ideal mother in relation to her experience with her real mother in day-to-day life (AF*b*, 296). By creating a guardian angel in the shape of her Granny, she fulfilled her own exhortation: "I have to be my own mother." The angel is an ideal mother: She protects and provides unconditional love. Freud, however, has pointed out that in the family romance fantasy:

> The faithlessness and ingratitude are only apparent. If we examine in detail the commonest of these imaginative romances, . . . we find that these new and aristocratic parents are equipped with attributes that are derived entirely from real recollections of the actual and humble ones; so that in fact the child is not getting rid of his father [*sic*] but exalting him. Indeed the whole effort at replacing the real father by a superior one is only an expression of the child's longing for the happy,

vanished days when his father seemed to him the noblest and strongest of men and his mother the dearest and loveliest of women. He is turning away from the father whom he knows today to the father in whom he believed in the earlier years of his childhood; and his fantasy is no more than the expression of a regret that those happy days have gone. Thus in these fantasies the overvaluation that characterizes a child's earliest years comes into its own again.

(Freud 1959b, 9, 240–241 [1908])[5]

As usual Freud's theories have to be translated in order to apply them to the mother-daughter relationship.[6] Once we have done this, his insights will be applicable to Anne's creation of a guardian angel.

According to Freud adolescents often criticize their parents and idealize others. On the surface it seems they are distancing themselves from their parents, but often this behavior is in fact directly related to them. Anne Frank's behavior can be seen in this context too. In her maternal grandmother, Anne found a substitute for her own mother. As a guardian angel, her grandmother functioned as an ideal mother.

As a little girl, Anne was banished from the symbiotic relationship with her mother, and probably not very gently at that. She then began to project her need for maternal love onto her grandmother. In puberty this projection was repeated. Each times, in 1933 and in 1943, this transference took place against the backdrop of mortal fear and the persecution of the Jews.

Anne Frank's guardian angel could appear in dreams and thoughts. It is as if she played a *"fort/da* game" (Freud 1964, 23, 14–17 [1920]) with her guardian angel. Freud observed his grandson Ernst playing a game of disappearance and appearance, throwing a reel or spool of thread away and retrieving it, accompanied by shouts of "o-o-o-o" (interpreted to mean *fort* [gone]) and *da* [there]. Freud interpreted this game as the child's way of coping with his mother's presence and absence. He believed it revealed a drive to gain mastery; Ernst tried to exert power over the mother by using an object and language.

According to Irigaray, girls do not play this game because the mother-daughter relationship is different. Because both mother and daughter are females, it never enters the daughter's mind to replace her mother with an object that can be thrown away at will. After all, she would also be renouncing part of herself. The *"fort/da* game" is no more than Freud's interpretation. As such, it is a perfect example of his linear reasoning, in which there is only one way for the child to grow: away from the mother. This can not be applied to a girl. Her growth is not focused on gaining mastery over her (m)other, but rather on giving birth to her self. Failure to do so may cause depression. This happens if a girl is unable to experience the loss of the mother as a partial loss. Instead, she experiences it as a total loss of self; in other words, the transition from symbiosis to the symbolic comes to a halt.

Such a depression may occur during adolescence, as discussed in the previous chapter. Using this theme I will now explore Anne Frank's spiritual development and in particular her creation of a guardian angel. Following Irigaray's thinking, I draw a connection between the mother, *fort/da* and religious discourse. In "Belief Itself " (Irigaray 1993b, 23–53 [1980]), she wrote: "The most important *fort-da* . . . refers, past the mother's presence, in the mother, beyond-veil, to the presence of God, beyond the sky, beyond the visual horizon" (Irigaray 1993b, 32 [1980]).[7]

While Freud, in his analysis, paid closest attention to the spool of thread, Irigaray focuses on the environment in which the game is played. Freud mentioned a curtained cot, behind whose curtain or screen the spool of thread disappears. This intermediary object, the screen, appeals to Irigaray's imagination: she visualizes a white, transparent veil, which leads to two associations.

First of all little Ernst might have been acting out his birth, with the thread acting as the umbilical cord and the veiled bed as the womb. Secondly— and this association is very relevant in Anne Frank's case—the image of white, translucent veils reminds Irigaray of angels.

To Ernst the screen mediated between the presence and absence of the spool of thread (the mother) and, perhaps, between the inside and outside of the mother. Similarly, angels mediate between life on earth and the afterlife in heaven. Angels are usually misunderstood, according to Irigaray. They are seen as messengers from God, but actually they stem from the mother. As usual the immediate, the sensory, and the natural nurture the mediated, the intelligible, and the cultural, and as usual this goes unrecognized (Van der Haegen 1989, 174). Angels mediate vertically, by rising from the original dwelling (the womb) up to the ultimate dwelling (heaven), and by eternally repeating this movement. In this interpretation of the divine discourse, there is space for the body that creates life. Angels are the vehicle by which the maternal enters the symbolic order of language and culture.

It was through this creativity that Anne Frank stayed in contact with the maternal dimension in herself. Denial of the mother is a cultural requirement that has an impact on the daughter's self-perception (Van der Haegen 1989, 178). For Anne this resulted in depression which she warded off by creating a guardian angel. This is the wonderful *"fort/da"* that Irigaray writes about. She sees the angel, rather than the phallus, as the appropriate symbol to signify transitions and processes between the sensory and the imaginable, between the semiotic and the symbolic. The transition from the semiotic to the symbolic is not governed by possessing or being the phallus, but by "the mystery of a first crypt, a first and longed-for dwelling place" (Irigaray 1993b, 32).

By casting her grandmother as a guardian angel, Anne was able to stay in touch with the semiotic without getting submerged in it. Since the symbolic order, including religious discourse, has traditionally centered on the phallus, there is no history of symbolization on the female side. As a consequence women are forced into a dilemma. They must choose either to repudiate and hate the semiotic (the maternal dimension), with the attending risk of depression, or to identify with the semiotic with the risk of regressing to a presymbolic stage. Anne managed to avoid these perils by inventing a guardian angel who saw her through the process of becoming a woman.

Frank did not, as a surface reading might suggest, simply exclude her mother from her religious life. Rather, she elevated her mother. Through her grandmother, Anne turned her mother into an ideal, a guardian angel who never totally disappears, but can always be invoked in thought or dream.

> If we are not to be accomplices in the murder of the mother we also need to assert that there is a genealogy of women. Each of us has a female family tree: we have a mother, a maternal grandmother and great-grandmothers, we have daughters. . . . Let us try to situate ourselves within that female genealogy so that we can win and hold on to our identity.   (Irigaray 1993b, 19)[8]

Anne managed to write herself into the maternal genealogy. As she became aware of her female identity, she completed the circle. Originally born from a uterine shell, she was being born again: a girl giving birth to the woman in herself. In the next section I deal in greater detail with the link between corporeality and spirituality by focusing on another aspect of this connection: my discovery that Anne's physical development into womanhood coincided with her spiritual development.

"God Knows Everything, but Anne Knows Better" [9]

In March 1944, a year before her death, Anne Frank reflected on the years behind her. The year before she went into hiding suddenly seemed unreal, a "heavenly existence" (AF*a*, 515). In the Secret Annex, she had, in her own words, grown wise. In reference to the latter half of 1943, she wrote:

"I became a young woman, an adult in body, and my mind underwent a great, a very great change, I came to know God! I started to think, to write, and I discovered myself" (AF*a*, 518).

When Anne exclaimed, "I came to know God!" she did not mean that she had been unaware of his existence before, but that she had redefined her attitude and become more conscious of him. In the latter half of 1943, Anne underwent a change: a process of internalization. As a child she had experienced God and the Jewish religion as a part of her upbringing, but it had not touched her deeply. As an adolescent she started to think about religion on her own. This development can be seen in Anne Frank's unfinished novel *Cady's Life,* which she worked on in late 1943 and early 1944 (AF*a*, 587–588). The novel's main character, Cady, goes through a development similar to the writer's. After a car accident Cady goes to a sanatorium for rehabilitation. During this crisis her religious beliefs change:

> I've thought about God a good deal lately, but never talked about Him. At home I learned when I was very little to pray to God every night before I went to bed. It was a habit, just like brushing my teeth. I didn't really stay with God, I don't think He was in my thoughts at all, because *people* could give me all I needed at that time. Now that I've had this accident and I'm alone so much, I have plenty of time to think about these things. On one of my first evenings here, I got stuck in my prayer, and then I noticed that I was thinking about something entirely different. So I made a change, I began to think about the deeper meaning of the words, and then I made a discovery that there's a frightful lot more than I'd ever imagined in this seemingly simple child's prayer. From then on I prayed for different things, things I myself thought beautiful, and not just a general prayer.   (Frank 1994, 76–77)

From the latter half of 1943 on, Anne developed a personal relationship to the divine, a process she summarized in her exclamation "I came to know God!" But why at that time? She had been in hiding for some time by then, so what made this period different from before? She described the second half of 1943 as the period in which she became a young woman, an adult in body. She saw her first menstrual periods in particular as a sign of physical maturity.

Becoming Woman, Becoming Divine

Having menstrual periods was extremely important to Anne Frank. On October 4, 1943, she wrote enthusiastically about Nico van Suchtelen's book entitled *Eva's jeugd* [Eve's youth]: "Also it says that Eva has a monthly period, oh, I'm so longing to have it too, then at least I'd be grown up" (AF*a*, 268).

A few weeks later she discovered the first signs of her pending menses (AF*a*, 287). She was full of expectations about becoming an adult. At first she was curious and excited. Later this mood gave way to an introspective, introverted sense of happiness. In a diary entry in early 1944, she penned her reaction to an article by journalist Sis Heyster about girls in puberty. She recognized herself in this description of pubescent girls "becoming quiet within and beginning to think about the wonders that are happening" to their bodies:

> I think what is happening to me is so wonderful, and not only what can be seen on my body, but all that is taking place inside. . . . Each time I have a period (and that has only been three times) I have the feeling that in spite of all the pain, unpleasantness and nastiness I have a sweet secret, and that is why although it is nothing but a nuisance to me in one sense of the word, I always long for the time that I shall feel that secret within me again. (AF*a*, 442)

This passage evokes an almost spiritual awareness of her own body. Anne felt she was becoming a woman and was deeply touched by it. In the same entry, she wrote of the ecstasy she felt on seeing nude figures of women: "It strikes me sometimes as so wonderful and exquisite that I have difficulty not letting the tears roll down my cheeks" (AF*a*, 443; see also p. 89).

The time of the first menstrual periods can be considered one of life's big crises because it marks the transition from childhood into adulthood. This maturation process is accompanied by a spiritual crisis, a need to redefine oneself (Washbourn 1979). Adolescents struggle with questions like: "Who am I? What is my relationship to others? What is my place in the world?" To answer them they need a symbolic order or a frame of reference. In the next section, I use Irigaray's reflections on divine discourse to describe the solutions Anne found to redefine herself and others. It will become apparent that her first menstrual periods were a rite of passage, the essence of which was her encounter with God. To Frank spirituality and corporeality were closely connected. Having her period, or becoming a woman, amounted to what Irigaray calls becoming divine: She simultaneously discovered herself and God. The divine and the physical are not mutually exclusive, but mutually inspiring. Anne Frank experienced the process of becoming a woman as a miracle: She felt that the female body became spiritualized. In other words, she interpreted her menstruation as a sign of the divine consummation of her female identity.

This is a revolutionary way of thinking in the context of Judaism, the religion in which she was raised. In Judeo-Christian tradition, after all, menstruating women are considered unclean. Menstruation is taboo. The book of

Leviticus includes a set of special laws for menstruating women, the *nidda,* which explicitly link discharges ("issues") with impurity.[10] Anne-Claire Mulder (1986) explains the purity laws and the politics of the body they imply in light of the "sexual in-difference" of Judeo-Christian thinking, in which woman is regarded as deviant from man. Menstruation is considered proof of her otherness, which accounts for a concept of feminine discharges and of woman herself as the opposite of (w)hol(i)ness. This is clearly a case of "sexual in-difference." Otherness, the anomaly of womanhood, is not respected but regarded as inferior. I believe that Anne's writings show traces of sexual difference: In defiance of Western tradition, she regarded her menstruation as a sign of divine completion.

Anne Frank's diary entries about monthly periods are far removed from biblical laws. She experienced her first periods as the manifestation of a divine force. She knew that, in a way, these feelings were subversive; she wrote of "her secret," which she dared to share only with Kitty. She did not openly show the quiet happiness she derived from her periods. She banished her *"jouissance,"* her pleasure,[11] into her innermost self. Anne apparently felt the weight of the centuries-old, Western Judeo-Christian tradition and realized that the beauty, the wonder, and the spirituality of menstruation had to be kept secret.

As members of the Reform Jewish community, the Franks were not terribly dogmatic. This probably allowed Anne enough freedom to still experience her physical transition to womanhood as a divine process. Thus, she practiced what Luce Irigaray has described as "a sensible transcendental—the dimension of the divine par excellence" (Irigaray 1993a, 115).[12]

A Sensible Transcendental

The conglomerate of ideas that in French is called *transcendental sensible* is very complex and hard to translate. It consists of two paradoxical ontological terms. There is the noun *transcendental,* in the sense of supra- or extrasensory, imperceptible through any of the five human senses. In English this word is mainly used as an adjective. Then there is the adjective *sensible* in the sense of the sensory, the tactile, that which can be perceived by the human senses. In traditional Western thought a "sensible transcendental" is an oxymoron: a figure of speech that combines two terms that in ordinary usage are opposites. In her paradox Irigaray has united two spheres of life that have always been thought of as contradictory. At one end we find the field of matter, the body, and the senses; at the other we find the spiritual, the transcendental, and the divine. And it is not just the Judeo-Christian tradition that regards body and spirit as two totally separate categories. Western philosophy, especially since Descartes's adage "I think, therefore I am," has also supported and defended this split, in which the transcendental is placed higher on the hierarchical ladder than the sensory. This divisional criterion is one of the basic premises on which Western thought and action have been founded, with far-reaching consequences in the areas of ethics and politics. Western culture testifies to a profound contempt for the conditions of its existence: the earth and nature. Irreparable damage to these is the result. In Western thought, including science and religion, all hope is directed at spiritual labor and at a divine life after death. In our quest for a heavenly paradise, we ride roughshod over the earth.

In her rereading of the biblical myth of paradise, Irigaray postulates that the origin of evil lies in the separation of heaven and earth. The blissful state in which Adam and Eve lived preceded the split between nature and God. In paradise, God and nature were one. Adam and Eve were in God, or God was in them. The transcendental was "sense-ably" present in the "here and now" of paradise, until the moment of exile:

> How did this banishment occur? In the mode of "being like unto God." The position of God as a model to be repeated, mimicked. Thus set outside the self. Surely evil, sin, suffering, redemption, arise when God is set up as an extra-terrestrial ideal, as an otherworldly monopoly? When the divine is manufactured as God-Father?
>
> (Irigaray 1991, 173)[13]

Adam and Eve wanted to know the divine. In defiance of God's will, they sought this knowledge outside themselves rather than regarding the divine as an integral part of their own being. God punished them for their curiosity by exiling them from paradise: "The earth [became] a great deportation camp" (Irigaray 1991, 174).[14] In light—or rather in the darkness—of this mistake in paradise, Irigaray advocates mediation by a "sensible transcendental," or in other words, a return to paradise lost. Ever since their exile from paradise, humans have experienced recurrent deportations. Irigaray is looking for ways to spiritualize earthly, bodily existence so that devastation and destruction will no longer be part of our everyday experience.

As a philosopher of sexual difference, Irigaray has more than just an ecological motive to plead for a "sensible transcendental." The dichotomous and hierarchical way of thinking that separates nature from culture, body from spirit, and heaven from earth becomes all the more bitter when the underlying issue of sexual indifference is considered. After all, because Western discourse has placed women and the feminine on the side of earth, nature, and the body, they are considered inferior to the male, which is associated with the spiritual and the divine. On the basis of the physical power and drives attributed to women, they are treated as the inferior part of humanity. Both women and the feminine are barred from the public sphere. A menstruating woman is in a sense living proof of her overpowering corporeality and her weaker mental faculties. In this rigid type of thinking, men and women are separated based on false and unfair grounds: Women are denied strength of mind, while men are deprived of the body. As long as these Western ideologies exist, both denials will inevitably lead to more power and self-respect for men than for women.

Anne Frank's candid testimony about her monthly periods shows that her initial innocence and excitement about menstruation gave way to an awareness of the taboo. But, more important, the time she experienced the physical changes of womanhood coincided with the period in which she came to know God. So how was she able to reconcile feelings which were culturally defined as mutually exclusive? Why did she become aware of God at the same time she attained womanhood, a coincidence that conflicted with reigning cultural taboos? I will answer these questions by incorporating them in Irigaray's discourse on "divine women."

Finite and Infinite

Apparently Anne experienced the separation of body and soul, of the feminine and spirituality, differently than prescribed in the *nidda*. She did not feel uncleanliness or unholiness. On the contrary, at the time of her first menstrual periods, she was faced with two fundamental dimensions of human existence: the finite and the infinite. Her menses made her conscious of becoming a woman, aware that she was part of the female gender. This shaped her finiteness: She was not a man, she was becoming a woman.

According to Irigaray, every growth process needs an image or awareness of the ultimate goal:

> In order to become, it is essential to have a gender, or an essence (consequently a sexual essence) as *horizon*. Otherwise, becoming remains partial and subject to the subject. When we become parts or multiples without a future of our own this means simply that we are leaving it up to the other, or the Other of the other, to put us together.
>
> (Irigaray 1993b, 61 [1987])[15]

In taking this position, Irigaray opposes the classical notion of universality. In patriarchal Western tradition men supposedly speak for everybody, representing universal human values. Through this assumption women are silenced; they have no right to speak. This Western discourse assumes that there is only one generic gender: the male. Women are deprived of their own desires and ideals. They must live their lives in ways envisioned by men. Once women become aware that they are not derived from the male gender, neither spiritually nor culturally nor historically, there is room to create a female gender. This female gender cannot be described or confined; its potential is limitless. "This process of acquiring a new subjectivity in the love of our own sex is also defined [by Irigaray] as a process of 'becoming divine' by women" (Braidotti 1991, 260–261).

This process is not about defining and restricting: It is about creating opportunities to actualize the self. Irigaray speaks of "enshrining in law of virginity"[16] (Irigaray 1984, 60–61; see also Halsema 1995, 172–174). In this context virginity should not be seen as a transition, a preparation, or a commodity but as a phase of life in its own right. Virginity is a precondition for becoming a woman: "It pertains to the gestures with which a woman turns inward, gathers herself; protects herself physically and emotionally from everything that violates, desecrates, crumbles, creates chaos; restores herself, reorders and reassembles herself" (Vincenot 1990, 70; trans. MH).

Women, like men, have the right to cherish and actualize their own dreams, hopes, and ideals. What do women themselves want to become? Who do they want to be? These ideals could be called divine, if it were not for the fact that Western discourse has so far hardly begun to experiment with creating a God for women. But what is God, other than a name for an otherness that affirms the human? God is the unknown Other, conceived of as an image of ideal humanity. Although this ideal is ultimately unattainable and infinite, it does provide a path and a horizon. God is a way of imagining and striving for human perfection. In Judeo-Christian tradition men have had far more opportunity than women to project their ideals onto God. Out of respect for the female gender, her ideals and her image of good, space must be made for a God in the feminine gender. "Divinity is what we need to become free, autonomous, sovereign. No human subjectivity, no human society has ever been established without the help of the divine" (Irigaray 1993b, 62 [1987]).[17]

In my view Anne Frank's physical and spiritual development beautifully illustrate Irigaray's thoughts on "divine women." In the period when Anne became aware of her finiteness and womanhood, she also came to know God, the infinite. In order to grow and to become, she needed to be aware of both her feminine identity and an ideal infiniteness (see also AF*a*, 601). In the chapters on Etty Hillesum, I will return to Irigaray's reflections on "divine women," because Hillesum's spirituality can also be read as a discovery of the divine within herself. But first I wish to continue applying the concepts of the finite and the infinite to Anne Frank's development, because these had a far-reaching influence on the way in which she started to relate to other women. This brings me to the identification process, the other focus of this chapter.

H(anne)li [18]

So far Irigaray's "sensible transcendental" has helped me to explain the implications of the simultaneity of Anne's first menses and her growing consciousness of God. Now I want to turn to another synchronicity: Her renewed awareness of God and of her friend Hanneli.

In early 1944 Anne Frank looked back on the latter half of 1943 and wrote that she had come to know God. In the diary entries that cover that period, she mentioned God twice, both times in connection with thoughts about Hanneli.

Hanneli Goslar was like Anne Frank in many respects. Their names were very similar—Anne's full name was Anneliese—and their backgrounds showed great similarities as well: Hanneli and Anne were the same age; at the age of four, both had to flee Germany to resettle in Amsterdam because of their Jewish background. In Amsterdam, they became neighbors. They were classmates throughout their schooling. They went to the same kindergarten, Montessori school, and Jewish secondary school. In the diary entries dating from before the Franks went into hiding, Anne wrote regularly about her friend (AF*a*, 178, 179, 185). In one of her first entries, she introduced her classmates, mentioning Hanneli last:

> Hanneli Goslar is a bit of a strange girl, she is shy on the whole and very cheeky at home, but quite unassuming with other people.
> She blabs everything you tell her to her mother.
> But she has an open mind and I respect her a lot, particularly recently.
> (AF*a*, 187)

Soon after, Anne went into hiding and did not mention Hanneli for months, until November 1942, when the people helping the Franks brought them sad tidings about the Goslars. Anne subsequently told Kitty:

Dearest Kitty,

I don't think I've told you, but the Goslars had a dead baby, that's awful, and poor Hanneli, how busy she's going to be. (AF*a*, 291)

And the whole truth is even more cruel, because Hanneli's mother died in childbirth, leaving Hanneli, her father, and her two-year old sister.[19] It was not until November 1943, a full year later, that Anne wrote of Hanneli again. She was very worried about what had become of her friend and expressed fears that Hanneli had been deported. She was right. During a large-scale raid in South Amsterdam on June 20, 1943, Hanneli, her father, and her sister were all arrested and deported to Westerbork transit camp. When Anne wrote about her in November, Hanneli was still interned in Westerbork:

Dear Kitty,

Yesterday evening, before I fell asleep, who should suddenly appear before my eyes but Hanneli!

I saw her in front of me, clothed in rags, her face thin and worn. Her eyes were very big, and she looked so sadly and reproachfully at me that I could read in her eyes: Oh Anne, why have you deserted me? Help, oh, help me, rescue me from this hell!"

And I cannot help her, I can only look on, how others suffer and die, and must therefore sit idly by and can only pray to God to send her back to us. I just saw Hanneli, no one else, and now I understand. I misjudged her, was too young to understand her difficulties. She was attached to her girlfriend, and to her it seemed as though I wanted to take her away. What the poor girl must have felt like, I know; I know the feeling myself so well!

Sometimes in a flash I saw something of her life, but a moment later I was selfishly absorbed again in my own pleasures and problems.

It was horrid the way I treated her, and now she looked at me, oh so helplessly, with her pale face and imploring eyes. If only I could help her! Oh, God, that I should have all I could wish for, and that she should be seized by such a terrible fate. I am not more virtuous than she; she, too, wanted what was right, why should I be chosen to live and she probably to die? What was the difference between us? Why are we so far from each other now?

Quite honestly, I haven't thought about her for months, yes, for almost a year. Not completely forgotten her, but then never thought about her like this until I saw her before me in all her misery. Oh, Hanneli, I hope that if you should live until the end of the war, you will come back to us and that I shall be able to take you in and do something to make up for the wrong I did you.

But when I am able to help her again, then she will not need my help as badly as now. I wonder if she ever thinks of me, if so, what would she feel?

Good Lord defend her, so that at least she is not alone. Oh, if only You can tell her that I think lovingly of her and with sympathy, perhaps that would give her greater endurance.

I must not go on thinking about it, because I don't get any further. I only keep seeing her great big eyes and cannot free myself from them. I wonder if Hanneli has real faith in herself, and not only what has been thrust upon her?

I don't even know, I never took the trouble to ask her!

Hannelie, Hannelie, if only I could take you away, if only I could let you share all the things I enjoy.

It is too late now, I can't help, or repair the wrong I have done. But I shall never forget her again and I shall always pray for her!

(AF*b*, 422–423)

She was plagued by guilt over not having thought of Hanneli for so long; she also felt guilty about once having tried to steal away a girlfriend (see also Lindwer 1991, 16 [1988]), and because, in comparison with Hanneli, she was so much better off.

Anne identified with Hanneli ("Hanneli, no one else"). It is meaningful that she remembered the competition for someone's friendship; this indicates that Anne's and Hanneli's positions coincided not only factually but also in Anne Frank's mind. This identification was probably the main reason she had repressed all thoughts of Hanneli. She was very well aware that Hanneli's fate might just as well have been hers. This was such a frightening thought that she could hardly allow herself to think it.

Despite her fears, she could no longer repress thoughts of Hanneli in November 1943. One possible explanation for the resurfacing of Hanneli is that Anne Frank—as I discussed in the previous sections—had become aware of her feminine identity and therefore sought connections with other women of her generation. The "becoming-woman" was part of a wider growth process. She had left the narcissistic phase behind (see previous chapter); no longer just her parents' daughter, she was now a member of the female gender too. In her transition from primary to secondary love objects, Hanneli was one of the first people who came to mind; the great similarity between the girls formed a bridge between the narcissist phase and the consciousness of being a woman.

This also clarifies why God appeared at the same time as Hanneli. In several ways Anne needed God's help to deal with her thoughts about Hanneli; she called on him to help her counteract her feelings of guilt and fear. In the above quotation, God essentially functioned as the signifier of her good wishes to Hanneli. On her own she was powerless to realize these wishes. Only by linking her finiteness, her own limited potential, to God's infinite potential, could she bear to think of Hanneli. She asked God to mediate between herself and Hanneli. But it was precisely this mediation which created a space between the two girls. Analogous to the disruption of the original symbiosis by the symbolic order, or the law of the father, Anne created a "third term" that freed her from the mechanism of automatic identification with Hanneli. In "Divine Women," Irigaray has worded this structure as follows:

> If women have no God, they are unable either to communicate or commune with one another. They need, we need, an infinite if they are to share *a little*. Otherwise sharing implies fusion-confusion, division and dislocation within themselves, among themselves. If I am unable to form a relationship with some horizon of accomplishment for my gender, I am unable to share while protecting my becoming.
>
> (Irigaray 1993b, 62 [1984]; italics in original)[20]

Anne called on God as a third term, to break the symbiosis between herself and Hanneli; the breach created the possibility of contact (in the sense of thoughts and well-wishing) between them. Furthermore, God made up for her human finiteness; Anne asked him to give Hanneli what she was unable to provide: protection.

On Wednesday, December 29, 1943, Anne returned to the subject of Hanneli:

> And Hanneli, is she still alive? What is she doing? Oh, God, protect her and bring her back to us. Hanneli, I see in you all the time what my lot might have been, I keep seeing myself in your place. Why then should I often be unhappy over what happens here, shouldn't I always be glad, contented and happy, except when I think about her and her companions in distress? I am selfish and cowardly. Why do I always dream and think of the most terrible things—my fear makes me want to scream out loud sometimes. Because still, in spite of everything, I have not enough faith in God. He has given me so much—which I certainly do not yet deserve—and I still do so much that is wrong every day!
>
> You could cry when you think of your fellow creatures, you could really cry all day long. We can only pray that God will perform a miracle and save some of them. And I hope that I am doing that enough!
>
> (AF*a*, 436)

It is evident once again from this passage just how much Anne identified with Hanneli and how she projected her own fears onto her friend. Life in the Secret Annex was dominated by daily tensions and fears, and Anne suffered badly from them. Right from the beginning she had been writing about the overwhelming fear of detection. The people in the hideout were terribly frightened by any unexpected sound or incident. They were constantly wary of the people who worked in the office by day; they were distrustful of one young man in particular, a worker in the warehouse. During their period in hiding, the office was burgled a few times. These events too were deeply disturbing. She felt she had to put more faith in God, as this would give her greater inner peace and courage to go on living. But could God give her the protection that she, in Hanneli's name, prayed for? Would he? This was the question she struggled with. In her unfinished novel, *Cady's Life,* she tried to express God's complexity. Cady pondered the nature of God and, in the end, came to regard him as the creator of everything. Misfortune and luck, conscience and the darker side of the human character—all were God's creation (Frank 1994, 77–79).

Anne also addressed the issue of God in her diary: "Who has inflicted this on us? Who has made us Jews different from all other people? Who has allowed us to suffer so terribly up till now? It is God that has made us as we are, but it will be God, too, who will raise us up again" (AF*a*, 600).

She tried to have faith in God and accept her fate. But, as I have shown, God alone was not enough. It was beyond her comprehension that one and the same God would offer protection and allow so much destruction. So, beleaguered every day by fear of discovery and visions of a terrible future, she invoked a guardian angel. This angel, in the shape of her grandmother, enabled her to keep courage:

> What I have to bear is so hard, but then I am strong. . . . I know that I have God, God and Granny and so much more and that's what keeps me going. Without the voice that keeps holding out comfort and goodness to me I should have lost all hope long ago, without God I should long ago have collapsed.
>
> I know I am not safe, I am afraid of prison cells and concentration camps, but I feel I've grown more courageous and that I am in God's hands!   (AF*a*, 526)

The Last Months:
Westerbork, Auschwitz-Birkenau, Bergen-Belsen

The entry quoted above was written on March 12, 1944. In March 1945 Anne Frank died of typhus, which she had contracted at Bergen-Belsen concentration camp. No written testimony in her own hand has been recovered from the period after her arrest in early August 1944.

Arrest, deportation, and annihilation are the final unwritten chapters of Anne's diary—as they are of six million Jewish victims, of whom more than half were women and children (Lindwer 1991, xi [1988]).

Some women who knew Anne Frank in the last months of her life have found the courage to testify to the events of this period. Their memories were incorporated into a deeply moving television documentary directed by Willy Lindwer. I have made extensive use of the eponymous accompanying book, *The Last Seven Months of Anne Frank*[21] to trace the final months of Anne Frank's life.

As a reader of Anne Frank's diaries, I could have ended with the phrase she wrote on the inside back cover of her last diary: "Soit gentil et tiens courage!" (AF*a*, 699). However, her life did not end when she stopped writing her diary. She went the inescapable route millions of people—mostly Jews, but also Gypsies, homosexuals, communists, resistance fighters, and dissidents—had gone before her: She was deported and killed.

On August 4, 1944, the inhabitants of the Secret Annex were arrested and imprisoned in Weteringschans prison (Frank 1989, 50). Four days later, in the early morning of August 8, they were taken by train from Amsterdam Central Station to Westerbork transit camp. Resistance fighter Janny Brandes-Brilleslijper was on the same train. She remembered the girls wearing sweatsuits and backpacks. They made a sporty impression, as if they were going on a winter vacation (Lindwer 1991, 52).

Hiding from the Germans was an illegal act under occupation law. Therefore the eight inhabitants of the Secret Annex were put in the punishment barracks. Another resistance fighter, Rachel van Amerongen-Frankfoorder, met the Franks in the S (for *straf,* or punishment) barracks[22] and remembered Anne: "She was really so sweet, a little older than she was in the photo we've all seen, gay and cheerful" (Lindwer 1991, 92).

In the camp the former inhabitants of the Secret Annex now had to wear overalls and wooden shoes. The women had to do dirty useless labor in a workshop: Every day they had to clean batteries for hours.

On September 3, 1944, the eight inmates were transported to Auschwitz-Birkenau extermination camp. They were on the very last train from Westerbork to leave for that destination. Packed seventy people to a car, they barely survived the journey for exhaustion and lack of air.

On arrival in Auschwitz, a "selection" took place. Men and women were separated, and old people, children, and young mothers with children were set apart. The other women were herded together. A number was tattooed on their left arms.

Resistance fighter Ronnie Goldstein-van Cleef remembered the roll calls in Auschwitz-Birkenau:

> Anne often stood next to me and Margot was close by, next to her or in front of her, depending on how it worked out, because you stood in rows of five. Anne was very calm and quiet and somewhat withdrawn. The fact that they had ended up there, had affected her profoundly—that was obvious.   (Lindwer 1991, 185–186)

There were thirty-nine thousand prisoners in the women's camp. Anne and Margot had scabies and were put in the *Krätzeblock* (scabies block) for a while. Ronnie Goldstein-van Cleef:

> The Frank girls looked terrible, their hands and bodies covered in spots and sores from the scabies. They applied some salve, but there was not much that they could do. You just have all these blotches everywhere. They were in a very bad way; pitiful—that's how I thought of them. There wasn't any clothing. They had taken everything from us. We were all lying there, naked, under some kind of blankets. Two of us shared a blanket, lying in a single cot.   (Lindwer 1991, 192)

By late October 1944 the Russian liberation army was approximately sixty miles from Auschwitz. The Nazis tried to move as many women as possible out to other concentration camps. Anne and Margot were deported again. The journey took a long time, and the train came under fire because the English assumed it was transporting troops. Finally the transport reached Bergen-Belsen.

Janny Brandes-Brilleslijper remembered sitting on a sand dune on the heath, sharing a blanket with her sister Lien. From the dune she saw the Frank sisters walking toward them in the rain, also sharing one blanket. Janny was ten years older than the Frank girls and tried to give them some support. In return Anne and Margot tried to care for the younger children in the camp.

Rachel van Amerongen-Frankfoorder also met Anne and Margot in Bergen-Belsen:

> The Frank girls were almost unrecognizable since their hair had been cut off. They were much balder than we were; how that could be, I don't know. And they were cold, just like the rest of us.
>
> It was winter and you didn't have any clothes. So all of the ingredients for illness were present. They were in bad shape. Day by day they got weaker. [. . .]
>
> The Frank girls were so emaciated. They looked terrible. They had little squabbles, caused by their illness, because it was clear that they had typhus, you could tell even if you had never had anything to do with that before.   (Lindwer 1991, 103–104)

She described typhus as a disease that affects the brain, as a gradual wasting away, a sort of apathy.

Hanneli Goslar had been in Bergen-Belsen since February 1944. In the beginning it had not been as bad as other camps, but conditions had worsened under the growing influx of prisoners who were being relocated. The barracks were too small to accommodate their numbers. Tents were put up provisionally, although Hanneli did not remember them being set up—suddenly they were there. She did not know who was housed in them. Then autumn gales blew the tents over. Across the camp a double barrier of barbed wire was put up and filled with straw, effectively dividing the camp into two. The people from the tents ended up on the other side of the barbed wire. Eventually Hanneli discovered that there were Dutch people on the other side of the barrier. At night she went to the wire and called out to them. Mrs. Van Pels, from the Secret Annex, recognized her voice and called out to her that Margot was too ill to come, but that she would fetch Anne. Unable to see each other, the girls exchanged a few words. Hanneli: "It wasn't the same Anne. She was a broken girl. Probably I was, too, but it was so terrible" (Lindwer 1991, 27).

The girls cried. Apparently unaware that her father had survived, Anne told Hanneli that her parents were both dead. Hanneli told Anne that her mother was dead and that her father was not doing well. Anne's living conditions were worse than Hanneli's; she had hardly any clothes or food. She told Hanneli she was very skinny and bald. Hanneli collected some food, put it in a package, and threw it over the barrier. Someone else caught the package and Anne was unable to retrieve it. Hanneli managed once more to throw a package over, which Anne did catch. Hanneli and Anne met at the barbed wire three or four times. Then Anne and Margot's group was moved, and they never met again.

Unlike Auschwitz, Bergen-Belsen was not an extermination camp; it had no gas chambers. But death was everywhere. Tens of thousands of people were slowly dying. Disease, exhaustion, hunger, and the cold killed most people in the final months before liberation and in the weeks that followed. Anne and Margot died from exhaustion and typhus. They perished, Anne shortly after Margot, just a few weeks before the English liberated the camp. Janny Brandes-Brilleslijper remembered:

> At a certain moment in the final days, Anne stood in front of me, wrapped in a blanket. She didn't have any more tears. Oh, we hadn't had tears for a long time. And she told me that she had such a horror of the lice and the fleas in her clothes and that she had thrown all of

her clothes away. It was the middle of winter and she was wrapped in one blanket. I gathered up everything I could find to give her so that she was dressed again. We didn't have much to eat, and Lientje was terribly sick, but I gave Anne some of our bread ration.

Terrible things happened. Two days later, I went to look for the girls. Both of them were dead!

First, Margot had fallen out of bed onto the stone floor. She couldn't get up anymore. Anne died a day later. We had lost all sense of time. It is possible that Anne lived a day longer. Three days before her death from typhus was when she had thrown away all of her clothes during dreadful hallucinations. I have already told about that. That happened just before the liberation.   (Lindwer 1991, 74)

Few contrasts can be more painfully sharp and poignant than those between the hell in which Anne Frank suffered an ignominious death and the profound, creative, life-affirming diary entries in which she tried to imagine a heaven on earth.

In more than one way, Anne Frank's oeuvre can be interpreted as her attempt to position herself in a symbolic order in which exclusion mechanisms are at work.

One the one hand her texts can be read as a representation of a mother-daughter dynamic in a patriarchal society that insists on a radical break between them. Anne Frank did indeed distance herself from her mother; the passages in which Anne showed contempt for her speak for themselves.

On the other hand I have found in her writings various traces of resistance against this breach. As I described in chapter 2, the act of writing is in itself a way of maintaining contact with the semiotic while occupying the symbolic order. And as we can see from this chapter, the idealized guardian angel can ultimately be traced back to an attempt to symbolize the original wholeness by the creation of a divine wholeness on earth.

Anne Frank did not radically break with her mother but used her fantasy to avoid regressing to the presymbolic without losing touch with the semiotic. The fact that she often wrote slightingly of her mother is closely connected to this. In view of her situation—going through the process of adolescence and living in hiding under constant danger—it is understandable that she felt a desire for the kind of safety and protection offered by the original symbiosis with her mother. At the same time Anne felt a strong need to develop herself and cut the ties that restrained her. This is why she sometimes reacted to her mother, and to her mother's position, with such vehemence. The positive and the negative Oedipus complex were vying for the upper hand; Anne did not want to end up like her mother. She wanted to play an important role in the wider world—in the arts and culture. Her mother's traditional life was not an example she could follow. Still, she was seeking role models, to help her become a woman and learn how to live. Through her grandmother she took her place in the maternal genealogy: grandmother, mother, herself, and finally the guardian angel. Together they closed the circle between the first, uterine crypt and the last, divine dwelling place. In Judeo-Christian tradition, God is exclusively male defined. He is a strict, aloof father rather than a loving mother. Anne Frank had a particular need for an ideal mother, which is why she invented a guardian angel on a par with God.

The guardian angel fulfilled various needs. Feeling that this angel would always be there enabled Anne to face fears of discovery, arrest, and deportation. By relieving her loneliness and preventing her from regressing to the semiotic, the angel also helped her overcome the depressions caused by adolescence and being in hiding. The guardian angel, after all, symbolized the archaic desire for the safety of the mother's womb. In this light Anne Frank's passion for writing cannot be seen in isolation from the creation of the guardian angel either. Writing put her in touch with the semiotic. The danger of regression lurks, when—as is frequently the case with women—there is no symbolic compensation. In that sense the guardian angel acts as an additional counterforce to resist the pull of the semiotic.

Earlier I posited the mother's breast as an alternative to the phallus as a symbol of desire. Here I followed Irigaray's thinking and offered the angel in its mediating role between heaven and earth as another alternative to symbolize the transition from the semiotic to the symbolic. This is how Anne Frank found a way not to deny the desire for the maternal but to acknowledge it as a dynamic, driving force, and a source of inspiration.

❧ Intermezzo

Otto Frank was the only inhabitant of the Secret Annex to survive the hardships of the camps; the other seven were murdered by the Nazis. Eight years after the war, in 1953, the Dutch Red Cross reported on the fate of those taken on the last transport from Westerbork to Auschwitz, on September 3, 1944. Of the 1,019 deportees, only forty-five men and eighty-two women survived the camps. Among this small group of female survivors were Janny Brandes-Brilleslijper, Rachel van Amerongen-Frankfoorder, Lenie de Jong-van Naarden, Ronnie Goldstein-van Cleef, Anita Mayer-Roos, and Bloeme Ever-Emden. Hanneli Goslar, who had been deported earlier, also survived the war.

Many years later these women found the strength and courage to testify to their experiences before the cameras of Willy Lindwer (1988) and Jon Blair (1995). Elie Wiesel (1977) has characterized survivors first and foremost as witnesses. Surviving the camps was an act of resistance; while the Nazis were eradicating all traces of the mass murder, the will to survive was fed by the desire to give an account of this mur-

der after the war (Felman and Laub 1992, 44). Only afterward did it become clear how impossible a task this was. In the "post-traumatic century" (Felman and Laub 1992, 1), repression and testimony vie for the upper hand. To testify to the Holocaust is to relive the memories at the risk of further traumatization. A number of writers, such as Paul Celan, Jean Améry, Tadeusz Borowski, Primo Levi, and Bruno Bettelheim, who committed their concentration camp experiences to paper, ultimately found no relief. Suicide—in some cases decades after the war—seemed the only way out of an existence that had become unbearable (Felman and Laub 1992, 67).

The difficulty or impossibility of testifying to the terrors experienced is related not only to the repression mechanisms of personal trauma; it is also linked to the historical trauma that Auschwitz constitutes in Western culture. This period has sharply divided the time before from the time after. The Shoah cannot be reconciled with the prevailing Western notions of humanity and the world, in which all hope is based on human rationality's ability to bring about emancipation and progress: freedom, equality, and brotherhood. The Nazi system had proved capable of using rationality toward an irrational end: the extermination of part of humanity. In fact modern Western consciousness precluded such events, because it lacked a frame of reference in which the Holocaust could be imagined.

The absence of such a frame of reference and the resulting repression mechanisms account for both Anne Frank's death and the success of her diaries.

According to Bettelheim (1979) Otto and Edith Frank decided to hide the whole family in Mr. Frank's office building because they wished to continue their normal way of life as best they could. However, this greatly increased their chances of being discovered; most people who went underground split from their families and ended up in different, unknown locations.[1] It was not only their daily life together that the Franks wished to preserve; according to Bettelheim they must also have felt it extremely important to maintain their optimistic view of humanity, which made it impossible for them to face the reality of the concentration camps. This is why they opted for the wrong strategy to survive:

> Going on with intimate family living, no matter how dangerous it might be to survival, was fatal to all too many during the Nazi regime. And if all men are good, then indeed we can all go on with living our lives as we have been accustomed to in times of undisturbed safety and can afford to forget about Auschwitz. But Anne, her sister, her mother, may well have died because her par-

ents could not get themselves to believe in Auschwitz.

> (Bettelheim 1979, 250)

Bettelheim here referred to Anne Frank's remark that I discussed earlier, a comment that, taken out of context, has become world famous ("In spite of everything I still believe that people are really good at heart"). He understood that the Franks, though they listened to the English radio and were well aware of the war situation, had held on to the ideals of the Enlightenment. Still, there is an accusation in Bettelheim's words which is grossly unwarranted and arrogant; he holds the Franks responsible for their own survival, while in fact they were being persecuted (see also Ezrahi-Dekoven 1980, 201). Moreover, his own reasoning also smacks of a simplified Enlightenment ideal, namely that increased knowledge and insight would enable people to steer and shape their lives.

Bettelheim was one of the first to criticize the reception of Anne Frank's writings by placing them in the wider perspective of Western Enlightenment thought. He accused the postwar generation of turning Frank into a Broadway and Hollywood character who remained optimistic in spite of everything. The emphasis on her optimistic statement, made her world famous while, at the same time, the reality of the concentration camps and her death in Bergen-Belsen was repressed. My analysis of Frank's writings comes fifty years after the fact, which allows me to incorporate ideas derived from differential thinking; in other words, I did not work within the context of a philosophy of unity but a philosophy of difference. This is a postwar school of thought that fundamentally criticizes the classical way of looking at differences as a passing stage, which ultimately, by way of hierarchization and exclusion, leads to sameness. Extremes such as Nazism have illustrated the dangers of classical thought on difference (Braidotti 1993, 320; 1994a, 146–147). Both modernism and postmodernism, as well as German critical theory and French poststructuralism have tried to give a different meaning to sameness and otherness, whereby respect for everyone's humanity (equality, sameness) is combined with respect for individual differences in religion, age, gender, and ethnicity (otherness). Moreover, the differences are located not only between people but also within each person. Julia Kristeva developed this theme in *Strangers to Ourselves* (1991 [1988]). She emphasizes the importance of Freudian ideas to the attempt to understand Western xenophobia. With his discovery of the unconscious, Freud disrupted the assumed unity of the individual; awareness of the unconscious means acceptance of the strangeness in oneself. In this view, fear and hatred of foreigners can be construed as projections; the fear of that which is strange and uncontrollable in oneself is projected onto the strangeness of the other. "The foreigner is within me, hence, we are all foreigners. If I am a foreigner, there are no foreigners" (Kristeva 1991, 192 [1988]).[2]

Acknowledgment of the stranger in oneself paves the way for a change of attitude. Contrary to the ideals of the French Revolution—which ultimately granted civil rights to the Jews, prompting mass assimilation—Kristeva advocates cohabitation without imposed homogeneity. Under the influence of the contemporary political climate in "the kaleidoscope that France is becoming" (Kristeva 1991, 194 [1988]),[3] in which newcomers refuse to relinquish their own identity, Kristeva is intensely preoccupied with indigenous and immigrant people. Although she touches on the link with woman as the other, this is not her main focus. She clearly proclaims herself to be a "third generation feminist"; in her essay "Women's Time" (Kristeva 1981 [1979]), which in many ways foreshadows the themes she later elaborated on in *Strangers to Ourselves,* Kristeva explains her choice to disregard the women's issue. According to her the male-female dichotomy has lost all meaning, since Freud's discovery of the unconscious completely upset any notion of identity. This means that ultimately any discussion about difference is not about the gap between self and other but about the inescapable differences within each individual. Kristeva is certainly politically engaged, but in the final analysis she deals with the issue of difference in an ungendered, individual way. I return to this point later; first I want to show the difference between Kristeva's and Irigaray's approaches to this issue.

Irigaray's point of departure is a radically different one. For one thing she believes that difference and sexual difference are very closely related. And, what is more: "Sexual difference is one of the major philosophical issues, if not the issue, of our age" (Irigaray 1993a, 5 [1984]).[4]

These were the opening words of Irigaray's 1984 guest lecture at Erasmus University in Rotterdam, the Netherlands. In one of her most recent books, *I Love* to You, she wrote: "Sexual difference probably represents the most universal issue we can address. Our era is faced with the task of dealing with this issue, because, across the whole world, there are, there are only, men and women" (Irigaray 1996, 47 [1992]).[5]

Irigaray regards the degree of sexual difference in a given culture as an indication of the way in which differences are viewed. She gives the highest priority to practicing sexual difference, because she believes that sexual indifference is at the root of the imbalance and inequality in Western culture: "People never cease to divide themselves into secondary but deadly rivalries without realizing that their primary and insurmountable division is *into two genders*" (Irigaray 1993, 13, [1990b]).[6]

Accepting sexual difference in our thinking would cause a revolutionary reversal of values: Women would become equals, the body would be respected, nature would no longer be ignored. According to Irigaray the task we have to fulfill in our time is to effect sexual difference on earth. Men and women should become conscious that they are both sexual beings. Women are not the only ones with bodies; men, too, are through their bodies part of nature and its drives. Body and soul should not be regarded as separate entities. Only connecting body and spirit would make a "sensible transcendental" possible: The body, nature and the earth would all be spiritualized rather than raped, destroyed and polluted. In this way life on earth can become blissful. And this is what Irigaray is striving for in her latest works. The subtitle of *I Love to You* is: *Sketch for a*

Felicity Within History. Irigaray turns away from Western cultural tradition, which dictates that the body must suffer while awaiting divine salvation in heaven. She argues for working to create happiness in the present. Earth should not be a place of deportation but a locus for happiness.

In a very enlightening analysis of current developments in feminist theory, Rosi Braidotti (1994a, 146–172) distinguishes three necessary pillars of thinking about sexual difference: the difference between men and women, differences between women, and differences within each woman. Placing Kristeva and Irigaray in Braidotti's structure immediately clarifies their respective positions. While Kristeva ignores differences between men and women, Irigaray neglects the differences between women.

With her most recent stance in *Strangers to Ourselves*, Kristeva has again written herself out of the feminist debate, which is based on the assumption that there are specifically female experiences. What Braidotti calls the first phase has lost all relevance according to Kristeva, because the notion of difference belongs primarily to the personal. In this way, Kristeva denies the position of double-otherness that women in patriarchal society occupy: they are the other not only in relation to their unconscious, but also vis-à-vis man (Geyer-Ryan 1994, 161). In the previous chapters, I have shown that Anne Frank's inner world was a maze of identities in which she was trying to find her way. Neither her experience of adolescence nor her Jewishness can be seen in isolation from her female subject position. It is apparent from her writings that the other differences are steeped in the man-woman difference. In other words Anne Frank's oeuvre clearly shows that whatever position of otherness a woman occupies, this otherness is always multiplied by the fact that she is also a woman in a patriarchal society. This means that Anne Frank was an adolescent *and* a woman, Jewish *and* a woman.

> I do believe that Kristeva's relationship to psychoanalysis and to feminism is one of the greatest attachment to the former and the strongest ambivalence to the latter. In her most recent work it seems to me that the dutiful Lacanian daughter takes the upper hand over the critical feminist theorist. (Braidotti 1991, 238)

Using Braidotti's structure, we can see that Irigaray has also paid little attention to this double otherness, albeit for completely different reasons. Irigaray's most obvious difference from Kristeva is that she focuses intensively on the difference between men and women, thereby losing sight of the differences between women themselves. This shortcoming has become more apparent in the 1990s; women's studies currently puts a great deal of emphasis on investigating the differences between women (without ignoring women's shared position in patriarchal society). When American postcolonial theorists began to point out that feminist theory had a Western, white bias, the theory was expanded into a multicolored and multicultural discipline.[7]

Irigaray did not take part in this development because her priorities lay with investigating and affirming the difference between men and women. However, current developments in women's studies clearly show that the levels Braidotti distinguishes are interrelated, presuppose one another, and cannot be explored separately. My thoughts on Anne Frank reflect this: She was not only a woman, she was also young and Jewish.

Braidotti's "feminist nomadism" (1994a, 146–172) inspires a way of thinking about sexual difference that recognizes both the shared history of women in a patriarchal culture and their divergent experiences based on differences in class, age, ethnicity, and belief. In the part of this book on Etty Hillesum, the work of Hélène Cixous provides an important theoretical framework. In my view Cixous engages at all of Braidotti's levels, more so than either Kristeva or Irigaray. Her theoretical reflections and poetic meditations connect very well with my exploration of the double otherness in Anne Frank's and Etty Hillesum's texts. This is because Cixous herself is personally involved in a double outsider position. She calls herself a *juifemme,* a "Jewoman," a phrase that brilliantly captures how intertwined her Jewish background and her position as a female subject truly are. In chapter 6 I apply this notion to Etty Hillesum, but not before I describe Hillesum's writings in chapter 4 and analyze her development as a writer in chapter 5.

Hanneli Goslar
and Anne Frank
at Merwedeplein
in May 1940.
*(Copyright © AFF/AFS,
Amsterdam, the Netherlands)*

Margot and Anne Frank, 1940.
(Copyright © AFF/AFS)

Edith Frank-Holländer
in Zandvoort, June 1934.
(Copyright © AFF/AFS)

Rosa Holländer-Stern
with her granddaughters
Margot and Anne Frank
in Zandvoort, July 1939.
(Copyright © AFF/AFS)

Page from the first diary.

Page from the "loose sheets" (*b* version).

Etty Hillesum's handwriting. From the second diary,
part of the diary entry dated September 5, 1941.
(Jewish Historical Museum, Amsterdam)

Julius Spier, around 1940.
*(Jewish Historical
Museum, Amsterdam)*

Henny Tideman (Tide),
around 1939.
*(Jewish Historical
Museum, Amsterdam)*

Etty Hillesum (*right*) and a friend during a visit to Groningen in 1931.
(Jewish Historical Museum, Amsterdam)

The Hillesum family in 1931.
Left to right: Etty, Rebecca Hillesum-Bernstein,
Mischa, Jaap, Dr. Levi Hillesum.
(Jewish Historical Museum, Amsterdam)

Etty Hillesum

Chapter 4 ✦ A Hand, Which Wrote[1]

While World War II raged on, Etty Hillesum was fighting a war on paper. From March 1941 to September 1943, she kept a diary to gain more self-knowledge, in the hope that doing so would help her to overcome her physical ailments and depressions. Her diaries reflect a process of inner growth, in which the perfecting of her self created room for caring for others.

For Etty Hillesum writing was an act of resistance in more than one sense of the word. During a period of unprecedented anti-Semitism, in which the Nazis were out to annihilate every last Jew, she achieved self-renewal. She managed to conquer her depressive moods and give her life new meaning. As Nazi ideology degraded Jews to subhuman status, she strove to develop an ethic and a spiritual awareness, first in herself and later in others as well. While the Nazis sought to wipe out any aberration or deviation from the norm, Etty Hillesum was discovering a way of life and philosophy that elevated the other to a position of glory. Resisting the zeitgeist of death and destruction, she fought for a belief that remained life affirming.

Writing a diary was Etty Hillesum's way of giving meaning to a life that was in danger of becoming meaningless. As she was cut off from the past and future, writing was her only means of making the present worth living—at once a form of resistance and a survival mechanism. To Etty Hillesum, who was writing practically in the face of death, the diary was a means of achieving self-actualization in the full awareness that the Nazi regime was out to destroy her. This individual self-expression subverted the Nazi ideology of annihilation and genocide. Hillesum was not a resistance fighter in the usual sense, but she was no less ardent. It was with the pen, rather than the sword, that she battled to save humanity.

Ten of Etty Hillesum's diaries have survived. Others were lost, among them those she kept while interned at Westerbork. She also wrote numerous letters to friends and acquaintances. The choice to write in the form of letters is particularly significant in the context of the Shoah. While the diary genre is likely to appeal to those who are confined to the present time, letter writing is inspired by restrictions in space: Letters can travel where the sender is no longer allowed to go. As the Nazis practiced their politics of banishment by isolating the Jewish people in ghettos and concentration camps, Etty Hillesum's letters mediated between two worlds. From Westerbork she wrote letters to her loved ones in Amsterdam; from Amsterdam she wrote letters to her friends in the camp.

In the multimedia center of Amsterdam's Jewish Historical Museum there is a collection of the Hillesum diaries, letters, photographs, and other possessions. The complete edition of her diaries and letters (Hillesum 1986) fills almost six hundred pages of closely printed diary entries and more than one hundred pages of letters. The handwriting, which Hillesum herself characterized as "illegible wriggly lines," looks strikingly modern in some places, while in others it has a passing resemblance to Arabic. The vocabulary is surprisingly modern too:

> Sometimes I could hardly believe I was dealing with language from the 1940s. Some words and expressions seemed much more recent: "working on yourself," "being able to cope again," "consciousness-raising," "listening to your own rhythm," "dealing with your own inadequacies."   (Bakker 1992, 65; trans. MH)

Etty Hillesum's writings display two seemingly contradictory, tendencies. On the one hand the chronology of the diaries and letters creates a sort of funnel effect; the war is in the background at first but comes closer and closer, so that in the end the violence is no longer something that "rages outside [her] window" (H'83, 80) but that happens right before her eyes in Westerbork. On the other hand she started keeping a diary to work out her problems, and through writing she was able to find an inner peace and harmony she had not known before. Against the tide of war and violence, this life-affirming current can be found in the texts as well. While destruction was drawing near, Etty Hillesum learned to embrace life, "despite everything" (H'83, 80, 114).

Perhaps her ability to achieve inner growth at a time of such extreme destruction can explain why the diaries and letters have become a source of inspiration to so many people. This process of liberation was profoundly contrary to the Nazi repression; it is nearly impossible to reconcile Etty Hillesum's philosophy of life—which hinges on love and gratitude—with the conditions of persecution, the circumstances under which she lived and died. However, these two extremes are inextricably linked, as I will demonstrate in the following description of the diaries and letters. I have decided to provide a detailed description of the entire body of surviving diaries because not all of these diaries have reached the general public. The most likely reason for this is that the complete edition—of which there is still no English translation—is so large. Although the complete edition has not been widely read, the collections of excerpts, entitled *Het verstoorde leven* (1981), *Het denkende hart van de barak* (1982), and *In duizend zoete armen* (1984) have become extremely popular. However, only the first two of these books have been translated into English, as *Etty: A Diary 1941–43* (1983) and *Letters from Westerbork* (1987). I hope my overview of the surviving texts will do justice to the dynamism of Etty Hillesum's diaries and letters. In chapter 5 I explore her motives for writing, and in chapter 6 I analyze her spiritual development.

Etty Hillesum's Diaries
NOTEBOOK ONE: MARCH 8–JULY 4, 1941

Etty Hillesum's first diary is a notebook with a bluish-gray cover and four metal rings in the spine. The first text is not a diary entry but a letter to "Dear Mr. S." (EH, 3) in German. The letter reveals that "Mr. S.," or Julius Spier,[2] wants to help Etty Hillesum get rid of her psychosomatic symptoms. Apparently he had earlier suggested that she write down her thoughts and feelings as a means of ordering her inner chaos.

The first diary entry is dated one day later. It is dedicated for the most part to Spier, who is consistently referred to as S. in Hillesum's texts. She had only recently met him and was very impressed. Her attraction to him was both sexual and intellectual.

Instantly she began writing several pages at a time, putting to rest her fear—to which she had earlier confessed—that she would have trouble writing (EH, 4). After a week she also noted that once she got started, she was barely able to stop. She concluded: "My '*verstopfte Seele* [constipated soul]' is getting less '*verstopft* [blocked]' already" (EH, 23; trans. MH). She wrote daily, mostly in the first person but on occasion, when admonishing herself, in the second. It is clear that she used writing for self-improvement. She strove, by writing about daily events and her emotions, to find inner peace. She also tried to live as simply as possible and wished she could "roll melodiously out of

God's hand" (EH, 7, 9; H'83, 5). At times she succeeded in this, doing what she had to do and not thinking too far ahead. She tried to live more from the heart and less from the head: neither to drift nor to get lost in fantasies and daydreams but to keep both feet on the ground. Her diary helped. By keeping in touch with writing, she was able to stay in touch with herself! (EH, 43; H'83, 15). In addition to writing, she also drew comfort and support from reading. The acts of writing and reading converged in her need to quote. (EH, 14–15) She copied meaningful and beautiful passages into her diary. She quoted Freud and his (former) protégés Adler and Jung, but most of all she cited Spier's notes.

Etty Hillesum's first mention of the war was a week after she began keeping the diary. Strikingly, what worried her most was how deeply people hated the Germans (EH, 19; H'83, 8). For pages on end she wrote about this hatred, ending with:

> Summarizing, what I am trying to say is: Nazi barbarism evokes in us a similar barbarism, which would employ the same methods, if we were allowed to do what we wanted these days. We must inwardly reject this barbarism, we must not cultivate this hatred in ourselves, because it will not do anything to help our world get out of the mud.
>
> (EH, 22; trans. MH)

This theme came to be the leitmotif in all her diaries and letters. Just as fundamental as her resistance to the new regime was her resistance to hatred. Nazism brought out the worst in people, even in the Nazis' enemies. Etty Hillesum made a passionate plea for fighting the bad tendencies in one's own character as being as important as opposing the occupying forces.[3]

The therapeutic value of writing—its usefulness as a key to self-discovery and improvement—was not the only reason why Hillesum wrote. Writing also had another meaning to Hillesum, which she mentioned on the very first pages of the notebook, in the letter to Spier: She wanted to become a writer. These two drives—writing as therapy, writing out of ambition—overlapped in her texts, for Hillesum went beyond scrutinizing herself and actually explored her very urge to write. Once, she had wanted to use words to hold on to and possess things, but she now strove to find a mode of writing which could bring her inner freedom and independence. Her battle against possessiveness also had a bearing on her conduct toward Spier. Her attraction to him was strong, and she was repeatedly tempted to make advances. However, Spier had a fiancée in London, Hertha Levi, whom he planned to marry. Etty wanted to help him stay loyal to Hertha, but sometimes her nearly irresistible desire to possess him physically made things difficult for both of them.

Between March 8 and March 26, 1941, she wrote almost daily. At the end of that month, she was struck by the news that Professor Van Wijk had died.[4] His death made her mourn for other Dutch scholars and writers, who, unlike Van Wijk, had died directly or indirectly as a result of the war: Bonger, Ter Braak, Du Perron and Marsman (EH, 55; H'83, 19; Hillesum 1986, 728).

This first period of writing started with a letter to Spier and ended with a letter to her parents. Addressing them in Russian, "*Dorogije roditeli* [dear parents]," Etty gave them the news of Van Wijk's death (EH, 56). Then, for several weeks, she did not write in her diary. The next entry did not come until May 8, 1941: "I must try to improve myself some more, there's no getting around it!" (EH, 57; H'83, 20). That day she wrote mainly about the difficulties of her complex relationship with Spier, of her sexual attraction to him and her need to keep him at a distance.

Although Etty had resolved to write every day, she did not stick to it. In her next diary entry, dated June 8, 1941, she wrote of needing contact with herself. She planned to meditate early in the morning, get some physical exercise, read some good literature, and write "a few words on these blue-lined pages" (EH, 60; H'83, 22).

Apparently, writing and mental well-being went hand in hand; as long as she wrote in her diary on a daily basis, she was fairly well in control of herself. Every time she stopped writing for a while, her first new entry was always about mental stress. After June 19 she stopped writing for a few weeks and did not resume again until July 4, 1941: "I am full of unease, a strange, infernal agitation, which might be productive if only I knew what to do with it. [. . .] Oh God, take me into your great hands and turn me into your instrument, let me write" (EH, 71; H'83, 26).

On that day she completed her first notebook.

AUGUST 4–OCTOBER 21, 1941

It was exactly one month later that Etty Hillesum began her second diary, a dark blue, spiral-bound notebook She opened with one of Spier's assertions: that love of mankind is greater than love for one man, because loving one person is ultimately a form of narcissism (EH, 72; H'83, 27). She applied this notion to herself and other women, while at the same time she acknowledged her own need to bond with one man. She wondered whether this typically feminine characteristic was a matter of nature or nurture: "Whether it is an ancient tradition from which she must liberate herself, or whether it is so much part of her very essence that she would be doing violence to herself if she bestowed her love on all mankind instead of on a single man" (EH, 73; H'83, 27).

She struggled with the "woman question," aware that women had as yet had little time or space for intellectual development:

> Perhaps the true, inner emancipation of women has yet to begin. We are not yet full human beings; we are still bitches. We are still bound and tied by centuries-old traditions. We are still waiting to be born as people, that is the great task that lies before us women.
>
> (EH, 73; H'83, 27–28; adapt. MH)

In this diary she thought long and hard about her relationship with Spier. At times she felt she was in love with him (EH, 106); the physical attraction between them was strong, sometimes almost too strong to withstand.

The writing process shows the same spiraling pattern as in the first diary. Whenever she was not feeling well, she turned to her diary. She called it a "rough draft," which she used to gain some clarity (EH, 74; H'83, 28). When she kept up the writing for a few days, she felt better; soon, it seemed, she did not need the diary any longer. Next she would experience a period of lust for life, in which she did not find the time or the peace to write. However, this caused her to lose contact with herself. Then she would start to feel bad again, all "bottled up," and would return to the diary. Writing appears to have been of vital importance to her mental health. "I will force myself to write every day, even if it's just a few words. Otherwise, I will get too full" (EH, 77; trans. MH).

Once started, she could hardly stop writing and would write for hours on end. (EH, 107) She also meditated as a means of coming to terms with herself. She called this *hineinhorchen*: listening within. By turning her attention inward, she found peace. The calming effect of these activities was interrupted in August, when she visited her parents in Deventer. She wrote of chaos in their home and her irritation at her mother's yapping. It took great effort not to let the situation sidetrack her:

> I want to become the chronicler of the things that are happening now (downstairs they're screaming blue murder, with Father yelling: "Go, then!" and slamming the door; that, too, must be absorbed and now I'm suddenly crying, sobbing. So that's how detached I am; actually you can't breathe properly in this house. Oh well, let's make the best of it); right, where was I? Oh yes, a chronicler.
>
> (EH, 91; H'83, 34; adapt. MH)

Etty's stay in Deventer evoked childhood memories.[5] She realized how disorganized the family in which she had grown up was, and she considered it her duty to bring order and harmony to the chaos she had internalized.

NOTEBOOK THREE: OCTOBER 21–DECEMBER 6, 1941

On October 21, 1941, Etty Hillesum wrote the last entry in her second notebook and immediately continued in the third. In this diary she dealt again with the internal conflict between independence and attachment (EH, 141; H'83, 46). She became increasingly convinced that she was not meant to spend her life with one man.

This diary, too, is characterized by her critical and painstaking self-analyses. For example, she discovered that she had an urge to reduce all contradictions to a unity and suspected that this urge was born from a feeling of insecurity (EH, 143–144). This was the theme that preoccupied her in the fall of 1941; she wanted to learn to accept life's complexities instead of favoring one and repressing another. She even applied this attitude to the persecution of the Jews. On Friday, October 24, 1941, she wrote: "Tonight new measures against the Jews. I have allowed myself to be upset and depressed about it for half an hour" (EH, 145; H'83, 47).

She forced herself not to linger over these measures, which increasingly isolated the Jews. She was determined not to let this isolation interfere with the work she considered most vital: shaping herself.

In this diary she also delved into her relationship with her parents. In late October she had a breakdown. She traced its cause to her mother, who had visited her a few days earlier. She criticized her mother for her unbalanced character but also acknowledged having much in common with her.

A few weeks later she wrote of her relationship with her father. She felt sorry for him because he did not have an easy home life. All the same she could not stand his company; his presence robbed her of all her life and energy. It happened again when he visited her in late November, but this time she also felt sympathy for him, in particular for his resigned attitude, which she saw as a reaction to inner chaos.[6] She shifted the focus from her parents to herself and voiced her intentions:

> From my parents' chaos, their failure to take a stance, I must shape myself by definitely taking a stance, by coming to grips with things, despite the recurrent feeling that it's all a waste of time, that's life for you, children. And so on, and so forth.
>
> (EH, 169; H'83, 57; adapt. MH)

Understanding the influence of her parents helped her undergo a healing process she described as follows: "Back into darkness, into your mother's womb, into *the collective*. Break free, find your own voice, vanquish the chaos within. I am pulled to and fro between these two poles" (EH, 145; H'83, 47).

On November 24 the diary reflects a turning point. Etty had decided to no longer accept tasks that she felt uncomfortable to her. Her attitude to Spier also changed slightly; she shook him off a bit. She was relieved at having made these decisions and felt more in touch with herself. Continuing by describing a prayer to God, she promised to live her life as best she could (EH, 162; H'83, 52).

In late November 1941, she mentioned having had a night of passion (EH, 163). A week later, she woke up in the middle of the night, dizzy and nauseous. She decided to abort her pregnancy; she fought the unborn life, first with quinine and cognac, and when that failed, with hot water and "blood-curdling instruments" (EH, 177; H'83, 60). She was convinced she had made the right decision, not only because of the war but, more important, because of her fear of hereditary mental illness. Her mother was admitted to a psychiatric hospital several times (Boas 1982, 260), and both of her brothers were psychiatric patients as well.[7] Etty herself had always been haunted by fears of a hereditary disease, but she conquered these fears through self-exploration. However, having children was something she never seriously considered:

> It feels to me as if I am saving a human life. How preposterous: to save a human life by doing my utmost to keep it from living! But all I want is to spare someone from entering this miserable world. I shall leave you in safety, in a state of unbornness, rudimentary being that you are, and you ought to be grateful to me. I almost feel tenderness toward you. I assault myself with hot water and blood-curdling instruments, I shall fight you patiently and relentlessly, until you are once again returned to nothingness, and then I shall feel that I have performed a good deed, that I have done the right thing. After all, I can't give you enough strength and, besides, my tainted family is riddled with hereditary disease.   (EH, 177; H'83, 60; adapt. MH)

NOTEBOOK FOUR: DECEMBER 8, 1941–JANUARY 24, 1942

The fourth diary—a dark green, spiral-bound notebook with a hard cover—describes a period during which the writer was, for the most part, doing and feeling well. No longer so easily daunted by physical or psychological complaints, she learned to accept her moods, sadness as well as happiness, exuberance along with despair.

More than ever she wrote about God, often invoking her prayer of November 24, 1941 (EH, 182).

Casually, she wrote that on the morning of December 8 "the unborn child was born" (EH, 180; trans. MH). She was far more preoccupied with her own growth and her work on language:

> [D]ays of . . . birth pangs about sentences and thoughts that refuse to be born and of making tremendous demands on yourself and of finding it of the utmost importance and necessity to find your own little voice, etcetera, etcetera.   (EH, 183; H'83, 60; adapt. MH)[8]

Still investigating the nature of her problems, she found that their roots lay in the excessive freedom her parents had given her in childhood. Because her parents had lacked a firm grip, they were unable to offer their children guidance (EH, 207–208; H'83, 64–65). Etty Hillesum also explained her frenetic efforts to create unity and order as a reaction to her parents' lack of direction, telling herself that "the only good unity [is] one which contains all opposites and irrational moments. Otherwise, it is just another case of the forcedness and fixity that misrepresents life" (EH, 208; trans. MH).

Etty also traced the cause of her depressions to her fear of being unable to express her moods and thoughts, which threatened to engulf her in chaos. She felt it absolutely necessary to find a form.

She spent Christmas in Deventer. Staying at her parents' was less devastating than before. Her feelings for her mother ranged from love to pity to irritation. Around New Year's Eve she devoted a great deal of thought not only to writing but also to reading (EH, 186). She brought writers, particularly Rilke and Dostoyevsky, to life; she wrote about them as if they were still alive, and her friends. Literary characters also came to life in her diary, for example Dostoyevsky's Prince Myshkin (EH, 223). She read books in much the same way that she dealt with people:

> One should approach books the way one approaches people. Not with preconceived notions or demands. Sometimes the first few pages are enough to form an impression of the whole book, and one gets attached to that idea and refuses to let go of it, and often that will undermine the writer's intentions. One should leave people full freedom, and books too.   (EH, 188; trans. MH)

On December 1941 she quoted a number of passages from Rilke's *Das Stundenbuch* [Book of hours]. The following lines in particular appealed to her:

> I will always want to reflect your whole form
> and never be too blind or too old
> to hold your heavy, swaying image.
>
> (EH, 201; trans. MH)[9]

She related this passage to her love for Spier. His importance to her is evident from the sheer number of words she used to describe him, but it can also be seen in drawings in her notebook. She drew his portrait—sometimes in profile, sometimes full-face—in the margins (Hillesum 1986, 818).

In January 1942 she mentioned that she intended to write something for Spier. On February 3 it would be a year since he had started treating her, so this text was meant as an ode to him. Aside from Spier she had also become friends with Liesl Levie and Henny Tideman, who was known as Tide. Liesl Levie was a woman toward whom Etty felt a mixture of fascination and friendship. And she was particularly fond of Tide, one of Spier's best friends (EH, 235–236; H'83, 70).

Almost unnoticed amid Etty Hillesum's positive thoughts about Spier are traces of his less pleasant character traits. His relationship with her also appears to have had a few nasty edges. For example, he once demonstrated to her how childishly Tide kissed. They also discussed Adri Holm, one of his more obedient students. Etty differed from Holm in that she did not unquestioningly accept everything Spier said. Spier and Hillesum talked about this on the phone:

> *Me: Ja die Holm, das ist so eine herrliche adorierende Gramophonplatte.*
> [Oh, that Holm woman is such a wonderful, adoring phonograph record.] Loud lowing on the other side. *Sagen Sie das nochmal* [Say that again].   (EH, 251; trans. MH)

On New Year's Eve she had accompanied Spier to his lung specialist. The doctor had told him that his complaints were nothing to worry about. Apparently his health was fine. Looking back on the previous year, she described it as the happiest of her life. It had been rich and fruitful. She felt that she had gained greater awareness (EH, 221; H'83, 66) and testified to her deep satisfaction and gratitude. On her birthday, January 15, 1942, she wrote just three sentences in her diary: "God, I thank you. Thank you for living within me. Thank you for everything" (EH, 240; trans. MH).

NOTEBOOK FIVE: FEBRUARY 16–MARCH 27, 1942

"Trying to refind myself by way of these words by Rainer Maria" (EH, 252; trans. MH) is how Etty Hillesum opened her fifth diary, which contains many quotations from Rilke. Particularly the following excerpt, about the relationship between the sexes, can be found in various entries:

> And maybe the sexes are more closely related than one thinks, and the great renewal of the world will perhaps consist of this: Man and girl—once liberated of all false emotions and feelings of unease—will no longer seek each other as opposites, but as siblings and neighbors, and they will come together *as human beings*, in order to simply, earnestly and patiently bear the burden of the sex they have been saddled with.   (EH, 258–259, 301; trans. MH/HL)[10]

Etty Hillesum thought it was woman's task to educate man. Although she felt unready to comment on these quotations, the following passage appears to be an elaboration on Rilke's thoughts:

> That I believed that this would be woman's historical task for the years to come: to guide man to his soul, by way of hers. And none of the eroticism need be lost. But one must put everything in its rightful place, einordnen. And I also believe that the most important and pioneering men of the future will be those who have such a strong feminine side—and at the same time are still real men, like him [Spier] and like Rilke for instance—that they act as the, how shall I say it, signposts to the regions of the soul. And not those "he-men," those Führers and heroes in uniform, not the ones they call "real men." But then, maybe real men only exist in the minds of women anyway.
>   (EH, 301; trans. MH)

She also wrote down a line from a poem by Rilke which she found especially meaningful: "There is one space which reaches through every being: the inner universe"[11] (EH, 286, 291; trans. MH), commenting: "These seem to me the most beautiful words that I know, probably because in their roundness and perfection they reflect exactly what I am experiencing ever more intensely" (EH, 291; trans. MH).

Her interaction with Rilke, though it existed only on paper, was intense. Inner reality meant more to her than surface existence. Only sporadically did she write about the war. However, on February 19, 1942, she mentioned that "that gentle boy from [the] 'Cultura' [bookstore]" had been tortured to death (EH, 253; H'83, 70). She also noted that eighty-five prominent citizens had been taken hostage following the January 30 assault on the Amsterdam headquarters of the Dutch National Socialist Movement's (NSB) student society (Hillesum 1986, 755). Among the hostages were history professor Jan Romein, and Johannes Tielrooy, professor of French language and literature, both of the University of Amsterdam. They were imprisoned in the Amersfoort concentration camp. Hillesum discussed the event with a fellow student, Jan Bool, and recounted this conversation in her diary. Although the following entry reveals why she devoted so few words to the atrocities, it also establishes again, with great clarity, the basic premise of her philosophy:

> I no longer believe that we can improve anything in the outside world that we have not first improved in ourselves. And that to me seems to be the only lesson to be learned from this war, that we must *only* look inside ourselves and nowhere else. . . . And it was not just theoretical knowledge either. Our professors are in prison, another of Jan's friends has been killed and there are so many other sorrows, but all we said to each other was: "It is too easy to feel vindictive."
>
> That really was the bright spot of today.
>
> (EH, 254; H'83, 71; adapt. MH)

From time to time she was confronted directly with German Nazis. She wrote with great compassion about a "young Gestapo officer" who shouted at her; her description ends with a philosophical observation on the nature of evil, which has its origin in people and therefore does not frighten her. What is terrifying is not the people, but the systems they devise, which can get out of control (EH, 269; H'83, 72–73).

Although she continued to fantasize about traveling the world with Spier and leading a nomadic life as a journalist (EH, 287), she also had no illusions about the realities of the war (EH, 289; H'83, 74).

She contemplated the past year, particularly the period in which she met Spier and, through him, attained a much better state of physical and mental well-being: "On the third of February, I turned one. I think I will keep February 3 as my birthday; it is a more important date than January 15, which is when my umbilical cord was cut" (EH, 255; trans. MH).

Apparently, she had already written and presented her "Ode to Spier," as we can gather from the quotations she took from one of Spier's letters and incorporated in her diary (EH, 287). Unfortunately, the "Ode" itself has not survived.

Early 1942 was a good time for Etty Hillesum. She wrote that she felt wide and spacious on the inside (EH, 255). She still had the occasional headache or stomachache, but it was no longer overwhelming. She was better able to put her ailments in perspective. She wanted to use this new inner strength to help others to get in touch with themselves and to start them on the path to healing. "Things should get to the point where one is always ready to help one's fellow human beings to develop; and the more developed one is, the better one will be able to help others" (EH, 263; trans. MH).

In her diary Hillesum also wrote about her relationships with "my two gray-haired friends" (EH, 259), Han Wegerif and Julius Spier, who were both of her father's generation. She had lived with the former since 1937. Wegerif was a widower, who had employed her to live with him as a *femme d'honneur*, to keep house.[12] However, what started as a business relationship evolved into a love affair (EH, 719). Still, she addressed him as "Papa Han."

Although she did not want to give in to her sexual attraction to Spier, she was not always able to control her feelings. In her diary she wrote more than once of her longing. She tried to keep her thoughts and actions pure and not to overemphasize her sexual urges. She also tried not to project her attraction to Spier onto Han, but there were times when she could not prevent this from happening (EH, 266–267).

Sometimes she addressed God in her writings, for example when she exclaimed: "O Lord, please let me live more in the spirit!" (EH, 259; trans. MH). She also wrote of not kneeling in prayer (see chapter 5 for Jewish and non-Jewish aspects of Hillesum's relationship to God) for months, because she had continually been praying inwardly. But in late February 1942 she knelt down again: "This morning I suddenly found myself kneeling in front of the unlit heater in the living room and I said: My dear God, give me some patience and teach me to love the simple things in life" (EH, 260; trans. MH).

Her relationships with women also deepened. Holm, Tide, and Levie became increasingly important to her (EH, 270). Although she often thought that Tide's way of experiencing religion was childish, she also learned from Tide's unquestioning faith in God and her gratitude (EH, 275–276).

NOTEBOOK SIX: MARCH 27–APRIL 30, 1942

On the very first pages of Hillesum's sixth diary, a notebook with a bright red cover, we are confronted with Rilke. Further on in this diary she writes that she become gradually entwined with Rilke's work. She was continuously, deeply, and completely absorbed in it (EH, 337; H'83, 90). She liked to quote him because he expressed exactly what she felt. Reading and quoting Rilke was almost a primary need. She realized that she was reading Rilke's letters when she was twenty-eight, the same age he was when he wrote them (EH, 340). Although she felt a certain kinship with him (EH, 343; H'83, 92), she also recognized that she had not attained what he had at her age: a medium, a voice. She comforted herself with his words that one should be patient (EH, 356; H'83, 100).

Another thing she had in common with Rilke was a love of Russian culture. Etty Hillesum studied and taught Russian and dreamed of traveling to Russia so that she could become a mediator between Russians and Europeans. She would also have liked to bring Rilke back to Russia: "For he was always so homesick for it" (EH, 339; trans. MH).

Rilke inspired her life and her writings: "For the time being my passion is this: to read and internalize the whole of Rilke, everything he wrote, every letter; and then to strip him away, to forget him, and to go back to living from my own substance" (EH, 352; trans. MH).

A common feature of Hillesum's two major inspirations, Rilke and Spier, was their very strong feminine side. This was also her explanation for why women were so attracted to both. With regard to Spier, Hillesum kept struggling with the balance between body and mind. She strove to put the body at the service of her spiritual life. Her greatest ideal was for physical love to be an expression of spiritual love, for the body to be the expression of the soul. Like learning to be patient, she saw this, too, as a leitmotif (EH, 329).

While writing her sixth diary, she suddenly, paradoxically, concluded: "Keeping a diary is an art I haven't mastered" (EH, 318; H'83, 77; adapt. MH). She felt she should actually be writing down every event, every encounter, every detail in daily life, but she did not get around to this: "But then, my real life is something quite different. I think I should once and for all forget about writing down all my experiences. My real life is elsewhere" (EH, 318; H'83, 78; adapt. MH).

The war was present in the background. Lying in bed she heard the airplanes, the antiaircraft guns, the bombs. She stayed calm—even peaceful—and grateful. Her conviction that all catastrophes originate in people (EH, 320; H'83, 80) helped her to conquer her fears:

> And I think that is why I do not feel fear at a time like this: because everything that is happening is somehow so close to me. And however monstrously out of proportion it sometimes gets, it is so human in nature; it can always be traced back to something human. That is why many human actions do not frighten me, because I will always see them as acts that originate in people, in individuals, in myself, and that makes everything comprehensible and prevents actions from becoming isolated monstrosities that are no longer of humanity.   (EH, 320; trans. MH)

This philosophy also motivated her to try to achieve personal growth. She was utterly convinced that there was only one way to counteract the war: All people had to try to treat themselves and others with love and compassion. In this diary she constantly tried to improve herself. She was critical of her own actions and thoughts and, by writing, worked on self-actualization. She held herself accountable for being envious and vain, for wanting to impress others, or for foisting her moods on them. She tried to cope with her two love relationships and battled feelings of jealousy toward Hertha, Spier's fiancée in London.

Her monthly periods affected her strongly. Usually Etty was patient with herself and steadily worked to improve herself, but while she had her period, she desperately tried to find an "object," a voice (EH, 355; H'83, 100). She felt that she was a different person while she was menstruating (EH, 359).

In mid-April she met her parents and noticed that they no longer bothered her as much. Compassion and guilt had given way to acceptance and mildness: "Much has changed in my relationship with my parents, many of the suffocating ties have been loosened, and as a result I have gained the strength to love them more genuinely" (EH, 350; H'83, 97; adapt. MH).

On April 29, 1942, she mentioned that the Jews had been ordered to wear the yellow star from then on. She wrote of her inner strength, which would enable her to bear the threats and to attest to all the good that remained despite the restrictions. "Years from now schoolchildren will be taught about yellow stars and ghettos and Nazi terror and it will make their hair stand on end. But parallel to that textbook history, there is another one" (EH, 375; H'83, 109; adapt. MH).

Etty spent the evening "on which the 'yellow star' appeared" (EH, 375; H'83, 109) with intimate friends, intensely enjoying the profundity of their conversation and the aroma of real coffee: "And I said, 'Perhaps it is worth being part of history. One can at least see for oneself what else there is, besides that which ends up in the history books'" (EH, 375; H'83, 109; adapt. MH).

She tried to incorporate the yellow star into her life and to give this symbol of the persecution of the Jews a meaningful place. She saw suffering as an integral part of life and felt mature enough to accept her destiny:

> What counts is the suffering, the love, the important emotions and the quality of those emotions. And the big emotions . . . are always ablaze . . . and every century may feed the flames with different fuels, but all that matters is the warmth of the fire. And the fact that, these days, it is yellow stars and concentration camps and terror and war is of secondary importance. And I do not feel less militant because of these thoughts, for moral rectitude and indignation are also "big emotions."   (EH, 376; H'83, 110; adapt. MH)

She even wrote that she was happy to be Jewish and glad that Spier was a Jew too. She decided that she wanted to stay with him in the period that lay ahead, to weather the storm together. She wanted to take care of him and deliver him safely to Hertha, his fiancée, after the war.

NOTEBOOK SEVEN: MISSING

Before Etty Hillesum left for Westerbork camp for the last time, in the spring of 1943, she asked her roommate Maria Tuinzing to hold on to her diaries for her and to give them to her friend Klaas Smelik should she not survive the war. She hoped that Smelik, who was a writer, could have them published. Johanna Smelik, Klaas's daughter and Etty's friend, typed out parts of the diaries, and Klaas Smelik contacted various publishers, but no one was interested in publishing Hillesum's writings (Hillesum 1986, xvi). In an interview with the Dutch feminist magazine *Opzij* Johanna Smelik said:

> You shouldn't go stirring up Jewish matters, they said. And you should realize that, every time, I left the original diaries with them. That's how trusting I was. At home I didn't even keep them in a safe, I put them in a leather bag. Out of carelessness I have lost one of the diaries. The seventh. It contained things that touched me so deeply. And she also wrote such sweet things about me in this diary. I always kept it next to my bed, like a Bible.   (J. F. Smelik 1993, 120; trans. MH)

NOTEBOOK EIGHT: MAY 18–JUNE 5, 1942

This diary covers a period when Nazi threats and terror were increasing day by day (EH, 380; H'83, 113). But Hillesum focused on herself. She tried to pray, and in doing so found peace and protection. Like writing, praying became another means of staying in touch with herself and of not getting bogged down in everyday worries and routine. Nonetheless she felt responsible for Spier and wanted to be his wife, at least for the duration of the war. Spier, however, wanted to stay faithful to Hertha. Etty pondered the paradoxical nature of their situation. Unable to make up her mind, she was torn between a longing for togetherness and a desire for solitude (EH, 400). She dreamed of going somewhere far away—Russia—should Hertha come to the Netherlands; at the same time she chastised herself for cherishing such unrealistic hopes:

> Later, yes, later. What can we know about later? My God. What sunny optimism we still have in our fantasies. The future? A barracks in Drenthe—36 families to a barrack? Hunger, murder or exile? In any case you should not be wasting your strength on fantasies—fruitless, masochistic fantasies—should you? You'll need every bit of your strength just to make it through these times.   (EH, 387; trans. MH)

In this diary—a dark green, spiral-bound notebook only half as thick as the previous three—she again wrote about the act of writing: the passion to write and the patience it required (EH, 384). And repeatedly she drew the conclusion that she could not stop writing: "And if I were to write down every thought inside me that is screaming to be put into writing, I would never be able to stop, would I?" (EH, 397; trans. MH).

She did not close her eyes to the harsh reality of life:

> I try to face up to your world, God, not to escape from reality into beautiful dreams—though I believe that beautiful dreams can exist alongside the most horrible reality—and I continue to praise your creation, God, despite everything.   (EH, 403; H'83, 114)

Despite all the misery and terror, she was determined to maintain contact with the beautiful and meaningful side of life; again and again, she drew support from Rilke.

NOTEBOOK NINE: JUNE 5–JULY 3, 1942

On June 5 Etty Hillesum completed her eighth diary and continued in her ninth, a notebook with a green cover and four rings. She did not feel very good, "sad and off-center" (EH, 414; trans. MH), and used the diary to ease her restlessness. When Wegerif sneered at her constant need to write about herself, she tried to explain to him that her writing was less egotistical than it seemed. Her diary helped her to gain insight into her mood swings and to prevent them from ruling her life: "This is my muddling book. A sort of trash can for all sorts of waste products of my plagued mind" (EH, 445; trans. MH).

But Wegerif's swipe had stung her; afterward she kept trying to express why she wrote and what it taught her. She defended her writing a few days later with an important point: Taking yourself seriously is the first step toward creating a more humane world. She realized that most people were unable to follow this reasoning; she wrote that they were too preoccupied with world politics to think about themselves. While many people at that time considered self-actualization an unaffordable luxury, she suspected them of living in denial:

> And they are sticking their heads in the sand, all those people who use the weight and the seriousness of "these times" as an excuse to ignore their own little problems and leave them lying around, unsolved, in the corners of their souls. It takes a different sort of courage to take your own small and so-called insignificant problems seriously in the face of these important events. But, in the final analysis, these events— big, external occurrences which loom ahead, even though we ought

to feel an inner bond with them—are not these events the product of our own doing? And so on. See Jung, page so and so.

(EH, 437; trans. MH)

Although Jung's writings were a source of inspiration for her, they were not the main one. Her great teachers remained Spier and Rilke (EH, 472). She reminded herself that her reading and writing should extend beyond her desk. Her insights into human nature should find expression in her daily life and permeate her actions (EH, 422). At the same time, she was aware that her focus on herself, though necessary, had its limits: "One should not hide one's agitation and sadness, but shoulder and bear them. But not give in to them completely, as if they were all there is to the world" (EH, 423; trans. MH).

Etty Hillesum believed this was something humanity should learn, and she wanted to teach it. Those whose own spiritual development was under way, should help others take the same route. "And this will ultimately become my way of doing 'social work.' I am incapable of doing it any other way" (EH, 425; trans. MH).

She held on to this thought, even in late June, when the Nazi terror made itself felt through the drastic restriction of personal freedoms. She was deeply convinced that a long-lasting, stable peace would only be possible once people had worked on themselves and replaced their inner hatred with love (EH, 458; H'83, 123).

She wrote about Liesl Levie, "Liesl, that small elf, a moonlight bather on warm summer nights" (EH, 474; H'83, 127), whom she liked more and more and to whom she occasionally felt sexually attracted. She also continued to describe her love and desire for Spier. She sometimes had difficulty dealing with Spier's loyalty to his fiancée in London; for this Etty admonished herself and admitted to feeling a sort of "wounded female pride" (EH, 438; trans. MH). She also blamed herself for having cliché notions about the relationship between the sexes; she felt these notions detracted from the love between her and Spier.

This diary shows once again the remarkable amount of time Etty spent improving herself. For example, she realized that she relied on others for attention and support when she was not feeling well. Her conclusion was that it would be better to get in touch with herself at these moments, and not to ask others for the love she lacked. Another problem she struggled with was premenstrual stress. She felt she was only partly responsible for her actions on the day before her period. But she also admonished herself for this and vowed to not to give in to premenstrual restlessness (EH, 453). Again and again she tried to play down her erotic feelings for Spier. On June 23 she wrote a long letter to Hertha in her diary. She put herself in Hertha's position and admitted that she had been unfair. She had not been thinking of how hard it was for Hertha, who was so far away from the one she loved. She told Hertha of her plans to marry Spier and be his wife for the duration of the war and travel to Russia as soon as Hertha came back (EH, 466–468; H'83, 124–126).

In this diary Etty occasionally wrote of her love for Russia. She dreamed of becoming a mediator between the Russians and Western Europeans. In light of the suffering she saw around her—after the Nazis stepped up the terror in the early summer of 1942—she reflected on the difference between Russians and Westerners. While the Russians accept suffering as part of life and fully experience all the attending emotions, she wrote, Westerners prefer to deal with suffering through philosophical contemplation rather than emotion.

The Jews in Holland were frightened by decrees that progressively restricted their freedom of movement. Rumors about deportations abounded. English radio broadcasts reported that hundreds of thousands of Jews had been murdered and also mentioned the method: gassing. The way in which Hillesum coped with this news makes the last entries of this notebook very impressive. It is as if she found new strength. Deeply aware of the fate that awaited her, she was able to enjoy the smell of the jasmine in her backyard as never before (EH, 484; H'83, 128). She wanted everything to have a place: the jasmine as well as the suffering. On July 3 she filled the last pages of this notebook:

> Yes, I am still at the same desk, but it seems to me that I am going to have to turn a new leaf and find a different tone. I must admit a new insight into my life and find a place for it: what is at stake is our impending destruction and annihilation, we can have no more illusions about that. They are out to destroy us completely, we must accept that and go on from there. [. . .]
>
> I work and continue to live with the same conviction and I find life meaningful—yes, meaningful—although I hardly dare say so in company these days.
>
> Living and dying, sorrow and joy, the blisters on my feet and the jasmine behind the house, the persecution, the unspeakable horrors— it is all as one in me and I accept it all as one mighty whole and begin to grasp it better if only for myself, without being able to explain to anyone else how it all fits together. I wish I could live for a long time so that I would have the opportunity to explain it all someday, and if I am not granted that wish, well, then somebody else will do it, carry on from where my life has been cut short. And that is why I must try to live a good and complete and faithful life to my last breath: so that those who come after me do not have to start all over again, need not

face the same difficulties. Isn't that also doing something for future generations?   (EH, 486–487; H'83, 130–131; adapt. MH)

NOTEBOOK TEN: JULY 3–JULY 29, 1942

By the time Etty wrote in this diary, a brown, spiral-bound notebook, the imminent threat had become reality. She resolved to accept everything. As if she were trying to get used to the idea, she repeated time and again: "And destruction is also part of life" (EH, 494–496; trans. MH). Personally she was quite extreme in her acceptance of history as it unfolded: "After all, my personal fate is not the issue; it doesn't really matter whether it is I who is destroyed or another. What matters is the destruction itself" (EH, 488; H'83, 131; adapt. MH).

In this diary she made several attempts to come to terms with her own death and to accept it as part of her life (EH, 489, 503; H'83, 132, 141). At the same time she worried about Spier, who was in pain and looked exhausted and weak. But she warned herself not to make any demands of life in this respect either. Once she had started to accept life as it came, she could no longer draw any lines or set boundaries; she could not say: enough is enough.

> You have to be consistent to the end. You can say: I could bear any-thing else, but if something were to happen to him or if I had to leave him, that would be the last straw. But even in that case you simply have to go on. It is one or the other these days: Either you leave all your scruples behind and become totally egotistical and self-serving or you must learn to forgo all personal desires and surrender completely. And to me, that surrender does not mean resignation or wallowing in my own grief and loss, but offering whatever assistance I can wherever God happens to put me.   (EH, 504; H'83, 142; adapt. MH)

Hillesum felt that she had suddenly become much older and wiser, as if great inner changes were taking place. She worried most about her poor phys-ical condition. Because the Jews were forbidden to use public transporta-tion, she had to walk long distances and this gave her headaches and blisters. She feared she would not last more than three days in a work camp. She tried to counter her concerns about her physical weakness by focusing on her mental strength:

> It doesn't matter whether my untrained body will be able to carry on, that is really of secondary importance; the main thing is that even as we die a terrible death we are able to feel right up to the very last moment that life has meaning and beauty, that we have realized our potential and lived a good life.   (EH, 500; H'83, 138)

She prepared for deportation to Westerbork. Thinking of what she should pack to take along, her greatest concern was whether there would be room for the Bible, her Russian dictionaries, and Rilke's writings. Once again spiritual sustenance was her highest priority (EH, 507; H'83, 144).

Her faith in God was growing so quickly, she wrote, that even she needed time to grow accustomed to it. Wishes, desires, and ties fell away from her; she found it easier and easier to take everything as it came. Nevertheless she was hurt when the people around her could not relate to her new convictions: "Why can't people understand that acceptance does not preclude elementary, moral indignation and a fundamental militancy?" (EH, 519; trans. MH).

She wavered between courageousness and depression, calm and despair, but each time managed to regain her balance. On July 10 she wrote:

> A hard day, a very hard day. We must learn to shoulder this *Massenschicksal,*" our common fate, and learn to ignore all our personal childishness; everyone who seeks to save himself must surely realize that if he does not go another must take his place. As if it really mattered which of us goes. Ours is now a common destiny, and that is something we must not forget. A very hard day. But I keep getting back in touch with myself in prayer. And that is something I shall always be able to do, even in the most cramped space: pray. And that part of our common destiny which I can carry myself, I strap ever more tightly and firmly to my back, it is becoming part of me, I take it along wherever I go.
>
> And I shall wield this slender fountain pen as if it were a hammer, and my words will have to be so many hammer strokes with which to beat out the story of our fate and of a piece of history as it is and never was before. Not in this totalitarian, massively organized form, spanning the whole of Europe. Still, a few people must survive if only to be the chroniclers of this age. I would very much like to become one of their number.   (EH, 511; H'83, 146–147; adapt. MH)

What if she could escape the fate that was inescapable for so many other people? she wondered. Would she be able to live with herself? Despite this question, she let her brother Jaap push her into accepting a job with the Jewish Council[13] in order to postpone deportation. Etty Hillesum was strongly opposed to this; she did not like pulling strings and wanted to stay clear of the scheming and conniving associated with the Jewish Council. Moreover, she was well aware that the members and employees of the Jewish Council would, in the end, be deported as well (EH, 516; H'83, 150). Nevertheless, as the following entry shows, she gave in:

Everyone must follow the way of life that suits him best. I cannot actively take part in pretending to save myself, it seems so pointless to me and it makes me nervous and unhappy. My letter of application to the Jewish Council on Jaap's urgent advice has upset my cheerful yet deadly serious equilibrium. As if I have done something immoral.

(EH, 519; H'83, 152; adapt. MH)

On Thursday, July 16, she was ordered to report for deportation to Westerbork, but a few hours later the notice was declared void because the Jewish Council offered to employ her. She was very ambivalent about the job. On the one hand she accepted it as a miracle, as God's mercy, but on the other she said to Jaap: "I shall have to do a great many favors for a great many people after this. Something has gone awry in this society, it is not just" (EH, 525; H'83, 156).

On Sunday, July 12, she wrote a Sunday morning prayer in her diary. She addressed God directly and wrote that she now understood that he could do little for people if they did not help themselves. She promised to help him find and safeguard the divine in herself and others (EH, 516–517; H'83, 151). She told God she would have many more conversations with him and promised to cherish him. Later she wrote that, to her, praying meant: "[A] . . . dialogue with my innermost being, which for the sake of convenience I call God" (EH, 523; H'83, 155; adapt MH).

From July 12 onward Etty regularly addressed God in her diary.

Starting in mid-July she went to the Jewish Council every day. She hated it but found comfort in Rilke's writings; despite the chaos and disaster; she managed to read on her breaks. She hated to witness the deadening of everyone's emotions, but tried to find some meaning in it by accepting that God had put her there for a reason (EH, 538). She had a hard time putting this into practice. She kept to herself as much as possible and withdrew into Rilke's letters. She also continued to question her decision to work for the Jewish Council: "Nothing can ever atone for the fact, of course, that one section of the Jewish population is helping to transport the majority out of the country. History will pass judgment in due course" (EH, 541; H'83, 166).

On July 23, 1942, Etty Hillesum prayed for Spier in her diary. He was in bad health, and she feared that he would soon die. She asked God not to take him away from her but also realized that such pleas went against her own beliefs (EH, 529; H'83, 160).

She reread her old diaries and was tempted to throw them away because she felt they were so immature. But she decided to keep them anyway, for later; they could be used to reestablish contact with herself when the hardship and desensitization ended.

This notebook was not filled entirely. There are about ten blank pages in the back.

NOTEBOOK ELEVEN: SEPTEMBER 15–OCTOBER 13, 1942

There is a gap of a few weeks between the last entry in the previous notebook and the first in this new notebook. Most likely her job at the Jewish Council and Spier's illness prevented her from writing. She volunteered to work for the Jewish Council in Westerbork and spent the first two weeks of August 1942 in the transit camp. In the third week she was given leave. She spent part of the time with her parents in Deventer and the rest in Amsterdam. She wrote that the preceding two months had been the most intense and richest of her entire life. She hardly wrote during that period. Her last entry in the previous notebook was dated July 29, 1942. The first entry in notebook eleven is dated September 15, 1942. "Perhaps, oh God, everything happening together like that was a little hard" (EH, 543; H'83, 167). She had fallen ill.

> I shall follow the tried and true method, talking to myself now and again on these faint blue lines. And talking to you, God. Is that all right? Leaving people aside, I only feel a need to speak to you. I love people so dearly, because in every human being I love something of you. And I seek you everywhere in them and often do find something of you.
>
> (EH, 543–544; H'83, 168; adapt. MH)

She wrote a lot that day: morning, afternoon and evening. At 1 A.M. she started to address Spier: "I once wrote that I wanted to read your life all the way through, including the last page. Now I have done just that" (EH, 545; H'83, 169; adapt. MH).

Spier had died that night. Hillesum said farewell to him in her diary and thanked him for everything he had done for her. She had experienced Spier as a mediator between herself and God; his death meant she would relate to God directly (EH, 545–546; H'83, 169). The diary entries from the period after Spier's death are almost all directly addressed to God. "Talking to you, God. Is that all right? Leaving people aside, I only feel a need to speak to you" (EH, 544; H'83, 168; adapt. MH).

She felt that she was left with God.

Spier's passing and her sojourn in Westerbork had exhausted her. It was midway through September, and her leave was over, but she was too ill to return to Westerbork and remained in Amsterdam. Because she worked for the Jewish Council and enjoyed privileges, her leave was extended. She detested the fact that she was ill, because she longed to go back to Westerbork. Her diary is filled with memories of the precious time she spent at the camp. She most wanted to be "the thinking heart of the barracks" (EH, 545; H'83, 169), but she also realized she would be a burden on the community if she went back ill. She fought her illness and battled with her rebelliousness:

> I ought not to make any demands. I must let things take their course and that's what I am trying to do with all my might.
> Not *my* will, but Thy will be done.
>
> (EH, 575; H'83, 190; adapt. MH)

The last sentence in her eleventh and last surviving diary is: *"Man muss seine Pausen wahrhaben wollen!!!* [One must be willing to take a break]*"* (EH, 583; trans. MH). This had been one of Spier's sayings. She had certainly taken it to heart; she quoted it more than once in her diaries. With Spier gone and her illness continuing unabated, she tried with all her might to accept her convalescence in Amsterdam as God's will. However, she could not stop herself from praying and appealing to God to make her better and send her back to Westerbork as soon as possible. She was determined not to evade what she saw as the common fate awaiting the Jews. She wanted to chronicle it and to help others. She saw it as her task to do what Spier had done for her: to mediate between human beings and God.

Her last entry is dated October 13, 1942. By November 20 she had recovered enough to return to Westerbork. However, due to the worsening conditions in the camp and her own physical weakness, she lasted only two weeks and had to return to Amsterdam for six months. On June 5, 1943, Etty Hillesum went back to Westerbork for the last time. It is unlikely that she did not keep a diary in the first half of 1943, but none has survived.

Etty Hillesum's Letters

The surviving letters and postcards from Etty Hillesum—around seventy in all—were written either in Amsterdam or Westerbork. Most of her Amsterdam letters were sent to Westerbork. They were addressed to Osias Kormann, whom she befriended during her stay at the camp. Most of Hillesum's letters from Westerbork were addressed to her housemates and friends in Amsterdam.

My description of Hillesum's correspondence begins with a letter to Hanneke Starreveld, quoted in full. It has never been published before, not even in the "complete" edition of Hillesum's writings. The undated letter reads:

Friday afternoon

Hanneke, you won't get angry with me, will you? I wanted to say some things to you. And please know that my intentions are good, even if the words I choose leave something to be desired, I still don't know at all how to say this. Because I have seen your face so much more relaxed and happier than when I saw you the past few times, I feel a great and honest need to talk to you. Sometimes I think you are on the wrong path again. How am I to account for these heavy words? Perhaps I am putting it too strongly if I say that, on a day like today, you look like you are constantly bumping into something that hurts. You look like you are frantically trying to find something but can't (even though there probably was a time when you had it). No, you don't look very happy then—while I know you with such a different expression. Which is why I feel the need to write to you. Had a stranger seen you this afternoon, he would have turned to me and said, "What's gotten into you? There goes a lively young woman, taking a stroll with her little boy and enjoying good poetry, so what makes you think she is unhappy?"

Immediately after you had left, the following came from my fountain pen in my illegible scribblings—now that I read it again, I think it was definitely not very well put, but my intentions are clear, so I will copy it down anyway—"Behind Hanneke's 'wanting-to-grow' there is such a strong drive and such ambition." But the point is not to seek rapid growth, no, the point is to unfurl slowly. I don't believe anyone has their peak or perfection ahead of them. Everyone has already experienced that, somewhere in the middle of their life or in their childhood, and they have gone past it. And as for growth, isn't that the same as trying to realize your own best moments? You are looking ahead, but shouldn't you sometimes be looking back and inside more?

Sometimes, Hanneke, I think that this ambition, wherever it comes from, often makes you overlook your own best and deepest moments and squander a lot of true happiness.

Sometimes I think that you are obsessed with the idea of having to make intellectual progress (by means of new ideas, books, lectures), while, if you would only listen patiently to what is going on inside you, you would find that you have made much more progress than you are giving yourself credit for now. (If only, in 10 years time, I could express these things as clearly and simply as I feel them now.)

Don't misunderstand me, Hanneke, I will never say that a human being shouldn't read books or try to gain new insights, but sometimes I think that you are going about it in a way that is actually hindering your inner growth rather than helping it, which is why deep down inside you remain dissatisfied. I know this so well from my own experience, from how I used to be. I know that by ending this spontaneous note here, I am stopping at a point when I should start, really, but I will leave it at this anyway for today. You're not just a casual visitor to me, and it unsettles me when I get the feeling that you are not at peace with yourself, while that is exactly what we are striving for. So, will you please pay attention to my intentions only? And you understand what they are, don't you?

In friendship

And if I'm barking up the wrong tree entirely, than please forgive me.

Etty

(trans. MH)

Starreveld came across this letter while sorting out her correspondence in the late summer of 1993.[14]

LETTERS FROM AMSTERDAM: AUGUST 1941–JULY 1942

The first three surviving letters are probably dated early August 1941. They were written partly in German and addressed to Julius Spier. Parts of these letters were incorporated in the dairy. The letters show Hillesum's admiration, love, and gratitude for everything Spier had done for her. His therapy and friendship had made her feel much better than she had been in the six months before they first met: "A kind of miracle happened to me. I think of S. with a quiet, deep love that is neither erotic nor being in love" (EH, 588; trans. MH).

Even her letters to her friends are full of him. In early 1942 she wrote to her fellow student Aimé van Santen. This letter is full of quotations from Spier, which she copied from her diary, because she thought they might help Aimé. Netty van der Hof, an acquaintance, received a letter full of good advice that was obviously inspired by Spier.

One of the surviving letters was written to Gera Bongers, a member of the "Spier club," the circle of people around Spier. In this letter, Etty described how she celebrated her first birthday, meaning February 3, 1942, the first anniversary of the day she met Spier. She also wrote what she had brought him as a present: "A big yellow envelope, containing my annual report; 15 pages from a notepad, written in calligraphy that cost me blood, sweat, and tears" (EH, 593; trans. MH).

The eighth and last letter from this period is again addressed to Spier and probably dates from July 1942. Hillesum wrote to say she would no longer be able to spend as much time with him, most likely because of her job with the Jewish Council. It is apparent from her letter that Spier had already fallen ill.

LETTERS FROM AMSTERDAM TO OSIAS KORMANN: AUGUST 1942

In late July 1942, Etty Hillesum was, at her own request, assigned to the Jewish Council department in charge of "Social Care for People in Transit." This meant she could leave for Westerbork, which she considered a privilege. She spent the first two weeks of August in the camp, where she met Osias Kormann, a Jewish refugee from Poland.[15] While on leave in Amsterdam, she wrote him two letters. They show that she had become very attached to Kormann in the short time she had known him and that she was anxious to return. On August 21 she returned to Westerbork, but in early September, she had to go back to Amsterdam again.

LETTERS FROM AMSTERDAM: SEPTEMBER–NOVEMBER 1942

All but one of the letters from this period are addressed to Osias Kormann. The first letter, dated September 11, 1942, was addressed to Tideman. It is Hillesum's ode to her "Dear big Tide-woman" (EH, 602; trans. MH). The letter expresses deep gratitude toward Tide and Spier, whom Hillesum considered her spiritual teachers. The letter also shows that Hillesum had accepted that her great friend was about to die. A few days later she wrote to Kormann in Westerbork to say that Spier had passed away. She added that she was physically in such bad shape that she was not yet able to return to Westerbork. She mentioned her physical weakness again in her next letters to him, but she also wrote that she hoped to regain her strength soon because her heart was in the camp. She knew that the conditions at Westerbork were deteriorating because so many people were being brought there at the same time. Hillesum tried to give Kormann courage, and through him, she tried to do the same for other friends.

Like her last diaries these letters show what type of person Hillesum had become—for example, the way in which she ended one of her letters to Kormann: "I often think the only thing you can really do is to let what little good there is in you flow out in all directions. Everything else takes second place" (EH, 612; trans. MH).[16]

LETTERS FROM WESTERBORK: NOVEMBER 1942

In late November, Hillesum was finally able to resume her duties in Westerbork. But only three days after her arrival, on November 23, 1942, she wrote to Wegerif and friends that she was not functioning well physically and might have to leave again soon. A few days later she wrote to the same people:

I find it impossible to write here, not for lack of time but because of all the different impressions I'm bombarded with. I'm sure I could talk for a year on end just about this one week. I am on the leave list for next Saturday. What a privilege to be able to get away from here and see you all again. I'm glad I didn't run away the first few days; once in a while I take to my bed for an hour, and then it's all right again.

(EH, 613; H'87, 16)

LETTERS FROM AMSTERDAM: DECEMBER 1942–MAY 1943

On December 5, 1942, she returned to Amsterdam. In late December, she wrote to Kormann, saying she had again been ill for a few weeks. Hillesum had been admitted to the hospital because of stomach pains. The likely cause was diagnosed as gallstones, a fact she treated with irony:

Yes, well: I'm living horizontally again, in the more or less companionable company of a gallstone. If this stone doesn't decide soon to dissolve somehow, it'll have to go to the hospital—and I will have to go with it. What is it my private patron saint has in mind for me?

(EH, 615; trans. MH)[17]

She wrote about the ironies of life; with so many Jews willing to give anything just to be admitted to an Amsterdam hospital so as to escape—only temporarily—deportation, she—who wanted nothing more than to go to Westerbork—ended up in a hospital bed.

In this period she wrote one of the two letters that would be published illegally a year later. Someone in Westerbork had asked her to report in writing on life in the camp. She wrote how hard it was to fulfill this task. What genre would be right to describe the indescribable?

One summer evening I sat eating red cabbage at the edge of the yellow lupin field that stretched from our dining hut to the delousing station, and with sudden inspiration I said, "One ought to write a chronicle of Westerbork." An older man to my left—also eating red cabbage—answered, "Yes, but to do that you'd have to be a great poet."

He is right; it would take a great poet. Little journalistic pieces won't do.　　　　　　　　　　　　　　　　　　　(EH, 618; H'87, 23)

Still she managed to describe Westerbork for pages and pages: the layout of the camp, the mud, the barbed wire, social life, the transports. But she always realized that words fell short: "Oh, you know, this is such a terribly sad and shameful piece of human history, that one does not know how to describe it. One is ashamed of having been present and not having been able to prevent it" (EH, 626; trans. MH).

Interspersed with the descriptions are pieces of her philosophy of life, so familiar from her diaries. Her aversion to hatred resurfaces in her letters:

> I know that those who hate have good reason to do so. But why should we always have to choose the cheapest and easiest way? It has been brought home forcibly to me here how every atom of hatred added to the world makes it an even more desolate place.
>
> (EH, 629; H'87, 36; adapt. MH)

Between January 16 and May 28, 1943, Hillesum wrote Kormann eleven letters from her bed in Amsterdam. These letters express her great friendship and interest in his life in Westerbork as well as her desire to return to the camp. The letters also mention her physical weakness.

In June 1943 she was finally well enough to go back to Westerbork. On June 5 she wrote a farewell letter to her friend Maria Tuinzing. The next day she left for Westerbork, this time for good (Hillesum 1986, xv).

LETTERS FROM WESTERBORK: JUNE–SEPTEMBER 1943

Just a few days later she wrote from Westerbork to Wegerif and friends:

> My very dear people,
>
> Did you go on waving to my two rosebuds for a long time? You were all so sweet to me; I held on to that thought during the whole train ride, but now the camp with its truly massive misery of transports coming and going has swallowed me whole again. I already feel like I have been here for a hundred years.   (EH, 639; H'87, 49; adapt. MH)

A few days later she wrote again, right after three thousand Jews had been deported to the East in cattle trains:

> Sometimes what goes on here seems totally unreal. I haven't been given any particular job, which suits me fine. I just wander around and find my own work. . . .
>
> The sky is full of birds, the purple lupins look so regal and peaceful, two little old women have sat down on the box for a chat, the sun is shining on my face—and right before our eyes, mass murder. The whole thing is simply beyond comprehension.
>
> I'm doing fine.   (EH, 642; H'87, 5–56; adapt. MH)

On Monday, June 21, 1943, she wrote to an acquaintance, Milli Ortmann, about "this, the darkest day of my life" (EH, 643; H'87, 57; adapt. MH). The previous night Liesl Levie had arrived in Westerbork with her husband and children. That morning Hillesum's parents and her younger brother, Mischa, had been deported from Amsterdam to Westerbork. Ortmann tried to get the

Hillesum family out of the camp on the basis of Mischa's musical genius. To make this possible the Hillesums were put on the so-called Barneveld list.[18] If the request was granted, they would be moved to Barneveld camp, where conditions were much better than in Westerbork. Mischa was given permission to go to Barneveld, but without his parents. He did not want to leave them, so he decided to stay in Westerbork, where he enjoyed certain privileges. Ortmann and her sister Grete Wendelsgelst tried to get Mischa's parents on the Barneveld list as well. In her letter to Ortmann, Hillesum emphasized that she wanted to stay in Westerbork under any circumstances and was not asking for a transfer for herself: "Remember: not me!" (EH, 644; H'87, 57). That same day Hillesum also wrote to Christine van Nooten, a teacher of Latin and Greek at the school she had attended and where her father, Dr. Levi Hillesum, had been the principal. Etty informed Van Nooten of the arrival of her parents and brother and asked her to send some food for them. A few days later she confessed to Wegerif: "I can see in myself the effects of worry about the family. It gnaws at you worse than anything else" (EH, 647; H'87, 61).

She wrote about daily routines and problems and that she was doing well:

> And in spite of everything you always end up with the same conviction: Life is good after all,* it's not God's fault that things go awry sometimes, the cause lies in ourselves. Of this I am still convinced, even now, even as I'm about to be packed off to Poland with my entire family.   (EH, 648; H'87, 63; adapt. MH)

In late June, Hillesum wrote letters to Wegerif, Ortmann, and Van Nooten, all of whom tried to give the family both material and spiritual support by sending letters, food packages, and other goods. For example, Van Nooten sent them goggles to protect them from the sand, dust, and dirt that blew in from the heath and caused eye infections (Hillesum 1986, 796).

In early July she reported that her privileges would soon be withdrawn, once the Westerbork branch of the Jewish Council was dissolved. This would make her a "regular" Westerbork inmate. She would no longer be allowed to leave the camp or to send and receive an unlimited number of letters.

In her letters she asked for baked goods, which she hoped might still be available in Amsterdam or Deventer. She did this for her mother, realizing full well that life outside Westerbork was not easy either. She was apologetic about these requests: "Sorry about this, but it isn't for myself" (EH, 655; H'87, 75; adapt. MH).

---

*While Anne Frank's "In spite of everything . . ." is so often misinterpreted because it is quoted out of context, Hillesum writes this so often that it was clearly her conviction.

Hillesum knew that as a *Kampinsassin* [camp inmate], she would be allowed to write only once every fortnight. Before her status changed Hillesum wrote a long letter to Klaas and Johanna Smelik; Klaas was a man with whom she had a love affair with when she was younger, and Johanna was his daughter, whom Hillesum later befriended. She gave them a description of camp life and the deportation trains to the East, wondering how many people would survive such a journey. She also wrote about the humor she shared with her father, and about her philosophies and fantasies of life:

> We may suffer, but we must not succumb. And if we should survive these times unscathed in body and soul, but above all in soul, without bitterness and without hatred, then we are entitled to have our say after the war. Maybe I am an ambitious woman: I would like to have just a tiny little bit of say. . . .
>
> I shall try to convey to you how I feel, only I am not sure if my metaphor is right. When a spider spins its web, does it not cast the main threads ahead of itself, and then climb along? The main path of my life stretches ahead of me, like a long journey, and already extends into another world. It is just as if I have already digested everything that is happening here and that is yet to happen. As if I had been through it and come to terms with it already, and was now helping to build a new and better society, beyond this one.
>
> (EH, 657; H'87, 78; adapt. MH)

She also wrote another long letter to Wegerif in the first week of July 1943. She was almost unable to bear the repeated nightmare of the weekly transports and her incessant worries about her parents and Mischa:

> The hardest labor camp is better than this suspense every week. It didn't bother me so much before, because I had accepted the fact that I would be going to Poland. But living in fear for your loved ones, knowing that they are headed for infinite suffering that will make life here look idyllic, is something you can't bear for long. I sometimes feel like quietly packing my backpack and getting onto the next transport to the East. But enough; it's not right for a human being to take the easy way out. (EH, 658–659; H'87, 80–81; adapt. MH)

She also wrote that she had fainted and that her eczema was acting up again. In this long letter she tried to convey an image of herself and Westerbork:

> One could write fairy tales here. It sounds strange, but if you wanted to convey something of Westerbork life, the best way to do it would be in a fairy tale. The misery here is so hyperreal that it has become unreal. Sometimes I walk through the camp laughing secretly to myself because of the completely grotesque circumstances. One would have

to be a very great poet indeed to describe them; perhaps in about ten years I could give it a try. (EH, 662; H'87, 88; adapt. MH)

She was interrupted "right in the middle of the fairy tales." The letter was obviously written in different places, in a few moments of privacy she managed to steal. "Ah, children, we live in a strange world—It is a complete madhouse here; we will be ashamed of it for the next three centuries" (EH, 663; H'87, 89; adapt. MH).

Hillesum constantly wrote to Ortmann and Van Nooten to ask for the necessities that were lacking in Westerbork, such as powdered soap and food for her parents. She also wrote that it was becoming increasingly difficult to keep her parents in Westerbork.

> Oh, Christine, if only they could stay here in case nothing comes of Barneveld. They might stand a chance of surviving here with the help of the outside world, however difficult everything may be. But once they're on that train, I expect nothing but endless suffering.
> (EH, 667; H'87, 92–93; adapt. MH)

In a letter to Ortmann, Hillesum communicated that her attempts to get Mischa and her parents transferred to Barneveld seemed to be futile. She tried to accept her parents' impending deportation.

By then she was allowed to write only one letter or two postcards every two weeks (EH, 673). She dealt with this restriction by sending one letter to a friend or acquaintance with the request to pass the letter on to others (EH, 677; H'87, 108). Once in a while she managed to have an illegal letter smuggled out of the camp.

In her letter of early July 1943, Hillesum had described her fear that her parents were about to be deported. This fear gave way to more optimism in her letters of late July and early August. One reason for this optimism would have been the fact that no deportations took place between July 20 and August 24 (Hillesum 1986, 805). The Westerbork inmates were given a breather, and Hillesum, too, took a physical and mental break. In this period she wrote a letter to Tideman:

> Darling Tide,
> I thought at first I'd have to skip my writing today, because I'm so terribly tired, and also because I thought I would have nothing to say this time. But of course I have a great deal to write about, but I'd rather let my thoughts freely go out to you; you're bound to pick them up anyway. This afternoon I was resting on my bunk, and suddenly I just had to write the following thoughts in my diary; now I send them to you:

"You have made me so rich, O God, please let me share out your beauty with open hands. My life has become an uninterrupted dialogue with you, O God, one long dialogue. Sometimes when I stand in some corner of the camp, my feet planted on your earth, my eyes raised toward your heaven, tears run down my face, tears of deep emotion and gratitude. At night, too, when I lie in my bed and rest in you, O God, tears of gratitude run down my face, and that is my prayer."

(EH, 682; H'87, 116; adapt. MH)

This letter indicates that Hillesum kept a diary in Westerbork, but none of her camp diaries have survived (Hillesum 1986, 806).

On August 24, 1943, she wrote a very moving letter to Wegerif about everything involved in preparing a transport to the East. This was the first deportation after the month in which no trains had left for the East. As the letter clearly shows, the regime as more vicious than ever:

There was a moment when I felt in all seriousness that after this night, it would be a sin ever to smile again. But then I reminded myself that some of those who had gone away had been smiling, even if only a handful of them this time. . . . And some of them might perhaps even smile in Poland too, though not many from this transport, I think. . . .

I have told you often enough that no words and images are adequate to describe nights like these. But still I must try to convey something of it to you. One always has the feeling here of being the ears and eyes of a piece of Jewish history, and there is also the need sometimes to be one small voice. We must keep each other informed of everything happening in the various corners of this world, everyone has to tell his part so that after the war, the story will be complete.

(EH, 686–687; H'87, 124; adapt. MH)

She described how the sick, the elderly, the handicapped, as well as babies and pregnant women, were driven into the cattle cars.

Whenever misfortune strikes, people have a natural instinct to lend a helping hand and save what can be saved. But tonight I shall be helping to dress babies and to calm mothers—and that is what I call "lending a helping hand." I could almost curse myself for it. We all know that we are yielding up our sick and defenseless brothers and sisters to hunger, heat, cold, exposure, and destruction, and yet we dress them and escort them to the bare cattle cars—and if they can't walk, we carry them on stretchers. What is going on, what conundrums are these, in what sort of fatal mechanism have we become enmeshed? . . .

If I were to say that I was in hell that night, what would I really be telling you? I said it aloud to myself once, that night, concluding almost soberly, "So, this is what hell is like."

(EH, 688–689; H'87, 126–127; adapt. MH)

Hillesum described the vulnerability and the fear but also the courage of the deportees. She also described the "green-uniformed men":

> On earlier transports, some of the guards were simple, kindly types with puzzled expressions, who walked about the camp smoking their pipes and speaking in some incomprehensible dialect. One would have found their company not too objectionable on the journey. Now I am transfixed with terror. Oafish, jeering faces, in which one seeks in vain for even the slightest trace of humanity. At what fronts were they raised? In what punishment camps were they trained?
>
> (EH, 694; H'87, 134; adapt. MH)

She ended the letter with a description of how the doors of the freight cars were closed on the densely packed mass of people inside.

> There are just a few thousand of us left here. A hundred thousand Dutch members of our race are toiling away under an unknown sky or lie rotting in some unknown soil. We know nothing of their fate. It is only a short while perhaps before we find out, each one of us in his own time. For we are all marked to share that fate, of that I have not a moment's doubt.   (EH, 697–698; H'87, 139; adapt. MH)

In December 1943 this letter, along with Hillesum's letter from late December 1942 (EH, 616–629; H'87, 21–37), were published illegally and distributed throughout Nazi-occupied Holland.

Hillesum wrote another few letters to Van Nooten and one more to Tuinzing. In the first days of September, she sent another two postcards to thank people for parcels.

On Tuesday, September 7, 1943, the whole Hillesum family was deported, except for Jaap, who was still in Amsterdam. The pretext for their deportation was the letter that Etty's mother, Riva Hillesum-Bernstein, wrote to Hans Rauter (commissioner general of public safety and lieutenant general of police) in the Hague. She had requested a little more freedom of movement, like the privileges afforded her son Mischa. Infuriated by the Jewish woman's impertinence, Rauter ordered the immediate deportation of the entire family (Hillesum 1986, 809–810). Hillesum managed to throw two postcards out of the train, one addressed to her housemates in Amsterdam and one to Christine van Nooten (EH, 702; H'87, 146). This was the last sign of Hillesum.

The complete edition of Hillesum's diaries and letters also contains a letter from Hillesum's friend Jopie Vleeschhouwer, describing the Hillesums' departure from Westerbork. Hillesum had at first been taken aback when she found that she would be deported together with her family, because she found her parents' and brother's suffering unbearable. However, she recovered quickly and accepted the inevitable. While she took care of her family's luggage, friends packed her bag:

> And there she was, walking onto the "Transport Boulevard," which only fourteen days earlier she had described in her idiosyncratic and unforgettable way. She was cheerful, talking and smiling, with a kind word for everyone she encountered; she was full of sparkling humor, tinged with wistfulness, perhaps, but she was the Etty we all know and love. "I'm bringing my diaries and my Bibles and my Russian grammar and Tolstoy and I have no idea what else is in my bag."
>
> (Hillesum 1986, 711–712; trans. MH)

Chapter 5 ❧ *Chronicler*

In June 1943 Etty Hillesum left Amsterdam for Westerbork, this time for good. Before her departure she gave her diaries to her friend and housemate Maria Tuinzing. She asked Maria to give them to her friend Klaas Smelik, should she not survive the war. She hoped that Smelik, a writer, would be able to get the diaries published. In the 1950s Smelik approached various publishers but was turned down by every one of them.[1] Etty Hillesum's wish was not fulfilled until 1981, almost forty years after she left for Westerbork, when Smelik's son Klaas junior approached publisher J. Geurt Gaarlandt (Hillesum 1986, xvi). Initially Gaarlandt published selections from her diaries and recovered letters, which were translated into fourteen languages. In 1986 the complete works were published in Dutch. The books got an overwhelmingly large, and mostly positive, response. Hundreds of reviews and articles about Hillesum's work were published. In 1988 an international conference in Rome focused on her life and writings.[2] Playwrights, sculptors, and composers alike responded to her oeuvre.[3] In a reaction to this wave of publicity, Gaarlandt remarked:

> It is astonishing to read how many different facets there were to her life and work. Literary, mystical, philosophical, historical, theological, psychological and therapeutic associations have provided material for countless articles. Kafka, Meister Eckhart, . . . Kierkegaard, Dostoyevski, Rilke, Jung, Seneca, . . . Bonhoeffer: she is compared to and associated with all of these people, the great names from the worlds of literature, philosophy and theology. It has been said that her diaries should be considered one of the most important documents of this century.
>
> (Gaarlandt 1989, x; trans. MH)

My approach to Hillesum's work is not based on comparisons between Hillesum and like-minded thinkers.[4] Although such comparisons are often fruitful because of the new insights they can produce, they are also, in a sense, risky. In Hillesum's case the risk is that her writing will be incorporated into a certain school of thought or religious belief, and that, in the process, similarities will be overemphasized and differences overlooked. This could obstruct a clear view of the authenticity of her work. Incidentally, Etty Hillesum's writings would not be the first to be co-opted in this way; a comparison often becomes an annexation of the work. It is not uncommon for women's writing to be usurped by inclusion in a canon stressing its patriarchal lineage—a modus operandi that fits in with "reductive reasoning," in which similarities outweigh differences. Comparisons can be deadly: They fixate and categorize. The oft-reached conclusion that a literary work represents "a variation on a theme" foregrounds the familiar theme at the expense of the variation. I am interested in the variation, the difference, the "otherness" of the text.

Despite the avalanche of comparisons, however, some reviewers of Hillesum's work stressed its originality, such as the Dutch literary critic, Kees Fens:

> The writer cannot be pigeonholed. The originality and intensity of her life and thinking are so great that in the end, she leaves us puzzled. From quite a few angles, many people will be able to find quotations to support their own points of view, but those are contradicted elsewhere. Despite her religious personality, and her obviously great religious literacy—she repeatedly quotes the Bible and Saint Augustine—she ultimately cannot be categorized. She did not design a doctrine, nor did she write a philosophy. She wrote herself. She essayed herself on the empty pages of her diary, which is so personal that the reader cannot help feeling embarrassed now and then.
>
> (Fens 1989, 9; trans. MH; see also Reitsma 1989, 110)

I deal with the religious nature of the diaries and letters in the next chapter; the emphasis in this chapter is on the issue of authenticity. Hillesum's writerly authenticity can be found primarily in her keenly observant eye, combined with a great talent for writing.[5] These two closely linked elements are dynamic, not static, phenomena; they changed and developed over the course of time.

Hillesum was very observant, both of herself and her surroundings. In her second diary she wrote about this gift:

> I want . . . to become the chronicler of many things that are happening now. [. . .] I notice that, over and above all my subjective suffering, I have an irrepressible objective curiosity, a passionate interest in everything that touches this world and its people and my own motives. Sometimes I believe I am here on earth to carry out a certain task.

Everything that is happening around me has to crystallize in my mind so that, later, I can write it down. Poor head and poor heart, you two will go through so much more in this life. Lucky head and lucky heart, you also have a beautiful life.　　　　(EH, 91; H'83, 34; adapt. MH)

We saw in the previous chapter that when Etty Hillesum first started keeping a diary, she wrote mostly about herself. At first, her observational skills were inner-directed, aimed at solving her psychological problems. Once she had sorted herself out, she started focusing on the outside world. This is particularly clear in her letters from and about Westerbork.

This shift in emphasis from inner to outer world is attended by a change in writing mode. While Dutch literary critic Karel van het Reve confessed to being irritated by "the adolescent nature of the beginning of this diary," he praised the later diaries for their "simple and translucent prose" (Van het Reve 1989, 42–43). However, in his review Van het Reve neglected to mention that he had copied this criticism from Hillesum herself. In her second diary, for instance, she wrote: "My biggest problem is that I still can't say things, can't formulate them in such a way that the words become transparent and the reader can see through to the essence of what I'm saying. Put far too bluntly, girl" (EH, 88; trans. MH).

In her tenth notebook—hundreds of pages and almost a year later—she noted: "I started rereading my diaries and I must admit that I am sometimes embarrassed by the adolescent nonsense I wrote. I wanted to tear them all up" (EH, 537; trans. MH; see also Bendien 1989, 174–175).

Dutch novelist Marga Minco pointed to the improvement in Etty Hillesum's writing skills:

> Toward the end both tone and writing become increasingly serrated, particularly in the letters from Westerbork that were recovered later. It seems that she found her voice. She wrote: "And one other thing: I believe that I have finally reached that simplicity that I always longed for."
>
> The destiny she herself suspected, hoped for and anticipated was to one day be able to act as the "literary witness" of her time; this is clear from what she wrote on July 27, 1942: "Later, I will become the chronicler of our fate. I will forge a new language within me and I will safeguard it if I don't get a chance to write anything down."
>
> 　　　　　　　　　　　　　(Minco 1989, 4–5; EH, 527, 540; trans. MH)

What is the connection between this "new language" of which Hillesum wrote and the response to her diaries and letters—which made it clear that many people were deeply touched by the originality of her writing? Could the originality of her oeuvre be ascribed to this new, different language in which she expressed her thoughts and feelings? To explore these questions I make dual-purpose use of Hélène Cixous's critical works: First I employ her thoughts to provide answers to the above questions. At the same time, however, I try to elucidate Cixous's well-known but often vague concepts; the famous notion of *écriture féminine,* for example, is used constantly without any explanation of what Cixous actually means by it.

A Different Language

The question "How does the text affect me?" is both the foundation and the core of Hélène Cixous's approach to literature.[6] By starting with this question, Cixous deemphasizes the more common question about the meaning of the text. This reversal is not unusual for those working within the framework of a philosophy of difference. Traditionally, scientific and scholarly thought has revolved around the "'what is?' question" (Van der Haegen 1989, 18–21). This question was aimed at revealing the essence, the truth, the core of the matter. As far as literature was concerned, every poem and every novel was assumed to have a hidden meaning, which the author put there to be discovered by the serious reader. But modern literary theory holds different notions: "Reading is no longer a noncontextual, neutral activity, with the reader in the role of a well-drilled operator, decoding what is objectively present in the text" (Meijer 1988, 11; trans. MH).

Cixous's theory of reading runs along the same lines. She argues that reading should not be done from a position of mastery. Like other philosophers of difference, she places her main emphasis on the relativity of truth: "Truth is not a totalising concept" (Cixous 1990b, 28). A text does not contain a single, objectively verifiable meaning but is always open to multiple interpretations, which depend on the reader's individual position and situation (Van Heijst 1992, 178). So there is no such thing as an objective reader; she or he is necessarily a context-bound subject. The interpretation process is an interplay of numerous factors, conscious or unconscious, explicit or implicit: class, age, gender, ethnicity, and religion. Meaning is not a static given anchored in the text but a dynamic process that evolves from the reader's engagement with the text. In this type of reader-response theory, the emphasis is no longer on the text in isolation; instead attention is turned to the process that takes place between reader and text. In other words, modern literary theory foregrounds "the reader's encounter with the text" (Meijer 1988, 56). This is not just a shift from objectivity to subjectivity. Although there may be as many interpretations of the text as there are readers, the personal is always shared with others too (Meijer 1988, 66). When one focuses on the question "How does the text affect me?", deferring the issue of what the text means, the contextuality of textual interpretations is recognized and accentuated.

In Dutch literary theory Maaike Meijer has provided the beginnings of an answer to the question "How does the text affect me?" She describes the reading process in terms of discontinuity rather than continuity or recognition (Meijer 1988, 14; Van Heijst 1992, 90–91). The reader's experience of being moved by a text cannot be explained as a case of identification with the text. That would be too simple. After all, it is often not the familiar and known in a text but rather the strange and unknown that touches the reader. Could Meijer's remarks about poetry apply to other texts as well, such as Hillesum's diaries and letters?

> When a reader is deeply touched by a poem, this reader accepts a poetic view of reality as the mold for the still wordless mass she knows resides somewhere in her innermost being. This may seem like "recognition," but actually we are moved by a text when our inner amorphousness finds shape, when it is born into language. A poem can say what you would have liked to think. It can preconceive, preview, presense something for you. It can inwardly push you over the edge, it can radicalize a path already taken, it can fling you into the unimaginable. If a text said only what you already knew, reading would become superfluous.   (Meijer 1988, 14–15; trans. MH)

An interpretation aimed only at revealing "the" meaning would do injustice to many poems, and to Hillesum's oeuvre for that matter. Meijer calls this the paradox of interpretation (Meijer 1988, vol. 1); traditional interpretation strives for rationality, nonambiguity, and accuracy, and in so doing ignores the power of poetry, which lies in its "otherness," the strangeness of its language. But are these specific poetic features also what make her work so special? Is her writing seen as authentic because of its ungrammaticalities, because of the music in the letters? Or is it because of some other reason? My attempt to provide a more detailed analysis of the "otherness" of Hillesum's texts is based on Cixous's view of literature. She distinguishes between two modes of writing: a dominant and a marginal mode, calling the dominant one "masculine" and the marginal one "feminine." (In light of what follows, I must point out that "masculine" and "feminine" do not simply refer to a biological distinction, but first and foremost to the social constructs of femininity and masculinity, in other words: to gender.) These modes of writing have their roots in two possible outlooks on life. Cixous uses the terms "masculine libidinal economy" and "feminine libidinal economy," showing her familiarity with psychoanalysis. In her interpretation of sexual difference, she uses Freudian and Lacanian psychoanalytical concepts but gives them a completely new twist.

The "Pleasure Principle"

Whereas both Freud and Lacan were mainly concerned with describing existing structures and identities, Cixous's psychoanalytical discourse is aimed more at exploring possibilities for change. Out of political and ethical principles, she refuses to accept the existing power structures as givens because they fundamentally exclude women.

According to Cixous both Freud and Lacan only noticed the most obvious structure of living and thinking, which she herself describes as the "masculine libidinal economy": Men's wishes, desires, and needs dominate cultural exchange. Freud's and Lacan's pyschoanalysis has made it abundantly clear that this masculine discourse is to a great extent determined by the fear of castration. The masculine economy is based on the fear of death; it is an economy of defying death. It is in a sense capitalist in nature; it is a practice of appropriation, whose creed— "more is better"—justifies the accumulation of wealth. Cixous has described this relationship between people, and between people and material possessions, as the realm of ownership: "We are still living in the Empire of the Selfsame [*Propre*]. The same masters dominate history from the beginning, inscribing on it the marks of their appropriating economy: history, as a story of phallocentrism, hasn't moved except to repeat itself" (Cixous 1986a, 79 [1975a]).[7]

This realm revolves around one focus: the same, the self, one's own, and ownership. It is an economy of conservation, of small-mindedness, in which strategic, calculating behavior is aimed at maximum profit, power, and results.

While Freud used the Greek oedipal myth to illustrate his arguments, Cixous makes use of an old Chinese fable:

> The Chinese king asks General Sun Tse, who is known for his excellence in training soldiers, to form an army out of his 180 wives. Sun Tse lines the women up in two rows, each headed by one of the king's two favorite wives. He teaches them the language of the drumbeat: two beats—right, three beats—left, four beats—about face. The women, however, do not listen to the general at all. They are far too busy laughing and chattering. The general repeats his lessons a few times, but to no avail. The more he talks, the more the women double up with laughter. Such behavior is tantamount to mutiny, and punishable by

death. The king hears of this and is most displeased that all his wives
have been sentenced to death. But Sun Tse remains firm and tells the
king: "You put me in charge of turning your wives into soldiers and I
am carrying out that order." Sun Tse is a man of absolute principle.
He obeys the law, which prescribes that his two favorite wives be put
to death. He beheads them with his saber and replaces them with two
others. Sun Tse then repeats the exercise; now the women obey him
absolutely. As if they have never done anything but practice the art of
war, they turn right, left, and about face, precisely on the drumbeat and
without a single mistake.   (Cixous 1981b, 42 [1974])

Cixous believes that Sun Tse exemplifies the masculine libidinal economy,
as he lives on/by the beat of the drum: Counting, calculating, and strategic
thinking are his forte. This masculine order leaves women little choice:
"castration or decapitation" (Cixous 1981b [1974]). Masculine fear of castration
is taken out on women by either desexualizing or decapitating them, by taking away their sex or beheading them. The moral of the story is that women
cannot win; either they literally lose their head by the sword, or they live
on—but without their self-esteem, their identity: "Women have no choice other
than to be decapitated, and in any case the moral is that if they don't actually
lose their heads by the sword, *they only keep them on condition that they lose
them*—lose them, that is, to complete silence, turned into automatons" (Cixous
1981b, 42–43 [1974]; italics in original).[8]

Women are turned into robots, willing instruments at the service of male
institutions. Their otherness is banished. The Chinese fable illustrates that
the feminine libidinal economy knows a different way of communicating:
exchange rather than cold calculation, pleasure instead of profit. This fable
describes the feminine in positive terms: happiness, vivacity. Unlike Freud
and Lacan, who always associate the feminine with the negative, the lack, the
absence, the shortcoming, Cixous places the feminine libidinal economy elsewhere: It is the affirmation and the source of life.

Fear of death is alien to women; men teach it to them. The feminine
economy has more to do with abundance, with sharing, living and
laughing. The feminine economy is therefore an economy of positive
lack. It is an economy that knows loss of self, because risks are taken;
this includes the risk of leaving oneself, of spilling over into an other,
of overextending oneself, of overindulging. The other and otherness
are not feared as they are in the masculine economy. There is room for
freedom, including the other's freedom. The other and otherness are
left intact, respected. This is not a life-and-death battle for appropriation but the playful game of differences: "[E]ach would take the risk of

other, of difference, without feeling threatened by the existence of an otherness, rather, delighting to increase through the unknown that is there to discover, to respect, to favor, to cherish."

(Cixous 1986a, 78 [1975a])[9]

While in the masculine libidinal economy differences are hierchically arranged, the feminine libidinal economy leaves room for the other to take a position of equality. There is more tolerance, more room for the other's movements. Because this economy is much less egocentric, this way of living attests to humility, to meekness (Cixous 1988a, 25), to the awareness of being part of a cosmic universe.

The feminine libidinal economy has a subtle relationship with ownership. Disconnection and separation are tolerated. It is not an economy of appropriation but of giving and the gift. In the masculine economy the gift is suspect because it creates inequality and upsets the balance of power; in the feminine economy the gift is a generous gesture, a pleasurable deed of magnanimity, signifying abundance.[10]

The Other Bisexuality

The feminine libidinal economy is not exclusively for women; nor is the masculine libidinal economy only for men. These two economies are two ways of living, greedily or generously, which can be practiced by any human being. "The other economy" is called feminine because women are more open to it, for various reasons. Basing her argument on both sex and gender, Cixous has established a perceptive interconnection between the two economies and the sexes. Due both to biologically and culturally determined traits, women can more easily develop the feminine economy, while the masculine economy more often occurs in men. The most important reason is probably that women have always been "outside the law" and, therefore, have less experience living with the immediate threat of death, which is what the fear of castration really is. The cultural exclusion system makes it more likely that a so-called feminine economy can be found among women. Women's existence has not been marked by the death threat, but more by dispossession and un*self*ishness: "Already she is another" (Cixous 1986a, 90 [1975a]).[11] Even before birth woman is the other, because phallocentric culture forces her into the straitjacket of otherness. She is denied the right to become herself from the very beginning; woman is dependent on man, she is man's other. She is denied access to the cultural order; she is not called on to enter the symbolic order.[12] Women are not invited to the phallocentric party. However, if women miss the rites of passage, they are also spared the fear of castration. The fact that women suffer cultural oppression may be the very reason why they are more capable of giving than men are (Conley 1984, 18). This gives women the opportunity to develop a new mode of life: It is, after all, more acceptable for women not to want power, not to want to fight.

Another reason is biological. Inside and outside, self and other are less clearly separated in a woman's body. Perhaps this makes women less afraid of their inner beings and of the other: They are familiar with the inside of their bodies, and what is more, they have the opportunity to encounter the other within their bodies (for example, during pregnancy). A woman's relationship with another can be rooted in physical connection and life, in respect for the other. However, masculinity and femininity are only in a very limited sense biologically determined, and biological differences are not always signified culturally; for these very reasons Cixous does not exclude men from a feminine libidinal economy. On the contrary, she believes that this other economy was first introduced by men, to express their femininity. Cixous sees a far greater potential for reconciliation between men and women than does someone like Irigaray, for example.[13] To Cixous male and female biology do not form a binary opposition but are on a continuum. On one end of this continuum there are more men, while on the other there are more women, but no clear lines of demarcation can be drawn. Cixous recognizes the links, the similarities between men and women; they have their humanity in common. However, a similarity does not necessarily lead to straightforward identification (Cixous 1989a, 135). Cixous leaves room for both the similarities and the differences.

She developed these reflections on sexual difference in her response to Freud's notion of bisexuality, a notion she rejected. In her view male bisexuality differs from female bisexuality; here she resists Freud's tendency to level off the differences. Rather, Cixous advocates "maintaining and cultivating their differences" (Stevens 1989, 416; trans. MH) on the assumption that both sexes are capable of incorporating the other: Women can embody the masculine, men the feminine:

> Bisexuality on an unconscious level is the possibility of extending into the other, of being in such a relation with the other that I move into the other without destroying the other: that I will look for the other where s/he is without trying to bring everything back to myself.
>
> (Cixous 1981b, 55 [1974])[14]

The cultural taboo surrounding bisexuality is a different issue. Cixous wants this taboo discarded because she believes in the usefulness of bisexuality in her definition. She keeps pointing out that women do not own the feminine libido, just as the masculine libido is not exclusively men's property:

> What is most important for me, what allows me to continue to live and not to despair, is precisely the conviction that it does not depend on the anatomical sex, not on the role of man and of woman, but that it depends in fact on life's chance, which is everybody's responsibility.
>
> (Cixous 1984, 133)

But what does Cixous mean when she posits that libidinal economies depend on life's chances?

The School of Loss

Some people are given the chance, or are fated, to enter "the school of losing" (Cixous 1988b, 150). Usually more women than men attend this special school, because culture is more likely to place women on the side of lack and reticence: "Now if you are a woman, you are always nearer to and farther from loss than a man is. More and less capable of loss. More attracted, more repulsed" (Cixous 1991a, 39 [1976]).[15]

At the school of loss (or losing), students are taught to mourn. They are taught to put a positive spin on a lack: how to transform loss into a virtue. Cixous, who believes that life can be an "education in loss," often questions the author's "education" in her textual analyses. In the 1985–86 academic year, she dealt with this question in her biweekly seminars, discussing texts inspired by "homelessness": "The majority of the texts we will work with this year, were written because of, result from, homelessness. They owe their existence to homelessness" (Cixous, seminar 10/20/1985; trans. MH).[16]

During that year Cixous regularly referred to Etty Hillesum. Although she described Hillesum's texts as poetically imperfect (a point I will return to later), she also called them unforgettable. Hillesum, she said, had discovered the secrets of life precisely because she was writing in the face of death (Cixous 1992, 113). As a Jewish woman Hillesum graduated from the school of loss and learned to assign a positive meaning to lack. Cixous is convinced that the experience of loss and mourning can make one aware of life's riches. Through one's having to let go, to part with one's possessions, it is possible to gain a deeper understanding of the wealth and joys of living. In this context, Cixous called Hillesum's diaries and letters a "bible of *savoir vivre*" (Cixous 1992, 122, seminar 11/23/1985), a text that bespeaks the art of enjoying life, as the following quotation makes clear:

Every clean blouse I put on is a kind of celebration. And so is every occasion I have to wash with scented soap in a bathroom I have all to myself for a precious half-hour. It's as if I were reveling in these civilized luxuries for the last time. But even if I have to forgo them one day, I shall always know that they exist and that they can make life pleasant and I shall think of them as a great boon even if I can't share in them any longer. For whether or not I share in them isn't really the point, is it?   (EH, 493; H'83, 135–136; adapt. MH)

Hillesum mourned for all the blessings of civilization, for although she was still surrounded by them, she knew this would not last. Cixous points out that Hillesum turned an everyday act into a ceremony, a celebration of joys, and a valediction to pleasure. In recounting all her losses, she was also counting her blessings. The hundreds of diary pages that Etty Hillesum wrote at her desk in Amsterdam before she was sent to Westerbork reflect the process that shaped her ultimate outlook on life. She had to work hard to let go of the people and material possessions around her. Particularly from Hillesum's first diary, it is clear that she had been a "greedier" person.

The Difference Between Then and Now[17]

Hillesum described February 3, 1941, as the day of her rebirth (EH, 255). That was the date on which she had first met Spier, her beloved friend and therapist, who influenced her deeply. He was helping her to overcome her physical complaints and depressions. When writing about her tense, fearful, and possessive way of life, she wrote mainly in the past tense. It was a way of life she had put behind her, outgrown. With Spier's therapeutic help, she was only just beginning to explore a life of inner freedom and trust. Full of euphoria, she greeted this new disposition as a better one, as a new energy she was collecting within her and giving off (EH, 28). It was as if her encounter with Spier had pushed her into another libidinal economy. She experienced the changes that were taking place within her as true revolutions:

Dear me, I used to be such a poor wretch compared to now. Let me appreciate this one last time, because soon this will be my normal state of being. . . . I used to be afraid all the time that my powers would desert me, and then they did desert me, of course. Now I don't think about that anymore, and my energy is simply replenished for every task that I take on. Some sort of miracle has happened to me.
                                        (EH, 15; trans. MH)

Particularly in the first diary, she repeatedly compared her old outlook on life with the new. She was in the middle of a transition from one state of consciousness to another. The old patterns had not disappeared entirely; once in a while she still regressed to her own "darkest Middle Ages" (EH, 148; trans. MH). A pressing question ran through her mind, blocking her thoughts and paralyzing her actions: "Is it all worth it, really?" (EH, 38; trans. MH). She discovered that this big question was actually a void, but she was still haunted by it occasionally. At these moments she felt discontented and suffered from "the feeling that everything was devoid of meaning, the sense that life was unfulfilled, all that pointless brooding" (EH, 45; H'83, 16; adapt. MH). These mood swings can easily be linked to the characteristics of what Cixous calls the masculine libidinal economy. It is the economy of shortcomings, the fear of missing out on something. Hillesum wanted her life to be so full of living and peacefulness that there would simply be no room for questioning its meaning. With all her might, and inspired by Spier, she battled her fears and tensions. She consciously learned to live in the present; by carefully and attentively carrying out her daily tasks, she learned to experience the fullness of the moment. This filled her life and dispelled her fears and uncertainty about the future. She tried to go with life's flow and not to worry too much. This was difficult, especially in wartime, something she was well aware of: "For that is quite a feat: to be truly, inwardly happy, to accept God's world and to enjoy, without turning a blind eye to all the suffering that is going on" (EH, 47; trans. MH).

The outside world had little positive news to offer. In 1941 the Nazi extermination machine was gaining momentum in the Netherlands. On Wednesday, March 19, 1941, Hillesum complied with the decree that "everyone of Jewish or partly Jewish descent" (Hillesum 1986, 724) report to the authorities. She was well aware of the fate awaiting the Jews (EH, 33). However, she shifted the emphasis to her inner life, which enabled her, that same afternoon, to write the following cheerful passage:

> Life is good. I have now achieved something that I used to strive for with all my might, but could not find, namely to be completely focused on, and fulfilled by that which I am doing at any one time; while enjoying the peaceful certainty lying dormant in my subconscious that, afterwards, new tasks will await me, and that these will again fulfill me completely. And so, life has suddenly become very full.
>
> (EH, 34; trans. MH)

By then she was living life quite differently. This can be seen in the shift away from emptiness and toward fullness, or rather toward experiencing the fullness of the void. However, something else was changing too: her inner-directedness. More than ever she was starting to feel like a part of a cosmic whole. One of the first discoveries she made about herself had to do with greed:

> And here I have hit upon something essential. Whenever I saw a beautiful flower, what I longed to do was press it to my heart or eat it all up. It was more difficult with a piece of beautiful scenery, but the feeling was the same. I was too sensual, I would almost say too greedy. I yearned physically for all I thought was beautiful, wanted to own it. . . . It all suddenly changed, by what inner process God only knows, but it is different now.   (EH, 25; H'83, 10–11; adapt. MH)

In *I Love to You* Luce Irigaray describes the image of Buddha and the flower to illustrate the convergence of sensuality and spirituality. Buddha looks at the flower but does not pick it. He enjoys without possessiveness: "He gazes at what is other to him without uprooting it" (Irigaray 1996, 24).[18] Sensuality need not be sacrificed to spirituality, as so often happens in Western culture; instead it can be cultivated as a spiritual source of energy. Hillesum gradually grew toward an outlook that could be called a feminine libidinal economy. She continued to enjoy, but without the need to possess, even at the erotic and sexual level. She did not reject eroticism or physical pleasure, only their attending possessiveness. She strove to love without wanting to own. Irigaray gave voice to this outlook in the title of one of her recent publications: *I Love to You* may be grammatically incorrect, but it springs from Irigaray's search for a different declaration of love, since "I love you" exhibits too many characteristics of the ownership economy. In this grammatically correct sentence, "you" is reduced to the object. In the poetically ungrammatical "I love to you," "you" becomes an indirect object and the preposition "to" creates space between subject and object, leaving room for respect. Etty Hillesum noticed that she had learned to enjoy without wanting to possess:

> And this greed, which is the best way I have of describing it, suddenly fell away from me. A thousand tyrannical chains were broken and I breathed freely again and felt strong and looked about with shining eyes. And now that I don't want to own anything any more and I am free, now I suddenly own everything, now my inner riches are immeasurable.   (EH, 26; H'83, 12; adapt. MH)

Here she was a bit too optimistic. The change did not happen overnight. She continued to struggle with her possessiveness; in writing she tried to develop in the right direction. At one point she confessed to having "eating problems"; sometimes she binged, even though she was not hungry and knew she would end up with a stomachache. She put this uncontrollable gluttony in a wider perspective: "Ultimately it is purely symbolic. Greed probably figures in my intellectual life as well, as I attempt to absorb a massive amount of information with consequent mental indigestion" (EH, 153; H'83, 49).

A memory surfaced of her mother, at some social occasion with other housewives, completely engrossed in eating. Etty watched her mother's total abandon and was horrified by the image. Looking back, she realized that her mother had been driven by fear: "That fear of missing out on things makes you miss out on everything. Keeps you from reality" (EH, 154; H'83, 49).

Etty's mother was a Russian Jew who had fled the pogroms in her country and moved to the Netherlands when she was still young. She had more than enough reason to be terrified. Even though history threatened to repeat itself, Hillesum resisted. She did not want to follow in her mother's footsteps, even if the outward circumstances were the same. She wanted to face and conquer her fears and to be happy without possessions. She had once wanted to understand, absorb, and subjugate everything. "And the dead simple fact is that now I undergo everything" (EH, 27; trans. MH). This does not mean that she became passive. Time and again she fought for human values, an uphill battle in that particular period. She was trying to distance herself from Nazism, a completely derailed version of the masculine libidinal economy. Hatred in particular was something she fought with every fiber in her body: "One thing is certain: you should help increase the stock of love on this earth. Every ounce of hatred you add to the excess of hatred makes this world more inhospitable and uninhabitable" (EH, 497; trans. MH).

While the mechanisms of hatred held society in their grip, Etty Hillesum focused on love. Nazi bigotry caused many in Holland, even among her own circle of friends, to despise the Germans. Sometimes she went along with this but afterward disliked herself for not resisting. She tried to unlearn this behavior (EH, 22–23). Rather than racism and xenophobia, she advocated respect for the other. She took this outlook on life very far, so far that many people could no longer follow her. She accepted everyone for what they were, even those who embraced Nazism. She propagated compassion rather than hatred:

> To put it very bluntly, at the risk of hurting my fountain pen: even if an SS officer were kicking me to death, I would look up into his face and wonder, full of fearful disbelief and human interest: My God, man, what terrible things happened to you in your life that you do these things? (EH, 23; trans. MH)

She fought demoralization and destruction with her fountain pen. She upended the world. Uninterested in the grand and massive scale, she focused on details and individuals. While the Nazis were planning a mass murder she knew was inescapable, she emphasized the individual. Turning away from those who clamored about the war and violence, she argued for turning inward:

> The rottenness of others is in us too, I continued my sermon. And I see no other solution, I really see no other solution but to turn inward, to your own core, to extinguish all the rottenness there. I no longer believe that we can improve anything in the outside world that we have not first improved in ourselves. And that to me seems to be the only lesson to be learned from this war, that we must *only* look inside ourselves and nowhere else.   (EH, 254; H'83, 71; adapt. MH)

The power of Etty Hillesum's writings lies precisely in these reflections, which coincide with Cixous's feminine libidinal economy. In these passages she rejects the destructive power of hatred and opts for the gift of love; she battles against greed and learns that one can enjoy without owning; she experiences and puts trust in the fullness of her existence. These are all aspects of a way of living Western culture has marginalized. Considering the hardship and persecution the Nazi regime imposed, such an outlook on life is very difficult to comprehend. The fact that Hillesum could grow in this way, even during the Holocaust, lends her texts their special distinctiveness. This also explains the aura of saintliness that has often been ascribed to Hillesum.

My Dear Desk, the Best Place on Earth[19]

The two economies Cixous describes manifest themselves in cultural expressions such as texts. Cixous connects the masculine libidinal economy with a masculine mode of writing and the feminine libidinal economy with an *écriture féminine,* although she also confesses to disliking these terms.

She modifies the term "feminine writing" by labeling it "so-called feminine writing" or, even more carefully, "a decipherable libidinal femininity discernible in texts by both women and men" (Stevens 1989, 419; trans. MH).

Again Cixous is trying to avoid the one-to-one correspondence between men and a masculine mode of writing and women and a feminine mode of writing. As I discussed earlier, Cixous's ideas on bisexuality imply that masculinity and femininity are part of every human being. "And if we are sent back to sexual identity cards, it is just a cultural curse" (Cixous 1988a, 25).

In terms of the practice of writing, matters are even more complicated. In order to stay afloat, many women throughout history have had to accentuate their masculine sides, while men could sometimes afford to take a few more risks and show their repressed feminine side. In this section, I will certainly heed Cixous's warning against too easily linking women to *écriture féminine*. Her statements to this effect cannot be misinterpreted:

> Most women are like this: they do someone else's—man's—writing, and in their innocence sustain it and give it voice, and end up producing writing that's in effect masculine. Great care must be taken in working on feminine writing not to get trapped by names: to be signed with a woman's name doesn't necessarily make a piece of writing feminine.   (Cixous 1981b, 52 [1974])[20]

Obviously the two modes of writing occur both in men and women. Therefore, Cixous prefers to describe a masculine style of writing as "a style marked by the pain of reduction" and a feminine style of writing as "the style of live water" (Cixous 1988a, 25).

The "reductive" style is the result of a masculine libidinal economy. A book in this style is characterized by rigid structures and a text divided into chapters, by strict demarcations; a story with a beginning, a middle, and an end; and linearity and nonambiguous use of language. These books are in the grip of the castration scene: "This gives rise to forms which are dry, stripped bare, marked by the negative" (Cixous 1988a, 25).

This type of book is written by authors who, after writing, become their own editors: They read to rephrase and remaster the text. As soon as the author has finished the text, he or she reenters it to reappropriate and control it. This is not the type of writing that Cixous appreciates, although she admits that even feminine writing needs a certain dose of masculinity in order to be published:

> Then, if you want to write books, you equip yourself, you trim, you filter, you go back over yourself. Severe test, you tread on your own flesh, you no longer fly, you no longer flow, you survey, you garden, you dig, ah, you clean and assemble, this is the hour of man.
>   (Cixous 1991a, 54 [1976])[21]

She asks of writing the same thing she desires of desire: that it not commit itself exclusively to the logic of "the selfsame." Such writing features a style of "living water." It is an (over)flowing mode of writing: "This style of live water gives rise to works which are like streams of blood or water, which are full of tears, full of drops of blood or tears transformed into stars. Made up of phrases which spill forth dripping in luminous parataxis" (Cixous 1988a, 25).[22]

Such texts are much less sutured than "classical" texts. They originate in detachment and the greatest possible passivity. Paradoxically this passivity is linked to activity; it requires the author to be willing and daring enough to surrender to language as it unfolds, in a process that is not about proving, explaining, and comprehending but about the surrender itself (Cixous 1991a, 57 [1976]). Texts in this mode have no real beginning, no division into chapters, and no real end. The writing flows and attests to tolerance and freedom. It is precisely these characteristics that make it hard, if not impossible, to define écriture féminine; the very act of defining places the reader in another economy: phallocentrism. It is impossible to use a frozen language to write about the style of living water,[23] which is, of course, not to say that there is no such thing as practicing feminine writing: "It does and will take place in areas other than those subordinated to philosophico-theoretical domination. It will be conceived of only by subjects who are breakers of automatisms, by peripheral figures that no authority can ever subjugate" (Cixous 1981a, 253 [1975b]).[24]

Although I do not know whether I meet the criteria Cixous sets for conceptualizing feminine writing, I would still like to give it a try—by drawing a connection between this mode of writing and the way in which Hillesum produced texts. Her inward focus was linked to a commitment to the outside world. She was not a hermit but someone who practiced her political conviction; to change the world, she felt, she had to start at home. I believe that her way of living coincided with the feminine libidinal economy, which is characterized by a great deal of tolerance for the other. This economy can generate a mode of writing which opens itself to the otherness of language. This raises a few questions: Did Hillesum's texts show any signs of linguistic change or liberation? In other words did she begin to write in the style of "flowing water"? Did she break with automatisms and subvert authorities? Does her writing constitute écriture féminine? Did she invent a new mode of writing that undermined the old? Did she inscribe the feminine into the language of her diaries and letters?

Death's Wordlessness

When she needed a mode of writing for reflection, Etty Hillesum chose to write a diary. This allowed her to write for hours; her words flowed freely onto the notebook paper and filled hundreds of pages. She was concerned with neither beginnings nor endings, structure nor style. She wrote down anything she wanted to commit to paper: "I must make sure I keep up with my writing, that is, with myself, or else things will start to go wrong for me: I still run the risk of suddenly losing my way completely" (EH, 43; H'83, 15; adapt. MH).

She started the diary to square things with herself, to conquer her depressions and master her inner chaos: "This is my muddling book. A sort of trash can for all sorts of waste products of my plagued mind" (EH, 445; trans. MH).

Unlike others, Cixous sees Hillesum's diary as no more than a diary (Cixous, seminar 10/20/1985); it was not a training ground for writing as, for instance, Kafka's diary had been. Hillesum did not attempt to develop her style, but wrote simply and naturally; this is evident from the numerous repetitions that characterize her diary. Although she had an ambition to become a writer, she was very modest about her diary: "And a diary, well, a diary is really just there to sort out all kinds of moods, at least that's the case with me" (EH, 416; trans. MH).

The flowing mode of writing is often particularly evident in "*la prénatalité*" (Cixous 1994, 327), or prenatal period: the preliminaries for the oeuvre. Ordering has yet to take place, form has yet to crystallize, and the text is still chaotic. This aspect of *écriture féminine* is definitely visible in Hillesum's diaries, even though the diary genre has a certain built-in structure, namely time. Within the confines of the genre, Etty Hillesum let her thoughts and feelings pour out onto the empty pages of the notebooks. This was precisely why she had been advised to start keeping a diary: to structure her inner chaos. To her, diary writing was a matter not only of language but also of the psyche: The words that flowed from her pen were like the contractions preceding her rebirth.

Because Etty Hillesum wrote not only for the sake of writing but also for healing purposes, the changes in her lifestyle were initially more visible than those in her prose. She remarked on this herself: "I can't write, but I can live. And this real life of mine will one day give birth to words" (EH, 456; trans. MH). In her oeuvre, the feminine libidinal economy is manifest in the content rather than her writing style.

The new way of living that Hillesum had learned since meeting Spier greatly influenced her experience of writing. At first her urge to write had been motivated by possessiveness:

> I think I know what all the "writing" was about as well: it was just another way of "owning," of drawing things in more tightly to oneself, to possess them in that way. And I'm sure that that used to be the very essence of my urge to write: I wanted to creep silently away from everyone with all my carefully hoarded treasure, to write it all down, keep tight hold of it and have it all to myself.   (EH, 26; H'83, 12)

Whereas Hillesum wrote in the past tense about the link between her desires to write and to possess, Cixous believes that her original motive for writing had not quite disappeared at the time she wrote the diaries. She points out that Hillesum's philosophy of life, of accepting loss and enjoying what was left, tied in with her passion for diary writing. Cixous is convinced that the one could not have existed without the other. According to her Hillesum needed the fullness of language to accept the void of life.

I want to explore this notion by using the distinction that Etty Hillesum herself drew between her inner world and the outside world. Her inner world was initially chaotic, shapeless, and unstructured. This caused her to suffer depressions and suicidal feelings. Meeting Spier put her in a different state of mind. He advised her to start keeping a diary to understand herself and take control of her life. In her first diaries she still faced the dilemma between Eros and Thanatos: "Back into darkness, into your mother's womb, into *the collective*. Break free, find your own voice, vanquish the chaos within. I am pulled to and fro between these two poles" (EH, 145; H'83, 47).

In chapter 2 I described the same psychic condition with regard to Anne Frank. Etty Hillesum, too, needed to write in order to live. She transcended the depressive position, which is essentially the human condition, by filling the void with language. This corresponds with Lacan's description of the child entering the realm of language. When the child realizes that the primary condition of wholeness is an illusion, it turns toward language. It seems as if language can close the yawning chasm, suture the open wound. The child hopes that by using language she or he can coincide with her- or himself again, regain the wholeness. Language arises in places of lack, of absence; writing, too, is a reaction to a paradise lost. It is both a way of reestablishing a connection and a mourning ritual. It is like a vehicle that braves hell in search of a second paradise (Cornell 1988, 130). Hillesum found that second paradise; in writing she achieved inner peace and quiet. She succeeded in battling depression by filling the void with words.

However, her writing had a bearing not only on her inner world, but also on the outside world, the world of war, the persecution of the Jews, fears, threats, and millions of dead. Apart from their therapeutic function, the diaries were also Hillesum's refuge in her inner world. Although she started keeping a diary to gain access to herself, writing also fulfilled her need to withdraw. The quest for personal growth gave her an excuse, so to speak, to retreat into her diary, to close herself off from the outside world. Writing allowed her to leave behind the confusion, persecution and destruction of the real world: "There is a sort of seclusion from the outside world, a sense of being veiled, but despite the dreaminess and the stillness, inside me everything has an almost mathematical clarity" (EH, 189; trans. MH).

While most people were so preoccupied by the terrors of the war that they lost touch with themselves, Hillesum preached:

> And of this I am becoming more and more certain: a line from a poem is just as much a reality as a cheese ration, or chilblains. Just as actual. Too often we experience our poetic and dreamlike and creative moments as unreal in the cold light of day, and therefore ban too much from the circle of our personalities at times. And so we suffer from a split that should not have to exist, if only we expanded that circle so that everything had its place there. (EH, 193; trans. MH)

Still, in her early diaries she, too, tended to split herself into two, although her schism manifested itself inversely to most people around her. She built a wall of words between her inner life and the outside world, and withdrew into the safety of herself. Cixous hit upon the thought that "death, the expiration date" might be the actual author of the diaries:

> Perhaps this expiration date, this death that awaited her, is the author of this diary, of this abundance born from necessity. It is a defense, a fortress against anxiety. Perhaps, in the face of death— which is silence—there was an avalanche of words, to sustain life at death's door. (Cixous, seminar 01/25/1986; trans. MH)[25]

In this way Cixous interprets Hillesum's prolific writing as a fortification against death. The diary is a survival mechanism, a wall erected to conquer the fear of dying. Hillesum produced thousands, perhaps millions, of words to prevent silence, the wordlessness of depression and death from overtaking her. According to Cixous her diary is not "a work of art" but a *"journal de sécours,"* a journal of self-help.

This interpretation raises the question of whether Hillesum's diaries can be considered *écriture féminine. Ecriture féminine* focuses on subversiveness and fantasy rather than on a description of reality. Hillesum's writing, however, is concerned with describing reality—albeit an inner reality—in order to solve psychological problems and to find a voice. Cixous is well aware of this context; in her critique she expressed regret that she could not find the silence in Hillesum's work, the blank space between the lines. Cixous questioned her own right to be so critical of this work, knowing full well that Etty Hillesum was living on borrowed time. Everything was compressed and crammed full; after all, Hillesum was writing on the brink of death. There was no time for silence.

On the other hand, it is clear from the very first pages of the diaries that Etty Hillesum aspired to become a writer. Her diary had a dual function:

Aside from its highly personal nature, it was also a "finger exercise in author-ship" (Reitsma 1989, 110; trans. MH). This is precisely what prompted Dresden to question whether these were really only diaries (Dresden 1991, 39). Cixous also touched on this matter in her seminars, but her doubts focused on another issue: whether Etty Hillesum's oeuvre could be called literature. Cixous had difficulty reconciling her opinion—that the diaries were less than spectacular from a literary point of view—with Hillesum's writing aspirations. She also had trouble criticizing the texts because, as she discovered, they *are* very impres-sive in content. The way in which Hillesum gave meaning to her suffering is very special, but:

> No, not all texts and poems of freedom-in-suffering are necessarily works of "literature." In this rarified zone, one cannot always distin-guish between what is and what is not a work of literature. Perhaps one should classify texts as either from the heart or not, at which point one would return to the extraordinary texts written by Margaret Buber-Neumann, Etty Hillesum and others.   (Cixous 1993a, 27)

Cixous's reaction to the diaries is a complex matter. Her problem is that she does not believe that diaries have any literary value, while Hillesum repeatedly mentioned that she wanted to be a writer (Cixous, seminar 01/25/1986).

I think Cixous's difficulty is related to the distinction between *écriture féminine* and literature. Hillesum's texts display the flowing, giving, unstop-pable stream of words that typifies "feminine writing," but this does not make them literature. Cixous wondered whether Hillesum would ever have become a great poet. Her diary is full of little poems, though these are formless and unfinished[26], but Cixous could not find the telltale blank space between the lines. A poem constitutes a certain relationship to silence, which was (as yet) absent in Hillesum's writing. Her oeuvre is on the threshold of literature, because the last phase, "the hour of man" (Cixous 1991a, 54 [1976]), the structuring, the distillation, is missing.

Hillesum knew this. She felt that her words and usage were insufficient and invoked Rilke's help to express her thoughts and feelings, in precisely the same way that a poetic text functions, according to Maaike Meijer: "It can preconceive, preview, presense something for you" (Meijer 1988, 14–15) Rilke's poems reflected what Hillesum herself had wanted to say about her inner world, her inner reality. She radically shut out the outside world and concentrated only on her *Weltinnenraum* (inner universe), a favorite term borrowed from one of Rilke's poems:

Durch alle Wesen reicht der eine Raum: Weltinnenraum. [One space extends through every being: the inner universe.] These seem to me the most beautiful words that I know, probably because in their roundness and perfection they reflect exactly what I am experiencing ever more intensely.[27]   (EH, 291; trans. MH)

Rilke described that which Hillesum had not yet been able to put into words, so for the time being she borrowed his words: "One day, I'll find my own words for the things I have to say; until then, I'll borrow them from Rainer Maria" (EH, 533; trans. MH; see also EH, 417).

She described herself as someone in training; she called Rilke and Spier (whose role is discussed in more detail in the next chapter) her two teachers:

Apart from S., my great teacher throughout this period has been Rilke. . . .

I have noticed more and more that Rilke has been one of my greatest teachers in this past year.   (EH, 471, 565; trans. MH)

Although she often copied poems and excerpts from Rilke's letters, she also thought about her own use of language. At one point she and a friend were looking at some Japanese prints when she suddenly realized: "That's how I want to write. With that much space round a few words. I hate a lot of words" (EH, 413; H'83, 116; adapt. MH).

This last sentence might seem absurd amid the thousands of closely scrawled words in her notebooks, but it was meant seriously. Increasingly she longed for a style of writing that tended toward wordlessness. As the increasing peril she lived in taught her to be humble and to accept death as part of life, she sought a new language in which to express this outlook. Although she was still writing many pages a day in her diary, she was contemplating a different style of writing to reflect her new lifestyle: "[L]ater, when I have survived it all, I shall write stories about these times that will be like faint brushstrokes against the great wordless background of God, Life, Death, Suffering and Eternity" (EH, 510–511; H'83, 146).

She did not have time to create this new language; there was only time for a first attempt:

Words should simply emphasize the silence. Just like that print with the sprig of blossom in the lower corner. A few delicate brush strokes— but with what attention to the smallest detail—and all around it space, which is not a void, but let's say an inspired emptiness.

(EH, 413; H'83, 116; adapt. MH)

Etty Hillesum accepted death as a meaningful part of life, and it was in much the same spirit that she wanted to write—in a way that would accentuate emptiness and its beauty. Her writing was a continuation of how she was already living: in the realm of the feminine libidinal economy, where life's joys and grieves can coexist. Again and again this is clearly demonstrated by the contents of her writing. She parted with all that she valued. She was in her senior year at the school of loss.

> Just a few days ago I thought to myself: the worst thing for me will be when I am no longer allowed pencil and paper to clarify my thoughts— they are absolutely indispensable to me, for without them something inside me will eventually explode and I will be destroyed.
>
> But now I know that once you begin to drop your demands and your expectations, you can let go of everything.
>
> (EH, 502; H'83, 140; adapt. MH)

She strove to find a voice, a mode of writing, to express this way of life. She made first attempts, well aware that she might not have time to develop them any further. This relationship between writing and living is one Cixous recognizes. "Writing follows life like its shadow, extends it, engraves it. It is a question of living to the end without losing sight of life for a minute, which is immense work" (Cixous 1989b, 6).

Like Hillesum, Cixous draws a comparison between the art of painting and writing (Cixous 1991a, 104–131 [1986b]). Cixous realizes that it is hard to avoid clichés in the medium of language; this is why she is interested in painting. She argues that writers should imitate painters, emulate their attention to detail and their focus on the moment, their refusal to stigmatize ugliness and their ability to see meaning in everything. It is on the matter of ugliness that Hillesum and Rilke part ways. Hillesum took up the challenge of the horrible, while Rilke fled from it. In this sense Hillesum evolved further than Rilke. This difference is largely due to the historical contexts in which they lived, as Hillesum acknowledged. Without envy, she concluded in one of her last diary entries:

> I always return to Rilke. It is strange to think that someone so frail, who did most of his writing within protective castle walls, would perhaps have been broken by the circumstances in which we now live. Is that not further testimony that life is finely balanced? Evidence that, in peaceful times and under favorable circumstances, sensitive artists may search for the purest and most fitting expression of their deepest insights so that, during more turbulent and debilitating times, others can turn to them for support and a ready response to their

bewildered questions? A response they are unable to formulate for themselves since all their energies are taken up in looking after the bare necessities. Sadly, in difficult times we tend to shrug off the spiritual heritage of artists from an "easier" age (as if simply being an artist is an easy task in any age!) with a disdainful "What use is that sort of thing to us now?"

It is an understandable but shortsighted reaction. And utterly impoverishing. (EH, 583; H'83, 196; adapt. MH)

Cixous aptly remarked that although Hillesum owed a great deal to Rilke, he was also greatly indebted to Hillesum.

Etty was reading Rilke and she thanked him. Rilke owes an immense amount to Etty Hillesum, since she gives him a life. An exchange of life exists between the two and, admirably, the chain is not broken. That is how strong the continuity between poetry and the soul can be.
(Cixous 1992, 113; see also EH, 316)

Cixous admires poets for being in touch with their femininity and channeling the feminine. Rilke, however, was not open to everything; he limited himself by focusing only on beauty. He avoided ugliness (Cixous 1991a, 75 [1979]). In Etty Hillesum's writing, too, there is an attempt to avoid the unsightly, although she knew from the outset that she could not avoid it forever. At first she did her best to keep the horrible news from the outside world at bay, to foster her psychological well-being and inner growth. From the summer of 1942 on, she gradually realized that the outside pressures were becoming too great to ignore. This realization marked the beginning of a period in which she went beyond Rilke. She consciously faced the horrors of the present and future without, however, losing sight of the beauty of living. Cixous arrived at the very same discrepancy when comparing her favorite author, Clarice Lispector, to Rilke: both wrote about beauty, but while Rilke avoided the unsightly, Lispector immersed herself in it and emerged to truly encounter the beautiful. According to Cixous, Lispector exemplifies the writer who works like a painter: She had an eye for the smallest detail, for the shortest moment, and for the most unappealing aspects of reality:

There is Rilke, but there is Clarice. There is only: There is fear, there is cult, there are limits, there is the reserved expanse of the *Weltinnenraum*: the world-in-the-intimacy-of-myself-Rilke. There is closure; the hand holds, writing elects through reading and contains. But there is Clarice, there is audacity, boundless vertigo, there is yes. . . . There is the Clarice-risk. Clarisk: through the horrible to Joy.
(Cixous 1991a, 75–76 [1979])[28]

At first Hillesum emulated Rilke's writing style, but later she developed a mode of writing reminiscent of Clarice Lispector's. First, she focused on her inner world, which she re-created as a second paradise. This rebirth allowed her to open up to the outside world, and at that moment she parted ways with Rilke, who stayed inside and explored his private world within the safety of castle walls and homes. Hillesum, however, ended up in Westerbork, where she lived and wrote of the harsh reality.

Letters from Westerbork

On July 14, 1942, the first Jews were deported from Amsterdam to Westerbork. Hillesum was probably among the people who received a notice to report. Her brother Jaap urged her to apply for a job with the Jewish Council, which she did the very same day (Hillesum 1986, 774). Two days later, she was offered a job as a typist. She accepted it, even though she had mixed feelings; on the one hand she saw the job as a gift from heaven, but on the other hand she was well aware of the Jewish Council's bizarre position. On the evening before her first day at work, she wrote in her diary: "Do you have other plans for me after all, God? Can I accept this? I will still be prepared to take on other tasks. Tomorrow I must descend into hell, and if I am to do the work properly, I shall have to get a good night's sleep" (EH, 254; H'83, 156; adapt. MH).

At the end of the month she announced: "Nothing can ever atone for the fact, of course, that one section of the Jewish population is helping to transport the majority out of the country. History will pass judgment in due course" (EH, 541; H'83, 166).

Working for the Jewish Council in Amsterdam was a horrible experience. She managed to brave the work and the atmosphere by reading Rilke at every opportunity: "I keep following my own inner voice even in the madhouse in which I work, with a hundred people chattering together in one small room, typewriters clattering, and me, sitting in a corner reading Rilke" (EH, 532; H'83, 162).

It took her only a few weeks to realize that she did not belong there. She did not want to stay in Amsterdam while the less fortunate were all being taken away. She requested a transfer to Westerbork transit camp and in late July 1942 was given employment as a social worker there (Hillesum 1986, 774).

In Westerbork she witnessed the persecution of the Jews firsthand. There was hardly any opportunity to withdraw and to write a letter. Nonetheless, she managed to find a few minutes now and then to put her thoughts and experiences on paper. It is clear from the surviving letters that she did not close her eyes to the misery. She heard many of her fellow prisoners exclaim: "We don't want to think, we don't want to feel, it's best to forget" (EH, 264; H'87, 31). But she tried not to forget, not to repress the horror. She wanted to stay open to all aspects of living, not only the suffering but also the beauty. She kept her mind and senses attuned enough to enjoy life in the middle of the Shoah:

> The sky is full of birds, the purple lupins look so regal and peace-ful, two little old women have sat down on the box for a chat, the sun is shining on my face—and right before our eyes, mass murder. The whole thing is simply beyond comprehension.
>
> (EH, 642; H'87, 56; adapt. MH)

She wanted not to harden, not to avoid anything. In her diaries, she had so often contended that suffering was part of life; now that she was living the suffering, she wanted, however hard it might be, to confront the pain. She had crying bouts and sometimes fainted but she kept fighting the moral danger of becoming numb. She did not want to give in to hate and bitter-ness. She refused to be dragged along by the forces of death and hatred: "What matters is not whether we preserve our lives at any cost, but *how* we preserve them. I sometimes think that every new situation, good or bad, can enrich us with new insights" (EH, 624; H'87, 30–31).

Although she understood why people felt hatred, she clung to her con-viction that only love could make the world a better place (EH, 629). Her trust in life and her capacity to find joy in it were immeasurable. From Westerbork camp she kept her friends informed about her life and thoughts:

> All I wanted to say is this: The misery here is quite terrible; and yet, late at night when the day has slunk away into the depths behind me, I often walk with a spring in my step along the barbed wire. And then, time and again, it soars straight from my heart—I can't help it, that's just the way it is, like some elementary force—the feeling that life is glorious and magnificent, and that one day we shall be build-ing a whole new world. Against every new outrage and every fresh horror, we must put up one more piece of love and goodness, which we must wrest from ourselves. We may suffer, but we must not suc-cumb. And if we should survive these times unscathed in body and soul, but above all in soul, without bitterness and without hatred, then we are entitled to have our say after the war. Maybe I am an ambi-tious woman: I would like to have just a tiny little bit of say.
>
> (EH, 657; H'87, 77–78; adapt. MH)

The many letters Hillesum sent from Westerbork to Amsterdam prove that she had more than "a tiny little bit of say." She was being too modest; her letters from Westerbork are magnificent. Circumstances forced her to choose another genre: letters. The diaries had been focused mainly on her inner life—Rilke's *Weltinnenraum*—which was safe and offered a refuge from the harsh reality of the day; by contrast the letters are grounded in this unpleasant reality. They are full of terrible details that were written with great sensitivity, as if Hillesum wanted to spare the people she wrote to. The letters stand apart from the diaries mainly because they explicitly address other people: her friends in Amsterdam. Cixous spoke highly of the way in which Hillesum reported on daily life in Westerbork (Cixous, seminar 10/24/1987). The letters are very tactful because they are addressed to people destined to live, people who are not in hell. Although the letters are much more graphic than the diaries, the writer practiced restraint. With dignity she asked her friends to send food, drink, and other necessities; she apologized profusely for the burden this put on them. All the while she could still identify with the people outside the camps; these were hard times for them too, even if they could take a vacation. "I suddenly remember that it's the 'summer holidays' in the outside world. Do you have any plans? You will tell me everything, won't you?" (EH, 660; H'87, 83).

She struggled with the continuity between living her life in Westerbork and writing about it. She was living the unlivable and wanted to describe the indescribable (Cixous, seminar 11/19/1988). Westerbork made her pose the question "In what form could one describe the camp to arrive at a readable description?" Again and again she faced the problem of writing, of reporting on Westerbork. She often wrote that it was almost impossible to write down everything that happened. In a letter dating from late November 1942 she wrote:

> Father Han, Käthe, Hans, Sister Maria,
>   Just a quick hello. I find it impossible to write here, not for lack of time but because of all the different impressions I'm bombarded with. I'm sure I could talk for a year on end just about this one week.
>   (EH, 613; H'87, 16; adapt. MH)

She tried anyhow, and what follows is a letter full of little scenes from Westerbork: her daily routine, the places where she found the peace to write, the arrival of Jews from other transit camps. Each paragraph contains enough material to base an entire chapter on. She concludes: "This is hardly a real letter. . . . No, it is impossible to write from here; it would take the better part of a lifetime to digest it all" (EH, 614; H'87, 18).

Six months later she had discovered two forms she considered appropriate for recording her experiences: fairy tales and poetry:

> One could write fairy tales here. It sounds strange, but if you wanted to convey something of Westerbork life the best way to do it would be in a fairy tale. The misery here is so hyperreal that it has become unreal. Sometimes I walk through the camp laughing secretly to myself because of the completely grotesque circumstances. One would have to be a very great poet indeed to describe them; perhaps in about ten years I could give it a try.   (EH, 662; H'87, 88; adapt. MH)

Nourishing Books

At the time Etty Hillesum fantasized about the fairy tales and poems she would later write about Westerbork, she had only a few months left to live. She did not leave any fairy tales. The diary she kept in Westerbork has never been found; only her letters survived. It took a long time for her words to reach a large audience, but once they did they became an important part of our reflections on the Holocaust. During the same period in which Hillesum's work found its way to a larger audience, the *écriture féminine* school of thought also gained a foothold (Stevens 1989, 111). Was this because the time was ripe for a different way of living and writing? I return to this issue in the epilogue, but first I would like to offer four answers to the question I raised at the beginning of this chapter: What makes Etty Hillesum's mode of living and writing so unusual?

First, Hillesum's oeuvre is extraordinary because of the circumstances in which it was written. Her life and work attest to the paradox that Cixous has expressed as follows: People who are forced to live under difficult circumstances are most likely to apprehend the essence of life. That is why we should listen to these people: to the homeless, the vagabonds, and the exiles. While the people around her sank into hatred and turmoil, Hillesum kept battling her own negative tendencies. Ultimately her answers to the great questions in life were affirmative: She accepted life unconditionally and intuitively sensed that love, rather than hatred, restores vitality. To her, life was not about control and exercising power; it was about living in love, gratitude, and humility, however hard that might be.

The second answer, which follows from the first, concerns the political aspect of her work. Cixous distinguishes two types of politics: polemic and poetic (Cixous 1982, 298). The first type comprises war, active resistance, and guerrilla warfare, while the second type is meditative and reflexive. The second is less conspicuous, but no less vital. Hillesum's texts are steeped in these poetic politics. Her outlook on life attests to what Cixous describes as "active passivity" (Cixous 1991a, 113 [1986b]; see also EH, 29, 591). This way of life was not universally appreciated in Hillesum's circle of friends. The people around her accused her of indifference and passivity (EH, 514; H'83, 149) and offered to help her go into hiding. But she stuck with her conviction: "And my acceptance is not resignation or helplessness. I still feel deep moral indignation at a regime that treats human beings in such a way. But events have become too overwhelming and too demonic to be stemmed with personal resentment and bitterness" (EH, 515; H'83, 150; adapt. MH).

Hillesum took a moral and representative stance. The path she followed opens our eyes to the difficulty but also to the possibility of making such a choice. In a creative, original, and idiosyncratic way, she sought a mode of living and writing that would break with old, obsolete structures. What she was looking for could not be found in the masculine libidinal economy, and certainly not in its Nazi extremes, but in a feminine libidinal economy which championed both life and suffering. To Hillesum, peace was not just the absence of war but rather a state of mind, a radically different attitude.

My third answer as to the source of Hillesum's authenticity is related to the giving, nourishing aspect of her work. Cixous feels that the letters in particular have a nourishing quality. Hillesum's published letters belong to a genre Cixous dubbed "nourishing books," which, paradoxically, are often written by the literally and figuratively starving: "These are books that, in their passivity, are militant and that, ultimately, give us real recipes for spiritual survival. These are nourishing books: books by starving people that feed us" (Cixous, seminar 10/15/1988; trans. MH).[29]

To my mind the diaries and letters are, as a whole, an inexhaustible source of life's wisdom and experience, while each of the two genres has its individual merits. In the diaries Hillesum fearlessly explored her inner universe. In her letters she reported in detail on the world around her. When she was writing her diaries, at her beloved desk in Amsterdam, there was still time to philosophize. She used this time intensively, thinking about life and death, writing and living.

Some of the letters she subsequently sent from Westerbork show signs of being what she had described as "faint brushstrokes against a great wordless background." She no longer had time to withdraw and write for hours on end. Even sending letters was a restricted activity. Hillesum did not have time to live and develop her style of writing further. She did what she could in such a short time. She made a start and contemplated how she would want to write. She reflected on how she would want to live; once she had found a new mode of living, she sustained it for as long as she could. Her texts, about living and writing, are inexhaustible. She gave it her all:

> I wish I could live for a long time so that I would have the opportunity to explain it all someday, and if I am not granted that wish, well, then somebody else will do it, carry on from where my life has been cut short. And that is why I must try to live a good and complete and faithful life to my last breath: so that those who come after me do not have to start all over again, need not face the same difficulties. Isn't that doing something for future generations too?
>
> (EH, 487; H'83, 131; adapt. MH)

Yes, Hillesum did "something" for future generations. Her life and writings attest to an enormous, almost explosive growth toward a feminine libidinal economy, a way of living abundantly in times of death and destruction. After fully accepting her own death, she taught us how to live: "The question a woman's text asks is the question of giving—'What does this writing give?' 'How does it give?'" (Cixous 1981b, 53 [1974]).[30]

What Etty Hillesum gave is extraordinary, but the fact that she gave at all is even more astounding. It is unimaginable that someone could keep giving so much when she no longer had anything to lose. Her mode of living and writing attest to abundance and generosity. This is especially obvious in the *content* of her writing, where she reports on her inner growth toward an all-encompassing, unconditional love of life and humanity. But in her *style of writing,* too, we see traces of a feminine libidinal economy. This is manifest not only when she reflects on a writing style to convey her experiences but also in the transition from the diaries to the letters. At first she wrote for keeps, motivated by an urge to possess, but later she increasingly wrote to give, to share with others. This shift in emphasis attests to an openness to the other and others. She addressed these letters to someone; in writing she focused on the other. At the same time her letters dealt more than ever with the external conditions in which she lived. She no longer closed herself off in her protective inner world but looked reality straight in the eye.

The last answer to the question I posed has to do with the special reading experience produced by Hillesum's texts. Her diaries and letters lead into the world of a woman, a "sculptress of the soul" (De Costa 1993a), who first chiseled herself and then took on the task of helping others in their personal growth and inner development. Like a midwife she assisted others in rebirthing. *Se laissez lire par Etty Hillesum,*[31] to let oneself (be) read (by) Etty Hillesum, is to open up to and be swept along by this undercurrent in her texts. To read Hillesum is to be pushed over an inner edge where there is no recognition; instead you—the reader—are transported out of the familiar into a world that rewrites you. Here, there is no reader interpreting the text, but a text that alters the reader. This is precisely the type of discontinuity that Meijer described as pertaining to reading poetry (Meijer 1988, 14). Hillesum's texts appeal to the "stranger in ourselves" (see Kristeva 1991), the repressed and twisted part of ourselves that we usually outgrow during our development into adulthood. Hillesum's texts go beyond adulthood to "the second innocence" (Cixous 1991a, 114 [1986b]), an innocence that, by following the path of understanding and experience, returns to simplicity and the nakedness of existence. What Etty loved to do most was "assemble the puzzle of life by reading its pieces: people" (EH, 552; trans. MH). Letting oneself be read by Etty Hillesum means reestablishing contact with the other and the alien both inside and outside oneself. Her oeuvre is an interdisciplinary, multidimensional study of the other. I discuss this further in the next chapter, in which I explore the divine Other invoked by Etty Hillesum.

Chapter 6 ❧ The Girl Who Could Not Kneel

A spiritual development can be discerned in Etty Hillesum's texts. As I described in chapter 4, God plays a fairly modest role in the early notebooks. She mentions him here and there; he is present, but in the background. In her later diaries God becomes one of the main characters, for it was to him that she addressed her writings.

Hillesum was very conscious of the spiritual path she was taking. She wanted to write a book about it, a novella entitled *The Girl Who Could Not Kneel* (EH, 153; H'83, 48).[1] She never got to write it. In this chapter I explore the spiritual process that runs through Hillesum's oeuvre. Although I am not the first to do this, I will not follow in my predecessors' footsteps. By and large their approach has been to compare and contrast Etty Hillesum's inclination toward the divine with other spiritual schools of thought, for instance those of Saint Augustine, Dostoyevski, Kierkegaard, Seneca, and Rilke.[2] My approach is different in that I am not out to find parallels, for reasons I mentioned in the previous chapter; comparison heightens the risk of obscuring the "difference" in Hillesum's thinking, and differences are precisely what interest me.

Another issue I do not wish to focus on is Hillesum's perceived (lack of) Jewishness. She has been criticized for not being Jewish enough, which raises the question: What is Jewish?[3] This in turn suggests that a straightforward, clear answer can be given—an illusion, certainly with regard to Hillesum. Her stance toward Jewishness was not static or immutable but dynamic. In that sense it would be more accurate to speak of her *becoming Jewish,* as a process, rather than her *being Jewish,* as a permanent, unchanging state. The path she traveled to become Jewish, however, was not the beaten path, a fact that has led many to interpret her spiritual development as a growth away from

207

Jewishness, not toward it. I believe we should be looking at this issue the other way around; my interest is not in what Jewishness consists of, but in what Hillesum wrote about her relationship to Jewishness. In dealing with this issue we should focus primarily on her texts. One important reason for choosing this mode of reading is to resist, or subvert, the Nazi idea that Jews are all the same and all clearly distinguishable from the "Aryan race." The Nazis tried on the one hand to wipe out all differences—in the sense that all Jews had to be murdered, without exception. On the other they greatly exaggerated difference when it came to comparing Jews with non-Jews. Hillesum's texts contrast sharply with these rigid views. In a period when she was robbed of all freedom, she still had the freedom of mind to go her own very personal way; therein lies the power of her writings. Hillesum's spiritual growth was not a matter of seeking sanctuary. On the contrary, her texts owe their existence to homelessness. Her oeuvre shows a spiritual development that is extraordinarily eclectic in nature and produces the following paradox: The more she turned toward the Jewish people and its body of ideas, the more receptive she became to Christian and other non-Jewish influences.

Etty Hillesum was of Jewish descent, but her parents were not very strict in matters of faith. For example, they did not keep kosher. Hillesum was definitely influenced by her father, an erudite man, well versed in the Bible.[4] Still, she was first and foremost a freethinker. She did what Cixous later (1981a [1975b]) called on other women to do, namely *voler* (steal): to take from the culture whatever is useful, regardless who it belongs to. (I will return to the two meanings of the French verb *voler*—to steal and to fly.) Hillesum was so hungry for spiritual nourishment that she was heedless which cuisine it came from. Essentially she was not interested in whether a certain thought was Jewish, Christian, or Buddhist; her priority was the text, not the provenance.

Out of respect for her development, I wish to avoid this kind of categorization. The fact that her spirituality cannot be forced into one particular mold indicates precisely how original and organic her thoughts were; this is what I wish to emphasize. I will do so by linking Hillesum's thoughts on God to her position: She was the other, in more than one sense.

In the first place Hillesum lived in a society that was and still is ideologically rooted in the distinction between Jews and Christians. This differentiation covers an entire spectrum: from the tolerance exemplified by the civil rights of the French Enlightenment to anti-Semitism as blatantly propagated in the German hegemony during World War II. To the Nazis, Hillesum was a Jew because she had Jewish parents and grandparents—that was all that counted. That was ultimately the reason why she was first denied a normal, daily existence and later denied life altogether.

Second, Western society has traditionally been a patriarchal order, in which men and masculine values set the tone. Women are considered subordinate and dependent "other halves." This position, too—being a woman and as such "the other"—influenced Hillesum's spiritual development.

In the cultural configuration outlined above, Judaism occupies an extremely complex position with regard to issues of difference and gender. In Western culture Christianity is the dominant religion, and Judaism is marginalized. In that sense, Judaism is the other in Western culture. However, Jewish and Christian thought also have something in common: the patriarchal nature of their religious ideas. While Jewish men may be excluded from aspects of the culture at large because they are Jews, within their own faith they are respected for being men. This is less true for Jewish women; they occupy a double outsider position, for they are "the other" both as Jews and as women, on the periphery of dominant culture. This is the third sense in which Hillesum is the other.

Cixous captured this position beautifully with the coinage: *juifemme,* a contraction of *juif* [Jew] and *femme* [woman].[5] This neologism is so splendid because it seems to connote strength and the courage to bear, even to relish, the position of the other—both as a Jew and a woman. I was inspired by this word: The term "Jewoman" provided me with an angle from which to explore and analyze the depth, authenticity, and courage of Hillesum's spiritual growth. My theory is that she reacted like many other assimilated Dutch Jews: She found that the war brought to the forefront her Jewishness, which had until then always been in the background.[6] Over the course of the war, Hillesum gradually decided that she did not want to escape the fate of the Jews: She turned down all offers of help to go into hiding. She consciously opted to go to Westerbork out of solidarity with the great majority of Jews who lacked the money and connections to flee the country or go into hiding.

The war against the Jews had an effect on Hillesum which went beyond her solidarity with the Jewish victims. The Nazi terror also influenced her religious beliefs. While many people were doubting the very existence of God, she created a new one. "Isn't it almost ungodly, in times like these, to still believe in God so strongly?" (EH, 484, trans. MH).

Hillesum did not bid God farewell and was therefore not godless, but she did give the classical Almighty Father "a makeover"; she crafted a more appropriate God for the circumstances. This new God, who was dependent on

people, made her accountable: He gave meaning and purpose to her life on
the brink of death.

Outlawed

In "Coming to Writing" (1991a [1976]), Cixous describes the process by
which she became a writer. She puts this autobiographical development in the
context of Western culture, in which women are less entitled than men to
speak/write.[7] Hélène Cixous was born in Oran, Algeria, in 1937. Her parents
were Jewish—her mother an Ashkenazic Jew of Austro-Hungarian ancestry
and her father Sephardic, of Spanish descent. Their daughter was "born among
languages"; from birth she was exposed to Yiddish, German (her mother's
native language, since she was a refugee from Nazi Germany), French, and
Arabic. The atmosphere outside the home was threatening: Imperialism,
colonialism, anti-Semitism, racism, and sexism were all rampant. It is to this
background that Cixous attributes her passion for texts. In her early years,
against the backdrop of political turmoil, fear, and war, she also experienced
the loss of her beloved father. To her, the only thing she could clutch, was
language. Everything was lost but words. From a very early age, Cixous had
a love of language: Reading was her life buoy, but she dared not give in to
the urge to write. As a woman, after all, she had no reason to write. She had
no place in the symbolic order. Cixous refers to Moses, who received his text
from God's hands. When he came down from Mount Sinai, he carried two
tablets of stone, inscribed by God himself (AV, Exodus 32:15–16). Women's
fear of writing has a long history and is connected to their reverence for
tradition. For women it takes audacity to want to write, since they have been
excluded from language from the start. "I wouldn't have had the [nerve] to go
claim my book from God on Mount Sinai" (Cixous 1991a, [1976]).[8]

This does not mean that Moses was not intimidated by language. When
God commanded Moses to speak for him, Moses tried in vain to decline:

> Moses replied to Hashem, "Please, my Lord, I am not a man of words,
> not since yesterday, nor since You first spoke to Your servant, for I am
> heavy of mouth and heavy of speech."
> Then Hashem said to him, "Who makes a mouth for man, or who
> makes one dumb or deaf, or sighted or blind? Is it not I, Hashem?
> So now, go! I shall be with your mouth and teach you what you
> should say."   (Exodus 4:10–12)[9]

Moses kept on protesting, incurring God's wrath but also prompting God
to propose a compromise: Moses' brother, Aaron, would become his spokesman.

Despite her prophesying talents (Exodus 15:20), Miriam, sister of Moses and Aaron, was given no voice to speak of.[10]

Unlike Moses, whose calling to language was an obligation put on him by God, Cixous perceives her passion for language as a need from within. She experiences her desire to write as an inner, physical urge; she goes to great lengths to control this urge, for she does not meet the standards required for admission to the world of writers:

> You can desire. You can read, adore, be invaded. But writing is not granted to you. Writing is reserved for the chosen. It surely took place in a realm accessible to the small, to the humble, to women. In the intimacy of the sacred. Writing spoke to its prophets from a burning bush. But it must have been decided that bushes wouldn't dialogue with women. (Cixous 1991a, 13–14 [1976])[11]

As she describes in *Coming to Writing,* Cixous ultimately could no longer keep her desire to write in check. Despite God's prohibitions she let her words pour out onto the empty pages. She discovered that her writing stemmed from different sources than God. In order to write she had to free herself of Jewish traditions, in which women are denied access to writing. The Jewish God that Cixous knew could not be reconciled with her urge to write. This unbridled desire finally placed her outside the divine discourse.

The difference between Cixous and Hillesum is great. Etty's God was a giving God who made no distinction between men and women. Hillesum was able to ask without hesitation for his assistance in her linguistic development: "God, you have given me the talent to read, please could you also give me the one to write?" (EH, 577; trans. MH).

Nothing in her writings suggests that she felt exiled from God's realm because she was a woman. Her relationship with God and her passion for writing did not clash. On the contrary, in her first diary she was already openly appealing to him for support: "O God, take me into your great hands and turn me into your instrument, let me write" (EH, 71; H'83, 26).

In her last diary, in which she described her experiences in Westerbork, "between heaven and heath" (EH, 558; trans. MH), she again innocently asked for God's help:

> How can I ever describe all this? So that others can feel too how lovely and worth living and just—yes, just—life really is? Perhaps one day God will give me the few simple words I need. And bright and passionate and serious words as well. But above all, simple words.
> (EH, 558; H'83, 177–178; adapt. MH)

Later it occurred to her that only a poem would be able to capture the reality of the camps. She doubted whether she could be that poet:

> There is no poet in me, just a piece of God that might grow into a poet.
> And a camp like this one needs a poet, one who experiences life, even here, as a bard and is able to sing about it.
>
> (EH, 575; H'83, 190; adapt. MH)[12]

Both Hillesum and Cixous want to write. Cixous experiences God as the obstacle standing between her and the pen. To Hillesum, on the other hand, God was the one to whom she could turn for help. Cixous's image of God resembles the traditional figure: a strict father who lays down the law, issues commandments and prohibitions—and in so doing, often excludes women. This is a God who rules the realm of the masculine libidinal economy.[13]

Although Hillesum and Cixous are both of Jewish descent, their images of the divine are vastly different. There is nothing in Hillesum's texts to indicate that she was concerned with the antifemale dimension of either Judaism or Christianity. She experienced God as the creator of heaven, earth, and herself, and was grateful to him for that. She also felt gratitude for her dormant talents:

> Why did you not make me a poet, my God? But perhaps you did, and so I shall wait patiently until the words have grown inside me, the words that can proclaim everything I feel I have to bear witness of: how good and beautiful it is to live in your world, God, despite everything we human beings do to one another.
>
> (EH, 545; H'83, 169; adapt. MH)

Not only does Hillesum's notion of God deviate from traditional notions; it is also hard to reduce to a single, unambiguous image. Her experience of the divine is a coalescence of several God-images; the diaries make mention of a transcendental God—a God outside her—as well as an immanent God— "the most essential and deepest in me" (EH, 549; H'83, 173). She experienced God as her creator, but her writings also contain passages in which she feels she is a divinity herself:

> And yesterday afternoon when I went to buy S.'s cheese and walked through beautiful South Amsterdam, I felt like an ancient god, shrouded in a cloud. No doubt that's recorded somewhere in our mythology: a god going forth, shrouded in a cloud. It was a cloud of my own thoughts and feelings which enveloped and accompanied me, and I felt so warm and protected and safe in that cloud.   (EH, 95; H'83, 35; adapt. MH)

In the Old Testament, and especially the book of Exodus—which describes the delivery of the Hebrews from Egypt—God is often described as shaped like a pillar of a cloud: "By day God went before the people in a pillar of a cloud" (AV, Exodus 13:21–22).[14] Hillesum's comments on Judaism include various references to the Hebrews' exodus from Egypt and their journey through the desert. It is this biblical story that evoked strong associations with the reality Etty Hillesum herself knew: the flight, exile, deportation, and destruction of the Jewish people. Later, during her time in Westerbork, she compared the nearby heath to a desert. Describing a walk she took with her father along the barbed wire fence, she wrote:

> Later we joked about the aptness of our surroundings. Westerbork sometimes seems like no more than a desert, despite the purple lupins and campions and the elegant birds that look like seagulls. "The Jews in the desert, we know this landscape, we've been here before."
>
> (EH, 656; H'83, 198; adapt. MH)

My impression is that Hillesum's Jewish identity was deeply rooted in the outsider position—which Jews have always occupied in our culture—and occupied to an extreme in Hillesum's day. However, her decision to identify with the outsider was also fueled by Christian sources, which pivot on Jesus' suffering and self-sacrifice. One telling example of this is Hillesum's reaction, in her diary, after Spier told her of a beautiful letter sent by his fiancée: "If I were a true Christian, I would be glad for him. But I am still much more woman than Christian, and woman in the most narrow-minded and ignorant sense of the word at that" (EH, 101; trans. MH).

Hillesum apparently thought of jealousy as a typically feminine trait, unworthy of a real, self-effacing Christian. She repeatedly placed her battle to replace hatred with love in a Christian context. The New Testament was a source of inspiration for her, for example the gospels of Matthew and John. She was also deeply influenced by Saint Augustine and Meister Eckhart. Etty Hillesum's relationship to Judaism and Christianity can be summed up as follows: inspired by Judeo-Christian thought on love and suffering,[15] and under pressure from Nazi barbarism, she opted for the Jewish people and accepted their fate as hers.

Hillesum's paradoxical, multidenominational, and somewhat elusive experience of the divine has had its detractors. Of the critics who have questioned the Jewishness of her spirituality, the most outspoken is probably Henriëtte Boas, an well-known Jewish Dutch publicist. According to Boas the popularity of Hillesum's texts among non-Jewish readers[16] is due to the so-called "Jessica motif":

But the general reverence she is now enjoying—there was even talk of putting up a statue in her honor in Deventer—strongly reminds me of the Jessica motif, which, in some form or other, is present in all modern literature: the angelic daughter from an evil Jewish family manages to break away from and rise above her background, often finding "the true faith" by converting to Christianity, or at least to non-Judaism. (Boas 1982, 278; trans. MH)[17]

I think Boas is mistaken.[18] Etty Hillesum did not convert to Christianity, and what is more, the "Jessica motif" has hardly played a role in the responses to her diaries and letters.[19] As in the previous chapter, I propose a reading of Hillesum's oeuvre that transcends the tendency to place her within a school of thought, religious faith, or literary genre. The practice of labeling is contrary to her beliefs: "Every 'ism' necessarily carries an element of deception because: Nothing is true and neither is that" (EH, 171; trans. MH; see also EH, 167–168; H'83, 56).[20]

At one point she listened to two people discuss Judaism and Christianity. She enjoyed the debate but at the same time wondered whether it was not bending the truth to divide life into "isms." Yet, she also felt a need for "a fenced-in space of [her] own, violently seized and passionately defended" (EH, 168; H'83, 56) to stave off vagueness, aimlessness, and chaos. It is my belief that she ultimately found this space, neither in Judaism nor in Christianity but in mysticism. I return to this point later. In any case she took the freedom to absorb knowledge from various sources and did not worry about their origin or copyright. This sparked criticism, not just in recent years, but in Hillesum's day too (see, for example, EH, 560–561; H'83, 180).

Etty Hillesum read the Old Testament: "Something so powerful emanates from the Old Testament and something so down-to-earth and folksy. It is peopled with great characters, poetic and austere. Actually, it is a really exciting book, the Bible is, it is so rugged and tender, simple and wise" (EH, 499; H'83, 138; adapt. MH).

She described her meditations as Buddhist interludes. The accusation that Hillesum turned away from Judaism to convert to Christianity is dogmatic, incongruous with the world in which Etty Hillesum lived and thought. Consider the following quotation:

I believe I can bear and cope with anything life and these times have in store for me.
And when the turmoil becomes too great and I am completely at a loss, then I still have my two folded hands and bended knee. It is a

posture that is not part of our Jewish tradition. I have had to learn it the hard way. (EH, 580; H'83, 194; adapt. MH)

Although Hillesum learned to kneel in prayer from her Christian friend Henny Tideman (whose influence is described in the next section), and from Julius Spier, who was inspired by parts of the New Testament, I deduce from the previous quote that Christian sources of inspiration did not lead Hillesum away from Judaism, since she still explicitly spoke of "us Jews." Her spirituality is rooted in the spirit of eclecticism.[21] Even as an outlaw she felt "above the law." No laws could curb her freedom: "Yesterday my heart was a sparrow, caught in a vise. It is on the wing again, flying wherever the fancy takes it" (EH, 539; H'83, 165).

Referring to a biblical text, Hélène Cixous connects women, birds, and writing. In Leviticus 11 God distinguishes between clean and unclean animals and declares the latter unfit for consumption. Leviticus 11:13 shows that God, speaking through Moses and Aaron, ordered the Israelites to abstain from eating a great number of fowl. Cixous comments that no reasons are given; it is the law because it is written in the Bible, because God says so—the Law of the Father in full glory. Just like most fowl, argues Cixous, women and a particular kind of writing are excluded from the realm of the divine. This style of writing was discussed in the previous chapter, which explored the hypothesis that an *écriture féminine* stems from a different, diverging outlook: the feminine libidinal economy. Like most birds and most women, this mode of writing—which has an inner source—cannot be found in the "He-Bible" (Cixous 1993b, 113). The common denominator in women, birds, and this mode of writing is their potential to undermine and subvert, which is seen as a threat to the established order.

As I touched on in the introduction to this chapter, Etty Hillesum's openness to different religions and philosophies of life can be explained in light of Hélène Cixous's reflections on the French verb *voler*. Cixous relates the double meaning of this verb (to fly and to steal) to a way of living practiced by women (Cixous 1986a, 96–97 [1975a]; 1981a, 258–259 [1975b]). The realm of culture belongs mainly to men; women are left outside. They can only take part in the culture by gate-crashing or trespassing like burglars or thieves: "For centuries we [women] have been able to possess anything only by flying; we've lived in flight, stealing away" (Cixous 1981a, 258 [1975b]).[22]

Because it has traditionally been men who are expected to organize and to structure our culture and society, women have been in a better position to transgress boundaries, break laws, and disrupt order; after all, these are not "innate" to women. When a woman like Hillesum enters the culture, she is not slotted into a preassigned space because there is no such space waiting for her. This gives her the freedom to position herself wherever she wants. So what is to stop her from acting like a magpie, stealing what catches her eye and storing it in her nest? Since she does not belong anywhere, she is free to come and go as she pleases. Just as Hillesum occasionally borrowed a book from Spier's bookcase,[23] to browse in it and quote from it, so she found inspiration in widely divergent philosophies and religions without regard to their mutual reconcilability.

> Women take after birds and robbers just as robbers take after women and birds. They go by, fly the coop, take pleasure in jumbling the order of space, in disorienting it, in changing around the furniture, dislocating things and values, breaking them all up, emptying structures, and turning propriety upside down.
>
> (Cixous 1981a, 258 [1975b])[24]

Hillesum's open-mindedness, her quest for sources of inspiration and wisdom, should not be interpreted as a denial of her Jewish roots. Her thirst for knowledge did not limit itself to Jewish literature; that much is true. As Rachel Feldhay Brenner points out in *Writing as Resistance* (1997), the prewar assimilation of the Jews may have encouraged them to identify with Christianity. The Christian values of universal brotherly love and forgiveness were particularly well suited to the realm of emancipation and humanism, where the ideals of liberty, equality, and fraternity were propagated. In Hillesum's immediate circle, there was a clear exponent of this type of thinking: Julius Spier. The debate on Judaism and Christianity mentioned earlier was between Spier and Werner Levie, both Jewish refugees from Germany. In this dialogue, Spier defended Christ, while Levie sided with the Jews (see also EH, 166; Hillesum 1986, 742).

Hillesum was the other as a Jewish woman in an anti-Semitic culture, but as a Jew she was also considered the other in Jewish culture to the extent that she was open to Christian sources of inspiration.

Based on Cixous's autobiographical account of her "coming to writing" and her reflections on the connections between birds, women, and writing, I conclude that Hillesum's urge to write stemmed from an inner source, which was, however, not independent of God. This sets Hillesum apart from Cixous, who externalizes God; to Cixous, God is a force that determines which human beings and animals are chosen and clean and which are not. As a writing woman Cixous feels excluded. Hillesum, however, opted for a different image of God (which I explore later); it was an image that allowed her to remain a woman, a writer, and a Jew.

"Dear Big Tide-woman!"

In a letter to Henny Tideman, shortly before the death of their mutual friend Spier, Etty Hillesum wrote:

> Dear big Tide-woman! You know that you are also one of the precious gifts of life that God has given me? I say it so openly and matter-of-factly: God. You were the one who taught me to say it, any time of day or night, you and our dear Friend, whom I've already let go of, by myself on the Dutch heath, at night under the stars; and for whom I now pray, from moment to moment, that God may call this last bit of suffering, mortal shell home. (EH, 602; trans. MH)

This letter shows how great Tide's influence on Etty's religious development had been. Henny Tideman and Julius Spier brought Hillesum into contact with God. In the next section I focus on the triangle between Spier, Etty, and God; here I deal with Tide's beliefs. She was a Christian and strongly influenced by the Oxford group, to which she belonged.[25] This group strove to attain the highest possible forms of love, unselfishness, honesty, and cleanliness (Hillesum 1986, 737).

Hillesum met Tideman when she became part of Spier's circle of friends. She soon felt the influence of Tide's personal faith. Hillesum once wrote: "I suddenly feel totally faint on account of the 'soul' and the God that Henny is so intimate with, and from S.'s love and goodness" (EH, 147; trans. MH).

At the beginning of their friendship, Hillesum was rather ambivalent toward Tide's brand of religion. Only very gradually did she begin to appreciate it. When she first learned of Tide's informal relationship with God, she reacted with a combination of irritation and envy; she considered it childish and "not grand enough" (EH, 275–276; trans. MH), but at the same time she also longed for Tide's simple faith in God. In light of her own character, however, she felt she could never attain this ideal: "I wished that a little of S.'s faith would flow to me, not Tide's variety, hers is unattainable for me, I am just not childish and simple enough" (EH, 126; trans. MH).

Sometimes she resisted her own intellectual powers, which she felt to be an obstacle to achieving inner peace and simplicity. Taking a lesson from Tide, she addressed herself as follows: "Promise me, Etty, that today you won't pick up any books and won't let any title affect you. Turn your ears and all your senses inward for a change and try to find peace within yourself again" (EH, 127; trans. MH).

Every day Tide took time to listen to God. She called these meditative moments her "silent time" and felt that the thoughts which then entered her mind came from God (EH, 113, 207; Hillesum 1986, 737). Hillesum also tried to find time for silence, prayer, and meditation. It may well be that she took her cue from Henny Tideman. At one point she mentioned a letter from Tide, whose naïveté irritated her tremendously, and yet:

> In some other way, this letter has perhaps influenced me anyway. I caught myself praying very hard for Käthe this morning and thinking that before I go to the Levies this Friday, I will pray very ardently and intensely before I leave, that our meeting may be blessed, because so much could depend on it.   (EH, 276; trans. MH)[26]

In the course of her writing, Hillesum gradually adopted not only Tide's habit of praying but also her gratitude toward God. In Etty's first diaries she occasionally commented on the gratitude that played such an important role in Tide's faith (see, for example, EH, 261), but later she herself spoke words of gratitude to God. At first she wrote *about* Tide, *about* God and *about* gratitude, for example in the following entry: "At the end of a day like today, Tide would have said in an almost businesslike tone: Dear God, thank you for those delicious cherries, for the sun and for the fact that I could be with *him* all day long" (EH, 500; trans. MH).

Later in her diary she addressed God directly and—in Jewish and Western history's darkest hour—proffered him a thousand signs of gratitude:

> How can I thank you, my Lord, for all the goodness that you bestow upon me, endlessly. For all the friendship, for the many fruitful thoughts, for that great feeling of love that is in me and that I can convert every step of the way, for everything.   (EH, 552; trans. MH)

Just after returning from her first visit to Westerbork camp, she wrote to Tide:

> I am so peaceful inside and, however strange it may sound, so happy. Happy, because God is giving me the strength to bear everything and look everything straight in the eye and because, just as with you, my gratitude will always exceed my sorrow.   (EH, 603; trans. MH)

At one point Hillesum talked to Spier about how Henny Tideman had influenced her:

> Just now in a conversation with S.: if it hadn't been for my exacting and disciplined mind, I, with *my* sensitivities, would have become a "weinerliche Theosophin [whining theosophist]." Denken Sie nicht [Don't you think]? A roar of laughter: Das hätten Sie doch nie werden können, es ist doch die Mischung bei Ihnen [You could never have become that, you're such a mixture].   (EH, 417; trans. MH)

Most theories about Hillesum's spirituality mention only the impact of Julius Spier. In our culture it is quite common to look for "the man behind the woman," particularly with regard to women's creativity.[27] This has happened in Hillesum's case as well. In this section I quoted several of Hillesum's references to Tide's influence. Significantly, none of these were included in the English translations of Hillesum's work. Without trivializing Spier's importance, I have highlighted the inspiration Hillesum drew from Tideman—an influence on which little has so far been written.[28]

The next two sections deal with the inspiration Etty Hillesum drew from Spier. Although by focusing on the mentor-student component of their relationship, I may appear to have fallen into the old phallocentric trap after all, I demonstrate that—far from being a passive, obedient student—Hillesum had her own reasons for taking his advice. It was Cixous who, in her seminars, first drew attention to this aspect of Hillesum's spirituality. I elaborate on Cixous's vision, though I ultimately find it unsatisfactory, concluding with my own views on Hillesum's spirituality. The point I would like to emphasize is that Hillesum's God was born at the moment when Hillesum decided to take her own path.

Spier the Teacher

Tide's religious notions share a number of characteristics with Spier's: "Spier advised his students to withdraw for 15 minutes or half an hour in the morning and to read a religious or philosophical text, ponder it and write down their reflections" (Hillesum 1986, 737; trans. MH).

This quote shows not only the similarities but also the differences between Tide's and Spier's ways of practicing religion. While Tide's faith could be characterized as childlike and simple, Spier gave his an apparently more mature twist by involving intellectual activities such as reading, reflecting, and writing. To Hillesum, Spier was, among other things, a man of texts, of writings. This was also literally true; in the fall of 1941 Spier was out of room and transferred all his books to Hillesum's quarters. Hillesum learned from Spier through his notes, which she copied (EH, 34). He once gave all his friends a Christmas gift: He had a text typed out, "The Gospel of the Holy Twelve," and added the following mottoes: "The Old passes and makes way for the NEW" and "Blessed are those who read, hear, and DO" (EH, 213; trans. MH; Hillesum 1986, 749–750).

Hillesum wrote of conversations with Spier, both in person and by telephone, about the book of Job and about Faust, Pushkin, and modern poetry (EH, 265–267). One morning, after she had spent the night at his house, they read from the Bible (EH, 498; H'83, 137). Spier lived by the text: "He [Spier] said: This is a time to apply: Love your enemies. And when *we* say that, then one will have to believe that such a thing is possible" (EH, 532; Bible quotation: AV, Matthew 5:44).

She had an intellectual bond with Spier. He encouraged her to read and think. But although she highly valued intellect and reason, she also saw their limitations; in this she was probably influenced by Tide.

> You shouldn't live from your brains, but from deeper and more eternal sources. But you can still gratefully accept your brains as a precious instrument for dissecting the problems your soul unearths. In more down-to-earth words, this may mean that I should trust my intuition more.
>
> Actually, it also means believing in God, without this weakening you. On the contrary, it gives you more strength.   (EH, 133–134)[29]

Spier may well have advocated great simplicity, but only in words, in theory; Tide really lived and practiced this simplicity. In any case it is clear that Etty Hillesum saw Spier as her teacher. "I still have to ask him a million things and learn so incredibly much from him. Why am I not making wiser use of my time" (EH, 129; adapt. MH/SL).

In modern terms we could perhaps call Spier a guru, Etty's enlightened teacher. Indeed, a number of her diary entries show that she closely associated Spier with God:

> Ich will dich immer spiegeln in ganzer Gestalt und will niemals blind sein oder zu alt, um dein schweres schwankendes Bild zu halten.—Rilke said it to God, but on the train and during those few days in Deventer, these lines guided me with regard to our friendship [between herself and S.]: um dein schweres schwankendes Bild zu halten.
>   (EH, 211; trans. MH; see also EH, 381)[30]

During Spier's illness and after his death, Hillesum often wrote about his importance to her; she referred to him as a mediator:

> I still had a million things to ask you and to learn from you, but now I will have to do everything by myself. But you know, I feel so strong: I know I will manage to do it. Whatever energies I possess I owe to you: you have set them free. You taught me to speak the name of God without embarrassment. You were the mediator between God and me, and now you, the mediator, have gone and my path leads straight to God. It is right that it should be so. And I shall be the mediator for any other soul I can reach.
>   (EH, 545–546; H'83, 169; adapt. MH)

The spiritualization Hillesum diagnosed in herself many times is reflected in her relationship with Spier. The physical attraction and love they initially felt evolved in the end into a spiritual mentor-student relationship.

Triangle

During her Saturday seminars in the 1980s, Cixous spun out her thoughts about the relationship between Spier and Hillesum, accentuating the finiteness that characterized their relationship from the beginning: "Even during the relationship, which dies before he does, there is ever present between Etty and S. that life that returns to death, that initial separation that has a form" (Cixous, seminar 03/22/1986; trans. MH).[31]

The separation that loomed ahead for Hillesum and Spier right from the start was partly due to the fact that they were twenty-seven years apart: Spier was almost her father's age. Moreover, he was engaged to be married to Hertha Levi. Because of the war Spier and Levi could only write to each other; she had fled to London, while he had ended up in Amsterdam. For these reasons alone the relationship between Spier and Etty Hillesum had to be temporary. Despite that, the two were considering a marriage for the duration of the war, in the hope that this would allow them to stay together in the concentration camps. Through several diaries Hillesum struggled with her conflicting desires: to make a commitment to someone and to be alone. In the end the scale tipped in favor of solitude:

> All sorts of things are becoming clear to me. For instance this: I don't want to be S.'s wife. To put it quite soberly and bluntly, the age difference is too great. . . . I see him growing old now. He is an old man whom I love, love infinitely, and to whom I shall always be united by an inner bond. But "marriage," what the worthy citizen calls marriage? I must in all seriousness and honesty own up to the fact that that is not what I want. And the fact that I am going to have to go my own way gives me a great feeling of strength. Sustained hourly by the love I bear him and others. So many couples rush off to be married at the last moment, in haste and desperation. I would rather be alone and there for everyone.
>
> (EH, 541; H'83, 165–166; adapt. MH)

Life ratified her decision, as Spier died of lung cancer in September 1942, one day before the Gestapo knocked on his door to deport him to Westerbork (Hillesum 1986, 778). However, the end of their relationship did not come at the moment of Spier's death. Right from the start the relationship had been permeated by an inherent finitude.

Spier was the mediator between God and Etty Hillesum. When he died, Hillesum calmly concluded that she was left with God: "There's no one left to help me. . . . It's not as if this makes me feel impoverished. Rather I feel the richer and more peaceful for it: what's left is God and I, all alone together" (EH, 577–578; trans. MH).

Cixous regards this passage as Hillesum's transition to a relationship with God, in which God takes up all available space. Cixous asserts that although God had always been present in the background, he only started to take a prominent place after Spier died:

> Once he [Spier] is dead, the kingdom of God arrives and sud-denly there is this immense opening up to God, who was already present. And at that moment, God occupies every available inch of space, but which God, and how?
> (Cixous, seminar 01/25/1986; trans. MH)[32]

I discuss Hillesum's answer to Cixous's questions later, but first I want to focus on Cixous's own answers. She explained the nature of Hillesum's God by analyzing the triangle connecting God, Spier, and Hillesum. According to Cixous, Hillesum's spiritual growth began during her relationship with Spier, which takes up a great proportion of her texts, and later developed into a direct relationship between her and God. To elucidate the relation-ship between Spier and God, Cixous alludes to the title of her first book, *Le Prénom de Dieu* [God's first name] (1967): "If you allow me to parody myself, I would say that S. is God's initial, his first name" (Cixous, seminar 03/22/1986; trans. MH).[33]

Cixous names Hillesum's spiritual growth the history of S. God. The two most important characters in Hillesum's diaries and letters ultimately blend into one name: S. God—first name S., last name God. This process can be divided into two periods. The first belongs to S., God's first name, while the second belongs to God. In the first period there are allusions to God, to invoking God, but he does not occupy all the available space. This is only possible once S. figures less prominently. S. died in the late summer of 1942, but Cixous argues that Hillesum had let go of him far earlier. From the very beginning of their relationship, she tried in an almost unconscious but notice-able way to remove S. in order to make way for God, as the following diary entry shows: "I don't think that I shall rely on another human being in my life, but on myself and God" (EH, 101; trans. MH).

This process of detachment, of letting go, intensified in early July 1942, when Etty Hillesum realized what was really going on in the Holocaust:

> Yes, I am still at the same desk, but it seems to me that I am going to have to turn a new leaf and find a different tone. I must admit a new insight into my life and find a place for it: what is at stake is our impending destruction and annihilation, we can have no more illusions about that. They are out to destroy us completely, we must accept that and go on from there. (EH, 486; H'83, 130; adapt. MH)

At that moment Hillesum really needed God; according to Cixous she then symbolically killed S. to make room for God. When she first became fully aware of what was in store for the Jews, she started to prepare for the worst kind of parting: death. Inside she started to let go of everything and everyone, while at the same time she practiced surviving such a separation. On the same day she wrote: "the man [S.] whom I know I will long for so terribly much that I could die" (EH, 513; trans. MH), she also jotted down:

> But also: we're only human. I am already training myself to face the fact that I will go on, even if I am separated from the one without whom I now think I cannot live. From minute to minute I free myself more from him outwardly by focusing ever more strongly on an inner continuation of that bond and that closeness, regardless of how far apart we will be. (EH, 513–514; H'83, 148; adapt. MH)

Hillesum felt the need for someone in her conscience whom she could talk to, someone present deep within her. S. had been the pillar, the buttress supporting the dialogue she would now have to conduct with God. Cixous believes that Hillesum's longing for God can be interpreted as a desire to marry God. Roman Catholicism knows a tradition of marriage to God in the shape of his son Jesus Christ, but Judaism does not.[34] This could perhaps explain Hillesum's fantasies of marrying S., of S. being the carrier of her dream. With this analysis Cixous also helps to explain the way in which Hillesum wrote about Spier's death in her last diary. Between the lines there is tenderness and joy. In a sense his death can be interpreted as the answer to her dreams. This is a magnificent but also chilling realization. Cixous cites the diary entry Hillesum made a few hours after Spier's death and concludes that his tragic fate is to have been relegated to anonymity, a place he had never actually escaped. She cites the fact that Hillesum never called Spier by his name (a fact I connect with the Jewish tradition of not pronouncing God's name—in keeping with the Third Commandment: Thou shalt not take the name of the Lord thy God in vain (AV, Exodus 20:7). This similarity demonstrates once more the extent to which Hillesum experienced Spier and God as one. In all her diaries she called him "S." For a long time they addressed each other with the formal German *Sie*, and only later did they use the informal *Du*.

And your *Du* was to me one of the most caressing words any man
had ever used toward me. And as you know, there had been quite a
few. You always signed your letters with a question mark, and I mine
as well. You began your letters with "Just listen to this . . !": your characteristic "Hören Sie mal," but your last letter you began with "Dearest."
To me you are nameless, as nameless as the Heavens above. And I want
to put all your portraits away and never look at them again, for they
are too material.   (EH, 547; H'83, 171; adapt. MH)

One matter that is relevant here is connected to contemporary developments in the field of feminist theology: the possible and desirable transformation of a "He-God" into a "She-God" in order to counterbalance the lopsided
association of God with masculinity. According to Gross (1979) the Kabbalah
teaches that exile is the fundamental condition of human existence. One of
the main reasons for this is the alienation of the masculine from the feminine
in God. The world would be healed if these two dimensions of God were
reunified. Because the Jewish religion is fundamentally theistic, that is to say
that the absolute can be represented as a person who enters into a covenant
of love and responsibility with people, it is of great importance that God can
be imagined not only as a man but also as a woman (Gross 1979:168). Even
if the word "God" is ultimately just a name for something so absolute and
infinite that it is beyond human comprehension and language, the only
approach to the divine is through human experience. Although Hillesum
was ahead of her time in many respects and thought about God in quite novel
ways, she did adhere to the image of a male God. In my view this has much
to do with Spier. Spier was her great love and source of inspiration. She sublimated the conversations she used to have with him into dialogues with God.
When Spier was about to die, she wrote: "And talking to you, God. Is that
right? Leaving people aside, I only feel a need to speak to you" (EH, 544;
H'83, 168; adapt. MH).

God Is Born in Etty

In this section I explore the complexity of Etty Hillesum's spiritual growth
in more detail by emphasizing the extent to which it was entwined with her
self-actualization. In the previous section we saw that Cixous answered her own
question about the nature of Etty's God, and established that Spier and God
are inextricably linked. Without rejecting this view, I would like to add another
one, based on Hillesum's own answers to Cixous's question. Her diary entry
dated September 17, 1942—two days after Spier died—gives a very lucid account
of her outlook on life and her image of God: "And that probably best expresses

my own outlook on life: I repose in myself. And that part of myself, that deepest and richest part in which I repose, is what I call 'God'" (EH, 549; H'83, 173; adapt. MH).

She saw God as the essence of everything and everyone, as the be-all and end-all of existence: "Those inner sources, which I prefer to call God" (EH, 566; trans. MH). Perhaps this clarifies to whom Hillesum directed her comments when—particularly after Spier's death, but also earlier—she addressed God in her diaries. Her God often seems to be a sort of God the Father, an external God, the Other. However, her God is in fact the core, the essence of every human being. Perhaps the confusion arises because she anthropomorphized God, a convention she might have adopted from Tide. Still, she applied this personification—the animation of an abstract entity or lifeless object— not only to God, but also to books, a pebble, and the like.[35]

In her analysis of Hillesum's relationship with God, Cixous regards Spier's death as the starting point of Hillesum's true spiritual growth. Spier's death is seen as the moment when she really turned to God. Cixous believes that the time leading up to his death was just a preparatory phase, and she argues, convincingly, that before Spier's death Hillesum mainly wrote *about* God, while after his death she wrote *to* God. Still, I want to modify Cixous's ideas for a number of reasons.

In the first place Hillesum had already expressed her wish to write a novella about her spiritual development back in November 1941. Her story idea reveals the confluence of a need to write and a love of God:

> And there is God. "The girl who could not kneel but learned to do
> so on the rough coconut matting in an untidy bathroom." . . . This inner
> process, the story of the girl who learned to kneel, is something I would
> love to write down in all its details.   (EH, 156; H'83, 50; adapt. MH)

This shows that Hillesum's spiritual development was well under way by the end of 1941. Apparently she felt she had enough to say on the subject to fill a book. Thus I reject the assumption that Hillesum's spirituality evolved later and only really came into its own after S.'s death (September 15, 1942). On this point I differ with Cixous, who posits: "Etty's diary clearly indicates a development. God is born very late, there is a history of God in the text, and by the time God fills up all the space he takes in the end, he has become completely domesticated" (Cixous, seminar 01/25/1986; trans. MH).[36]

I believe that Hillesum's spiritual growth began long before Spier's death and even culminated before he died. My assertion is supported not only by Etty's fantasy of writing her novella, but also by her references to Tide. This is the second reason I do not share Cixous's opinion. To take Hillesum's spirituality seriously only after September 1942 is to deny Tide's inspiration. Her impact on Hillesum's experience of religion dates back to 1941.

A third reason lies in one particularly gripping diary entry, which I see as the mark of a radical move—clearly visible in the text (EH, 161–163; H'83, 52)—toward greater involvement with God. This change took place almost a year before Spier's death.

It began with a sort of mental spring cleaning. Etty Hillesum felt she had taken on too much and was spreading herself too thin. She decided that psychochirology, or chiromancy,[37] was not for her and that she would cancel her appointments with the woman whose lady-companion she was.[38] This return to herself took place on Monday morning, November 24, 1941. On the afternoon of that same day, she suddenly addressed God and made him a promise:

> You know, God, I will do the best I can. I will not try to withdraw from this life. I will continue to be part of it and try to develop all the gifts that I have, if I have any. I won't sabotage. But please, give me a sign once in a while. And please make some music come out of me, let whatever is in me, find a voice, it so longs to be expressed.
> I'm in a very weird mood, all of a sudden.   (EH, 161; trans. MH)

The next morning she continued to write: "Something is happening to me and I don't know if it's just a passing mood or something real. It feels like I have been yanked back on track. I feel a little more self-reliant and independent" (EH, 161; H'83, 52; adapt. MH).

She described the prayer she had murmured the night before as she cycled through the unlit streets; it was a promise to do her best and an appeal for help from God. She pledged to be good to others but acknowledged her own limitations: "I don't want to be anything special, I just want to try and be true to the person inside me who is seeking to reach her fullest potential" (EH, 162; H'83, 52; adapt. MH).

My argument is that Etty Hillesum's God was born the very moment Etty chose to be herself. She experienced this God not as a father figure but as her own essence, her innermost being, her deepest self. The moment she canceled a few appointments, after realizing they were not for her, she opened up to the God inside her. She refused any longer to fulfill other people's expectations of her and saw it as her duty to become herself, in other words: to fulfill her potential, to grow personally, to use her talents. This is what Luce Irigaray calls becoming divine.

Irigaray's 1984 lecture on divine women was based on Ludwig Feuerbach's *The Essence of Christianity,* a text that can be used to gain more insight into Hillesum's spirituality. Feuerbach, Marx's mentor, brought God down to earth. With revolutionary zeal he argued that it was not God who had created people, but people who created God in their own image, after their own likeness. Feuerbach argued that humankind needs a God in order to position itself as a species, that God is the projection of people's ideals and dreams. This interpretation of religious thought is especially appealing to Irigaray,[39] but she finds in it—as in all other ideas she absorbs—the flaw of sexual indifference, the male bias nearly omnipresent in Western discourse. Although Feuerbach spoke of people, it is clear that he was referring to men only; women are not included in his argument. The fallacy of equating people with men has had a particularly strong influence on people's conceptions of God. When God, in Feuerbach's view, is created by humankind to define the species, to position themselves as finite in relation to the infinite, all implications of sexual difference are overlooked. In other words, in the phallocentric attempt at self-definition, the differences between men and women are ignored—while it is sexual difference that sets boundaries and thus makes definition possible.

> To avoid that finiteness, man has sought out a unique male God. God has been created out of man's gender. He scarcely sets limits within Himself and between Himself: He is father, son, spirit. Man has not allowed himself to be defined by another gender: the female. His unique God is assumed to correspond to the human race (*genre humain*), which we know is not neuter or neutral from the point of view of the difference of the sexes. (Irigaray 1993b, 60–61 [1987])[40]

The traditional, powerful God of the establishment is a statue erected to celebrate and glorify the male sex. This He-God, God the Father, molded after the ideals of the male, demands of women what men demand of them. In this divine discourse, women are a derivative, secondary class. This precludes any potential for actualization *as a woman*. Women are expected to conform to masculine ideals. Such a God does not command women to become themselves, to use their talents, to discover who they are.

What options are there for women who refuse to be subjugated? What course of action is there for women who feel the divine surge within them but can find no channel for it within their Judeo-Christian environment? In "Divine Women" Irigaray reflects on a way for women to express their spirituality, a way that does not lead to loss of self but promotes self-actualization and personal growth instead. Feuerbach's investigation into the meaning and significance of God to hu/mankind prompted Irigaray to posit the following:

> God forces us to do nothing except *become*. The only task, the only obligation laid upon us is: to become divine men and women, to become perfectly, to refuse to allow parts of ourselves to shrivel and die that have the potential for growth and fulfillment.
>
> (Irigaray 1993b, 68–69 [1987])[41]

Traditionally only men were given this task. It is high time that women, too, accepted this obligation and started living it. This means that women have to assert their right to enter the symbolic order. We need not reject Feuerbach's image of God, we need only make it accessible to both men and women. Women also need a God on whom to project their ideals, dreams, and desires. They also need a God who acts as a horizon, an ultimate goal, an incentive to engage in becoming human, becoming man as well as becoming woman.

Virginia Woolf already knew very well what women need: "a room of [their] own." To this, Irigaray has added "*un Dieu au féminin*" (Irigaray 1987, 85), "a God in the feminine gender." (Irigaray 1993b, 72). Hillesum did have a room of her own, which she enjoyed wholeheartedly because it offered her the quiet space she needed to stay in touch with herself. But the act of writing at her desk also served another purpose: She was also seeking a God of her own. On November 24, 1941, after making a few drastic changes in her life and reaching some illuminating conclusions about herself, Hillesum professed her faith. She realized that doing so much work for others threatened to alienate her from herself. Her job as a companion was at odds with her primary need for a dialogue with herself. Her contributions to Spier's chirological work, which consisted of her typing out reports on other patients, were hard to reconcile with her urge to get to know and understand herself. She discovered that she did not want to be more than herself, but no less either: only herself in her fullest potential. This was no resignation she professed to. On the contrary, by forgoing the tasks that were "not for her," she hoped to discover her own strengths and put them to use, without false pretenses, for her own and others' benefit. This return to her own roots suggests an encounter between herself and the God within her. The God to whom Hillesum prays is not a transcendental God or a wrathful God who lays down the law from above, but an immanent God, a God deep within herself, who is consistent with her own dreams and thoughts. This "becoming divine" brings to mind an ability women have, which Irigaray has termed "*la re-touche*": "reflexive touching, a woman's touching of her self by her self" (Vincenot 1990, 69;

trans. MH; see also Whitford 1991, 139, 153, 161). This motion is the opposite of the scattering that characterizes so many women's lives; women tend to spread themselves too thin in order to meet others' expectations and needs, forgetting that they too have needs. In contrast, *la retouche,* or "auto-affection," is a woman's "return upon herself" (Whitford 1991, 153), her spinning on her own axis. Putting this into the context of "divine women," this gyration is women's attempt to create their own pivot, their own God.

I would like to return to a point I made earlier. I have shown that Hillesum increasingly felt God to be a part of herself. This begs the question of why she chose to adhere to a male God and did not change him into a female. One might find an answer in the limitations she saw in the word "God" anyway: "Sometimes I find the word God so primitive, it is only a likeness, an approximation of our greatest and most continuous inner adventure. I believe I don't even need the word 'God,' it often strikes me as a primitive grunt, a crutch" (EH, 463; trans. MH).

Another possible explanation has to do with the cliché views that Etty Hillesum held, particularly in the first few diaries, about men and women (see also De Costa 1993a). These prompted her to write the following, for instance: 'We are not yet full human beings; we are still bitches. We are still bound and tied by centuries-old traditions. We are still waiting to be born as people, that is the great task that lies before us women" (EH, 73; H'83, 27–28; adapt. MH).

As I discussed before, Luce Irigaray explores the opportunities for women's self-actualization, and its difficulties, from an angle of sexual difference. Irigaray reasons that the traditional image of women has little to do with women themselves, but owes much to phallocentric cultural constructs, which define women as deviant from the male norm. True womanhood has hardly been explored: "I am born a woman, but I must still become this woman that I am by nature" (Irigaray 1996, 107).[42] According to Irigaray women should not deny their womanhood. On the contrary, they should develop it and work on becoming-woman. In my view it was because Hillesum was still caught up in the traditional notions of masculinity and femininity that she spoke not of becoming woman but of becoming human. It is interesting to see that when her physical and mental condition improved, her ideas about women also changed. In her depressed state she had a negative attitude toward women; she rejected the traditional female role. This attitude changed over the course of time: The more she grew personally, the more she believed that women had a special task to fulfill in society and culture (EH, 301, 312). I am convinced that Hillesum's spirituality is linked to both her becoming woman and her becoming divine, and that it shows an active sense of responsibility rather than passivity and victimization. In the next section, I will demonstrate that the double bind of being a "Jewoman" pushed Hillesum toward mysticism. She braved the dangers inherent in the position of the mystic by symbolically taking on motherhood.

Between Mysticism and Motherhood

The altar and the ark: two inner sanctums from which women are banned. Where is the place of worship for women who are awash in spirituality? Traditionally they have found sanctuary in mysticism. After all, mystical experiences are outside the religious establishment and a source of confusion. The symbolic order of Western religious discourse is undermined by the outlandish, untraceable tendencies of mysticism: the unconscious semiotic potential of spirituality. In mysticism, women can subvert the power of the masculine and speak for themselves: "This is the only place in the history of the West in which woman speaks and acts so publicly" (Irigaray 1985a, 191 [1974]).[43]

The feminine mystic disregards the men around her and addresses God directly. The woman mystic's union with God can be interpreted as the woman's union with herself (Irigaray 1985a, 200–201[1974]). The mystic experiences her encounter with God as authentic and immediate: It takes place outside the established institutions and without mediation. Hillesum felt this aspect of mysticism very strongly after Spier's death: "You were the mediator between God and me, and now you, the mediator, have gone and my path leads straight to God. It is right that it should be so. And I shall be the mediator for any other soul I can reach" (EH, 545–546; H'83, 169).

Irigaray pointed to the paradoxical risk of self-loss that must be faced by the woman mystic in patriarchal Judeo-Christian tradition. Fleeing into mysticism to escape masculine dominance, her desire for God can be so great that she loses her own identity. Irigaray's coinage *"la mystérique"* (Irigaray 1985a, 191) combines the mystic with the hysteric: Both defy the establishment and reject conformism. They take part in neither subjugation nor devout devotion but live on the edge of insanity, balancing dangerously between suffering and passion.

Hillesum's writings seem to move away from hysteria and toward mysticism. She defies the dangers of hysteria by transforming her dependent daughterhood into a responsible motherhood. Her early diaries show her to have been an unstable young woman with psychosomatic complaints.[44] She often felt confused, empty, depressed, and lacking form. Periods of high energy and zest for life alternated with depressions during which she suffered headaches and stomachaches and contemplated suicide. Guided by Spier she learned to uncover the causes of her unstable, restless life. Her mother's internal despair and chaotic behavior cast a gloom over Hillesum's development. She once wrote, almost with malice: "To me, mother exemplifies what not to become" (EH, 148; trans. MH). She feared having inherited the psychiatric disorders that afflicted her mother and two brothers. Etty's mother, Riva Bernstein, was, it has been generally confirmed, unbalanced and hard to deal with. In Deventer rumor had it that the principal's wife was mad (Lagrou 1985, 25; trans. MH).[45]

This harsh judgment says more about the people who spread the rumor than about Riva Bernstein. As a refugee from Russia, she probably stuck out like a sore thumb in Deventer. From her childhood she had known the terror of anti-Semitism. After pogroms drove her from her birthplace, Pochep, she fled Russia in 1907, disguised as a soldier, her head clean shaven (Hillesum 1986, 747). She lost touch with her brother and her parents, who also fled to the Netherlands but later moved on, probably to the United States. These traumatic events had marked her for life and left their stamp on the family. The chaos in her psyche was reflected by an untidy and disorganized household. Hillesum also suffered from this: "Slowly I'm beginning to understand my childhood a little, those recurrent bouts of headaches and listlessness for weeks on end, the feeling of drowning in chaos" (EH, 217; trans. MH).

From the moment Hillesum met Spier and started keeping a diary, she began battling her inner complexes, trying to reeducate herself. This critical and relentless self-analysis finally freed her from the burdens she had been carrying since childhood. She replaced the chaos, emptiness, and shapelessness that had once marked her life with an inner peace and harmony that stayed with her until the end. Although she did not break with her parents and others, she did release herself from feelings of guilt, frustration, and dependence. This caused her to see herself more and more as a loner. However, this separation process was counterbalanced by her spiritual growth, which made her aware that everything was interconnected in a meaningful whole and imbued with a divine essence.

Others have already pointed out the similarities between Hillesum's texts and mystical literature in general and Jewish mysticism in particular. They have focused on her desire for unity, her turning in on herself and her image of an immanent God.[46] In my view the most important source of Hillesum's mysticism can be found not in mystical texts—although it is common knowledge that at the end of her life she was reading Meister Eckhart (EH, 654; Hillesum 1986, 800)—but in the circumstances in which she lived. I will now show how her position as a "Jewoman" and her religious experiences are connected and also how this link allowed her to sidestep the pitfall of mysticism mentioned by Irigaray.

During World War II many people found it hard to reconcile their traditional Judeo-Christian faith—which upheld an image of an almighty, just God— with their wartime existence, in which all the world seemed to be sinking into a pool of pain and suffering. After all, what kind of God would allow dictators to grab power, the innocent to be condemned, and the young to be murdered? In one of her letters from Westerbork, Hillesum described the struggle with God that so many people experienced: "There was a woman who'd had to feed her four-month-old child on cabbage soup for days. She said: 'I keep calling, "Oh God, oh God"—but does he even exist anymore?'" (EH, 640; H'87, 50; adapt. MH).

While many desperately questioned God's existence, Etty Hillesum grew toward an experience of life in which good and evil, beautiful and horrible could coexist. It appears that she was able to stay in touch with the divine without closing herself off to the dramatic suffering and death surrounding her. However, with so much evil around her, she too would eventually have to face the unavoidable question of God's place and meaning. To save God, and to withstand the harshness of outer reality, she turned him into an almost human character living deep within herself. In her writings Hillesum is the creator of this divine character. Cixous notes: "That is absolutely right, she is the author of God" (Cixous, seminar 03/22/1986; trans. MH).[47] Cixous concludes that Hillesum's God differed considerably from the biblical, Old Testament version.[48] I would not go that far. God in the Old Testament has many faces. He is sometimes a powerful, sovereign outsider ruling his subjects; this God is indeed absent from Hillesum's writings. However, in Exodus, a book of the Bible that particularly appealed to Hillesum, we find a God who does not forsake his people but follows them into exile. This "desert God" (Reitsma 1989, 118; trans. MH) joins the people on their journey and shares in their suffering. This image of God can be found in Hillesum's work: Her God is in the camps.

Cixous compares Hillesum's longing for God's presence to the development of her favorite author, Clarice Lispector. Lispector died of lung cancer in middle age: like Hillesum she wrote in the face of death. However, Cixous feels that Lispector went much further than Hillesum, because she went beyond God. Cixous ascribes this difference to the fact that Lispector was older and more experienced than Hillesum. I find this argument hardly convincing. Cixous's second argument is more acceptable to me: The rapidly growing threat to Hillesum's life precipitated an early maturity. She became aware that she would have to go the last leg of life's journey alone. To make this absolute solitude bearable, she invoked God as her witness.[49] She needed someone who would not forsake her, whom she could address in a familiar, informal tone, whom she—in the manner of Saint Augustine's love letters to God (EH, 579; H'83, 193)—could write to. The dialogical nature of her relationship with God is similar to Hasidism, which holds that direct contact with God is possible.

Hillesum arrived at her image of God in a way similar to the emergence and history of Hasidism, a Jewish mystical movement that arose amid the persecution and pogroms of eighteenth-century Poland. Then, too, people felt the need for a God who was present and for a way to encounter him in daily life, in daily suffering. Hasidism was, in a sense, a resistance movement. To oppose destruction, hatred, inhumanity, and murderousness, Hasidism proclaimed the sanctification of daily life, love of people, faith in God, hope and joy.[50] It was also a reaction to Jewish religious life in which Talmudic studies were given the highest priority; hence, Hasidism has also been described as a "Jewish revivalist-pietistic movement" (Eliach 1989, xv). As for the debate about how Jewish or Christian Hillesum's work is, I would prefer to transcend this distinction by focusing on her kinship with mysticism (and with Hasidism in particular). This kinship is apparent in another aspect of Hillesum's image of God, in which Jewish mysticism and her womanhood converge: the mother-child dynamics. My exploration of this aspect of Hillesum's spirituality once again highlights her position as a "Jewoman."

Hillesum's God is not only a God who shares in the suffering, he is also a dependent God (see also Burnier 1988, 83–84). Her growth toward independence, which took wing during her prayer of late November 1941, went hand in hand with a growing awareness of God's dependence:

> Well, God, there doesn't seem to be much you yourself can do about our circumstances, they're part of life. I don't hold you responsible either—later you can hold us accountable. And it is becoming clearer to me with practically every heartbeat: you cannot help us but we must help you and we must defend your dwelling place inside us to the last.   (EH, 517; H'83, 151; adapt. MH)[51]

Etty Hillesum promised God that she would not ask for anything, only help him. In light of her circumstances, she had little choice. By making even the smallest request of him, she would have risked losing him. Therefore she completely reversed the traditional roles—in her personal life too. She wondered what God intended with her and countered with a question of her own: "And perhaps that is what it depends on: what I intend with you?" (EH, 562; H'83, 182; adapt. MH). It is not God's but people's responsibility when hell rather than paradise visits the earth. Hillesum felt God to be very small and dependent, and so she offered him protection. It is as if she were pregnant with God: "It is a life with God and in God and with God within me" (EH, 463; trans. MH). She offered to protect him and to guide him safely through all the hardship. She wanted to safeguard him from all outside evil, so that he could survive the war unscathed. Her relationship with God is not vertical but circular: Although he is her creator, he is not viable without her. Surrounded by the mechanisms intent on destroying the Jewish people, Hillesum continued to focus on the new life she felt within her: "I would so much like to stay alive, in order to help prepare for a new era and to keep that solid core in me whole and to pass it on to that new era, which I know will come. For it is already growing within me, day by day, I can feel it" (EH, 526; trans. MH).

This symbolic pregnancy contrasts sharply with the real abortion she had around the time of her profession of faith (late November 1941). A few days after her prayer, she spent the night with one of her lovers, which resulted in an unwanted pregnancy. This led to the following outpouring of emotion:

> The mother instinct is something of which I am completely devoid,
> I think. I explain it like this to myself: basically, life is a vale of tears
> and all human beings are miserable, so I cannot take on the responsi-
> bility of bringing yet another unhappy creature into the world.
>
> (EH, 173; H'83, 58; adapt. MH)

Her feelings about motherhood were probably influenced not only by her fear of hereditary madness, but also by the war. Very caringly, responsibly, and paradoxically, full of love for the unborn child, she opted for its death (see EH, 177). The fact that Hillesum did not want to become a mother in the literal sense of the word does not detract from her pro/creative abilities, which she did put to use. Her reasons for rejecting actual motherhood were the same as those for assuming symbolic motherhood in the last year of her life. This interpretation of Hillesum's life story, as expressed in her writings, is inspired by Irigaray's philosophical reflections on the relationship between womanhood and motherhood. While Irigaray's illustrious predecessor Simone de Beauvoir advised women against motherhood because she felt that it stood in the way of emancipation, Irigaray rejects this strategy because of its intrinsic danger of "turning women into men." Irigaray advocates a revaluation rather than a rejection of motherhood. This revaluation should create room for both women and their potential motherhood in the symbolic order, which would also radically change this order:

> We also need to discover and declare that we are always mothers just by being women. We bring many things into the world apart from children, we give birth to many other things apart from children: love, desire, language, art, social things, political things, but this kind of creativity has been forbidden to us for centuries. We must take back this maternal creative dimension that is our birthright as women.
>
> (Irigaray 1993a, 18 [1980])[52]

Following in Irigaray's footsteps, philosophist Rina Van der Haegen also pleads for a place for women in the symbolic order where they can develop without having to deny who they are. In response to the traditional restriction of women to their role as mothers and their exclusion from the symbolic order, Van der Haegen has formulated a notion of "sociomaternal productivity":

> Independent of actual motherhood, of reproduction in the strict sense of the word—or, in other words, reproduction at her own expense—I want to use the word conglomerate "sociomaternal productivity" to create an opening for a social actualization of her pro/creative powers.
>
> (Van der Haegen 1989, 178–179; trans. MH;
> see also Withuis 1995, 196)

Is "sociomaternal productivity" not exactly what Hillesum's inward journey ultimately led to? In her "profession of faith" she very tentatively wrote of her wish to be able to help her fellow human beings. Her desire to be socially productive by treating all others with love was much stronger than traditional motherly feelings. In the end she went to Westerbork to be a social worker, to take on the impossible task of trying to ameliorate other people's suffering. Even in this concentration camp hell she did not lose touch with God; like a midwife assisting in childbirth, she tried to bring out God in the hearts of others. She was not a victim, but a strong woman with a great sense of responsibility, who kept trying to give meaning to her life and the lives of others.

Cixous places Hillesum's writings in the genre of "nourishing books": Etty Hillesum wrote in white ink. Nourishing books are those that map out paths to spiritual survival. Hillesum wanted to write about a way of living and thinking peripheral to the mainstream. She felt that history had to be rewritten, as the dominant discourse did not do justice to the fullness and wealth of life: "And I said, perhaps it is worth being part of history. One can at least see for oneself what else there is, besides that which ends up in the history books" (EH, 375; H'83, 109; adapt. MH).

She wanted to rewrite history in order to bring out reality's multiformity and contradictions, but that is not all. In her thinking she also radically transformed religious discourse. God was her creator and witness, but then she was also God's creator and witness. Her open-minded image of God was religious in the true sense of the word, because it connected heaven with earth, suffering with happiness, and God with people.[53] She did not avoid paradox or complexity, but gave them free rein, because she was convinced that was the only way to do justice to the multiplicity and ambiguity of reality as she experienced it.

The Lord Is My High Retreat

Etty Hillesum, her parents, and her brother Mischa were deported on Tuesday, September 7, 1943. Jopie Vleeschhouwer, her "dear companion" (EH, 643; trans. MH), wrote to Han Wegerif and other friends of Hillesum in Amsterdam to tell them how she had taken the news of her deportation and had said good-bye. Hillesum managed to throw two postcards from the train. One postcard was addressed to Han Wegerif and friends. On her way to Auschwitz she tried to reassure those who stayed behind: "We left the camp singing—the cattle trains are not so bad" (Hillesum 1986, 713; trans. MH).

The other postcard was addressed to Christine van Nooten, a teacher at the secondary school where Hillesum's father had been the principal and one of the people who had sent parcels to the Hillesums during their stay in Westerbork (Hillesum 1986, 795).

> Christine,
>   Opening the Bible at random, I find this: "The Lord is my high tower."
> I am sitting on my rucksack in the middle of a full freight car.
>   (EH, 702; H'87, 14; adapt. MH)

It is likely her Bible opened to a page in a book she had often been reading over the past few months: Psalms. Less than a week before her deportation, she had written Christien and remarked: "How splendid the Psalms are" (EH, 699; trans. MH; see also Hillesum 1986, 809).

In the Authorized (King James) Version, Psalms 18:2 reads: "The Lord is my rock, and my fortress, and my deliverer; my God, my strength, in whom I will trust; my buckler, and the horn of my salvation, and my high tower."

In the Dutch Bible, "high tower" is *hoog vertrek*, literally a "high room." However, the word *vertrek* also means "departure," lending Hillesum's last writing a certain ambiguity. An alternative translation in English might be: "The Lord is my high retreat." When "retreat" is read as withdrawal or departure, the sentence "The Lord is my high retreat" can be interpreted as an affirmation of her great faith in God. In a sense she was saying: In my departure I see the hand of God. More than a year earlier, when she first realized what awaited the Jewish people, she had already written:

> With each minute that passes I shed more wishes and desires and attachments to others, I am prepared for anything, for any place on this earth God might send me and I am prepared to testify, in any situation and until my last breath, that this life is beautiful and meaningful. And that it is not God's fault that things are the way they are now, but our own.   (EH, 507–508; trans. MH)

The postcard from the cattle train shows that even then, on the way to her death, Hillesum neither abandoned God nor blamed him for anything. The postcard was the last sign of life that her friends received from her. According to Red Cross records, Etty Hillesum died on November 30, 1943 (Hillesum 1986, xvi). This means that she managed to stay alive longer than the three days she thought she could survive in a concentration camp (EH, 492; H'83, 134). There had been times when she expressed a tentative hope of surviving: "I know I will often be cast down on God's earth, crushed and destroyed. I also believe that I am very resilient and will always manage to get back up" (EH, 522; trans. MH).

Etty Hillesum and 986 others arrived in Auschwitz in September 1943. Some of the deportees had already died from the hardships of the journey, and Hillesum's parents might have been among them. On arrival men and women were separated. Some of the men were sent to Warsaw to clear up the rubble after the quelling of the Warsaw ghetto uprising. The women were made to work so hard that few survived longer than two months. Only eight people from this transport survived the war (Hillesum 1986, 810).

Hillesum once described the weekly deportations from Westerbork as hell on earth: "If I were to say that I was in hell that night, what would I really be telling you? I said it aloud to myself once, that night, concluding almost soberly, 'So, this is what hell is like'" (EH, 689; H'87, 127; adapt. MH).[54]

Was she able to find words for Auschwitz?[55]

The second meaning of "The Lord is my high retreat" lies in the other definition of "retreat": "a place of retirement, quiet or security; a refuge, shelter, haunt." And also "(the time spent in) religious retirement" (*Webster's New International Comprehensive Dictionary of the English Language,* 1996). Hillesum reversed this image and turned it into: "I am the Lord's retreat or refuge." She did this for the first time on her twenty-eighth birthday, when all she wrote in her diary were the following sentences: "God, I thank you. Thank you for living within me. Thank you for everything" (EH, 240; trans. MH).

Hillesum's God was not just an external God; he was also part of herself, even her "better half." Such a God was more befitting to her than a transcendental God who laid down his laws from above or from outside. By creating this God, who resided deep within her, she became a "divine woman." Her architecture was open and hospitable, attesting to a feminine libidinal economy. While men tend to build walls around themselves, to close off and protect—both materially and symbolically: caves, huts, homes, women, villages, cities, language, and theory (Irigaray 1993a, 141 [1984])[56]—Etty Hillesum did not build a refuge for herself but for another: God. She built God a symbolic shelter in herself where she could retreat, but which did not hamper her freedom of movement. Her shelter was no prison with a mother confined to the kitchen; it was the point of departure, the birth, of her socio-maternal productivity. Amid so much brutalization, desensitization, hatred, and misery, she tried to bring out the divine in her fellow human beings: "The most essential and the deepest in me hearkening unto the most essential and deepest in the other. God to God" (EH, 549; H'83, 173).

And if it was not there to bring out, then she wanted to bring it to them:

> Sometimes people seem to me like houses with open doors. I walk in and roam through hallways and rooms. Every house is furnished a little differently, and yet they are all the same, and each one of them must be turned into a dwelling dedicated to you, God. And I promise you, yes, I promise that I shall try to find room and refuge for you in as many houses as possible. Actually, that is a nice metaphor. I walk up to the front door and seek shelter for you. There are so many vacant houses, I will bring you to them, you will be their main lodger.
> (EH, 550; H'83, 174; trans. MH)

While Cixous believes that Hillesum's texts are among those that owe their existence to homelessness (Cixous, seminar 10/20/1985; see also chapter 5), Hillesum did not feel homeless. Sitting on her rucksack among dozens of others who shared her fate, in a packed train headed toward annihilation, she tossed out postcards to tell her friends that the cattle car was not so bad—and to attest to a spiritual home: "The Lord is my high retreat." She created a God who suited her and her circumstances. Her last messages tell us how successfully she attained this goal. She did not have to leave him behind; he accompanied her to Auschwitz.

❧ Epilogue

La fin du siècle, the end of the century, calls for reflections on the preceding age. At the end of the twentieth century, we might ask what issues can be considered the most important of our time. Europe's biggest trauma of the twentieth century is the persecution and murder of six million Jews and millions of others for their perceived deviation from, and inferiority to, the "Aryan race." Perhaps as a reaction to this, Anne Frank's diaries were for decades read from a universal perspective: as a book written by a child who came to writing in extraordinary circumstances, while neither her Jewish background nor her female subjectivity received much attention. Etty Hillesum's writings met with the same fate: Emphasis was placed on the author's spiritual growth. As a saint or mystic, she was stripped of any specifically Jewish or female subjectivity. It is precisely this double bind, their double otherness, that I have explored in order to arrive at a new reading of Anne Frank's and Etty Hillesum's texts.

The twentieth century is an era of paradox. It brought the Holocaust, but it has also rung in radical and encouraging developments worldwide, including advances in feminism and women's studies. In the most recent feminist wave, sex and gender differences have been linked to other differences, such as religion and ethnicity. This "brand" of feminism advocates the acceptance of differences without falling prey to inclusion or exclusion mechanisms or to binding definitions or restrictions. It challenges us to deal with differences in a way that gives life, rather than causing death and destruction. Questions such as "What is a woman?" and "What is a Jewish woman?" are rejected, because every woman can provide a different answer, or even several answers. Anne and Etty were women, but this biological fact means nothing until we read what it is they themselves had to say on the subject. They both regarded themselves as Jewish, and for that reason it is impertinent to question whether they were "real Jews." What did they themselves write about their Jewish and female subjectivity? I intentionally avoid using the word "identity" because this term can be misleading. There is no single, essential Jewish or feminine identity, or, to paraphrase Irigaray, "This (Jewish/Feminine) Sex Which Is Not One" (Irigaray 1985 [1977]). The essence is the difference within the difference (Trinh 1989), the essence is pluriformity and ambivalence. Rosi Braidotti calls on feminists and other intellectuals to cultivate a nomadic consciousness (Braidotti 1994a, 146–172). A nomad can bond for life without pinning herself down, but gives life her own meaning, assigns it her own idiosyncratic significance, all the while feeling free to take another, a different path.

This book is my attempt to read, from a nomadic awareness, the texts of two authors with a history of exile. Anti-Semitism and Nazism chased them and their families through Europe: first from east to west (Riva Bernstein fled Russia for the Netherlands; the Franks left Frankfurt am Main for Amsterdam) and later from west to east (Amsterdam, Westerbork, Bergen-Belsen, Auschwitz-Birkenau), until they were finally murdered. The Nazis took away their nationality, but these two women created a new one: "Nationality: literary" (Stevens 1995a). They felt at home in language. In the land of writing, they could grow and develop, they could freely express their inner feelings without being hemmed in by restrictive measures. They did not pin themselves down with their fountain pens, but committed themselves to inscribing their spirituality and sexuality and in the process transgressed boundaries and broke taboos. While in our culture, womanhood and Jewishness go hand in hand with restriction and exclusion, Anne Frank and Etty Hillesum managed to transform their exile into a nomadic consciousness. This is the strength and the inspiration that speaks from their texts even now, more than fifty years later. Locked up in death's antechamber, they kept themselves alive by writing themselves, until they were denied even pen and paper. The diaries, the letters, and the stories are the silent witnesses of a Jewish girl and a young Jewish woman who became writers. "Letting oneself (be) read (by) Anne Frank and Etty Hillesum" implies opening up to life's paradoxes, to an existence whose ambiguity makes it a cause for sadness as well as joy.

❧ NOTES

ABBREVIATIONS USED IN THE NOTES

AF   *The Diary of Anne Frank: The Critical Edition* (New York: Doubleday, 1989)

AF*a*   Original version of the diary

AF*b*   Version edited by Anne and Otto Frank

AF*c*   Version originally published as *Anne Frank: The Diary of a Young Girl* (New York: Doubleday, 1952)

Frank 1989   Secondary sources in *The Critical Edition*

EH   Klaas Smelik, ed., *Etty: De nagelaten geschriften van Etty Hillesum, 1941–1943*, 3rd rev. ed. (Amsterdam: Balans, 1991)

Hillesum 1986   Introduction or notes in *Etty: De nagelaten geschriften van Etty Hillesum*

H'83   Arnold J. Pomerans, trans., *Etty: A Diary 1941–43*, from *Het verstoorde leven* (London: Jonathan Cape, 1983)

H'87   Arnold J. Pomerans, trans., *Etty Hillesum: Letters from Westerbork*, from *Het denkende hart van de barak: Brieven van Etty Hillesum* (London: Jonathan Cape, 1987)

INTRODUCTION

1. "To die" masks the fact that their deaths were murder. In reference to the death of Anne Frank and her sister, Margot, Mirjam Pressler wrote: "Anne and Margot did not 'die,' as they say. They were murdered. True, they died of exhaustion and typhus; they were not shot or clubbed to death or herded into a gas chamber by any one individual. Unfortunately our language does not have a word for this: There is no expression for actions that create a situation in which death is not only taken for granted but is systematically planned and carried out" (Pressler 1993, 19 [1992], trans. MH).

2. Frank van Vree (1995, 165–167) has described the history of the various names for the persecution and destruction of the Jews under the Third Reich. Israel's official name for it is *Shoah* (catastrophe, destruction), which is commonly used in France as well, a fact Van Vree attributes to Claude Lanzmann's 1985 film of the same name. In the English language the usual term is "Holocaust," but Van Vree thinks this term should be avoided because it suggests a sacrifice to God. Van Vree opts for following Lyotard and calling the Nazi genocide "Auschwitz." In this book I refrain from choosing one name, because I believe no term can express the unspeakable horror of this mass destruction.

3. See, for example, Heinemann (1986) and Rittner and Roth (1993).

4. I would like to thank Dineke Stam of the Anne Frank House. She pointed out the sex-specificity of the Nazis' anti-Semitism in her comments on my paper on Anne Frank and Etty Hillesum during the Gender and War workshop held under the auspices of RIOD on October 28, 1995.

5. See also Bock 1995, 117–144.

6. Where a published English translation of Etty Hillesum's writings was available—either from *Etty: A Diary 1941–43* (H'83) or *Etty Hillesum: Letters from Westerbork* (H'87)—we have either used it verbatim or adapted it. In some cases Arnold J. Pomerans's translations were used unaltered, in which case the Dutch source is cited, followed by a citation of the English edition (H'83 or H'87). However, Pomerans's translations were frequently inaccurate or could stand improvement, in which case we indicated our adaptation of his work by adding "(adapt. MH)" or "(adapt. MH/SL)" to the author-date citation. Note that these adaptations vary from the replacement of an occasional word to an almost completely new translation. For readability's sake it was impossible to indicate every individual change by means of brackets in the quotations themselves. It was necessary, however, to include the somewhat cumbersome references to both Dutch and English versions of the text, because in some places the existing English translation omitted parts of the Dutch text.

Since not all of Hillesum's writings have been translated into English, we had to translate some of the quotations from her work from the original Dutch. We indicated this by citing the Dutch source, followed by "(trans. MH)." In the interest of brevity we used "trans. MH" rather than "trans. MH/RC," which would more accurately have reflected our joint effort. [MH]

7. "L'histoire personelle de Freud, le Juif errant de Galicie à Vienne et à Londres, en passant par Paris, Rome et New York (pour ne citer que quelques étapes clés de son épreuve de l'étrangeté culturelle et politique), conditionne cette préoccupation d'affronter le malaise de l'autre en tant que mal-être à partir d'une permanence de l'«autre scène» en nous" (Kristeva 1988, 268–269). Note that Kristeva is in error about Freud's birthplace; he was born in Moravia, which was, at the time of his birth, part of the Austro-Hungarian Empire and is now part of the Czech Republic.

8. In 1972 Joke Smit, one of Holland's most important representatives of the second feminist wave, compared the "minority status" of blacks to that of women (Aerts and Saharso 1994, 11).

9. Influenced by the women's movement in the United States, feminists in Europe started to look more carefully at the differences between women, such as age, class, and ethnic and religious background. "Classical" feminist writings were reinterpreted. For example, see Spelman (1988), particularly chapter 3: "Simone de Beauvoir and Women: Just Who Does She Think 'We' Is?" (57–79).

10. "Ecrire, rêver, s'accoucher, être moi-même ma fille de chaque jour. Affirmation d'une force intérieure capable de regarder la vie sans mourir de peur, et surtout de se regarder soi-même, comme si tu étais à la fois l'autre,—indispensable à l'amour—et rien de plus ni de moins que moi" (Cixous 1991, 14).

11. "Respecter Simone de Beauvoir, c'est poursuivre l'oeuvre théorique et pratique de justice sociale qu'elle a menée à sa façon, c'est ne pas refermer l'horizon de libération qu'elle a ouvert pour beaucoup de femmes, et d'hommes" (Irigaray 1990b, 14).

12. "On ne nait pas femme: on le devient" (Beauvoir 1968, 285, [1949]).

13. "[J]e suis née femme, mais je dois encore devenir cette femme que je suis par nature" (Irigaray 1992, 168).

14. Julius Spier was a Jewish refugee from Germany. Etty Hillesum had an excellent command of German, which is why they often communicated in German, both when speaking and writing. The interjection of the word *einordnen* must be seen in this context.

15. See Alvin Rosenfeld (1991), *Popularization and Memory: The Case of Anne Frank,* and also Frank 1989, chapter 6, by David Barnouw, "The Play," 78–83.

16. Anne Frank is "the other" in yet another way: Because of her young age she is not always taken seriously. This was the case in the Secret Annex, and still is in the reception of her work. For example, see Dresden, who criticized the diaries for lack of Jewishness, and added: "But what more could one expect of such a youngster" (Dresden 1991, 239, trans. MH).

17. The musical *Je Anne* [Yours, Anne] by the Royal Ballet of Flanders also bears witness to this change from one-dimensionality to a more complex perspective. The Anne Frank character is vivacious and cheerful but at times also scared or impolite. In contrast to the Hackett play, this production reflects the Jewishness of the people in hiding. Its ending resembles the Bouhuys version of the play: Otto Frank, the only survivor, names the seven others who hid in the Secret Annex and the camps where they died.

   By contrast the Japanese animated film *The Diary of Anne Frank* (Akinori Nagoki, 1995) is proof that even today the distortion of Frank's writings continues. The film's romantic and simplistic script is distinguished by a total lack of depth and background. For example, it remains a mystery why Frank had to go into hiding. Some scenes resemble a promotional spot for the city of Amsterdam: Anne Frank can be seen walking from her home to the hiding place on the Prinsengracht along the most attractive, scenic route.

   The Flemish musical and Art Spiegelman's *Maus* comic strip show that the Holocaust can be incorporated into the most improbable genres in a manner that does justice to its complexity and horror. The Japanese animated film is proof of the opposite.

18. "The 500 pages of triple entries in *The Critical Edition* (twice the number in most paper-back editions) resemble a Talmudic text" (Enzer 1991, 214).

19. "La différence sexuelle représente une des questions ou la question qui est à penser à notre époque" (Irigaray 1984, 13).

20. In late 1943 two of Etty Hillesum's letters from Westerbork concentration camp were published illegally by the Dutch Resistance. The same two letters were later published again in a literary magazine called *Maatstaf: Maandblad voor Letteren (Maatstaf* 7 no. 1 [Apr. 1959]: 3–41), after which they were also published as a book, entitled *Twee brieven uit Westerbork van Etty Hillesum* [Two letters from Westerbork by Etty Hillesum], with a preface by David Koning (The Hague: Bert Bakker/Daamen NV, 1962). In 1978, another edition of the same two letters appeared: *Etty Hillesum, Twee brieven uit Westerbork* was again prefaced by David Koning, but published by another company (Utrecht: Knippenberg [Bulkboek no. 73], 1978).

21. For example, in Sellers (1988, 150) and Conley (1992, xii, 23, 69, 91–92, 112–113).

22. "J'ai eu la 'chance' de faire mes premiers pas en plein brasier entre deux holocaustes, parmi, au sein même du racisme, avoir trois ans en 1940, être juive, une partie de moi dans les camps de concentration, une partie de moi dans les 'colonies'" (Cixous 1991, 34).

23. This biographical background is reflected in the title of the French-Dutch edition of *La venue à l'écriture: Tussen talen ontstaan* [Born among languages] (Cixous 1991b). The English translation is titled *Coming to Writing* (Cixous 1991a).

24. "Tu es, toi aussi, juifemme, menue diminutive, souris parmi le peuple des souris, assignée à la crainte du grand méchant chat. A la diaspora de tes désirs; aux déserts intimes. Et si tu grandis, ton désert grandit aussi. Si tu sors du trou, le monde te fait savoir qu'il n'y a pas de place entre ses états pour ton espèce" (Cixous 1991, 16).

25. For a translation of Rilke's *Weltinnenraum* in a larger context, see chapter 5, note 27.

26. "Sa structure à elle, sa nature ce qui va donner forme à son destin porte ce nom, que je me permettrais de lui donner, de 'sainteté'" (Cixous seminar 03/22/1986).

27. "Mais très rapidement elle va devenir une non-femme et une sainte" (Cixous seminar 03/22/1986).

CHAPTER 1   ODE TO MY FOUNTAIN PEN

1. Slips of the pen and grammatical errors in the quotations from Anne Frank's works are entirely her own.

2. Many people were appalled to hear that young people were being forced to leave for Germany without their parents. Etty Hillesum reacted to the news in her own, idiosyncratic way: "Have I really made so much progress that I can say with complete honesty: I hope they will send me to a labour camp so that I can do something for the 16-year-old girls who will also be going? and to reassure the distracted parents who are kept behind, saying, 'Don't worry, I'll look after your children'?" (H'83, 145).

3. In *The Critical Edition,* the word *tabeh* ('bye)—a loanword from Indonesian that entered the Dutch language during the Dutch colonization of the East Indies—has been omitted from Frank's letter to Emmy. Because this tends to make the reference "Just as in 'Joop ter Heul'" (AF*b*, 238) rather incomprehensible, we have adapted the translation slightly. [MH]

4. Lies Goslar also appears in the diaries as Hanneli. For the friendship between Hanneli and Anne, see chapter 3.

5. In a letter from Westerbork, Hillesum wrote that there were three books in their barracks, one of which was *Quicksilver* by Cissy van Marxveldt, and she noted: "People almost come to blows for browsing rights to Cissy van Marxveldt" (H'87, 105–106).

6. Berteke Waaldijk was one of the first historians to read Anne Frank in the context of women's studies and literature. She paid special attention to Frank as a writer, dealing in detail with the link between the *Joop ter Heul* novels and Frank's diaries (Waaldijk 1993). She wrote this article during her stay in the United States, using the English-language *Critical Edition* of Frank's work. Waaldijk was obviously thrown off by the omission in this edition; see note 3 (Waaldijk 1993, 332; see also Van Marxveldt 1985, 13 [1919]).

7. In 1985 all five *Joop ter Heul* novels were reissued in one volume. The last, entitled *Joop ter Heul's Daughter,* was published just after the war, two years before Van Marxveldt died.

8. I would like to thank Dineke Stam for pointing this out to me.

9. See AF*a*, 223. On September 28, 1942, she wrote a letter to "the whole club," giving the first and last names of all the young women and their boyfriends.

10. When Anne started rewriting her diaries, she drew up a list of name changes. There she included a Henk as well: It is an alias for Miep Gies's husband, Jan (Frank 1989, 60).

11. We added "either" because this more accurately reflects the meaning of the Dutch: Frank was making a distinction between the girls who belonged to "the whole club" and those who did not, namely Emmy, Jetje, and Jacqueline.

12. Van Maarsen (1990, 103) mentioned a Jetteke, Margot's best friend. This passage was not included in the English translation (Van Maarsen 1996).

13. The name Marian(ne) resurfaces in the diary (AF*a*, 647) when Frank writes to Kitty about the contents of her novel, *Cady's Life.* In this context Marianne is Cady's Jewish friend.

14. In the *b* version, the name Gabi appears once: She is the two-year-old sister of Hanneli Goslar, Anne Frank's friend (AF*b*, 205). Frank also mentioned the Goslar baby in a letter to Marianne (AF*a*, 267).

    The helpers of the inhabitants of the Secret Annex borrowed books from the library for them; therefore Frank had only temporary access to the *Joop ter Heul* novels, which she read at a single sitting (AF*a*, 242). So perhaps she remembered only the names but not the exact relationships, as Maaike Meijer has suggested.

15. Bep Voskuijl, a young woman, was one of the helpers.

16. In *The Critical Edition* the Dutch word *roman* was translated "romance"; it should be "novel." See also note 1. [MH]

17. In the Dutch *a* version Frank quoted the English radio announcement as "*the* day," editors later modified this to "D-day" (*c* version). [MH]

18. Dresden (1991, 39–40) wrongly accused Anne Frank of lacking political interest (see De Costa 1994, 6–7).

19. The translation in *The Critical Edition* does not acknowledge the existence of Anne Frank's "book of beautiful quotations" and translates the Dutch *mooie zinnenboek* as "diary."

20. See Hondius 1990, particularly chapter 2.

21. *The Critical Edition* translates *sprookjes* as "stories"; I prefer to call them "fairy tales." *De Prins* was a weekly magazine. See also Frank (1960, 7). [MH]

22. Frank defended *Cady's Life* by writing: "It isn't sentimental nonsense for it's modeled on the story of Daddy's life" (AF*a*, 647). In her December 24, 1943, diary entry, she recalled a conversation from a year earlier, when her father had told her about his first love. This was probably one of the few times that Otto Frank discussed his personal history with his younger daughter. She longed for him to confide in her again. (AF*a*, 433). See also an entry from a few months later, when, looking back on the first half of 1943, she wrote: "I . . . did my utmost to turn Daddy into my confidant, failed, was alone and (nearly) every evening did nothing but cry" (AF*a*, 518).

23. *The Critical Edition* wrongly translates "als het ooit wel af komt" as "if it ever comes off at all." The Dutch phrase actually means: "if I ever get to finish it."

24. She used the same words as Joop ter Heul (see Af*b*, 180).

25. Zlata Filipović—the girl from Sarajevo who, like Anne Frank, kept a diary during wartime—adopted the idea of giving her diary a name: "Hey diary, you know what I think? Since Anne Frank called her diary Kitty, maybe I could give you a name too." (Filipović 1994, 27) She opted for "Mimmy," which reminds one of both "mama" and "Kitty." For the link between Kitty and the mother, see chapter 2.

26. Partly based on the function of Kitty in Anne Frank's diaries, Patricia de Martelaere (1993, 149–168) questioned whether a diary writer writes for herself only. Considering the issue she discussed, she should have distinguished between the *a* and *b* versions, but failed to do so.

27. *Anne Frank is niet van gisteren* [Anne Frank was not born yesterday] is the title of a children's novel about the life of Anne Frank by Mies Bouhuys (1982). The back cover reads: "It is all there in hurried, almost vertical letters, the way you write when you're very young and at odds with every grownup and yourself. Every 13-year-old, whether fifty years ago, today or in the future, will sometimes write or think this way. Anne Frank was no different when she started exploring the world" (trans. MH).

28. In *The Critical Edition,* the Dutch "Is me dat een manier van optreden!" is translated as "Shall I take up that attitude?" It would be better approximated by "That is no way to behave!" [MH]

29. Sinterklaas is the Dutch name for Saint Nicholas, and stands for St. Nicholas Day, December 6. On this traditional family holiday, gifts and poems are exchanged to celebrate the birthday of the patron saint of children.

30. In late 1987 Joke Kniesmeyer, who worked for the Anne Frank House, found at Amsterdam's Waterlooplein flea market the possessions of Charlotte Kaletta, Pfeffer's lover, including photographs and letters. Based on this information, Nanda van der Zee wrote a book on Pfeffer, titled *De kamergenoot van Anne Frank* [Anne Frank's roommate] (1990), partly out of a wish to correct the rather negative picture Frank had painted of him.

31. The metaphor of the caged bird is a recurring image in women's literature: "From Mary Wollstonecraft's *Maria* to Brontë's *Jane Eyre*—to Anne Frank's *Diary of a Young Girl* I find that the caged bird makes a metaphor that truly deserves the adjective female," wrote Ellen Moers (1976, 250). I would like to point out that Anne Frank's desire to be a bird has less to do with her respectable upbringing and its attending restrictions than with her position as a Jewish girl in hiding, a fact that Moers ignored.

32. I have kept the Dutch title "Kaatje," rather than use the existing translation "Kitty" (Frank 1994), to avoid confusion with the other Kitty, to whom the letters in the diary are addressed. [MH]

33. One of Anne Frank's pastimes was to spy on the neighbors with a telescope or to look at the people walking on the street through a crack in the curtains.

34. Rhea, daughter of Uranus and Gaea (of heaven and earth), is Zeus's mother.

35. In 1959 Miep Gies located this scene in Anne Frank's room; in 1987 she remembered it taking place in the Franks' parental bedroom.

CHAPTER 2   IN WHITE INK

1. For a detailed description of the semiotic in Kristeva's theories, see Van den Brink 1986, 38–46.

2. Pamela Pattynama fills this void by using the views of Kristeva and others to study "feminine fantasies expressed in the characters of adolescent girls" (Pattynama 1992, 14; trans. MH).

3. This chapter shows multiple approaches to psychoanalysis. I use psychoanalysis as a method to uncover deep structures. However, I also criticize it as a discourse and try to rewrite it in light of sexual difference theories that allow women to be included in the Symbolic Order. I use psychoanalysis to understand the adolescent's psychological makeup, while also employing it as a reading method. By looking for slips of the pen, distortions, coincidences, and omissions in Anne Frank's text, I try to bring to light her unconscious desires.

4. "Nicht ohne guten Grund ist das Saugen des Kindes an der Brust der Mutter vorbild-lich für jede Liebesbeziehung geworden. Die Objektfindung ist eigentlich eine Wieder-findung" (Freud 1942, 123 [1905]).

5. Freud invariably refers to "the child" by the personal pronouns "he," "his," and "him." Because this chapter is about Anne Frank, I have opted wherever possible to take a more heterogeneous view, using the female forms as well.

6. "Gleichzeitig mit der Überwindung und Verwerfung dieser deutlich inzestuösen Phantasien wird eine der bedeutsamsten, aber auch schmerzhaftesten, psychischen Leistungen der Pubertätszeit vollzogen, die Ablösung von der Autorität der Eltern, durch welche erst der für den Kulturfortschritt so wichtige Gegensatz der neuen Generation zur alten geschaffen wird" (Freud 1942, 128 [1905]).

7. I would like to repeat—perhaps unnecessarily—that any slips of the pen and gram-matical errors in the quotes from Anne Frank's works are her own.

8. Anne Frank gave their names in full, but at the request of a number of the people involved, the names were replaced with initials chosen at random (see Frank 1989, 187 n.).

9. Karl Silberbauer, a member of the Sicherheitsdienst (Security Service, or SD), was in charge of the August 4, 1944, arrest of the people hiding in the Secret Annex. He recalled a short conversation with Otto Frank: "He also told me that he and his family, including his daughter Anne, had spent a good two years in the hiding place. When I refused to believe him, he pointed to the marks that had been made on the doorpost, showing how much Anne had grown since they had gone into hiding" (Frank 1989, 22–23).

10. "On se souvient que la séparation avec l'objet ouvre la phase dite dépressive. En per-dant maman et en m'appuyant sur la dénégation, je la récupère comme signe, image, mot" (Kristeva 1987a, 74).

11. For the influence of Lou Andreas-Salomé on psychoanalysis in general and on the study of narcissism in particular, see Hermsen 1993, 37–51.

12. "Das 'Anale' bleibt von da an das Symbol für alles zu Verwerfende, vom Leben Abzuscheidende" (Freud 1942, 88 [1905]).

13. In *The Critical Edition,* the Dutch "Het is bij ons toch wel heel goed ingedeeld" is erroneously translated as "With us, it's all pretty much divided." This should read: "With us [women], it's all pretty neatly constructed." [MH]

14. "Uns Laien hat es immer mächtig gereizt zu wissen, woher diese merkwürdige Persönlichkeit, der Dichter, seine Stoffe nimmt" (Freud 1941, 213 [1907]).

15. "Träumer am hellichten Tag" (Freud 1941, 219 [1907]).

16. "Ein starkes aktuelles Erlebnis weckt im Dichter die Erinnerung an ein früheres, meist der Kindheit angehöriges Erlebnis auf, von welchem nun der Wunsch ausgeht, der sich in der Dichtung seine Erfüllung schafft; die Dichtung selbst lässt sowohl Elemente des frischen Anlasses als auch der alten Erinnerung erkennen" (Freud 1941, 221 [1907]).

17. See chapter 1, note 32.

18. Laureen Nussbaum assumes that the last part of the diary (the last notebook, a version only) was also written with possible publication in mind: "There is no 'b' version of the last four months in the 'Secret Annex.' However, it stands to reason that Anne, while rewriting and editing her old texts, was committing her new writings to paper in a way that took future publication into account" (Nussbaum 1995, 38, trans. MH).

19. Katherine Dalsimer (1986, 44–76) provides a psychoanalytic interpretation of Anne Frank's diaries in which she also discusses this passage. Because she did not have access to *The Critical Edition,* she places this particular entry in the context of other diary entries that *were* written in January 1944. Therefore her interpretation does not stand up.

20. Peter Blos (1962, 87, 95) also discusses the diary's "acting out" function, but assigns only one meaning to "acting out," namely the prevention of girls' premature heterosexual behavior. Kristeva puts "acting out" in a much wider context, although the example she gives points in the same direction (Kristeva 1990, 10). Anne Frank's diaries prove that writing as a way to avoid "acting out" can also apply to other areas of life, such as the mother-daughter relationship.

21. D. W. Winnicott saw a connection between transitional and fetish objects: "The transitional object may eventually develop into a fetish object" (Winnicott 1953, 92–93).

22. "La création littéraire est cette aventure du corps et des signes qui porte témoignage de l'affect: de la tristesse, comme marque de la séparation et comme amorce de la dimension du symbole; de la joie, comme marque du triomphe qui m'installe dans l'univers de l'artifice et du symbole que j'essaie de faire correspondre au mieux à mes expériences de la réalité. Mais ce témoignage, la création littéraire le produit dans un matériau tout autre que l'humeur. Elle transpose l'affect dans les rythmes, les signes, les formes. Le 'sémiotique' et le 'symbolique' deviennent les marques communicables d'une réalité affective présente, sensible au lecteur (j'aime ce livre parce qu'il me communique la tristesse, l'angoisse ou la joie), et néanmoins dominée, écartée, vaincue" (Kristeva 1987a, 32–33).

23. "Vater der persönlichen Vorzeit" (Freud 1940b, 259 [1923]).

24. "Le désir maternel du Phallus" (Kristeva 1983b, 44).

25. "De pouvoir recevoir les mots de l'autre, de les assimiler, répéter, reproduire, je deviens comme lui: Un. Un sujet de l'énonciation. Par identification-osmose psychique. Par amour" (Kristeva 1983b, 31–32).

26. "En résumé, l'identification primaire paraît être un transfert au (du) père imaginaire, corrélatif à la constitution de la mère comme un 'ab-jet.' Le narcissisme serait cette corrélation (au père imaginaire et à la mère 'abjet') qui se joue autour du vide central dudit transfert" (Kristeva 1983b, 46).

27. See chapter 1, note 29.

28. In *The Critical Edition,* the Dutch *gehaspel* has been translated as "bickerings." In this context "gibberish" is closer to the meaning. [MH]

29. "Le matricide est notre nécessité vitale, condition sine qua non de notre individuation" (Kristeva 1987a, 38).

30. In her tales Anne Frank also let her imagination run wild. See the opening sentence of the story "Blurry, the Explorer."

31. This vision is strongly reminiscent of the object-relation theory developed by Melanie Klein and D. W. Winnicott. (See the first section of this chapter.) *From Klein to Kristeva* (Doane and Hodges 1992) is an attempt to clarify the link between object-relation theory and Kristeva.

32. "Même si la mystification phallique a contaminé généralement les bons rapports, la femme n'est jamais loin de la 'mère' (que j'entends hors-role, la 'mère' comme non-nom, et comme source des biens). Toujours en elle subsiste au moins un peu du bon lait de mère. Elle écrit à l'encre blanche" (Cixous 1975b, 173).

CHAPTER 3   GUARDIAN ANGEL

1. Grandmother resurfaces only in November 1943, as the generous provider of a fountain pen that Anne was very attached to and always used. The pen accidentally ends up in the heater and burns. In memory of her precious pen, Anne Frank wrote a story titled "Ode to My Fountain Pen: In Loving Memory" (see also AF*b*, 413–414).

2. In *The Critical Edition,* this passage is annotated with Otto Frank's: "A severe internal disease" (Frank 1989, 435). Neither the Anne Frank House nor RIOD was able to help me clarify this rather vague comment.

3. "Die Ablösung des heranwachsenden Individuums von der Autorität der Eltern ist eine der notwendigen, aber auch schmerzlichsten Leistungen der Entwicklung. [. . .] Für das kleine Kind sind die Eltern zunächst die einzige Autorität and die Quelle alles Glaubens. [. . .] Kleine Ereignisse im Leben des Kindes, die eine unzufriedene Stimmung bei ihm hervorrufen, geben ihm den Anlaß, mit der Kritik der Eltern einzusetzen. [. . .] Nur zu oft ergeben sich Gelegenheiten, bei denen das Kind zurückgesetzt wird oder sich wenigstens zurückgesetzt fühlt, wo es die volle Liebe der Eltern vermisst, besonders aber bedauert, sie mit anderen Geschwistern teilen zu müssen" (Freud 1941, 227–228 [1908]).

4. Cf. the ninth letter in *Brieven aan mijn kleinzoon* [Letters to my grandson], in which Abel J. Herzberg writes about his Hasidic grandfather: "A great, wide distance has formed between us and Hasidism and even between us and religion in general. But my grandfather has always been there and has stood beside me and over me. When I married, when the children were born, when father and mother died, when the children had children and also when you were born. He went with me into the German camps and protected me. And he is here now, while I write this. I never stopped being a child and he never stopped blessing me" (Herzberg 1990, 124, [1964]; trans. MH).

5. "Es ist nur scheinbare Treulosigkeit und Undankbarkeit; denn wenn man die häufigste dieser Romanphantasien . . . im Detail durchgeht, so macht man die Entdeckung, daß diese neuen und vornehmen Eltern durchwegs mit Zügen ausgestattet sind, die von realen Erinnerungen an die wirklichen niederen Eltern herrühren, sodass das Kind den Vater eigentlich nicht beseitigt, sondern erhöht. Ja, das ganze Bestreben, den wirklichen Vater durch einen vornehmeren zu ersetzen, ist nur der Ausdruck der Sehnsucht des Kindes nach der verlorenen glücklichen Zeit, in der ihm sein Vater als der vornehmste und stärkste Mann, seine Mutter als die liebste und schönste Frau erschienen ist. Er wendet sich vom Vater, den er jetzt erkennt, zurück zu dem, an den er in früheren Kinderjahren geglaubt hat, und die Phantasie ist eigentlich nur der Ausdruck des Bedauerns, dass diese glückliche Zeit entschwunden ist. Die Überschätzung der frühesten Kindheitsjahre tritt also in diesen Phantasien wieder in ihr volles Recht" (Freud 1941, 231 [1908]).

6. Marianne Hirsch uses Freud's "family-romance theory" in her analysis of mother-daughter discourses. She connects the necessity of leaving the mother, as Freud posits, with the frequent absence or death of the mother as described in many nineteenth-century

novels by women writers: "The heroine who wants to write, or who wants in any way to be productive and creative, then, must break from her mother, so as not to be identified with maternal silence" (Hirsch 1989, 45).

As a child of the twentieth century, Anne Frank had enough of a sense of fantasy not to force a radical break with her mother, but to draw her mother into the symbolic order by creating a guardian angel.

7. "Le plus formidable *fort-da* s'envoie . . . de la présence de la mère, dans la mère, outre-voile, à celle de Dieu, outre-ciel, outre-horizon visible" (Irigaray 1987, 44).

8. "Il est nécessaire aussi, pour ne pas être complices du meurtre de la mère, que nous affirmions qu'il existe une généalogie de femmes. Il y a une généalogie de femmes dans notre famille: nous avons une mère, une grand-mère, une arrière-grand-mère maternelles et des filles. [. . .] Essayons de nous situer dans cette généalogie féminine pour conquérir et garder notre identité" (Irigaray 1987, 31).

9. Hannah Pick-Goslar, one of Frank's best friends, remembers hearing these words from her mother, who was very fond of Anne (Lindwer 1991, 17).

10. "And if a woman have an issue, and her issue in her flesh be blood, she shall be put apart seven days: and whosoever toucheth her shall be unclean until the even. And every thing that she lieth upon in her separation shall be unclean: every thing also that she sitteth upon shall be unclean. And whosoever toucheth her bed shall wash his clothes, and bathe himself in water, and be unclean until the even. And whosoever toucheth any thing that she sat upon shall wash his clothes, and bathe himself in water, and be unclean until the even. And if it be on her bed, or on any thing whereon she sitteth, when he toucheth it, he shall be unclean until the even. And if any man lie with her at all, and her flowers be upon him, he shall be unclean seven days; and all the bed whereon he lieth shall be unclean" (AV, Leviticus 15, 19–24; see also Mulder 1986 and Plaskow 1991, 174–175).

11. "Jouissance" can be described as "a specific female representation of the unconscious" (Braidotti 1991, 248). This also indicates that women's pleasure is often tabooed or repressed into the culturally determined unconscious. In that sense, the unconscious can be regarded as feminine.

12. "Un transcendantal sensible, dimension du divin par excellence" (Irigaray 1984, 111).

13. "Comment arrive l'exil? Sur le mode du 'être semblable à Dieu.' La position de Dieu comme modèle à répéter, mimer. Donc situé hors de soi. Le mal, la faute, la souffrance, la rédemption n'adviennent-ils de la constitution de Dieu comme entité idéale extra-terrestre, comme monopole extra-mondain? De la fabrication du divin comme Dieu-Père?" (Irigaray 1980, 185).

14. "La terre devient lieu de déportation" (Irigaray 1980, 186).

15. "Pour devenir, il est nécessaire d'avoir un genre ou une essence (dès lors sexuée) comme horizon. Sinon, le devenir reste partiel et assujetti. Devenir parties ou multiples sans futur propre aboutit à s'en remettre à l'autre ou l'Autre de l'autre pour son rassemblement" (Irigaray 1987, 73)

16. "L'inscription juridique de la virginité" (Irigarary 1989a, 75–76).

17. "Ce dont nous avons besoin pour devenir libres, autonomes, souveraines. Aucune constitution de subjectivité ni de société humaine ne s'est élaborée sans assistance du divin" (Irigaray 1984, 74).

18. Anne Frank spelled Hanneli's name inconsistently, sometimes writing "Hanneli" and sometimes adding an "e" ("Hannelie"). I have opted for Hanneli throughout.

19. All biographical details about Hanneli are derived from Lindwer 1991, pp. 9–34.

20. "Si les femmes manquent de Dieu, elles ne peuvent communiquer ni communier entre elles. Il faut, il leur faut, l'infini pour partager *un peu*. Sinon, le partage entraîne fusion-confusion, division et déchirement en elle(s), entre elles. Si je ne me rapporte pas à quelque horizon d'accomplissement de mon genre, je ne peux partager en protégeant mon devenir" (Irigaray 1987, 74).

21. "This book contains the complete interviews conducted for my film documentary *The Last Seven Months of Anne Frank*. [. . .] Through the filmed interviews, an attempt is made to reconstruct a period during the Second World War. The six women all knew Anne Frank in the last seven months of her life, and although they tell of their own experiences, many aspects of their stories also reflect the story of Anne Frank" (Lindwer 1991, ix).

Seven years later another moving film document about Frank was released: *Anne Frank Remembered* (Jon Blair, 1995, UK). Many of Lindwer's witnesses reappeared in this production.

22. Rachel also met Leo Beek there. She had worked at the Bijenkorf department store for thirteen years. Beek had been her personnel manager. He held a high military rank, and during the war he worked on a secret plan to liberate the Netherlands. He was arrested in January 1943. Beek spent a few weeks in camp Westerbork's penitentiary. His mixed marriage was not enough to save him; he was married to the writer Cissy van Marxveldt, a gentile. On August 15, 1944, he was executed by firing squad in Overveen. Only after the liberation did Cissy van Marxveldt find out that her husband was dead. Her son wrote about this in his biography: "Although she lived for another three and a half years, she never wrote another word." (J. van Marxveldt 1991, 124–125; trans. MH). During the war, Cissy van Marxveldt had been working on her last novel, entitled *Ook zij maakte het mee* [She too went through it], which deals with the war and is dedicated to: "My husband, Leo Beek, field officer in the Dutch Army, who was executed by a German firing squad in Overveen on August 15, 1944" (trans. MH). The book was published in 1947, one year before Cissy van Marxveldt died.

INTERMEZZO

1. The women who went underground and who were interviewed by Ziporah Valkhoff could not relate to the story of the most famous girl who went into hiding, Anne Frank, because Anne's situation was so exceptional: She went into hiding with her parents and her sister, the whole family staying in the same place (Valkhoff 1992, 14).
2. "L'étrange est en moi, donc nous sommes tous des étrangers. Si je suis étranger, il n'y a pas d'étrangers" (Kristeva 1988, 284).
3. "Le kaléidoscope que devient la France" (Kristeva 1988, 288).
4. "La différence sexuelle représente une des questions ou la question qui est à penser à notre époque" (Irigaray 1984, 13).
5. "La différence sexuelle représente probablement la question la plus universelle que nous puissions aborder. C'est au traitement de celle-ci que notre époque est affrontée. En effet, dans le monde entier il y a, il n'y a que, des hommes et des femmes" (Irigaray 1992, 85).
6. "Les peuples se partagent sens cesse en rivalités secondaires mais meurtrières sans prendre conscience que leur première et irréductible partitions est *en deux genres*" (Irigaray 1990b, 14).
7. This development is also clearly reflected in the work of my colleagues in women's studies at Utrecht University, in particular the work of Gloria Wekker and Elsbeth Locher-Scholten.

CHAPTER 4   A HAND, WHICH WROTE

1. "Other girls had visions of a husband and children. But I always had this one vision: a hand, which wrote. I always saw a thin hand and many papers and that hand just wrote and kept on writing" (EH, 123; trans. MH).
2. Julius Spier (1887–1942) was a Jewish refugee from Germany who worked as a therapist. He had studied with Carl Gustav Jung for two years. Spier was very talented at

palm reading, which enabled him to come up with revealing characterizations. On Jung's advice he became a chirologist (Hillesum 1986, 729; Spier 1982). In Amsterdam he gave courses in hand analysis.

3. Her convictions are similar to Kristeva's point of view in *Strangers to Ourselves* (1991 [1988]). Kristeva seems to give not only psychological but also political priority to acknowledging the foreign, the abject in oneself. She sees this as a first, basic step toward a world order without exclusion mechanisms: Strangers do not walk the streets but inhabit one's own soul. For a more detailed explanation of these views, see the Intermezzo.

4. He taught Russian to Etty Hillesum and some other students in Leiden. Van Wijk was the founder of Balto-Slavic studies in the Netherlands (Hillesum 1986, 720). Hillesum had a law degree but never put it into practice in her working life. She earned money as a private tutor in Russian, just as her mother had done when she first arrived in the Netherlands as a Jewish refugee from Russia. Etty's father, Levi (or Louis) Hillesum, had been one of her mother's students.

5. See the excellent biographical and historical thesis on Hillesum by Els Lagrou (Catholic University of Leuven [Louvain], Belgium, 1985), in particular chapter 1, section 1: "Jeugd in Deventer" [Childhood in Deventer].

6. In 1992 the late Jaap Meijer privately published two works about Levi Hillesum, to correct what he saw as Etty Hillesum's "diminished and distorted" image of her father (Meijer 1992b, 2).

7. Hillesum's older brother, Jaap, a medical student, voluntarily sought admission to a psychiatric ward when his attacks of schizophrenia got out of control. Her youngest brother, Mischa, spent long periods in psychiatric hospitals, including Het Apeldoornsche Bosch, a Jewish institution.

   The Amsterdam register of births, deaths, and marriages shows that there were psychiatric problems on both the maternal and the paternal sides of the family. One of Levi's older sisters, Grietje, was more than once admitted to an insane asylum for a number of years.

8. The metaphor of pregnancy in relation to writing occurs several times, for example on April 13, 1942: "In those days, I also had the feeling that one of these nights, I would just get up in the middle of the night and write a book. And the feeling that I was pregnant, mentally pregnant, and wanted finally to give birth to something" (EH, 345; trans. MH).

9. Ich will dich immer spiegeln in ganzer Gestalt
   Und will niemals blind sein oder zu alt
   um dein schweres schwankendes Bild zu halten.
                                              (EH, 201)

10. "Und vielleicht sind die Geschlechter verwandter, als man meint, und die große Erneuerung der Welt wird vielleicht darin bestehen, daß Mann and Mädchen sich, befreit von allen Irrgefühlen und Unlüsten, nicht als Gegensätze suchen werden, sondern als Geschwister und Nachbarn und sich zusammentun werden *als Menschen* um einfach, ernst und geduldig das schwere Geschlecht, das ihnen auferlegt ist, gemeinsam zu tragen" (EH, 258–259, 301).

    This is a quote from Rilke's *Briefe an einen jungen Dichter* [Letters to a young poet] (1929). By equating a girl rather than a woman with a man, Rilke lets inequality sneak into the text. I think that the world's greatest innovation might be when man and woman can live together as neighbors who mutually respect each other.

    I would like to thank Herbert Lehnert, Ph.D., for his help in translating and interpreting Hillesum's quotations of Rilke.

11. "Durch alle Wesen reicht der *eine* Raum: Weltinnenraum" (EH, 286, 291). (*Weltinnenraum* is Rilke's neologism, composed of *Weltraum* in the sense of "outer space, the universe," and *Innenraum*: interior space. My thanks to Herbert Lehnert for this explanation.)

12. What it meant to be an "honorable woman" can be deduced from Hillesum's own description of the job: "For the past few years, I have been earning my living by supplying some

warmth and atmosphere in a family which also employs a housekeeper" (EH, 24; trans. MH). She also had to do a few minor household chores (Hillesum 1986, 719).

13. Jewish Councils were Jewish administrative bodies instituted by the Nazis in all the countries they occupied. The Jewish Council was entrusted with executing German measures, such as the registration and deportation of the Jewish population to the concentration camps.

14. Hanneke Starreveld sent me a copy of the letter, on which she wrote: "I would so much like for you to read it in its entirety, because it shows so much love for the other."

15. Max Osias Kormann (1895–1959) was born in Poland and moved to Germany at a young age. As a stateless Jew, he was expelled in 1935. He boarded a transatlantic vessel, the St. Louis, bound for Cuba, in the hope of reaching New York, where his wife and children had found refuge. However, the Jewish refugees were refused entry to Cuba. A number of European countries, including the Netherlands, offered the refugees asylum. Kormann ended up in the Netherlands. He became one of the first inhabitants of Westerbork camp, which was set up by the Dutch authorities to accommodate Jewish refugees (for more information, see Hillesum 1986, 779, 863–864).

16. "I denke oft, das einzige, was man wirklich tun kann, ist das bischen Güte, das man in sich hat, ausströmen lassen nach allen Seiten. Alles andere kommt erst in dem zweiten Platz" (EH, 612).

17. "Ja, also: ich lebe jetzt wieder horizontal, in der mehr oder weniger gemütlichen Gesellschaft eines Gallensteines. Wenn dieser Stein sich nicht bald dazu entschliesst, sich irgendwie aufzulösen, dann muss er ins Krankenhaus—und ich muss dann auch mit. Was mein privater Schutzheiliger doch wohl mit mir vorhat?" (EH, 615).

18. The Nazis established various exemption lists, including the Barneveld list for talented Jews, giving the false impression that such lists were a guarantee of permanent exemption from deportation. Friends of the Hillesums did their best to get Mischa, a very talented pianist, and his whole family on the Barneveld list. To this end Milli Ortmann asked Willem Andriessen (pianist, composer, and music teacher) and Willem Mengelberg (conductor of the Amsterdam Concertgebouw Orchestra), who knew of Mischa's musical talents, to write letters of recommendation to the German authorities (see also Herzberg 1978, 131–133 [1950]).

CHAPTER 5   CHRONICLER

1. The multimedia center of the Jewish Historical Museum, where Etty Hillesum's legacy is kept, contains not only diaries, personal letters, and pictures but also letters from publishers, such as A. W. Sijthoff and E. M. Querido, to Klaas Smelik turning down his requests for publication of the diaries. The letters gave no reasons for the rejection. Smelik later told his son that the publishers were not interested in Hillesum's work because it did not contain enough horror. I would like to thank Dr. K.A.D. Smelik for this information.

2. There are proceedings from this conference (Van Oord 1990).

3. Willem G. van Maanen wrote *Etty: Toneelstuk over Etty Hillesum* (Etty: A Play) (Baarn: de Prom, 1988). After reading her diaries and letters, Pieter Starreveld, who had known her personally, made a sculpture of her head and writing hand; the artwork is now displayed in the Holocaust Museum, Washington, D.C. Ed de Boer composed Symphonie no. 1, op. 2D (*uit het dagboek van Etty Hillesum* [from Etty Hillesum's diary]).

4. See also Scholtens 1989, Schrijvers 1986, Swart 1991, and Van den Brandt 1990.

5. This is a frequently heard comment. For examples, see the book containing some of the reactions to Hillesum's writings (Gaarlandt 1989, 1, 4, 8–9, 43, 55, 64, 127–128, 147, 191).

6. See also Cixous 1981b, 45; 1982, 302; and Hablé 1988, 12–15.

7. "Nous vivons toujours sous l'Empire du Propre. Les mêmes maîtres dominent l'histoire depuis les commencements, y inscrivant les marques de leur économie appropriante:

l'histoire, comme histoire du phallocentrisme ne s'est déplacée que pour se répéter" (Cixous 1975a, 144).

8. "Une femme n'a pas d'autre choix que d'être décapitée, et d'ailleurs il faut le dire, la morale de l'affaire, c'est que si elles ne perdent pas la tête comme ça, à coup de sabre, elles ne la gardent qu'à condition de la perdre, c'est-à-dire, dans le plus total silence et transformées en machines" (Cixous 1974, 6).

9. "Chacun prendrait enfin le risque de l'*autre*, de la différence, sans se sentir menacé(e) par l'existence d'une altérité, mais en se réjouissant de s'augmenter d'inconnu à découvrir, à respecter, à favoriser, à entretenir" (Cixous 1975a, 143).

10. Cf. Dorien Pessers's views. In *De Wet van het hart* [The law of the heart], she criticizes the theory (to her mind, a feminist theory) that only equals can experience true love. She advocates a type of love in which reciprocity is strived for rather than equality: "The principle of reciprocity is less easily economically manipulated and shows more clearly that the pleasure of love lies in the alternation, and not the fixation of roles" (Pessers 1994, 86; trans. MH).

11. "Déjà elle est une autre" (Cixous 1975a, 162, 177).

12. Even in the early twentieth century, Freud still offered a psychoanalytical explanation for women's underdeveloped superego, creating a pretext for keeping women out of positions of power and authority (Freud 1964, 22 [1933]).

13. For a detailed description of Irigaray's views on sexual difference, see part 1, chapter 3, and the Intermezzo.

14. "La bi-sexualité au niveau de l'inconscient, c'est la possibilité de se prolonger d'autre, d'être dans un rapport avec l'autre de telle manière que je passe dans l'autre sans détruire l'autre; que je vais chercher l'autre là où ille est sans essayer de tout ramener à moi" (Cixous 1974, 15).

15. "Or, si tu es une femme, tu es toujours plus proche et plus loin de la perte qu'un homme. Plus capable et mons capable de perte. Plus attirée, plus repoussée. Plus séduite, plus interdite" (Cixous 1991, 74).

16. "C'est dans le sans abri que la plupart des textes que nous allons travailler cette année se sont avancés, se sont écrits. C'est grâce au sans abri, qu'ils ont pris naissance" (Cixous, seminar 10/20/1985).

17. "Just now, as I was sitting and enjoying the sun on the trash can in our tiny patio, leaning my head against the washtub and seeing the sun shine on the strong, dark, still leafless chestnut branches, I felt for just one very sharply outlined moment, the difference between then and now" (EH, 27; trans. MH).

18. "Il regarde l'autre que lui sans l'enlever à ses racines" (Irigaray 1992b, 49).

19. "My dear desk, the best place on earth" (EH, 701; H'87, 144).

20. "La plupart des femmes sont comme ça: elles font l'écriture de l'autre, c'est-à-dire de l'homme, et dans la naïveté, elles le déclarent et le maintiennent, et elle font en effet une écriture qui est masculine. Il faut faire très attention quand on veut travailler sur la féminité dans l'écriture, à ne pas se faire piéger par les noms: ce n'est pas parce que c'est signé avec un nom de femme que c'est une écriture féminine" (Cixous 1974, 12).

21. "Alors si l'on veut faire livre, on s'outille, on taille, on filtre, on revient sur soi, dure épreuve, tu marches sur tes chairs, tu ne voles plus, tu ne coules plus, tu arpentes, tu jardines, tu fouilles, ah tu nettoi et rassembles, c'est l'heure de l'homme" (Cixous 1991b, 100 [1976]).

22. Parataxis is "the independent arrangement of clauses, phrases, etc. without connectives" (*Webster's New International Comprehensive Dictionary of the English Language*, 1996).

23. "In terms of language, you once spoke of a 'frozen' language. I love that expression, it is a real find: the way in which language is coded does indeed block the paths to let life and living, and the body and the physical through, blocks the opportunities to make them *heard*." Philosopher Rina Van der Haegen in an interview with Hélène Cixous (Cixous 1982, 302).

24. "Elle a et aura lieu ailleurs que dans les territoires subordonnés à la domination philosophique-théorique. Elle ne se laissera penser que par les sujets casseurs des automatismes, les coureurs de bords qu'aucune autorité ne subjugue jamais" (Cixous 1975a, 169–170).

25. "Peut-être que cette échéance, cette mort qui l'attend est l'auteur de ce journal, de cette surabondance qui était nécessaire. C'est un défense, une formidable construction contre l'angoisse. Peut-être qu'en face de la mort qui est silence il y a eu une immense levée de mots pour faire vie en face de la mort" (Cixous, seminar 01/25/1986).

26. Cixous's example was this: "We walked along the quay in a balmy and refreshing breeze. We passed lilac trees and small rose bushes and German soldiers on patrol" (EH, 393; Etty, H'83, 113; Cixous, seminar 01/25/1986).

27. "A few lines from: 'Es winkt zu Fühlung fast aus allen Dingen':

    Durch alle Wesen reicht der *eine* Raum:
    Weltinnenraum. Die Vögel fliegen still
    durch uns hindurch. O, der ich wachsen will,
    ich seh hinaus, und *in* mir wächst der Baum."   (EH, 286)

    See also Hillesum 1986, 757. Rilke's poem quoted from *Gedichte 1906–1926, Sämtliche Werke II,* p. 92. In translation this stanza from "All Things Beckon Toward Feeling" reads:

    There is *one* space that reaches through all beings:
    the inner universe. Birds wing silently
    right through us. Oh, now I want to grow,
    I look outside, and *inside* me, the tree grows tall.
                            (trans. MH)

28. "Il y a Rilke: mais il y a Clarice. Il n'y a que: Il y a culte, il y a peur, il y a limites, il y a l'étendue retenue de la Weltinnenraum: le monde-en-l'intimité-de-moi-Rilke. Il y a clôture; la maint tient, l'écriture é/lit et contient. Mais il y a Clarice, il y a audace, vertige sans bords, il y a oui. . . . Il y a risque—Clarice. Clarisque: à travers l'horrible jusqu'à Joie" (Cixous 1986b, 135–136).

29. "Ce sont des livres qui, dans la passivité, sont combattants, et qui, finalement, nous donnent de véritables recettes de survie spirituelle. Ce sont des livres nourrissants: des livres d'affamés qui nourrissent" (Cixous, seminar 10/5/1988).

30. "La question que pose un texte de femme, c'est la question du don «qu'est-ce qu'elle donne?», «comment elle donne?», cette écriture" (Cixous 1974, 14).

31. One of Cixous's texts about Clarice Lispector is entitled: "L'approche de Clarice Lispector. Se laisser lire (par) Clarice Lispector. A Paixao Segundo C.L." (Cixous 1986b, 113 [1979]). In English this has become "Clarice Lispector: The Approach. Letting Oneself (be) Read (by) Clarice Lispector. The Passion According to C.L." (Cixous 1991a, 59).

CHAPTER 6   THE GIRL WHO COULD NOT KNEEL

1. "What a strange story it is, my story: the girl who could not kneel. Or put differently: the girl who learned to pray" (EH, 580; H'83, 194; adapt. MH).

2. See also Reitsma (1989), Scholtens (1989), Schrijvers (1986), K.A.D. Smelik (1989), and Snijders (1993).

3. See also Bendien 1989, 175.

4. Jaap Meijer (1992a; 1992b) discusses Levi Hillesum's rabbinical training. Meijer criticizes Etty Hillesum's representation of her father because he feels it does not sufficiently bring out his Jewish background. Meijer's texts were printed privately. I would like to thank Professor Klaas Smelik for sending them to me.

5. In December 1995 the Belgian radio broadcasting company BRT aired a series on *écriture féminine.* In part 2 Christa Stevens, a Dutch Cixous scholar, was interviewed by reporter Katleen van Langendonck. Stevens and Van Langendonck spoke about Cixous's

neologisms and the difficulty of translating them. They mentioned the word *juifemme*, which translates rather well into "Jewoman." However, the word *juifemme* is more seminal: The first syllable resounds not only *juif/juive* (Jew/ess), but also *je suis* (I am) and *je jouis* (I enjoy). It is an affirmation of the Jewishness and femininity in the acts of being and enjoying, which is lost in the translation.

6. This hypothesis was posed earlier by K.A.D. Smelik (1989, 213)

7. For an analysis of the patriarchal nature of Judaism, see Plaskow (1991).

8. "Je n'aurais pas eu le culot d'aller réclamer mon livre à Dieu sur le Sinaï" (Cixous 1991, 20 [1976]).

9. This version is taken from a recent translation from the Hebrew: *The Stone Edition Chumash*, trans. Nosson Scherman (Brooklyn, N.Y.: Mesorah Publications, 1993). This translation always refers to God (when identified by the four-letter name *yud-hay-vav-hay*) as "Hashem," literally "the name." My thanks to Michael Chesal for this information.

10. See Plaskow (1991, 38–39), who points to the possiblity of other interpretations of Miriam that are not included in the Torah.

11. "Tu peux désirer. Tu peux lire, adorer, être envahie. Mais écrire ne t'est pas accordé. Ecrire était réservé aux élus. Cela devrait se passer dans un espace inaccessible aux petits, aux humbles, aux femmes. Dans l'intimité d'un sacré. L'écriture parlait à ses prophètes depuis un buisson ardent. Mais il avait dû être décidé que les buissons ne dialogueraient pas avec les femmes" (Cixous 1991, 28 [1976]). Cixous refers to Exodus 3, in which God appeared to Moses in a burning bush.

12. Here I should refer to the poems by Maria de Groot and Christianne Méroz, collected in a volume entitled *Westerbork* (1985). The poems in this book were all written after the war, after Auschwitz. "What is written often appears uninvited," the poets wrote in their preface. In apparent defiance of Adorno—who concluded that it was impossible to write poetry after the Holocaust—they wrote a book of poems that, according to the back cover, "are meant to be a response to words that speak to us from beyond the barbed wire, words of pain and courage," for example the words of Etty Hillesum. The book is dedicated to her. In a less well-known text, incidentally, Adorno put his statement in perspective by emphasizing that while aesthetic art has been suspect since the Holocaust, the language of art offers the only opportunity to convey the unthinkable, the indescribable (Felman and Laub 1992, 33–34).

13. For a more detailed explanation of this notion, see chapter 5.

14. See also EH, 733; Exod. 40: 33–38; Num. 12:5.

15. In addition to religion, Hillesum was also influenced by the theme of Russian suffering, which she was familiar with from studies about Russian culture and the work of Dostoyevsky. She saw a clear difference between Russia and the West. While Western culture transposes suffering into words, reflections, and philosophies about suffering, "[the Russians bear] their suffering until the bitter end and buckle down to the entire weight of their emotions and suffer to the very core" (EH, 478; trans. MH; see also EH, 388–389; EH, 484; H'83, 128–129; EH, 510; H'83, 146; and EH, 524). Hillesum believed that in the West suffering was more likely to be sublimated; in Russia, on the other hand, suffering was accepted as a part of life and people tried to glean something positive from it. Incidentally, Hillesum's mother, Riva Bernstein, did not live up to this image of the Russian outlook on life. She brought from Russia the awareness of what it means to be a persecuted Jew. Like many Ashkenazic Jews who had fled Eastern Europe, she was much more alert to the likelihood of persecution than the Dutch Jews, who had lived in relative security for centuries and had very little memory of pogroms. When the persecution of the Jews became real in the Netherlands, Riva attempted several times to escape her fate. Initially she tried to "aryanize" herself and her family by proving that she did not have Jewish blood. She even wrote a letter from Westerbork to Police Lieutenant General Rauter, requesting a little more freedom of movement. Rauter rewarded this "impudence" by

ordering the immediate deportation of the entire Hillesum family to Auschwitz (Hillesum 1986, 809–810). In Etty Hillesum's philosophy of life, acceptance of suffering went hand in hand with moral indignation (see EH, 168–169; H'83: 56–57; EH, 349–350; H'83, 96–97; and EH, 656; H'83, 77).

16. Cf. Sem Dresden, who believes that the success of Anne Frank's diary is partly due to the limited Jewish element in her text (Dresden 1991, 239).

17. Although Deventer did not erect a statue of Etty Hillesum, the city did put up a momument along the river IJssel, made by Arno Kramer in 1985 and entitled *Het verstoorde leven* [An interrupted life]. Deventer also renamed the Schoutenplein, where Hillesum and her family lived from 1924 to 1932. It is now called the Etty Hillesumplein (See Hop-Dijkhuis 1995, 8, 73.)

    The "Jessica motif" refers to Shakespeare's *The Merchant of Venice,* in which Lorenzo, a Christian, falls in love with Jessica, daughter of Shylock, the Jew. In act 2, scene 3, Jessica exclaims:

    > Alack, what heinous sin is it in me
    > To be ashamed to be my father's child!
    > But though I am a daughter to his blood
    > I am not to his manners. O Lorenzo,
    > If thou keep promise, I shall end this strife,
    > Become a Christian and thy loving wife.
    >
    > (Shakespeare *MV* 2.3)
    > (See also Hans Bendien 1990, 173)

18. See also K.A.D. Smelik 1989, 211–212.

19. For the exceptions, see Bendien 1990, 172–173.

20. Multatuli's Idea I. The original text reads: "Perhaps nothing is totally true, not even that statement" (Hillesum 1986, 743 [ed.]; trans. MH).

21. Ellis (1989, 126) also remarked on this.

22. "[D]epuis des siècles que nous n'avons accès à l'avoir qu'en *volant*; que nous avons vécu dans un vol, de voler" (Cixous 1975a, 178).

23. "In a minute the '1,100 books' will arrive; I'll probably get drunk on them" (EH, 118; trans. MH).

24. "La femme tient de l'oiseau et du voleur comme le voleur tient de la femme et de l'oiseau: illes passent, illes filent, illes jouissent de brouiller l'ordre de l'espace, de le désorienter, de changer de place les meubles, les choses, les valeurs, de faire des casses, de vider les structures, de chambouler le propre" (Cixous 1975a, 178–179).

25. The Oxford group was founded by Frank Buchman (1878–1961), a Lutheran evangelist from the United States. He moved to England and founded a revival movement that appealed greatly to Oxford students, hence the name. In 1938 he launched a "Moral Rearmament" program as an alternative to communism, which he abhorred. His program propagated four standards of Christian life: total love, total unselfishness, total honesty, and total cleanliness.

26. Käthe Fransen was Han Wegerif's German-born housekeeper. For the history of "the Gretchens, the Liesls and the Käthes," the numerous German housemaids that lived and worked in the Netherlands between the world wars, see Barbara Henkes's doctoral thesis (1995).

27. For a well-known Dutch example of this tendency, see the reception of Maria Neeltje Min's poetry, discussed briefly in Maaike Meijer's *De Lust tot Lezen* [An appetite for reading] (1988, 107–111).

28. With the exception of Sieves's article (1985), particularly p. 117.

29. See also EH, 100; H'83, 38; EH, 139; H'83, 45–46; EH, 166; EH, 481; and EH, 510; H'83, 145.

30. The convergence of God and Spier is also evident in EH, 352–353; H'83, 98 (in which the Dutch *bidden* has been translated as "cry," while it should be "pray"); and EH, 367.

31. "Du vivant de cette relation qui meurt avant qu'il meurt, il y a sans cesse entre Etty et S. cette vie qui se retourne en mort, cette séparation initiale qui a une figure" (Cixous, seminar 03/22/1986).

32. "Lui [Spier] une fois mort, c'est le règne de Dieu, il y a tout d'un coup d'une ouverture immense à Dieu qui était déjà là. Et Dieu occupe à ce moment-là toutes les places, mais quel Dieu, et comment?" (Cixous, seminar 01/25/1986).

33. "Si vous me permettez de me parodier moi-même, je dirais que S. c'est le 'Prénom de Dieu'" (Cixous, seminar 03/22/1986).

34. Cixous's statement is debatable, since Israel is repeatedly depicted in the Torah as God's bride. I would like to thank Professor K.A.D. Smelik for pointing this out to me.

35. For example: "Yet another day so rich and brimming with inner experiences, my God, it almost gets unheimlich [creepy]. Good night, little lamp, I'm switching you off now, I'll see you in the morning!" (EH, 191; trans. MH) or "Good morning, untidy desk" (EH, 420; H'83, 117).

36. "Le Journal d'Etty indique d'une manière très nette un développement. Dieu naît très tard, il y a une histoire de Dieu dans ce texte, et il est tout à fait apprivoisé quand il commence à prendre l'ampleur qu'il prend à la fin" (Cixous, seminar 01/25/1986).

37. Spier called the brand of chirognomy he developed "psychochirology" (see Spier 1982).

38. See EH, 24, and Hillesum 1986, 723, 742.

39. In Hinduism she also came across the idea that people create gods rather than the other way around: "Per gli Indù, noi creiamo dèi, siamo noi che facciamo gli dèi e che ci facciamo dèi [Since for the Hindus, we create gods, it is we who make the gods, and make ourselves gods]" (Irigaray 1989c, 95; trans. Giuliana de Novellis). I would like to thank Anne Claire Mulder for bringing this article to my attention.

40. "L'évitement de cette finitude, l'homme l'a cherché dans un Dieu unique *masculin*. Le Dieu, il l'a créé de son genre [. . .] L'homme ne s'est pas laissé définir par un autre genre: féminin. Son Dieu unique correspondrait au genre humain dont nous savons qu'il n'est pas neutre du point de vue de la différence des sexes" (Irigaray 1987, 74).

41. "Dieu ne nous oblige à rien, sinon *devenir*. Aucune tâche, aucune obligation ne nous incombe que celle-là: devenir divin(e), devenir parfaitement, ne pas nous laisser amputer de parties de nous que nous pouvons épanouir (Irigaray 1987, 81).

42. "Je suis née femme, mais je dois encore devenir cette femme que je suis par nature" (Irigaray 1992b, 168).

43. "Ce lieu, le seul où dans l'histoire de l'Occident la femme parle, agit, aussi publiquement" (Irigaray 1974, 238).

44. See also Bendien 1989, 161–162.

45. Levi (Louis) Hillesum was a teacher of Latin and Greek and principal of the gymnasium (secondary school) in Deventer. He was dismissed in late November 1940, after the Nazi regime decreed that Jews were no longer allowed to hold such positions (see EH, 148; Hillesum 1986, 740; Lagrou 1985, 19; and J. Meijer 1992b).

46. See Heldring, Hahn, Reitsma, and Swart in Gaarlandt (1989). See also Van den Brandt (1990), Burnier (1988, 83–84), and Van Dongen (1989).

47. "C'est très juste, elle est l'auteur de Dieu" (Cixous, seminar 03/22/1986).

48. Initially Heldring also assumed that Hillesum's God was not an Old Testament God, but in a later publication he changed his view. Cf. Heldring's articles in Gaarlandt (1989, 22–23, 49).

49. For the issue of witnessing the Holocaust, see Felman and Laub (1992). Many camp inmates found the fact that the Nazis were removing all traces of the genocide—even the bodies were burned—unbearable. At the same time, however, this also fueled an intense will to survive in order to bear witness.

50. See Eliach (1989).

51. This aspect of God is also present in the Hebrew Bible. After all, did God not depend on Moses and Aaron to spread his word?

52. "Il est nécessaire aussi que nous découvrions et affirmions que nous sommes toujours mères dès lors que nous sommes femmes. Nous mettons au monde autre chose que des enfants, nous engendrons autre chose que des enfants: de l'amour, du désir, du langage, de l'art, du social, du politique, du religieux, etc. Mais cette création nous a été interdite depuis de siècles et il faut que nous nous réapproprions cette dimension maternelle que nous appartient en tant que femmes" (Irigaray 1987, 30).

53. Cf. Braidotti's "The divine in all humans is the capacity to see interconnectedness as the way of being" (1993, 180) with Hillesum's "The most essential and the deepest in me hearkening unto the most essential and deepest in the other. God to God" (EH, 549; H'83, 173).

54. See also Dresden 1991, 28–29.

55. Riet Okken believes that she is a reincarnation of Hillesum. She has written a book titled *Tussen scepsis en overgave* [Between skepticism and surrender] about Etty Hillesum's last months in Westerbork and Auschwitz (Okken 1988, 9).

55. See also Whitford (1991, 47, 164).

❧ BIBLIOGRAPHY

ANNE FRANK

1947. *Het Achterhuis: Dagboekbrieven 12 juni 1942–1 augustus 1944.* Amsterdam/Antwerp: Contact.

1949. *Weet je nog? Verhalen en Sprookjes.* Amsterdam/Antwerp: Contact.

1952. *Anne Frank: The Diary of a Young Girl.* Reprint, New York: Doubleday, 1993. Page references are to the 1993 edition.

1960. *Verhalen rondom het Achterhuis. Met 8 fascimile's naar handschrift.* Amsterdam/Antwerp: Contact.

1982. *Verhaaltjes, en gebeurtenissen uit het Achterhuis.* Amsterdam: Bert Bakker.

1986. *De Dagboeken van Anne Frank.* The Hague: Staatsuitgeverij/Amsterdam: Bert Bakker.

1989. *The Diary of Anne Frank: The Critical Edition.* Translated by Arnold J. Pomerans and B. M. Mooyaart-Doubleday. Edited by David Barnouw and Gerrold van der Stroom. New York: Doubleday.

1994. *Anne Frank's Tales from the Secret Annex.* Translated by Michel Mok and Ralph Manheim. 1983. Reprint, New York: Bantam.

1995. *Anne Frank: The Diary of a Young Girl: The Definitive Edition.* Edited by Otto H. Frank and Mirjam Pressler. Translated by Susan Massotty. New York: Doubleday.

Baruch, Grace K. 1968. "Anne Frank on Adolescence." *Adolescence* 3:425–434.

Berryman, John. 1976. "The Development of Anne Frank." In *The Freedom of the Poet.* New York: Farrar, Straus & Giroux.

Bettelheim, Bruno. 1979. "The Ignored Lesson of Anne Frank." In *Surviving and Other Essays.* New York: Alfred A. Knopf.

Boas, Jacob. 1996. *We Are Witnesses: Five Diaries of Teenagers Who Died in the Holocaust.* New York: Scholastic Inc.

Boonstra, Janrense, and Marie-José Rijnders. 1982. *Anne Frank Huis: Een museum met een verhaal.* The Hague: Sdu.

Bouhuys, Mies. 1982. *Anne Frank is niet van gisteren.* Amsterdam: Bert Bakker.

Brenner, Rachel Feldhay. 1996. "Writing Herself Against History: Anne Frank's Self-Portrait as a Young Artist." *Modern Judaism* 16:105–134.

———. 1997. *Writing as Resistance: Four Women Confronting the Holocaust. Edith Stein, Simone Weil, Anne Frank, Etty Hillesum.* University Park: Pennsylvania State University Press.

Chiarello, Barbara. 1994. "The Utopian Space of a Nightmare: The Diary of Anne Frank." *Utopian Studies: Journal of the Society for Utopian Studies* 5, no. 1:128–140.

Costa, Denise de. 1993. "Beschermengel: Over Anne Frank." *Lust & Gratie, Encyclopedie* (winter): 10–13.

———. 1994. "'We zitten hier als uitgestotenen.' Ballingschap en (zelf)censuur in de dagboeken van Anne Frank." *Lover: Literatuuroverzicht over feminisme, cultuur en wetenschap* 21, no. 2:4–7.

Dalsimer, Katherine. 1986. "Middle Adolescence: The Diary of Anne Frank." *Female Adolescence: Psychoanalytic Reflections on Works of Literature.* New Haven, Conn.: Yale University Press.

Dam, Heiman van. 1993. "De vrouwelijke seksuele ontwikkeling in de puberteit: een herbezinning op Anne Frank's dagboeken." *Psychotherapeutisch Paspoort* 2:125–152.

———. N.d. "The Jewish Identity of Anne Frank." Chapter in a forthcoming book.

Enzer, Hyman. 1991. "Review of The Diary of Anne Frank: The Critical Edition." *Contemporary Sociology: An International Journal of Reviews* 20, no. 2 (Mar.): 214–221.

Gies, Miep, with Alison L. Gold. 1987. *Anne Frank Remembered: The Story of the Woman Who Helped to Hide the Frank Family.* London: Guild.

Gilligan, Carol. 1990. "Joining the Resistance: Psychology, Politics, Girls and Women." *Michigan Quarterly Review* 29, no. 4:501–536.

Graver, Lawrence. 1995. *An Obsession with Anne Frank: Meyer Levin and the Diary.* Berkeley/Los Angeles/London: University of California Press.

Grobman, Alex, and Joel Fishman, eds. 1995. *Anne Frank in Historical Perspective: A Teaching Guide for Secondary Schools.* Los Angeles: Martyrs Memorial and Museum of the Holocaust.

Haas, Gerard C. de. 1979. "Anne Frank, vijftig jaar geleden geboren." In *Het vaderschap van God in de nadagen van het paternalisme.* Baarn: Ten Have.

Heebing, Sonja. 1994. "Anne, Esther en Mozes. Jonge dagboekschrijvers in oorlogstijd." In *Een halve eeuw geleden:De verwerking van de Tweede Wereldoorlog in de literatuur.* Edited by Hans Ester and Wam de Moor. Kampen: Kok Agora.

Hemmerechts, Kristien. 1992. "Mijn broer, Sarah, de maan en ik." In *Kerst en andere liefdesverhalen.* Amsterdam/Antwerpen: Atlas.

Houwaart, Dick, ed. 1982. *Anne in 't voorbijgaan. Emoties, gedachten en verwachtingen rondom het huis en het Dagboek van Anne Frank.* Amsterdam: Keesing Boeken.

Kooiman, J. 1995. "Het meisje werd maar vijftien jaar. Anne Frank en haar dagboek." In *Oorlog in fragmenten.* Kampen: Kok Voorhoeve.

Lindwer, Willy. 1991. *The Last Seven Months of Anne Frank.* Translated by Alison Meersschaert. New York: Doubleday.

Maarsen, Jacqueline (Jopie) van. 1996. *My Friend Anne Frank.* Translated by Debra F. Onkenhout. New York: Vantage Press.

Martelaere, Patricia de. 1993. "Het dagboek en de dood." In *Een verlangen naar ontroostbaarheid: Over leven, kunst en dood.* Amsterdam: Meulenhoff/Kritak.

Moffat, Mary Jane, and Charlotte Painter, eds. 1974. "Anne Frank (1929–1944)." In *Revelations: Diaries of Women.* New York: Vintage Books.

Nussbaum, Laureen. 1994a. "Anne Frank." In *Women Writing in Dutch.* Edited by Aercke Kristiaan. London: Garland Publishing.

———. 1994b. "Schrijven met Anne Frank: Leren van je leeftijdgenootje." *Levende Talen* 486 (Jan.): 4–8.

———. 1995. "Anne Frank, schrijfster." *De Groene Amsterdammer* (23 Aug.): 36–38.

Piszkalski, Henry J. C. 1980. *The Personality of Anne Frank in the Light of Theory of "Extreme Situations" by Karl Jaspers.* Washington, D.C.: n.p.

Pressler, Mirjam. 1993. *Daar verlang ik zo naar: Het levensverhaal van Anne Frank.* Translated by Anneriek de Jong. Amsterdam: Bert Bakker.

Rol, Ruud van der, and Rian Verhoeven. 1992. *Anne Frank.* Amsterdam: Anne Frank House.

Rosen, Norma. 1992. "The Fate of Anne Frank's Diary." In *Accidents of Influence: Writing as a Woman and a Jew in America.* Albany: State University of New York Press.

Rosenfeld, Alvin H. 1991. "Popularization and Memory: The Case of Anne Frank." In *Lessons and Legacies: The Meaning of the Holocaust in a Changing World*. Edited by Peter Hayes. Evanston, Ill.: Northwestern University Press.

Roth, Philip. 1979. *The Ghost Writer*. New York: Fawcett Crest.

Stam, Dineke. 1995. "Laat me mezelf zijn, dan ben ik tevreden." In *Sekse en Oorlog: Jaarboek voor Vrouwengeschiedenis* 15. Amsterdam: Stichting beheer IISG.

Steenmeijer, Anna G., ed. 1970. *Weerklank van Anne Frank*. Amsterdam: Contact.

Waaldijk, Berteke. 1993. "Reading Anne Frank as a Woman." *Women's Studies International Forum* 16, no. 4:327–335.

Wiggins, Marianne. 1991. *Bet They'll Miss Us When We're Gone*. London: Secker & Warburg.

Zee, Nanda van der. 1990. *De kamergenoot van Anne Frank*. Amsterdam: Lakeman Publishers.

ETTY HILLESUM

1962. *Twee brieven uit Westerbork van Etty Hillesum*. Introduction by David Koning. The Hague: Bert Bakker/Daamen N.V.

1981. *Het verstoorde leven: Dagboek van Etty Hillesum 1941–1943*. Introduction by J. Geurt Gaarlandt. Haarlem: De Haan.

1982. *Het denkende hart van de barak: Brieven van Etty Hillesum*. Introduction by J. Geurt Gaarlandt. Haarlem: De Haan.

1983. *Etty: A Diary 1941–43*. Introduction by J. Geurt Gaarlandt. Translated by Arnold J. Pomerans. London: Jonathan Cape.

1985. *Une vie bouleversée: Journal 1941–1943*. Translated by Philippe Noble. Paris: Éditions du Seuil.

1987. *Etty Hillesum: Letters from Westerbork*. Edited by J. Geurt Gaarlandt. Translated by Arnold J. Pomerans. London: Jonathan Cape.

1988. *Lettres de Westerbork*. Translated by Philippe Noble. Paris: Éditions du Seuil.

1991. *Etty: De nagelaten geschriften van Etty Hillesum: 1941–1943*. Edited by Klaas Smelik. 3rd rev. ed. Amsterdam: Balans.

1994. *Het denkende hart van de barak: De brieven van Etty Hillesum*. Rev. ed. Amsterdam: Balans.

Allewijn, Herrianne, et al. 1984. "Een voorbeeld voor de eeuwigheid? Over de huidige waardering voor de dagboeken van Etty Hillesum." *Werkschrift voor Leerhuis & Liturgie* 4, no. 2/3 (Nov.): 164–173.

Bakker, Sybe. 1992. "De innerlijke gebieden. Over het dagboek en de brieven van Etty Hillesum." In *Vuurproeven over literatuur*. Barneveld: De Vuurbaak.

Bendien, Hans. 1989. "Zelfverwerkelijking." In *Men zou een pleister op vele wonden willen zijn. Reacties op de dagboeken en brieven van Etty Hillesum*. Edited by J. Geurt Gaarlandt. Amsterdam: Balans.

———. 1990. "Mythe-vorming over de heiligheid van Etty Hillesum." *De Gids* 153, no. 3:170–181.

Boas, Henriëtte. 1982. "Etty Hillesum in niet-joodse en joodse ogen." In *Neveh Ya'akov: opstellen aangeboden aan dr. Jaap Meijer ter gelegenheid van zijn zeventigste verjaardag*. Edited by Lea Dasberg and Jonathan N. Cohen. Assen: n.p.

Brandt, Ria van den. 1990. "'Ik heb hem gebracht de schriften van Meister Eckhart.' Het Eckhartbeeld van Etty Hillesum." *De Gids* 153, no. 13:182–191.

Brenner, Rachel Feldhay. 1997. *Writing as Resistance: Four Women Confronting the Holocaust: Edith Stein, Simone Weil, Anne Frank, Etty Hillesum*. University Park: Pennylvania State University Press.

Burnier, Andreas. 1988. *Mystiek en magie in de literatuur*. Leiden: Martinus Nijhof.

Costa, Denise de. 1991. "Ceçi n'est pas une cigarette: Een detaillistische lezing van Etty Hillesum." *Lover: literatuuroverzicht voor de vrouwenbeweging* 18, no. 3:140–145.

———. 1993a. "Etty Hillesum, beeldhouwster van de ziel." In *Een beeld van een vrouw: De visualisering van het vrouwelijke in een postmoderne cultuur.* Edited by Rosi Braidotti. Kampen: Kok Agora.

———. 1993b. "Nageslacht: Etty Hillesum." *Lust & Gratie, Encyclopedie* (winter): 81–84.

Dongen, Marian van. 1989. "Tegenstelling in eenheid. Erotiek en mystiek in het werk van Etty Hillesum." *Lust & Gratie* 22 (summer): 8–23.

Dresden, Sem. 1990. "Etty Hillesum: identiteit als opgave en oplossing." *De Gids* 153, no. 3:159–169.

Fens, Kees. 1989. "Naar een woestijn van medemensen." In *Men zou een pleister op vele wonden willen zijn: Reacties op de dagboeken en brieven van Etty Hillesum.* Edited by J. Geurt Gaarlandt. Amsterdam: Balans.

Gaarlandt, J. Geurt, ed. 1989. *Men zou een pleister op vele wonden willen zijn: Reacties op de dagboeken en brieven van Etty Hillesum.* Amsterdam: Balans.

Hop-Dijkhuis, Siemy, ed. 1995. *Etty Hillesum '43–'93. Teksten van lezingen gehouden in de Herdenkingsweek november 1993 te Deventer.* Deventer: Boekhandel Praamstra.

Hulst, J. W. van. 1983. *Treinen naar de hel. Amsterdam, Westerbork, Auschwitz: een aantal beschouwingen die verband houden met het dagboek en de brieven van Etty Hillesum.* Amsterdam: Buijten & Schipperheijn.

Lagrou, Els. 1985. *Etty Hillesum, 1914–1943. Een historisch-biografische studie.* Master's thesis in Modern History, Faculty of Arts and Philosophy, Catholic University of Leuven (Louvain), Belgium.

Meijer, Jaap. 1992a. *Als Maggied vergeten: Doctor Levie Hillesum 1880–1943: De vader van Etty.* Heemstede: privately printed.

———. 1992b. *De Odyssee van een joods docent. Dr. Levie Hillesum 1911–1924.* Heemstede: Privately printed.

Minco, Marga. 1989. "De kroniekschrijfster van onze lotgevallen." In *Men zou een pleister op vele wonden willen zijn: Reacties op de dagboeken en brieven van Etty Hillesum.* Edited by Geurt Gaarlandt. Amsterdam: Balans.

Okken, Riet. 1988. *De kracht van de bestemming.* Deventer: Ankh-Hermes.

Oord, Gerrit van, ed. 1990. *L'esperienza dell'Albro: Studi su Etty Hillesum.* Rome: Sant'Oreste.

Reitsma, Anneke. 1989. "Ik bloei van binnen met de dood tot bloem." Pp. 99–132 in *Men zou een pleister op vele wonden willen zijn. Reacties op de dagboeken en brieven van Etty Hillesum.* Edited by J. Geurt Gaarlandt. Amsterdam: Balans.

———. 1992. "'Men moet zichzelf het vaderland zijn': Over Etty Hillesum en de innerlijke noodzaak van haar schrijverschap." *Periodiek Parodos* 31 (Apr.): 29–37.

Reve, Karel van het. 1989. "Het korte leven van Etty Hillesum." In *Men zou een pleister op vele wonden willen zijn. Reacties op de dagboeken en brieven van Etty Hillesum.* Edited by J. Geurt Gaarlandt. Amsterdam: Balans.

Scholtens, Wim R. 1989. "Søren Kierkegaard en Etty Hillesum, een vergelijking." In *Men zou een pleister op vele wonden willen zijn: Reacties op de dagboeken en brieven van Etty Hillesum.* Edited by J. Geurt Gaarlandt. Amsterdam: Balans.

Schrijvers, P. H. 1986. "Een filosoof in bezettingstijd: Over Seneca's brieven en het dagboek van Etty Hillesum." In *De mens als toeschouwer: Essays over Romeinse literatuur en Westeuropese tradities.* Amsterdam: Ambo, Atheneum-Polak.

Sieves, Joseph. 1995. "'Aiutare Dio': riflessioni su vita e pensiero di Etty Hillesum." *Nuova Umanità* 3/4 (May–Aug.): 113–127.

Smelik, Klaas A. D. 1989. "Reacties op Etty Hillesum." In *Men zou een pleister op vele wonden willen zijn: Reacties op de dagboeken en brieven van Etty Hillesum.* Edited by J. Geurt Gaarlandt. Amsterdam: Balans.

Smelik, Johanna F. 1993. "Het "zusje" van Etty Hillesum." Interview by Anke Manschot. *Opzij* (July/Aug.): 118–121.

Snijders, Jos. 1993. *Ik heb zo lief: De menselijke en gelovige groei van Etty Hillesum.* Den Bosch: KBS/Averbode: Altiora.

Steeg, Maria ter. 1994. "De verlokking van de liefde: De geestelijke ontwikkeling van Etty Hillesum." *Streven* 61, no. 4 (Apr.): 291–303.

Swart, Loet. 1991. "Een verzamelplaats voor het lijden van de mensheid." In *Tot op de bodem van het niets: Mystiek in een tijd van oorlog en crisis: 1920–1970.* Edited by H. H. Blommestijn. Kampen: Kok/Averbode: Altiora.

Taylor, Dennis. 1993. "Examined Lives." *Boston College Magazine* 52, no. 1 (winter): 33–40.

Tigchelaar, Herma. 1985. *Als zij spreekt is de ander veilig: Over de grenzen en mogelijkheden van taal: Een lezing van "Über Wahrheit und Lüge im außermoralischen Sinn" van Friedrich Nietzsche en "La venue à l'écriture" van Hélène Cixous.* Master's thesis in Social Ethics, Faculty of Theology, Utrecht University.

Ypma, Sytze. 1990. *Voorbij het verstoorde leven: Een zelfpsychologisch lezing van het zelfbeeld en godsbeeld van de ik-persoon uit "Etty, De nagelaten geschriften van Etty Hillesum, 1941–1943."* Master's thesis in Theological Psychology, Faculty of Theology, Groningen University.

HÉLÈNE CIXOUS

1967. *Le Prénom de Dieu.* Paris: Bernard Grasset.

1974. "Le sexe ou la tête?" *Les Cahiers du GRIF,* 13:5–15.

1975a. "Sorties." In *La jeune née.* Edited by Hélène Cixous and Catherine Clement. Paris: Union Générale d'Éditions.

1975b. "Le rire de la Méduse." *L'Arc* 61:39–54.

1976. *La venue à l'écriture.* Paris: Des Femmes.

1979. "Clarice Lispector: The Approach." *Poétique* 40:59–77. Reprint 1986 in *Entre l'écriture.* Paris: Des Femmes. Page references are to 1986 edition.

1981a. "The Laugh of the Medusa." Translated by Keith Cohen and Paula Cohen. In *New French Feminisms: An Anthology.* Edited by Elaine Marks and Isabelle de Courtivron. Brighton, England: Harvester Press.

1981b. "Castration or Decapitation?" Translated by Annette Kuhn. *Signs: Journal of Women in Culture and Society* 7, no. 1 (autumn): 41–55.

1982. "Voor mij gaat het lichaam bevrijden, de geest bevrijden en de taal bevrijden samen. Hélène Cixous in gesprek met Rina Van der Haegen." *Tijdschrift voor Vrouwenstudies* 11, no. 3:290–305.

1984. "An Exchange with Hélène Cixous." In *Hélène Cixous: Writing the Feminine,* ed. Verena Andermatt Conley. Lincoln/London: University of Nebraska Press.

1985–1988. Seminars 10/20/85, 11/23/1985, 1/25/86, 3/22/86, 10/24/87, 10/15/88, and seminar 11/11/88.

1986a. *The Newly Born Woman.* Translated by Betsy Wing. Introduction by Sandra M. Gilbert. Minneapolis: University of Minnesota Press.

1986b. "Le Dernier Tableau où le Portrait de Dieu." In *Entre l'écriture.* Paris: Des Femmes.

1988a. "Extreme Fidelity." Pp. 9–36 in *Writing Differences: Readings from the Seminar of Hélène Cixous.* Edited by Susan Sellers. Milton Keynes, England: Open University Press.

1988b. "Conversations." Pp. 141–154 in *Writing Differences: Readings from the Seminar of Hélène Cixous.* Edited by Susan Sellers. Milton Keynes, England: Open University Press.

1989a. *L'heure de Clarice Lispector.* Paris: Des Femmes.

1989b. "From the Scene of the Unconscious to the Scene of History." In *The Future of Literary Theory.* Edited by Ralph Cohen. London: Routledge.

1990a. "Ecoute avec la main." In 1989: *Etats généreaux des femmes.* Paris: Des Femmes.

1990b. "Difficult Joys." In *The Body and the Text: Hélène Cixous, Reading and Teaching.* Edited by Helen Wilcox et al. New York/London: Harvester Wheatsheaf.

1991a. *"Coming to Writing" and Other Essays.* Translated by Sarah Cornell et al. Edited by Deborah Jenson. Introduction by Susan Rubin Suleiman. Cambridge, Mass.: Harvard University Press.

1991b. *Tussen talen ontstaan.* Translated by Camille Mortagne. Amsterdam: Hölderlin.

1992. *Readings: The Poetics of Blanchot, Joyce, Kafka, Kleist, Lispector and Tsvetayeva.* Edited, translated, and with an introduction by Verena Andermatt Conley. New York/London: Harvester Wheatsheaf.

1993a. "We Who Are Free, Are We Free?" In *Freedom and Interpretation: The Oxford Amnesty Lectures 1992.* Edited by Barbara Johnson. New York: BasicBooks/HarperCollins.

1993b. *Three Steps on the Ladder of Writing.* New York/Chichester, England: Columbia University Press.

1994. "Questions à Hélène Cixous." Interview in *(En)jeux de la communication romanesque.* Eds Suzan van Dijk and Christa Stevens. Amsterdam/Atlanta: Rodopi.

Beckers, Mirke. 1988. *Vanuit dreigen en beheersen richting beminnen gedacht . . . Een vrouwelijke mythe-interpretatie aan de hand van teksten van Hélène Cixous.* Master's thesis in Comparative Literature/Women's Studies, n.p. (Copy from IIAV [International Information Center and Archives of the Women's Movement] in Amsterdam)

Brügmann, Margret. 1982. "'Tussen Liefde en Verlangen': Aspecten van vrouwelijk schrijven. Een vergelijking van Freud's en Cixous' Dora-benadering." In *Maria of Medusa: Op zoek naar nieuwe mythen.* Amsterdam: IAV.

Conley, Verena Andermatt. 1984. *Hélène Cixous: Writing the Feminine.* Lincoln: University of Nebraska Press.

———, ed., trans. 1992. *Hélène Cixous: Readings: The Poetics of Blanchot, Joyce, Kafka, Kleist, Lispector, and Tsvetayeva.* New York/London: Harvester Wheatsheaf.

Cornell, Sarah. 1988. "Hélène Cixous' Le Livre de Promethea: Paradise Refound." In *Writing Differences: Readings from the Seminar of Hélène Cixous.* Edited by Susan Sellers. Milton Keynes, England: Open University Press.

Hablé, Renée, et al. 1988. *Vrouwelijk denken in Parijs. Over écriture féminine en vrouwelijk leren.* Amsterdam: Metaphora, Social Policy and Context Publications.

Sellers, Susan, ed. 1988. *Writing Differences: Readings from the Seminar of Hélène Cixous.* Milton Keynes: Open University Press.

Shiach, Morag. 1991. *Hélène Cixous: A Politics of Writing.* London: Routledge.

Stevens, Christa. 1989. "Ecriture féminine. Schrijven om het lichaam." *Tijdschrift voor Vrouwenstudies* 10, no. 3:411–426.

———. 1994. "Questions à Hélène Cixous." In *(En)jeux de la communication romanesque.* Edited by Suzan van Dijk and Christa Stevens. Amsterdam/Atlanta: Rodopi.

———. 1995a "Hélène Cixous. Nationaliteit: literair." *De Gids* 158, no. 11/12:922–929.

———. 1995b. "Hélène Cixous: wegen naar een culturele politiek." In *De Marges van de Macht: Filosofie en politiek in Frankrijk 1981–1995.* Edited by Rob Devos and Luc Vanmarcke. Leuven (Louvain): Universitaire Pers.

Wilcox, Helen et al., eds. 1990. *The Body and the Text: Hélène Cixous, Reading and Teaching.* New York/London: Harvester Wheatsheaf.

LUCE IRIGARAY

1974. *Speculum. De l'autre femme.* Paris: Minuit.

1977. *Ce sexe qui n'en est pas un.* Paris: Minuit.

1980. *Amante Marine: De Friedrich Nietzsche.* Paris: Minuit.

1984. *Ethique de la différence sexuelle.* Paris: Minuit.

1985a. *Speculum of the Other Woman.* Translated by Gillian C. Gill. Ithaca, N.Y.: Cornell University Press.

1985b. *This Sex Which Is Not One.* Translated by Catherine Porter. Ithaca, N.Y.: Cornell University Press.

1987. *Sexes et parentés.* Paris: Minuit.

1989a. *Le Temps de la différence: Pour une révolution pacifique.* Paris: Librairie Générale Française.

1989b. "Equal to Whom?" *Differences: A Journal of Feminist Cultural Studies.* Special issue: "The Essential Difference: Another Look at Essentialism" 1 (summer): 59–76.

1989c. "Il divino fra di noi. Domande poste a Luce Irigaray nel corso di un incontro al Centro di studi femministi di Utrecht." *Inchiesta* 19, no. 85–86 (July–Dec.): 93–100.

1990a. "Goddelijke vrouwen." In *Renaissance: Drie teksten van Luce Irigaray vertaald en becommentarieerd.* Translated and annotated by Agnès Vincenot et al. Amsterdam: Perdu.

1990b. *Je, tu, nous: Pour une culture de la différence.* Paris: Bernard Grasset.

1991. *Marine Lover: Of Friedrich Nietzche.* Trans. Gillian C. Gill from the French *Amante Marine.* De Friedrich Nietzsche. [1984. Paris: Minuit.] New York/Oxford: Columbia University Press.

1992. *J'aime à toi: Esquisse d'une félicité dans l'histoire.* Bernard Grasset. Paris.

1993a. *An Ethics of Sexual Difference.* Translated by Carolyn Burke and Gillian C. Gill. Ithaca, N.Y.: Cornell University Press.

1993b. *Sexes and Genealogies.* Translated by Gillian C. Gill. New York: Columbia University Press.

1993c. *Je, tu, nous: Towards a Culture of Difference.* Translated by Alison Martin. New York/London: Routledge.

1994a. *Thinking the Difference: For a Peaceful Revolution.* Translated by Karin Montin. London: Athlone Press.

1994b. "De weg van het vrouwelijke." Pp. 155–166 in *Hooglied. De Beeldenwereld van Religieuze Vrouwen in de Zuidelijke Nederlanden, vanaf de 13de eeuw.* Edited by Hans Devisscher. Brussels: Snoeck-Ducaju & Zoon.

1996. *I Love to You: Sketch for a Felicity Within History.* Translated by Alison Martin from the French *J'aime à toi: Esquisse d'une félicité dans l'histoire.* [1992. Paris: Bernard Grasset.] New York/London: Routledge.

Brüggemann-Kruijff, Atie T. 1993. "Emmanuel Levinas en Luce Irigaray over de liefde en het man-vrouw-verschil." Pp. 101–118 in *Bij de Gratie van de Transcendentie. In gesprek met Levinas over het vrouwelijke.* Amsterdam: Vrije Universiteit Uitgeverij.

Burke, Carolyn, et al., eds. 1994. *Engaging with Irigaray: Feminist Philosophy and Modern European Thought.* New York: Columbia University Press.

Grosz, Elizabeth. 1989. "Luce Irigaray and the Ethics of Alterity." Pp. 140–183 in *Sexual Subversions: Three French Feminists.* Sydney: Allen and Unwin.

Hablé, Renée, et al. 1988. *Vrouwelijk denken in Parijs. Over écriture féminine en vrouwelijk leren.* Amsterdam: Metaphora, Social Policy and Context Publications.

Halsema, Annemie. 1995. "Luce Irigaray: Het recht om vrouw te worden." Pp. 163–180 in *De Marges van de Macht. Filosofie en politiek in Frankrijk 1981–1995.* Eds. Rob Devos and Luc Vanmarcke. Leuven (Louvain), Belgium: Universitaire Pers.

Mortagne, Camille. 1988. "Op de adem van de kosmos." *Lust & Gratie* no. 18 (summer): 36–49.

Vincenot, Agnès et al. 1990. *Renaissance. Drie teksten van Luce Irigaray vertaald en becommentarieerd.* Amsterdam: Perdu.

———. 1993. "Afscheid van de verstrooiing. Ethiek en esthetiek bij Luce Irigaray." *Lover: literatuuroverzicht voor de vrouwenbeweging* 20, no. 1:23–30.

Whitford, Margaret. 1991. *Luce Irigaray: Philosophy in the feminine.* London: Routledge.

JULIA KRISTEVA

1975. "Unes femmes. Propos de Julia Kristeva, recueillis par Eliane Boucquey et relus par leur auteur." *Les cahiers du GRIF* 7:22–27.

1979. "Le temps des femmes." *34/44: Cahiers de recherche de sciences des textes et documents, Université Paris* 7, no. 5 (winter).

1980. "(M)enige vrouwen." Dutch translations by Hugues C. Boekraad from the French "Unes femmes. Propos de Julia Kristeva, recueillis par Eliane Boucquey et relus par leur auteur." [1975. *Les Cahiers du GRIF* no. 7:22–27.] *Te Elfder Ure 27: Seksualiteit,* 25, no. 1 (Nov.): 141–150.

1981. "Women"s Time." Translated from the French "Le temps des femmes."

[1979. *34/44: Cahiers de recherche de sciences des textes et documents, Université Paris* 7, no. 5 (winter).] *Signs: Journal of Women in Culture and Society* 7, no. 1 (autumn): 13–35.

1983a. "J'aime donc je suis." Interview in *Art Press* no. 74:16–19.

1983b. *Histoires d'amour.* Paris: Denoël.

1985. "Entretien avec Julia Kristeva." Interview in *Les Cahiers du GRIF* no. 32:6–23.

1986. "Ik heb lief dus ik ben." Dutch trans. Hugues C. Boekraad from the French "J'aime donc je suis." [1983a. *Art Press* no. 74:16–19.] *Te Elfder Ure 40: Julia Kristeva* 29, no.2 (Dec.): 167–177.

1987a. *Soleil Noir. Dépression et Mélancholie.* Paris: Gallimard.

1987b. "On the Melancholic Imaginary." Pp. 104–123 in *Discourse in Psychoanalysis and Literature.* Ed. Schlomith Rimmon-Kenan. London/New York: Methuen.

1987c. *Tales of Love.* Trans. Leon S. Roudiez from the French *Histoires d'amour.* [1983b. Paris: Denoël.] New York: Columbia University Press.

1988. *Etrangers à nous-mêmes.* Paris: Fayard.

1989. *Black Sun: Depression and Melancholia.* Translated by Leon S. Roudiez from the French *Soleil Noir. Dépression et Mélancholie.* [1987a. Paris: Gallimard.] New York: Columbia University Press.

1990. "The Adolescent Novel." Pp. 8–23 in *Abjection, Melancholia, and Love: The Work of Julia Kristeva.* Edited by John Fletcher and Andrew Benjamin. London/New York: Routledge.

1991. *Strangers to Ourselves.* Translated by Leon S. Roudiez from the French *Etrangers à nous-mêmes.* [1988. Paris: Fayard.] New York/London: Harvester Wheatsheaf.

Brink, Gabriël van den. 1986. "Kristeva en de revolutie van de poëtische taal." *Te Elfder Ure 40: Julia Kristeva* 29, no. 2 (Dec.): 30–75.

Crownfield, David, ed. 1992. *Body/Text in Julia Kristeva: Religion, Women and Psychoanalysis.* Albany: State University of New York Press.

Doane, Janice, and Devon Hodges. 1992. *From Klein to Kristeva: Psychoanalytic Feminism and the Search for the "Good Enough" Mother.* Ann Arbor: University of Michigan Press.

Jardine, Alice. 1986. "Opaque Texts and Transparent Contexts: The Political Difference of Julia Kristeva." Pp. 96–116 in *The Poetics of Gender.* Edited by Nancy K. Miller. New York: Columbia University Press.

Jones, Ann Rosalind. 1984. "Julia Kristeva on Femininity: The Limits of a Semiotic Politcs." *Feminist Review* no. 18 (London): 56–73.

Lechte, John. 1990. *Julia Kristeva.* London/New York: Routledge.

Oliver, Kelly. 1993a. *Reading Kristeva: Unraveling the Double-bind.* Bloomington: Indiana University Press.

Oliver, Kelly, ed. 1993b. *Ethics, Politics, and Difference in Julia Kristeva's Writing.* New York: Routledge.

Poel, Ieme van der. 1995. "Julia Kristeva het leven als theorie." *De Gids* 158, no. 11/12: 941–948.

Te Elfder Ure 40: Julia Kristeva 29, no. 2 (Dec.), 1986.

Weir, Allison. 1993. "Identification with the Divided Mother: Kristeva's Ambivalence." Pp. 79–91 in *Ethics, Politics, and Difference in Julia Kristeva's Writing.* Edited by Kelly Oliver. New York: Routledge.

OTHER LITERATURE

Aerts, Mieke, and Sawitri Saharso. 1994. "Sekse als etniciteit. Een beschouwing over collectieve identiteit en sociale ongelijkheid." *Tijdschrift voor Vrouwenstudies* 15, no. 1:11–26.

Alphen, Ernst van, and Maaike Meijer, eds. 1991. *De canon onder vuur. Nederlandse literatuur tegendraads gelezen.* Amsterdam: Van Gennep.

Arnóthy, Christine. 1964. *Ik ben 15 jaar en wil niet sterven.* Dutch trans. Line Kamp-Kan from the French *J'ai quinze ans et je ne veux pas mourir.* [1954. France: n.p.] Rotterdam: Ad. Donker.

Beauvoir, Simone de. 1988. *The Second Sex.* Translated and edited by H. M. Parshley from the French *Le deuxième sexe.* [1949. Paris: Gallimard.] London: Picador Classics.

Berns, Egide, et al. 1981. *Denken in Parijs. Taal en Lacan, Foucault, Althusser, Derrida.* Alphen a/d Rijn/Brussels: Samsom.

Blommestijn, H. H., ed. 1991. *Tot op de bodem van het niets. Mystiek in een tijd van oorlog en crisis. 1920–1970.* Kampen: Kok.

Blos, Peter. 1962. *On Adolescence: A Psychoanalytic Interpretation.* New York: Free Press of Glencoe.

Bock, Gisela. 1995. "Gewone vrouwen. Daders, slachtoffers, omstanders en meelopers van racisme en de holocaust in nazi-Duitsland, 1933–1945." Pp. 117–144 in *Sekse en Oorlog. Jaarboek voor Vrouwengeschiedenis* No. 15. Amsterdam: Stichting beheer IISG.

Bouw, Carolien, et al., eds. 1994. *Van alle markten thuis. Vrouwen- en genderstudies in Nederland.* Amsterdam: Babylon-De Geus.

Braidotti, Rosi. 1991. *Patterns of Dissonance. A Study of Women in Contemporary Philosophy.* Cambridge: Polity Press.

———. 1993. "On the Female Feminist Subject, Or: From 'She-Self' to 'She-Other.'" Pp. 177–192 in *Beyond Equality and Difference. Citizenship, Feminist Politics and Female Subjectivity.* Edited by Gisela Bock and Susan James. London/New York: Routledge.

———. 1994a. *Nomadic Subjects: Embodiment and Sexual Difference in Contemporary Feminist Theory.* New York: Columbia University Press.

———, and Suzette Haakma, eds. 1994b. *Ik denk, dus zij is. Vrouwelijke intellectuelen in een historisch en literair perspectief.* Kampen: Kok Agora.

Brügmann, Margret. 1986. *Amazonen der Literatur. Studien zur Deutschsprachigen Frauenliteratur der 70er Jahre.* Amsterdam: Ropodi.

Buikema, Rosemarie. 1995. *De Loden Venus. Biografieën van vijf beroemde vrouwen door hun dochters.* Kampen: Kok Agora.

Buikema, Rosemarie, and Anneke Smelik, eds. 1995. *Women's Studies and Culture: A Feminist Introduction.* Trans. from the Dutch *Vrouwenstudies in de cultuurwetenschappen.* [1993. Muiderberg: Dick Coutinho.] London/New Jersey: Zed Books.

Christ, Carol P., and Judith Plaskow, eds. 1979. *Womanspirit Rising: A Feminist Reader in Religion.* New York/London: Harper and Row.

Costa, Denise de. 1989. *Sprekende stiltes: Een postmoderne lezing van het vrouwelijk schrift: Irigaray, Kristeva, Lyotard.* Kampen: Kok Agora.

Dalsimer, Katherine. 1986. *Female Adolescence: Psychoanalytic Reflections on Works of Literature.* New Haven, Conn.: Yale University Press.

Daly, Mary. 1974. *Beyond God the Father: Toward a Philosophy of Women's Liberation.* Boston: Beacon Press.

Deutsch, Helene. 1946–1947. *The Psychology of Women: A Psychoanalytic Interpretation.* London: Grune & Stratton.

Devisscher, Hans, ed. 1994. *Hooglied: De Beeldenwereld van Religieuze Vrouwen in de Zuidelijke Nederlanden, vanaf de 13de eeuw.* Brussels: Snoeck-Ducaju & Zoon.

Dresden, Sem. 1991. *Vervolging, vernietiging, literatuur.* Amsterdam: Meulenhoff.

Dresen, Grietje. 1990. *Onschuldfantasieën: Offerzin en heilsverlangen in feminisme en mystiek.* Nijmegen: SUN.

Eliach, Yaffa. 1989. *Hasidic Tales of the Holocaust.* New York: Oxford University Press.

Ellis, Marc H. 1987. *Toward a Jewish Theology of Liberation.* Maryknoll: Orbis Books.

Emden, Rachel van, ed. 1986. *. . . Die mij niet gemaakt heeft tot man . . . Joodse vrouwen tussen traditie en emancipatie.* Kampen: Kok.

Ester, Hans, and Wam de Moor, eds. 1994. *Een halve eeuw geleden: De verwerking van de Tweede Wereldoorlog in de literatuur.* Kampen: Kok Agora.

Ezrahi-Dekoven, Sidra. 1980. *By Words Alone: The Holocaust in Literature.* Chicago/London: University of Chicago Press.

Felman, Shoshana, and Dori Laub. 1992. *Testimony: Crises of Witnessing in Literature, Psychoanalysis, and History.* New York/London: Routledge, Chapman & Hall.

Feuerbach, Ludwig. n.d. *The Essence of Christianity.* Translated by Marian Evans from *Das Wesen des Christentums.* [1893. 2nd Ger. ed.] London: Kegan Paul, Trench, Trübner.

Filipovič, Zlata. 1994. *Zlata's Diary: A Child's Life in Sarajevo.* Translated and annotated by Christina Pribichevich-Zorič. New York/London: Viking Penguin.

Flinker, Mozes. 1985. *Dagboek van Mozes Flinker: 1942–1943.* Amsterdam: Amphora Books.

Freud, Anna. 1986. *The Ego and the Mechanisms of Defense.* 1937. Reprint, London: Hogarth Press; the Institute of Psycho-analysis.

Freud, Sigmund. 1953. "Three Essays on the Theory of Sexuality." In *The Standard Edition of the Complete Psychological Works of Sigmund Freud.* Vol. 7. Gen. ed. James Strachey. London: Hogarth Press.

———. 1955. "Beyond the Pleasure Principle." In *Standard Edition.* Vol. 18. London: Hogarth Press.

———. 1959a. "Writers and Day-dreaming." In *Standard Edition.* Vol. 9. London: Hogarth Press.

———. 1959b. "Family Romances." In *Standard Edition.* Vol. 9. London: Hogarth Press.

———. 1961. "The Ego and the Id." In *Standard Edition.* Vol. 19. London: Hogarth Press.

———. 1961. "Female Sexuality." In *Standard Edition.* Vol. 21. London: Hogarth Press.

———. 1964a. "Lecture XXXIII: Femininity." In *Standard Edition.* Vol. 22. London: Hogarth Press.

———. 1964b. "Moses and Monotheism." In *Standard Edition.* Vol. 23. London: Hogarth Press.

Geyer-Ryan, Helga. 1994. *Fables of Desire: Studies in the Ethics of Art and Gender.* Cambridge. U.K.: Polity Press, 1994.

Groot, Maria de, and Christianne Méroz. 1985. *Westerbork: Gedichten.* Baarn: De Prom.

Gross, Rita M. 1979. "Female God Language in a Jewish Context." In *Womanspirit Rising: A Feminist Reader in Religion.* Edited by Carol P. Christ and Judith Plaskow. New York/London: Harper & Row.

Hayes, Peter, ed. 1991. *Lessons and Legacies: The Meaning of the Holocaust in a Changing World.* Evanston, Ill.: Northwestern University Press.

Heebing, Sonja. 1991. "'Lief dagboek': Het dagboek als hartsvriendin in de adolescentie." In *Het is meisjes menens: Inleiding vrouwenstudies.* Edited by Ineke van der Zande. Amersfoort: Acco Bibliotheek, Jeugd en Samenleving.

Heijst, Annelies van. 1992. *Verlangen naar de val: Zelfverlies en autonomie in hermeneutiek en ethiek.* Kampen: Kok Agora.

Heilbrun, Carolyn G. 1988. *Writing a Woman's Life.* New York: Ballantine Books.

Heinemann, Marlene. 1986. *Gender and Destiny: Women Writers and the Holocaust.* New York/Westport, Conn./London: Greenwood Press.

Henkes, Barbara. 1995. *Heimat in Holland: Duitse dienstmeisjes 1920–1950.* Breda: Babylon–De Geus.

Hermsen, Joke J. 1993. *Nomadisch Narcisme: Sekse, liefde en kunst in het werk van Lou Andreas-Salomé, Belle van Zuylen en Ingeborg Bachmann.* Kampen: Kok Agora.

Herzberg, Abel J. 1978. *Kroniek der Jodenvervolging 1940–1945.* 1950. Reprint, Amsterdam: Meulenhoff.

———. 1990. *Brieven aan mijn kleinzoon.* 1964. Reprint, Amsterdam: Querido.

Hilarová, Dagmar. 1990. *Ik heb geen naam.* Translated by Miep Diekman and Olga Krijtová. 1980. Reprint, Amsterdam: Leopold.

Hirsch, Marianne. 1989. *The Mother/Daughter Plot: Narrative, Psychoanalysis, Feminism.* Bloomington: Indiana University Press.

Hondius, Dienke. 1990. *Terugkeer: Antisemitisme in Nederland rond de bevrijding.* The Hague: Sdu.

Hoogland, Renée C. 1994. *Elisabeth Bowen: A Reputation in Writing*. New York/London: New York University Press.

Hoogland, Renée, and Pamela Pattynama. 1992. "Curious Figures: Female Adolescence in Literature." Published on the occasion of *Alice in Wonderland: First International Conference on Girls and Girlhood*. Amsterdam: n.p.

Imbens-Fransen, Annie. 1995. *God in de beleving van vrouwen*. Kampen: Kok.

Isarin, Jet. 1994. *Het kwaad en de gedachteloosheid: Een beschouwing over de holocaust*. Baarn: Ambo.

Kuijer, Guus. 1980. "Het kind als onpersoon." Chapter in *Het geminachte kind: Acht stukken*. Amsterdam: Arbeiderspers.

Laqueur, Renata. 1965. *Dagboek uit Bergen-Belsen*. Amsterdam: Querido.

Martelaere, Patricia de. 1993. *Een verlangen naar ontroostbaarheid: Over leven, kunst en dood*. Amsterdam: Meulenhoff/Kritak.

Marxveldt, Cissy van. 1947. *Ook zij maakte het mee*. Haarlem: De Erven Loosjes.

———. 1985. *Joop ter Heul; De H.B.S.-tijd van Joop ter Heul; Joop ter Heuls problemen; Joop van Dil-ter Heul; Joop en haar jongen; De dochter van Joop ter Heul*. 1919–1925. Reprint, Helmond/Hoorn: Westfriesland.

Marxveldt, Jan van. 1991. *De Zoon van Joop ter Heul*. Helmond/Hoorn: Westfriesland.

McFague, Sally. 1987. *Models of God: Theology for an Ecological Nuclear Age*. London: SCM Press.

Meijer, Maaike. 1988. *De Lust tot Lezen: Nederlandse dichteressen en het literaire systeem*. Amsterdam: Sara/Van Gennep.

———. 1996. *In tekst gevat: Inleiding tot een kritiek van representatie*. Amsterdam: Amsterdam University Press.

Mens-Verhulst, Janneke van, ed. 1993. *Daughtering and Mothering: Female Subjectivity Reanalysed*. London: Routledge.

Miller, Alice. 1987. *The Drama of Being a Gifted Child and the Search for the True Self*. Translated by Ruth Ward. London: Virago.

Moers, Ellen. 1976. *Literary Women*. New York: Doubleday.

Moffat, Mary Jane, and Charlotte Painter, eds. 1974. *Revelations: Diaries of Women*. New York: Vintage.

Moi, Toril. 1985. *Sexual/Textual Politics: Feminist Literary Theory*. London/New York: Methuen.

Mooij, Antoine. 1975. *Taal en verlangen: Lacans theorie van de psychoanalyse*. Meppel: Boom.

Mulder, Anne-Claire. 1986. "Bloed vloeit uit haar lichaam." *Opstand* 13, no. 6:13–19.

Nieuwstadt, Michel van. 1991. *Rondom het dierenpark: Abdij-journaal*. Nijmegen: SUN.

Pattynama, Pamela. 1992. *Passages. Vrouwelijke adolescentie als verhaal en vertoog*. Kampen: Kok Agora.

Pessers, Dorien. 1994. *De Wet van het hart*. Amsterdam: Balans.

Plaskow, Judith. 1991. *Standing Again at Sinai: Judaism from a Feminist Perspective*. Reprint, New York: HarperCollins.

Polak, Fia. 1995. *Oorlogsverslag van een 16-jarig joods meisje*. Amsterdam: Kolenoe.

Presser, J. 1991. *De Nacht der Girondijnen*. 1957. Reprint, Amsterdam: Meulenhoff.

Rilke, Rainer Maria. 1929. *Briefe an einen jungen Dichter*. Leipzig: Insel.

———. 1930. *Briefe an eine junge Frau*. Leipzig: Insel.

———. 1933. *Über Gott*. Leipzig: Insel.

Ringelheim, Joan. 1984. "The Unethical and the Unspeakable: Women and the Holocaust." *Simon Wiesenthal Center Annual* 1:69–87. New York: Rossel Books.

———. 1985. "Women and the Holocaust: A Reconsideration of Research." *Signs: Journal of Women in Culture and Society* 10, no. 4:741–761.

Rittner, Carole, and John Roth. 1993. *Different Voices: Women and the Holocaust*. New York: Paragon House.

Rizzuto, Ana-Maria. 1979. *The Birth of the Living God: A Psychoanalytic Study*. Chicago: University of Chicago Press.

Rosen, Norma. 1992. *Accidents of Influence: Writing as a Woman and a Jew in America*. Albany: State University of New York Press.

Scherman, Nosson, trans. 1993. *The Chumash*. Brooklyn, N.Y.: Mesorah Publications.

Schloss, Eva. 1989. *Herinneringen van een joods meisje 1938–1945*. Amsterdam: Sua.

Schofield, Mary Anne. 1990. "Underground Lives: Women's Personal Narratives, 1939–45." In *Literature and Exile*. Edited by David Bevan. Amsterdam/Atlanta: Rodopi.

Segal, Hanna. 1988. *The Work of Hanna Segal: A Kleinian Approach to Clinical Practice*. 1981. Reprint, London: Free Association Books and Marcsfield Library.

Shakespeare, William. 1987. *The Merchant of Venice*. 1600. Reprinted in *The New Cambridge Shakespeare*. Edited by M. M. Mahood. Cambridge, England: Cambridge University Press.

Silverman, Kaja. 1988. *The Acoustic Mirror: The Female Voice in Psychoanalysis and Cinema*. Bloomington: Indiana University Press.

Sosin, Deborah Anne. 1983. "The Diary as a Transitional Object in Female Adolescent Development." *Adolescent Psychiatry* 11:92–103.

Spek, Inez van der. 1996. *A Momentary Taste of Being: Female Subjectivity, the Divine and the Science Fiction of James Tiptree Jr*. Ph.D. diss., Department of Theology and Women's Studies, Utrecht University.

Spelman, Elizabeth V. 1988. *Inessential Woman: Problems of Exclusion in Feminist Thought*. Boston: Beacon Press.

Spiegelman, Art. 1986. *Maus: A Survivor's Tale: Part I: My Father Bleeds History*. New York: Random House.

———. 1991. *Maus: A Survivor's Tale: Part II: And Here My Troubles Began*. New York: Random House.

Spier, Julius. 1982. *Worden wie je bent: Inleiding tot de handleeskunde*. Introduction by Carl Jung. Weesp: De Haan.

Trinh, Minh-ha T. 1989. *Women, Native, Other: Writing Postcoloniality and Feminism*. Bloomington: Indiana University Press.

Valkhoff, Ziporah. 1992. *Leven in een niet-bestaan: Beleving en betekenis van de joodse onderduik*. Utrecht: Stichting ICOCO.

Van der Haegen, Rina. 1989. *In het spoor van seksuele differentie*. Nijmegen: SUN.

Vintges, Karen. 1992. *Filosofie als passie: Het denken van Simone de Beauvoir*. Amsterdam: Prometheus.

Vree, Frank van. 1995. *In de schaduw van Auschwitz: Herinneringen, beelden, geschiedenis*. Groningen: Historische Uitgeverij.

Vriesland, Esther van. 1990. *Esther, een dagboek—1942*. Utrecht: Matrijs.

Wantoch, Erika. 1989. *1939: Freuds laatste jaar*. Baarn: Anthos.

Washbourn, Penelope. 1979. "Becoming Woman: Menstruation as Spiritual Challenge." In *Womanspirit Rising: A Feminist Reader in Religion*. Edited by Carol P. Christ and Judith Plaskow. New York/London: Harper & Row.

Wiesel, Elie. 1977. "The Holocaust as Literary Inspiration." In *Dimensions of the Holocaust: Lectures at Northwestern University*. Evanston, Ill.: Northwestern University Press.

Winnicott, D. W. 1953. "Transitional Objects and Transitional Phenomena: A Study of the First Not-Me Possession." *International Journal of Psycho-analysis* 34, part 2:89–97.

Withuis, Jolande. 1995. "Van springplank tot obstakel." In *De jurk van de kosmonaute: Over politiek, cultuur en psyche*. Antwerpen/Meppel: Boom.

Wolf, Ellie. 1995. *Voortijdig afscheid*. Kampen: Kok.

Wright, Elizabeth, ed. 1992. *Feminism and Psychoanalysis: A Critical Dictionary*. Cambridge: Basil Blackwell.

Young, James E. 1988. *Writing and Rewriting the Holocaust: Narrative and the Consequences of Interpretation*. Bloomington: Indiana University Press.

❧ INDEX

❧ ABOUT THE AUTHOR

DENISE DE COSTA is a researcher at the University for Humanist Studies in Utrecht, the Netherlands. She is currently working as editor and contributor on a new book about Etty Hillesum. She is the author of *Sprekende Stiltes: Een postmoderne lezing van het vrouwelijk schrift: Irigaray, Kristeva, Lyotard* [Silences that speak: a postmodern reading of feminine writing: Irigaray, Kristeva, Lyotard]. She received her Ph.D. degree in the Women's Studies department of Utrecht University. The present study, based on her dissertation, was originally published in Dutch in 1996.